CHASING CHARLIE

CHASING CHARLIE

A Force Recon Marine in Vietnam

Richard Fleming

McFarland & Company, Inc., Publishers
Jefferson, North Carolina

Frontispiece: The author, 1968.

All photographs are by the author or from the author's collection except as otherwise noted.

Library of Congress Cataloguing-in-Publication Data

Names: Fleming, Richard, 1946– author.
Title: Chasing Charlie : a Force Recon Marine in Vietnam / Richard Fleming.
Other titles: Force Recon Marine in Vietnam
Description: Jefferson, North Carolina : McFarland & Company, Inc., Publishers, 2018 | Includes bibliographical references and index.
Identifiers: LCCN 2018008688 | ISBN 9781476671871 (softcover : acid free paper) ∞
Subjects: LCSH: Fleming, Richard, 1946– | Vietnam War, 1961–1975—Personal narratives, American. | United States. Marine Corps. Force Reconnaissance Company, 1st—Biography. | Scouts (Reconnaissance)—United States—Biography. | Vietnam War, 1961–1975—Reconnaissance operations, American. | Vietnam War, 1961–1975—Regimental histories—United States.
Classification: LCC DS559.5 .F58 2018 | DDC 959.704/342092 [B]—dc23
LC record available at https://lccn.loc.gov/2018008688

British Library cataloguing data are available

ISBN (print) 978-1-4766-7187-1
ISBN (ebook) 978-1-4766-3148-6

© 2018 Richard Fleming. All rights reserved

No part of this book may be reproduced or transmitted in any form or by any means, electronic or mechanical, including photocopying or recording, or by any information storage and retrieval system, without permission in writing from the publisher.

Front cover: the author with M14; *background* Danang

Printed in the United States of America

McFarland & Company, Inc., Publishers
Box 611, Jefferson, North Carolina 28640
www.mcfarlandpub.com

Silent as the angels of death we led the long line of grunts to their fate.

Dirty, sweating, sullen, savage, bound to one another by unbreakable chains forged in the furnace of combat, they followed us without questioning toward the unnamed hill where the living would be split from the dead.

This book is dedicated both to their sacrifices, and to my wife, who soothed the nightmares that have plagued me since that day.

We would have died for each other.

Table of Contents

Preface   1

1—Monsoon   3
2—One Way Ticket to Nam   4
3—Da Nang   5
4—Battalion Recon   8
5—Pack Mule to the Rescue   11
6—Chief   14
7—The Club   17
8—Gear Up   20
9—Morning   26
10—Mount Up   28
11—Alone on the LZ   32
12—Sniper   39
13—Leaving Battalion   43
14—Welcome to Force   45
15—The Firing Range   52
16—Mortar   56
17—Contact   58
18—Golden Wings   62
19—Toothpaste   67
20—Hospital Visit   72
21—The Coop   74
22—Jonah   78
23—The *New Jersey*   81
24—Sic 'Em   87
25—River Rat   90

26—The Red Corvette   93
27—An Hoa   94
28—Buzzard Bait   101
29—A Christmas Carol   106
30—A Close Shave   108
31—Hell's Half Acre   110
32—Wounded   114
33—Cam Ranh Bay   116
34—Gassed   122
35—The Pit   129
36—Grunts   134
37—The Quick and the Dead   137
38—Blessed Sleep   140
39—Rats   142
40—Sink or Swim   146
41—Hot Water   150
42—Elephants on the LZ   155
43—Foresight…Foresight…   164
44—Everything Is Samee-Same   171
45—The Bucktoothed Sergeant   175
46—The Silken Boudoir   182
47—CAP   187
48—The Dog and Pony Show   191
49—The Fight   192
50—Truckin   197

Table of Contents

51—Tiger 199
52—Don't Blink 202
53—Sentry Post Alpha 206
54—Murder 209
55—Short Timer 213
56—Trinkets 217
57—Ho...Ho...Ho Chi Minh 220
58—Homecoming 224

Epilogue 226
Reconnaissance Creed 235
Navaho Blessing 236
Chapter Notes 237
Recommended Reading 240
Index 241

Preface

*Since then, at an uncertain hour,
That agony returns:
And till my chastely tale is told,
This heart within me burns.*
—Samuel Taylor Coleridge,
"The Rime of the Ancient Mariner"

It has been half a century since Charlie[1] and I hunted for each other through the jungles of Southeast Asia. A half-century is very long time. One would think that after all this time my memories of my time as a Marine scout in Vietnam would be vague. Yet I do not believe that a single day has passed when I have not thought about the war, the men who fought with me, and the determined soldiers who fought against us. I often wish this were not so, but thoughts, like so many other things in our strange lives, are beyond human control. I have now spent more than half my time on earth trying to understand the war and find peace within myself for my actions in it.

I began writing my stories as they happened. I would sit on a wooden footlocker, sip a warm beer and record my experiences in a large green notebook that I found in the mess hall. I had written the names of places I had run missions on the top of my footlocker; Charlie Ridge, Antenna Valley, Happy Valley, the Garden of Eden and so many more. Places not shown on standard maps, but well known to the bush Marines in I Corps.[2] When I finally inked the location of my last mission, I had twenty-seven names written on the top of my footlocker. I had been on more patrols than anyone else in First Force Recon.

My stories are written from the perspective of an enlisted man. My knowledge of the war was limited to what I could see a few hundred feet in front of me. Grand military strategies and formal battle plans never made it down to my level. Perhaps they were lost in the chaos of war. Perhaps they never existed in the first place.

I have written what I remembered, but only God himself knows the whole story. Memory is a fickle, selfish servant at best, and we are seldom its master. I have concealed the identities of the men I served with, and the officers I served under, in the hope that this will protect their privacy and obscure any failings. My own faults and limitations will soon become obvious to even the most casual reader.

Vietnam 1968

1. Monsoon

Your father who is in heaven makes his sun rise on the evil
and on the good and sends rain on the just
and on the unjust.—Matthew 5:45

The monsoon rains had arrived, turning the land around our base from a dusty desert into a shallow lake. Once the rains began, they never stopped. It seemed the sky and earth had reversed, the droplets hitting the ground with so much force they flew upward. Our line of tents swayed in the wind, back and forth, back and forth, tugging like chained animals at the heavy ropes holding them to the ground. The canvas heaved inward, buckling against the wind only to snap back like a living thing, throwing off the water in a shower of spray.

The trenches were the first to go, slowly filling with coffee-colored water and then suddenly disappearing. We hammered marker stakes into the ground around them so that we wouldn't fall into the water-filled pits. The sandbagged walls we had piled up so laboriously to protect our tents from shrapnel collapsed into the mud, and even our heavily built bunkers and observation posts started to sag. Small waves lapped at the bases of our wooden tent platforms. Instead of the water rising, the land itself seemed to be sinking.

It was impossible for our choppers to fly in these conditions, and we hadn't been able to go out on a mission in several weeks. The artillery company next to our compound was still active, firing rounds over our heads no matter what the weather, and a few fixed-wing aircraft were able to operate. In the distance, we heard the sound of a Puff[1] gunship shooting a tongue of fire into the green mountains looming over us. The rounds from Puff's Gatling guns sounded like a swarm of giant bees or the sudden ripping of a heavy canvas cloth.

With the coming of the rains, the temperature suddenly dropped. Our bodies had grown accustomed to the humid heat of the dry season and we were now always cold. We spent nearly all of our time in our tents, leaving them only if forced to by sentry duty or the call of nature. Instead of sloshing our way through the water to the chow hall we cooked our own food on the homemade stoves we made out of C-ration cans, fueled with the pea-sized pieces of C-4 plastic explosive that we dug out of our Claymore[2] mines.

As long as we stayed inside our tents, we could stay somewhat warm and our bodies would have at least a little time to heal. Most of us were suffering from jungle rot, a nasty fungal infection that took hold when skin never had a chance to dry. A few of the men played cards, others wrote letters or listened to music, but most huddled down in their blankets and tried to sleep.

The downtime gave me plenty of time to think. I had been in Vietnam for over seven months and still had nearly half my tour left. I wrapped myself in my blanket and, half-dreaming, let my mind wander back in time.

How had I ever gotten to this truly godforsaken place?

2. One Way Ticket to Nam

Hey Marine
Have you heard?
LBJ has passed the word
We're gonna go to Viet Nam
We're gonna kill some Viet Cong!
—Fragment from a Marine running song

My experience getting to Vietnam was probably not much different from tens of thousands of other young Americans, but one must begin a story somewhere, so let me begin it here. I waited in the rain at El Toro airbase in San Diego to board a commercial flight to Hawaii, a first stop on the way to Vietnam. I don't remember which airline it was, and it really doesn't matter. Every major company in the United States was scrambling to make as much money out of the Vietnam War as it could, and the airlines were no different.

A few civilians in business suits and a group of officers boarded ahead of us and were seated in first class. The rest of the plane was packed solid with nervous, pimply-faced teenaged Marines who spent the entire trip trying desperately to get the two stewardesses to pay attention to them. They were out of luck. After offering us the obligatory bag of peanuts, the stewardesses spent the rest of the flight in the forward compartment, serving their first-class passengers steak dinners and glasses of wine.

After many hours in the air we finally flew over the shoreline of Hawaii, low enough to see the deep blue water turn into brilliant green, low enough to see surfers riding white waves and sunbathers lolling around on the white sand. It sure looked nice, but that was the last we saw of the fabled island. As soon as we landed we were herded into a bare open space on the lower level of the terminal. We had to wait there while our plane was refueled for our flight to Guam, our last stop before Vietnam.

There was no place for us to sit except the floor. On the balcony above us, cheerful passengers arriving for their Hawaiian vacations peered down at the mass of men in uniform milling around beneath them. Some threw down flowers from the leis they had been given when they arrived, but most just ignored us and hurried past, anxious to get to their hotels on the beach.

Sitting around with nothing to do except wait, bored Marines started horsing around with one another and giving the finger to anyone looking over the railing. Someone mentioned that they felt like cattle in a pen, and soon the men began mooing like cows, the noise echoing throughout the terminal. Things could have gotten out of control, if we had not been told that our plane was ready and we trooped aboard.

We were in Guam[1] only long enough to drop off our stateside uniforms and personal effects. The men in the supply depot told us that everything would be waiting for us when we finished our tour of duty,[2] and we accepted their assurances without a second thought.

Within a few hours, we boarded another jet for the final leg to Vietnam. This time there were no civilians on board, and the stewardesses spent even less time in our cabin and even more time flirting with the officers in first class.

I never saw the coastline of Nam at all. One minute we were over the ocean and the next the pilots turned on final approach and the plane dropped out of the sky. A few of the Marines returning for a second tour hung on to their seats and told us not to worry, assuring us that the pilot was just coming in steeply to avoid rocket fire. We had no way of knowing whether they were serious or just pulling our chains, but what they said wasn't reassuring. Our plane slammed onto the runway and the pilot braked hard, throwing us forward in our seats. Despite the rumors and the rough landing, we taxied normally to a group of a squat green Quonset huts sitting at the edge of the runway.

The side door of the plane opened, and a blast of hot, humid air filled the cabin. It smelled like newly turned earth, mixed with the scent of hot asphalt and jet fuel. A ramp was wheeled up, and we left the air-conditioned cabin. A stewardess flashed us a bright, impersonal smile as we passed, and thanked us for flying with her. As I was leaving the air-conditioned cabin I wondered what she thought of us—most likely not much.

3. Da Nang

*Now we have a problem in making our power creditable
and Vietnam looks like the place.*—President John F. Kennedy, 1961

We gathered up our duffel bags and straggled into a small green wooden building built against the side of a hangar where a harried-looking corporal grabbed our paperwork and told us to wait in a holding area until he called our names. He promptly disappeared into a back room where we could hear an old air conditioner gasping away. There were wooden benches along the wall, but not enough of them. It was stifling hot inside the hut and I threw down my duffel bag and slouched down against one of the open doors where at least there was a bit of breeze.

Most of the Marines in the room were newbies[1] like me, new boots, new utilities, new haircuts, but in the corner a small group of helmeted and flak-jacketed bush Marines were also waiting. We looked at them curiously, but they kept to themselves and didn't speak to us. A whippet-thin Marine squatted down in the corner, a sniper rifle cradled protectively in his hands—Marine and rifle seemingly one weapon.

Every ten or fifteen minutes the glass panel keeping the air-conditioned coolness inside the office would slide back and a corporal would call out a list of names. Those summoned would get to their feet, take their paperwork and disappear out a side door. I had almost fallen asleep when the panel slid back once again. The corporal poked his head out and peering around asked if anyone in the room had a paratrooper rating. I walked over to the desk and told him that I was jump qualified. Without looking up, he stamped my orders, handed them to me and told me to board the truck waiting outside the hangar.

"Tell 'em you want Recon," he told me, sliding the panel shut.

I hauled my duffel bag to my shoulder and stepped outside. Another Marine quickly grabbed my choice spot near the doorway. A few hundred yards away a truck was idling. I showed the driver my paperwork and told him where I needed to go. He nodded, threw the butt of his cigarette away and told me to jump into the back. There were plain wooden seats on both sides of the truck and I sat down near the front, joined a few minutes later by the grunts who had been waiting with me in the shed. They looked at me impassively, and after a few minutes the truck started moving.

It had started to rain, a hot, steamy rain. The back of the truck was covered, but the heavy canvas was punctured in so many places that the water streamed all around us. Someone remarked that the round holes looked like they had been made by bullets, and perhaps they had. The Tet Offensive[2] had just ended only a few months earlier, General Giap's troops had attacked even the most secure American facilities and ended any illusions General Westmoreland might have held about quickly defeating the enemy forces.

The driver pulled out of the air base and soon we were moving through the city of Da Nang itself. Despite the rain, the streets were crowded with people. Old men with cone-shaped cane hats were carrying baskets on long poles. Entire families walked together down the center of the road. RVN[3] soldiers scooted past our truck on small motorbikes, their girlfriends in tight silk dresses sitting sidesaddle behind them. We passed a farmer carrying two small pigs in net baskets suspended from a pole across his shoulders. The pole flexed with the farmer's steps and the fat little pigs seemed to be enjoying the ride through the city as they bounced up and down. I doubted they would enjoy their final destination quite as much.

We passed small stalls that Vietnamese vendors had built along both sides of the road. Most of these were nothing more than a few feet of shelving covered with a tarp, although a few were small sheds. All were overflowing with American-made goods. Some vendors seemed to specialize in liquor; others offered cartons of cigarettes. One stall contained nothing but elaborately decorated jackets that were made out of military blankets. The entire city seemed like a giant outdoor bazaar. I couldn't imagine where all this stuff had come from.

Whenever the truck slowed down gangs of Vietnamese kids would run after it.

"Hey, Meereens! Twook?"[4] the little urchins shouted.

"What do they want?" I asked a big black Marine sitting next to me.

"Cigarettes," he answered in a bored voice. "Don't give 'em nothing; it just encourages more of 'em."

He suddenly stood up and waved his rifle menacingly at them. "Deedee!"[5]

"You fuckin' numba ten Meereen!" the urchins called back mockingly, one of them giving him the finger. The kids certainly seemed to be enjoying themselves. The group laughed, scattered, and re-formed a few yards down the road to wait for the next truck.

"You let these little cocksuckers get too close once too often and you'll find a grenade in your lap," the man next to me warned me in a morose voice, sitting down again.

We left the city and I looked out on a large, flat valley covered in shallow water, the fabled rice paddies of the Orient. As the clouds moved across the sky, the water in the paddies reflected their images like a giant mirror. In the far distance mountains thrust up against the horizon, their tops sheathed in wispy clouds. The truck followed a road that wound around the base of a large hill covered in thick green vegetation. Banana trees grew along the roadside. I saw my first water buffalo, the huge beast herded by a small boy sitting on his massive neck and controlling him with nothing more than a small stick that he tapped against the animal's side. The hot diesel stench of the city was replaced by a clean and spicy scent. Everything I saw entranced me.

The truck continued on, and the shops were replaced by military outposts. We drove past a huge ammunition post protected by rolls of barbed wire, its ominous-looking bunkers hunkered down into the earth like crypts built to hold the bones of giants.

We passed a compound of prefabricated steel buildings. The sign in front read: Freedom Hill PX.[6] The driver stopped there for a few seconds to pick up several more Marines, who jumped aboard with bottles of Coke and bags of pretzels in one hand and M-16s in the other. The truck moved slowly down the road, the driver stopping to pick up the occasional hitchhiking Marine, and slowing down to let guys jump off the back of the truck when they reached their destination.

We drove through a small Vietnamese village that I later learned was called Dogpatch[7] by the troops. A large sign at the entrance to the village forbade American troops from entering the compound, but the grunts ignored it and a group of them jumped off. Giggling Vietnamese girls scantily clothed in what looked to me like silk pajamas suddenly appeared, taking the men by the hand and leading them away.

I started to get worried that the driver had forgotten all about me, and finally asked the Marine sitting next to me if he knew where "Recon" was. He acted surprised by my question and told me that we had already passed it, but added that the truck would be turning around in a few miles and I could jump out on the return trip. Sure enough, the driver turned the truck around after a mile or so and we passed through Dogpatch once more, this time picking up a group of happy Army soldiers.

The Marine next to me poked me in the shoulder and told me to get my stuff ready. He pounded the truck cab with the butt of his rifle and yelled for the driver to slow down. I got up, grabbed my duffel bag and climbed over to the tailgate. The truck had slowed, but there was a five-foot drop from the top of the tailgate to the road. I hesitated for a moment but felt the truck start to speed up again. I threw my duffel bag over and jumped after it, landing hard in a heap at the side of the road. In a few weeks, I would be jumping on and off trucks without even thinking about it, but this time I had to pick myself up off the ground and rescue my orders from a muddy ditch.

With the truck gone, the road was suddenly very quiet. It was now getting to late afternoon. The rain was still falling, and the temperature was quickly dropping. After sweating all day in the hot hangar I was now feeling chilled. I walked back up the road until I came to a painted sign hanging from two wooden beams. The words *Camp Reasoner*[8] were hand-painted in bold black letters. Underneath were the biblical words: *Greater Love Hath No Man*. Underneath the quote was a brief description telling about the action in which Lieutenant Reasoner had sacrificed his life. A second sign was hung a little farther down the road: "Recon Battalion—Swift, Silent, Deadly."

I was inspired reading about Lieutenant Reasoner, and vowed that I would do my best to live up to the highest ideals of the Marine Corps: *Duty, Honor, Country*. I was excited about joining my first unit and looking forward to proving myself.

A small plywood sentry post stood at the top of the road leading down the hill. As I approached, a bored sentry stepped out of the hut. He automatically started to salute but noted my lowly PFC[9] rank and his hand dropped to his side. He glanced at the muddy orders I handed him and with four words waved me through.

"Welcome to Nam ... asshole."

4. Battalion Recon

Then out spake brave Horatius,
The Captain of the Gate:
To every man upon this earth
Death cometh soon or late.
And how can man die better
Than facing fearful odds,
For the ashes of his fathers,
And the temples of his gods
—Thomas Babington Macaulay,
"Lays of Ancient Rome"

Camp Reasoner was built into the side of a small hill[1] five miles outside of Da Nang City. A muddy road ran down from the guard shack to a group of green huts neatly arranged around a cleared parade ground. The Stars and Stripes hung limply from a flagpole on one side of the open area, the Marine Corps flag beneath it. Voices were coming from the mess hall farther up the hill, but it was raining heavily, and no one was hanging around outside.

After the less than inspirational welcome the sentry had given me, I hadn't bothered to ask him for directions, but as I walked down the hill I spotted a crudely lettered sign with the abbreviation *HQ*[2] over one of the doors and I could hear the steady click of a typewriter coming from inside the shack. I pushed open the screen door and entered a small room overflowing with boxes and papers. The typing stopped as I entered. A young Marine took a cigarette from his lips and looked up at me expectantly. He wasn't wearing any insignia, but I didn't think he was an officer, so I simply told him that I had just arrived in-country. He nodded and held out his hand without comment. I gave him my muddy papers and he clipped them to a board hanging over his typewriter. He pulled another clipboard from a nail in the wall and ran his finger down the list in front of him.

He told me that I would be assigned to the First Platoon and added that they were out on patrol but would be would be back again in a few days. He told me to take my stuff down to their hooch and then report back to him as soon as I'd settled in.

I nodded, grabbed my duffel bag again and stepped out into the rain. I had no idea where the First Platoon was located, but I was afraid of looking foolish and didn't go back inside to ask. In front of me, built into the side of the hill, was another line of small green buildings. A raised walkway connected the shacks together. The hill was so steep that in many places the boardwalk was nearly ten feet off the ground. At the bottom of the hill was a cleared landing area for helicopters and beyond the LZ, or landing zone, rice paddies glistened. A line of blue-gray mountains rose up in the far distance.

The rain was still falling, but the clouds were breaking up and blue sky appeared in the distance. The air was clear and sweet, carrying smells that were new to my senses. Tall palm trees overhung the walkway and strange leafy vines climbed the railings. Occasionally I heard music or the murmur of voices from inside the shacks, but because of the rain everyone seemed to be staying indoors.

I walked along the walkway looking for the First Platoon's hooch. The shacks all looked nearly the same. All of them built from cheap plywood and perhaps twenty feet in length and about twelve feet wide. The walls were about four feet high, leaving space for a screened area that ran around the building. A sloping metal roof overhung the walls on each side, and only a few feet separated each building from its neighbor. Despite the flimsy construction, the overall effect was one of neatness and order. Every hooch was numbered, and most had insignias of various kinds painted over the door. I finally found one that had a crudely painted skull with the words *Always First* written in white letters beneath it.

I climbed up and opened the door and stepped into a strange world. Standard Marine Corps cots were lined up five to a row along each wall and there was a footlocker at the foot of each cot, but other than these, it seemed like each person was free to create his own personal living space. Some areas were military neat, others messy. One area had an expensive-looking stereo system wired up with speakers hanging down from overhead beams. Another boasted a desk constructed out of discarded ammunition boxes. Nails peppered the walls, and everything from family photographs to flak jackets hung on the open studs.

Scattered around on the floor were half-opened boxes of C rations, and the rounds of ammunition scattered on the floor gave the overall impression that the occupants had left in a hurry. The hut was open to the open air on all sides but inside the building the air held the odor of damp canvas, overlaid with the smell of too many people living too long in too small a space.

There was only one empty cot left, so I didn't have to make any choice about which one to take. I dropped my duffel bag on the floor, took off my starched Marine cap, and put it on a small shelf that the previous occupant had probably tacked up for the same purpose. There didn't seem to be that much more than I could do, so I got up and walked back to the operations area.

The corporal was still typing away when I entered. He rummaged around behind his desk, came up with a rusty saw and told me that the captain needed firewood cut for his stove. He gestured outside at a tree limb that someone had dragged up and leaned against the building. I could hardly believe what he was asking me to do. The Marine Corps had trained me for nearly a year, flown me halfway around the world, and here I was cutting wood for somebody's stove! The saw was dull, and the wood was hard, but after about an hour of hard work in the rain I had cut it up into small pieces and stacked them just inside the doorway.

It was now nearly dark. I was soaked and sweating from sawing up the log with the next to useless saw. The corporal had left quite a while ago, and I began to suspect that he had just gotten me to do his job. Marines were entering the mess hall that I had passed on my way to the headquarters building. I went into the mess hall to get something to eat.

I filled my tray with food doled out by two young Vietnamese girls, sat down at an empty bench and looked around at the other men. They didn't look a lot different from the guys I had trained with, just a little thinner, their faces and arms a little more tanned. Some of the men carried M-16 rifles, balancing their trays in one hand and holding their weapon with the other. When they sat down to eat, the weapon rested butt down between their legs, and their rifle was the first thing they grabbed as they got up from the table.

The sun was setting over the mountains when I left the mess tent and walked outside to look at the sunset. The last rays lit up the rice paddies in the distance. I looked down the hill and saw the Vietnamese farmers leaving their fields and leading their water buffalos homeward. After a long day toiling in the rice paddies, I was sure that both of them were looking forward to the end of the day. As I passed the small parade ground, a small honor guard was taking down the Stars and Stripes for the evening. Our flag snapped in the breeze and seemed to glow in the light of the fading sun. I was proud to be an American, proud to be a Marine defending the farmers and their families and proud to be a recon Marine.

Night fell quickly, and as soon as it got dark a gasoline generator began running and lights appeared from within the shacks. I was tired, but unable to fall asleep for a long time. A scratchy recording played "Taps,"[3] but Marines kept coming and going down the walkway all night long, walking past to the head at the end of the ramp. From somewhere in the darkness came faint laughter and singing and the clink of beer cans. The night wore on and the human noises slowly faded, replaced by the hum of insects and the croaking of frogs.

5. Pack Mule to the Rescue

*Sometimes you have to hit the mule between the eyes
with a 2 × 4 in order to get his attention.*
—General Norman Schwarzkopf

I awoke to the scratchy sound of a reveille blasted through loudspeakers over by the parade ground. Pulling on my pants and grabbing a towel, I followed a line of half-dressed men to the showers. Making my way back to the hooch, I once again grabbed my plate and cup and walked to the mess hall for breakfast. When I returned, I saw the men in the platoon next to me cleaning their rifles, brushing their boots, and making the way to the parade ground for formation. I stopped a young sergeant who was urging his men out the door and said that I had just arrived and asked him what I should do. He advised me to stay in the hooch until formation was over and then go down to the armory and supply to get myself properly set up.

I waited around until the men returned and then made my way down to the armory, a substantial building built out of heavy wooden planks. The door had been reinforced with steel and the windows had iron bars bolted over them. I stepped into the room and found myself in a small area closed off by a long counter. It reminded me of a general store, but instead of food and other goods, the shelves contained boxes of ammunition, bandoliers of M-60[1] shells and racks of rifles, black M-16s on one side, M-14s in the middle and sniper rifles with gleaming scopes standing in the rack at the far end.

There is something about a fine weapon that exerts a fierce attraction on most men. It is an instinctual feeling, something sensual, perhaps even bordering on sexual. For thousands of years men have caressed their deadly tools, talked to them, even named them. Perhaps it is their purity of purpose, their merging of design and function that gives them such a hold over us. A Spartan hefting a perfectly balanced spear, or a Roman centurion honing his short sword, probably felt the same kind of pleasure that I did feeling the bolt of an M-16 slide smoothly back and forth in my hand.

During basic training at Parris Island we were taught how to rub layer after layer of linseed oil onto the rifle stocks of the older M-14s that we had been issued for training. The oil was heated by the motion of our hands rubbing against the wood. The rifle stocks responded to our attentions by turning a rich golden color and the wood responded to our attention by turning a rich golden color, almost as though the wood had a life of its own. The functional fiberglass stocks on the weapons sitting on the rack in front of me would never develop that lustrous sheen, but they wouldn't warp in the rain either.

In the corner, at a wooden bench a corporal was working on a disassembled M-60 machine gun, but he put down what he was doing and nodded when I told him that I had just arrived and needed to be assigned a rifle. He glanced over the new M-16s lined up on the shelf, but then seemed to reconsider and walked into the back room. He returned with the most beat-up rifle I had ever seen and his arms extended he held it out to me as though it were an offering. The plastic stock on the weapon he held out to me was deeply scratched and nicked from one end to the other, and even the original blueing on the barrel seemed to have been worn away.

"Is this the best you can do for me?," I asked, looking dubiously at the rifle he was holding out to me.

He patted the weapon in his hands affectionately.

"It may look a little ragged," he admitted, "but she has a hair trigger and will fire faster than any M-16 in the company. We aren't allowed to shave down the springs anymore … you're lucky to get it."

I left with my battered-looking weapon and a bandolier of magazines that I hung around my shoulder. I dropped the rifle off back at the hooch and started out again.

My next stop was the supply hut, a long, low building not much different from the other buildings lining the road. After I walked in, the door slammed shut, waking a pasty-faced sergeant who was dozing in an aluminum beach chair by the window. He sat up guiltily, listened to my request and in a soft southern drawl told me that he really didn't have much of anything left.

He got up from the chair with a sigh and disappeared into the back of the building, coming back in a few minutes with a flak jacket with a few plates gone, a beat-up backpack, some canteens, a mess kit, a wide brimmed camouflaged hat, and a battered helmet, on the back of which someone had written: *Don't follow me … I'm lost too!*

The supply sergeant settled back into his beach chair and told me that he might have some more jungle boots coming in next week and suggested that I try back then. I put on the flak jacket and helmet, stuffed everything else into the backpack and left him snoozing away.

As I walked back to the hooch I passed an old Vietnamese "papa-san"[2] carefully grinding an edge on a Ka-Bar knife. He worked slowly, carefully honing the blade. He looked up from his squatting position as I passed and smiled at me, startling me with his black smile. I later learned that most of the older Vietnamese were addicted to chewing tobacco mixed with betel nuts. Over time, the mixture stained their teeth a dull blackish brown, which the villagers found attractive.

I sat on my bunk and started writing a letter to my parents. I had not written to them in several weeks and wanted to let them know I was all right. I had just started the letter when I heard shouting and the sound of feet on the walkway. I opened the door to see Marines shrugging into flak jackets and helmets as they ran down the hill to the helicopter pad.

"Third Platoon's in trouble … Get your gear!" one of the Marines shouted up at me as he ran by.

My heart started pounding. I had no idea what to bring and what not to, and there didn't seem to be anyone around to ask. I grabbed my rifle and the meager gear that I had just been issued and ran out the door, following the stream of men running down to the LZ. Each man was with his platoon, but I was alone.

The scene below me seemed like utter confusion with men running around and struggling into their gear. I went over to a corporal who was frantically filling his pack with extra ammunition and asked him what I should do.

"How am I supposed to know?" he replied in exasperation.

He took the long tube of a LAW,[3] a rocket-propelled grenade, from the pile beside his gear, strapped it to my back and pulled two boxes of M-60 ammo out of the pile of ordnance by his feet.

5. Pack Mule to the Rescue

"Here, carry these," he said, stuffing more ammunition into my pack.

My web gear was loose and flapped around, and I hadn't even had a chance to adjust my pack. Nothing seemed to fit. The leather soles of the shiny jump boots I had been issued in the states skidded and slipped on the muddy ground. The LAW strapped to my back kept swinging around awkwardly, and with two ammo boxes in my hands I couldn't even hold my rifle. I felt like the water boy on a high school football team. I had no idea what I was doing and no one to ask. The corporal that I had first spoken to seemed to have disappeared. Everyone except me was attached to their own group and they gathered together in tight knots around their radiomen. Rumors began to circulate around the LZ: the Third Platoon was surrounded; the team had three casualties; they were running for their lives. None of the rumors were good.

We waited for hours at the LZ, the men in each platoon staying in their own group while I walked back and forth hoping to find someone who could tell me what to do. I'm sure there were some officers in the group, but no one was wearing any insignia and I didn't know who they were. I eventually decided to stick with whatever group was closest to me.

Two CH-46 helicopters had landed, and like everyone else I was soon covered in a fine dust stirred up by their spinning rotors. The temperature grew hotter as the sun rose higher in the sky. I finally sat down and waited like the rest of the men for something to happen.

Curiously, I was more concerned about my lack of jungle boots and about the ragged assortment of stuff I was supposed to carry than I was about the possibility of dying in combat. I hadn't even had a chance to fill up my new canteens. There was no water on the LZ and I didn't want to leave to get some because I was afraid that I might miss out on the action. What an innocent newbie I was!

The man next to me muttered to his friend that they should be sending in a company of grunts, and to my surprise I heard the other Marine reluctantly agree.

"Yeah, we ain't equipped for this shit."

I was shocked to hear these offhand comments. How could they not want to rescue their buddies? It was only after I had been in-country longer that I realized that they were just stating the obvious. No matter how much they might want to help their comrades, there were too few of us and we were too lightly armed to rescue anyone.

We sat in the sun and baked. Things seemed to have somehow calmed down in the last few minutes. A few Marines were still fiddling with their gear, but most were sitting around in small groups smoking and talking. Some, leaning back against their packs, had even fallen asleep. Suddenly there seemed to be a commotion at the far end of the LZ. I saw a small group gathering around a radio operator, and someone called out, "They're OK!"

Everyone whooped and yelled, giving one another the high five and shouting, "AhOooRah![4] over and over to one another. I was told later that this grunting cheer was brought over by Recon's SCUBA divers, who likened it to the distinctive sound made by a submarine's klaxon when the sub dove, others saying that it mimicked the hoarse grunting of a seal. Whatever the origin, the distinctive "AhOooRah" served to cheer and united us as much as the more famous "Rebel Yell," rallied Confederate troops during the Civil War.

After a few minutes, we heard another helicopter in the distance. It landed in a swirl of dust and the team came down the ramp, dirty, tired and surprised to see the entire company armed to the teeth waiting for them on the LZ. Someone passed the order to stand down and we all made our way back up the hill.

Looking back on this episode in the days that followed, I realized how fortunate I was not to have gone out on this half-baked rescue mission. I didn't have the training, the equipment, or the support that I would have needed to survive. I would likely have quickly gotten myself killed my first week in Nam.

———

6. Chief

*I am not an educated man. I never had the opportunity
to learn anything except how to fight.*—Pancho Villa

I was lying on my bunk when the door of the hooch swung open and a line of filthy men slowly shuffled into the hooch, each one carefully holding open the door for the next. They walked hunched over, leaning forward to carry the weight of their enormous packs as high as possible on their backs. Their rifles rested across their cartridge belts or were carried loosely in their hands. It seemed that everything they carried, from their packs to their utilities, was covered in slowly drying mud. Clods of mud forced out from the treads of their jungle boots left clumps of dirt on the plywood floor with every step they took.

Most of the men wore soft bush hats of green and brown. Grenades, flares, canteens, and cartridge belts hung from their web gear, and the men had Ka-Bar knives taped upside down to their shoulder straps. Multiple layers of camouflage paint covered their faces and arms. The whites of their eyes shining against the dull green and brown background gave them the startled look of trapped animals. They smelled of wet earth, sweat, insect repellent and something else, a rotten sweetness that I later recognized all too well as the smell of the Asian jungle.

I stood up nervously as they entered, but too tired to care, they only glanced at me as each man made his way over to his bunk. They hung their rifles on nails hammered into the two-by-four studs above their bunks. They shrugged their arms out of straps and their packs hit the floor with dull thuds. Releasing the clasps on their web gear, canteens, and cartridge belts joined the growing pile of gear at their feet. Grenades, ammunition magazines, Claymore mines, knives, pistols and flares were carefully laid on their bunks to be put away later. Finally, they sat down on their footlockers, took off their mud-encased boots and, sighing with relief, peeled off their socks. It was only after their gear was off and they began talking to one another that a few of them glanced over and nodded at me.

6. Chief

The screen door to the hooch opened again and a figure in tiger-striped utilities was outlined in the doorway. The bantering died away suddenly as he entered.

"Hey, Sarge!" someone called out in a hesitant voice as if warning the others.

Unlike the other men, the Marine who entered moved easily under the weight of his equipment and didn't seem tired at all. Instead of a bush hat he wore a green bandanna tied tightly around his forehead. His face was still covered in green and brown camouflage paint, but I had the impression that he was as young as I was. He saw me sitting on my cot and walked over, a questioning look on his face. His eyes fastened on to mine, a gray-blue stare that suddenly made me nervous.

"I didn't know if anyone was using this cot," I blurted defensively, thinking that maybe I had taken his.

"Don't matter; take any that's empty," he said dismissively, his eyes never leaving my face.

"You're the new guy they sent us?" he finally asked.

I nodded.

"I'm Sergeant Blaze," he told me simply.

He turned to the Marine on the bunk closest to me and ordered, "Get him squared away, Chief."

Giving me one last piercing look my new sergeant walked out the door. Once he had left, the men seemed once more to relax and began talking and joking to one another again. The Marine the sergeant had called Chief finished taking off his boots, grimacing as he did so. Groaning in relief, he pulled the last one off and stripped off the rest of his clothes, leaving a shining silver crucifix hanging with his dog tags against the darkness of his chest. He was a short, square man with broad shoulders and a huge chest. Dark eyes were set wide apart in his broad face. I had the overall impression that he was someone you were able to count on. He grabbed a bar of soap and, wrapping a green Marine towel around his waist, joined his teammates heading for the showers.

Chief returned about half an hour later and sat down cross-legged on the bunk next to me. Despite the shower, traces of green camouflage paint still covered parts of his neck and arms. I later learned that it would take more than a single shower for the paint to come off. He nodded at me and motioned ruefully at the reddened skin and blisters on his foot that he told me were due to something called jungle rot. He rummaged around under his bunk and came back with a pair of rubber flip-flop sandals that he carefully slipped onto his swollen feet with a sigh of relief.

The door slammed and the rest of the team came in flicking their towels at one another and joking around in a mishmash of English and Spanish with some Vietnamese thrown in from time to time.

"Hey, Chief, who's the Gringo?" one of them called out.

"He's your replacement, Fernandez. The sergeants decided to ship your ass to Hanoi."

"I can't wait, got to be better than this shit hole."

"That comedian is Fernandez," Chief mentioned, introducing me to a thin Marine who grinned and pulled a case of beer from under his cot and tossed me a Bud[1] as he threw cans to the other men. The beer was warm and sprayed out all over everything when I popped it open, but it sure tasted good going down.

It was hard for me to believe that these men were the same group of bedraggled, exhausted creatures who had struggled up the steps less than an hour ago. Freed from their eighty-pound packs, their feet out of their jungle boots, showered, shaved and dressed in clean utilities, they were now filled with life and energy.

Chief turned on an elaborate stereo system that took up a large section of his wall. It would have cost thousands of dollars back in the States, but he said he had bought it for a few hundred bucks when he was in Hong Kong on R & R. He turned on a high-end tape player and carefully adjusted the dials as country music blared from huge speakers attached to the ceiling. Fernandez left to get the mail that had piled up when they were out on patrol. He returned with a big stack, and soon the floor of the hooch became covered in envelopes and empty boxes.

Chief cut open a package from his mother and pulled out a small bottle with long, stringy peppers inside. The other men eagerly crowded over as he took a long red one from the bottle and passed the rest around. I hesitated as the bottle came around to me. Fernandez warned that the red ones were too hot and suggested a green one, pulling it out of the bottle and handing it to me. I gingerly took a small bite and immediately my mouth ignited. I grabbed for a canteen as the other men howled with laughter. The water only made things worse; my mouth was on fire and tears ran from eyes.

"What do you think?" Fernandez asked innocently.

"Can I have a red one?" I choked out.

Fernandez slapped my shoulders and laughed at my joke. For the first time since I joined the Marine Corps, I began to feel part of a group. In boot camp, we were all just individuals trying to survive the drill instructors' wrath. The pace of advanced infantry training made close friendship all but impossible. Perhaps it was the joke, perhaps it was their general good nature, but from that moment I felt welcomed, but I was later to learn that it would take more than a joke for me to really become part of their unit

Things gradually quieted down. Some of the men took off for the NCO[2] club; others left to visit their friends on other teams. In a few minutes only Chief, Fernandez and a Marine named Garcia were left with me in the hooch.

Looking at the pile of gear on my cot, Garcia pulled a wooden footlocker away from the far wall and slid it over to me. The chest had the name **Mariner** written in bold block letters on top of the lid. Garcia saw me looking at it, took a black marker and blacked out the name.

"He went home," Garcia replied quietly to my unasked question.

"Yeah, he went home," came a faintly hysterical laugh from Fernandez at the other end of the hooch, He paused for effect. "In a body bag."

"Why don't you just shut it!" Garcia responded angrily.

I took the footlocker, but it sure made me feel uneasy when I opened it and found a pair of socks, an old hat and some other stuff still left in the bottom. Chief noticed my expression and stood up abruptly, telling me that I'd be able get squared away later. He told me that they always had a few days off when they first got back from patrol and suggested that I join him and the other men at the club.

7. The Club

> *I have made fellowships ...*
> *... wound with war's hard wire whose stakes are strong;*
> *Bound with the bandage of the arm that drips;*
> *Knit in the webbing of the rifle-thong.*
> —Wilfred Owen, "Apologia Pro Poemate Meo"

The enlisted men's club at Camp Reasoner was nothing more than a plywood shack perched precariously on the edge of the steep hill overlooking the landing pad. As we approached the club, I saw a cardboard sign hanging from a nail to the right of the door. In bold black letters it read: *CLUB CLOSED*. Chief ignored the sign, opened the screen door and pushed me inside.

Inside it was cool and dark. A makeshift bar made of plywood ran along the far end. A tiny Vietnamese woman stood behind the bar busily cleaning beer glasses in a bowl of soapy water. She wore a spotless white top and black silk pants. We watched her scrub each glass furiously and then carefully rinse it. She raised her head questioningly as we entered.

"Hello, Gypsy!" Chief called out.

She nodded but continued scrubbing the glasses.

Someone started laughing outside and Fernandez and Garcia pushed into the room.

"What you got for me today, Gypsy?" Garcia called out teasingly.

"Nothing for you.... You Numba Ten! We closed. You no read sign?"

"What sign?" Garcia answered innocently, turning to Fernandez questioningly. "Did anyone see a sign?"

She wagged her finger at him. "I go get sign and show you...." She walked outside and then stormed back in a few seconds later.

"What you do with my sign?" she yelled furiously.

The two men turned innocently to each other and shrugged.

"You fuckin' Numba Ten GI!" she yelled, storming around the bar. "You get the hell outta here!"

"Oh, c'mon, Gypsy ... give us some slack—get us a beer," Garcia pleaded as she glared at him.

"You want beer ... you first give back sign."

Laughing, the two men went back outside, and we heard them hanging the sign again. After checking to make sure they had put everything back, Gypsy finally pulled back the cover of a storage chest filled with ice and pulled out two six-packs of beer.

Garcia winked at me, "She really likes me."

"I can tell," I responded.

The place was quickly filling up with more men from other teams. One table started singing a raucous drinking song and the men at the other tables joined in.

> Oh ... the Marine Corps flag is a dirty old rag,
> and the commandant is a fairy.
> He hates little girls, and he loves little boys, and his wife is still a cherry.
> So drink chug-a-lug drink-chug-a lug ...

Chief motioned to me to grab the beers and follow him out the back door. The rice paddies below us glistened in the clear air. Each paddy was a neat rectangle of water and rice shoots bordered by low dirt dikes that kept the water in. At this time of year, the rice shoots were just starting to come up and they showed a brilliant light green in the sun. The grass-like shoots poked through the water and waved in the soft breeze, a patchwork quilt of color and movement. The shallow waters of the paddies reflected the puffy white clouds and deep blue of the sky. A few farmers were working the land below us with their water buffalos.

In the adjoining paddy, an entire extended family, men, women, children and even grandparents, was planting their rice crop. They worked bent over, wading through the knee-deep water, carefully inserting individual sprigs of rice into the mud of their paddies. The farmers wore their traditional conical straw hats and were dressed in the black silk.

In comparison to the timeless farming scene below us, our compound cut an ugly slash across the landscape. Rolls of razor-sharp concertina wire wound haphazardly around the top of the cliff. The plywood and plastic club looked like it would topple over any moment. A huge pile of beer cans littered the steep slope beneath our feet. The Marines just threw the empties over the side of the hill, using the justification that no one would be able to climb up the cliff without causing the cans to make a racket. This, however, was a lame excuse. There were no sentry posts near this end of the compound, and no one would hear the noise even if the enemy did try to sneak up this side of the hill.

In the far distance, the flat plain of rice paddies and fields gave way to looming blue-green mountains that Chief told me marked "the bush," enemy-held territory. The clear air made distances deceiving, but even so, the possibility of enemy troops within my sight was unnerving.

There were a number of benches leaning against the wall of the club and a few rickety tables. The benches were in the shade, so Chief and I sat there to enjoy the view. A hot breeze blew up the cliff from the rice paddies below, but it was cool in the shade. Chief downed his first beer in two or three huge swallows, his head tilted back, his throat bobbing as he drank. When the can was empty he crushed it in his huge hand and flung it down the slope to join the others. He drank the second one more slowly, taking the time to savor every drop. The back door opened and Garcia and Fernandez sat down across from us.

I asked them how they had gotten into Recon. Garcia laughed softly and told me that the three of them had been in a grunt outfit, living in the jungle and humping the hills for weeks at a time. He heard that Battalion was asking for volunteers for Recon and that they had transferred over.

"We figured that it wouldn't be any worse than being a grunt, so we all volunteered and ended up here." He gestured expansively around him.

"Did you guys make the right move?" I asked curiously.

"Better than the grunts. We got better training, better equipment, better support."

"Better chance of being blown away," Fernandez joked.

"Tell me about the sergeant," I asked, helping myself to another beer.

"Blaze? He's OK," Garcia replied, adding, "…for a lifer."[1]

6. Chief

"He's crazy," Fernandez added seriously, and none of the men objected.

"This is his second tour, came over in '66 with the grunts. He came up for R and R,[2] about a couple of months ago. You know where he spent it?" Fernandez asked me.

I shook my head.

Fernandez pointed to the hill looming over the camp, "Right up there. Took some rations and a tent and spent the entire week up there alone."

He shook his head in disbelief and continued, "I asked him once why he re-upped for Nam and he told me he liked it here." Fernandez shook his head "Can you imagine that? He likes it here. Man, if that ain't nuts ... nothin' is."

By the end of the day, I had drunk so much beer that I was beginning to like it too. There was a big sign over the bar limiting the beers to four per man, but by going in multiple times we soon had accumulated enough to keep ourselves well supplied. No one seemed to care. I noticed some men walking off along the perimeter and the sweet scent of marijuana drifted back to us on the breeze. Fernandez and Garcia walked over in their direction.

Chief came back and sat down at the table.

"Everybody calls you Chief ... you don't mind?" I asked him.

"Nah ... well, maybe at first," he finally admitted, "But now I've got more important things to worry about. After a while, you don't sweat the small stuff. Nothin' I can do about it now anyway," he admitted ruefully, almost to himself.

"How come you joined up?" I asked, hoping to get to know him better.

"Sheer stupidity," he joked, and then thought for a moment. "My father was a Marine ... saw a lot of action in the Pacific."

"So he encouraged you to enlist?" I asked.

Chief shook his head and laughed dismissively. "He wanted me to get an education, go on to college, but I didn't listen."

He paused for a moment, and then continued.

"There was nothing for me at home anyhow. Most of my friends were drafted. I couldn't wait to join up and prove myself. Put on my dress blues, see the world ... impress the girls." He looked ruefully around him at the men horsing around the bar.

"So here I am seein' the world."

He turned away from me lost in his own thoughts.

"What did I know? I had just turned seventeen. I was only a kid,"

I wasn't particularly surprised at what Chief had said. My reasons for joining up were pretty much the same as his. I never heard any enlisted man say that he joined to protect America from communism or to fight for the right of South Vietnam to remain free. These slogans may have gotten good press back in the States, but they fell flat on Marines. We were all patriotic enough, I guess. We believed in our country and thought that we were doing the right thing by serving, but fancy slogans were far removed from the daily reality of our lives. We joined up for far simpler reasons: to prove ourselves, get away from home, maybe even to just impress the girls.

8. Gear Up

War is a rough teacher, and fits men's characters to their condition.—Thucydides

It was a sad little group who stood for inspection the next morning. With bloodshot eyes and ringing heads, we tried to fake our way through inspection. Sergeant Blaze had made sure that our rifles were clean and our boots shined, but the captain inspecting our sorry asses put us on a work party anyway.

Garcia and I were ordered to put up another layer of wire around the perimeter. I was issued a pair of heavy leather gloves and a pair of wire cutters. Garcia drew a twenty-pound sledgehammer. I held the long metal stakes as he struggled to hit the tops and drive them into the ground. The stakes were six feet in height and vibrated wildly from side to side with every stroke. They felt like they were alive and trying to avoid the hammer. If Garcia missed he would break my arm, but he was careful, slowly tapping the top until the bottom of the metal stake bit into the ground before pounding it in the rest of the way.

The concertina wire was nasty stuff. Thousands of blades of razor-sharp metal spikes ran along the supporting wire. The rolls of wire sprang apart when we cut the restraining clips. By the end of the morning, I had been scratched in half a dozen places and Garcia had a nasty cut on his arm. We got a case of empty beer cans from the club, filled the cans with pebbles and wired them to the topmost strands. The idea was that the slightest touch would cause the cans to rattle and alert the sentries, but the slightest wind caused them to shake as well. We became so accustomed to the rattling sound that their warnings went unnoticed.

At the end of the day Garcia turned to me and quite seriously mused, "You know, sometimes I get the strangest feeling that this wire isn't meant to keep the gooks out, but to keep us in. Crazy, isn't it?"

In the next few days I joined Chief and the other men as they took their utilities over to the Freedom Hill PX to get them cleaned and starched, grabbed some food, got a haircut or drew their pay. I gradually got to know the other men in the platoon. Unlike the friendly acceptance I had received from Fernandez, Garcia and Chief, most of the other men seemed to keep their distance, almost as though they were sizing me up.

It was now raining heavily and most of the guys were back inside the hooch, lying around their bunks, writing letters or cleaning their gear when Sergeant Blaze suddenly entered the hooch and told us to get ready for a new mission.

"We just got back in!," Fernandez complained, "Where are we goin now?"

"What the hell do you care?" Garcia muttered under his breath.

Blaze took a map out of his pocket and laid it on the floor as the team gathered around. He pulled a knife from his belt and using it as a pointer showed us the LZ.

"Ben Giang, a little east of the Song Cai River." He pointed to an area outlined in black ink labeled "Phuac Hao."

"Fuck You Valley, I knew it." Fernandez moaned softly.

Blaze ignored him and told us that Intelligence believed that the NVA (North Vietnamese Army) was moving into the area once again.

8. Gear Up

"They never left," Chief muttered under his breath.

In one fluid motion the sergeant rose to his feet, smoothly sheathing the knife he had been using as a pointer as he did so.

"OK—enough of this bullshit! You got your orders. Get the grid lines copied and draw your gear."

He turned to Fernandez. "Since you're such a wise guy, you can help Chief get the newbie ready. He'll be going out with us."

He paused, daring anyone to speak, but no one did.

I was a little annoyed that sergeant Blaze had referred to me only as "the newbie." Didn't he even remember my name?

Chief shuffled over to me. He was bigger than he looked, his size deceiving because of his rounded shoulders and habitual slouch. His face held a peculiar kind of resigned weariness. He didn't say anything to me as walked down to the armory together and I had the feeling he was somewhat embarrassed about sharing so much of himself to me last night at the club.

As soon as we returned to the hooch, Chief told me to put away the rifle and get out my pack. I pulled it out from under my bunk and handed it over to him. The previous day I had packed it with everything that I thought I would need on a patrol. Chief turned the pack upside down and my poncho, mess tin, toothpaste, flashlight, matches, nearly everything I had carefully put into it fell out onto the floor.

Fernandez carried a box of C rations over and threw it on the floor next to my things. Chief opened the cardboard with his big hands and again dumped everything onto the floor, where he began to sort out the cans.

"Beanies and weenies, spaghetti and rocks, fruitcake, some cans of fruit, take along some chocolate bars and crackers if you want. I wouldn't feed the rest of this crap to my dog," he grunted, kicking the rest of the nearly full box away.

I picked up my poncho from the pile on my cot and held it out to him questioningly, but he shook his head.

"The grunts wear ponchos; we don't, too much noise. No ponchos, no tarps, no tents," he explained.

"Hard core! Marine Corps!" Fernandez broke in, mocking the marching cadence we learned in boot camp.

Chief ignored him. He pulled out a quilted light silk blanket from beneath his bunk and tossed it to me. I had seen these blankets sold in the Da Nang marketplace but hadn't been issued one. He took a pair of socks from my pack and started stuffing cans that he had selected into them, explaining that the socks kept the cans from rattling against one another. He advised me to go light and not to try to carry too much food or water.

"Just more weight to hump around. Same for the water, some guys haul around gallons. The more they carry around the thirstier they get."

I asked him about the freeze-dried packets of food we had been issued in recon training.

He snorted dismissively. "Yeah, I got a whole case under my cot. We eat 'em if we don't feel like going to the mess hall, but they're no good in the bush. They use up too much water. I don't know about you, but I'd rather be hungry than thirsty any day."

"Now, you want something good, you capture some good VC rations," Fernandez broke in. "Shrimp and veggies with rice … sprinkle on some of their Muc Luc[1] fish sauce, and now you're talkin'." He smacked his lips. "Makes me hungry just thinkin' about it."

Chief held out his hand and asked me for my dog tags. I slipped them off my head and handed them to him. He unclipped the chain that had held them together and threw it away, restringing the tags on a piece of green parachute cord. He walked over to his bunk and pulled out a roll of green tape. "You don't want anything shiny and this will keep them from rattling," he explained, carefully taping the dog tags together.

He took the little P-38 can opener that came with every C-ration packet and threaded it onto the parachute cord. He carefully knotted the cord and handed the line back to me.

"This way you won't lose it. This little metal thing will keep you fed."

"And the Marine Corps needs the tags when you're dead," Fernandez rhymed jokingly.

Chief took the map that Sergeant Blaze had left by the door and laid it on his bunk. He rummaged around in his footlocker and came back with his own map, a small pair of scissors and a Magic Marker. Spreading the two maps out on the bunk, he carefully copied the rectangle drawn on the first map onto his own. He then cut around the outside of the lines that he had just drawn. He carefully sealed the small map fragment into the plastic bag, taping down the ends, explaining to me that if the paper got wet the contour lines would smudge up and the map would be useless.

Chief asked me if I knew the grid system.

I wasn't sure what he meant, but I told him that I could read a map. "You locate yourself latitude/longitude and then report top to bottom, left to right."

"Forget that boot camp crap; I don't even know why they still teach it," he told me contemptuously.

"If we've got a map, you can bet your sweet ass that Charlie's got one as well," he explained. "We radio in our lat/long position and the Cong will know exactly where we are.

"We don't use lat/long. We go off this rectangle," he told me, pointing to the square that he had drawn on the map. "See this 'X' that's our LZ? Counting down the number of grid lines down from left we get 1 and from the top 3. Our LZ position is therefore 1–3. Each of the squares is a thousand meters, or a 'click.' Each of us has an identical map, and one copy stays behind at base. Without one of our maps Charlie can't know our position, even if they monitor our radio transmissions."

"You don't need to carry along the whole map, only need the part we're going to be patrolling." Fernandez added,

Chief asked me to hand him my M-16. He swiftly inspected it to be sure that it was unloaded and then removed the sling. Taking a piece of green camouflage tape, he wrapped the sling buckles so they would not jingle. He took another long piece and taped up some of the air holes along the top and bottom of the grip, explaining that the tape would help camouflage the rifle.

He walked to the side of the hooch and came back with several boxes of ammunition.

"I've already got my magazines loaded," I told him.

"Get rid of 'em; they're probably old. On missions, we only use new ammo."

Chief flipped a round out of one of my magazines.

"How many rounds did you put in?" he asked, pushing down on the cartridges and testing the spring.

8. Gear Up

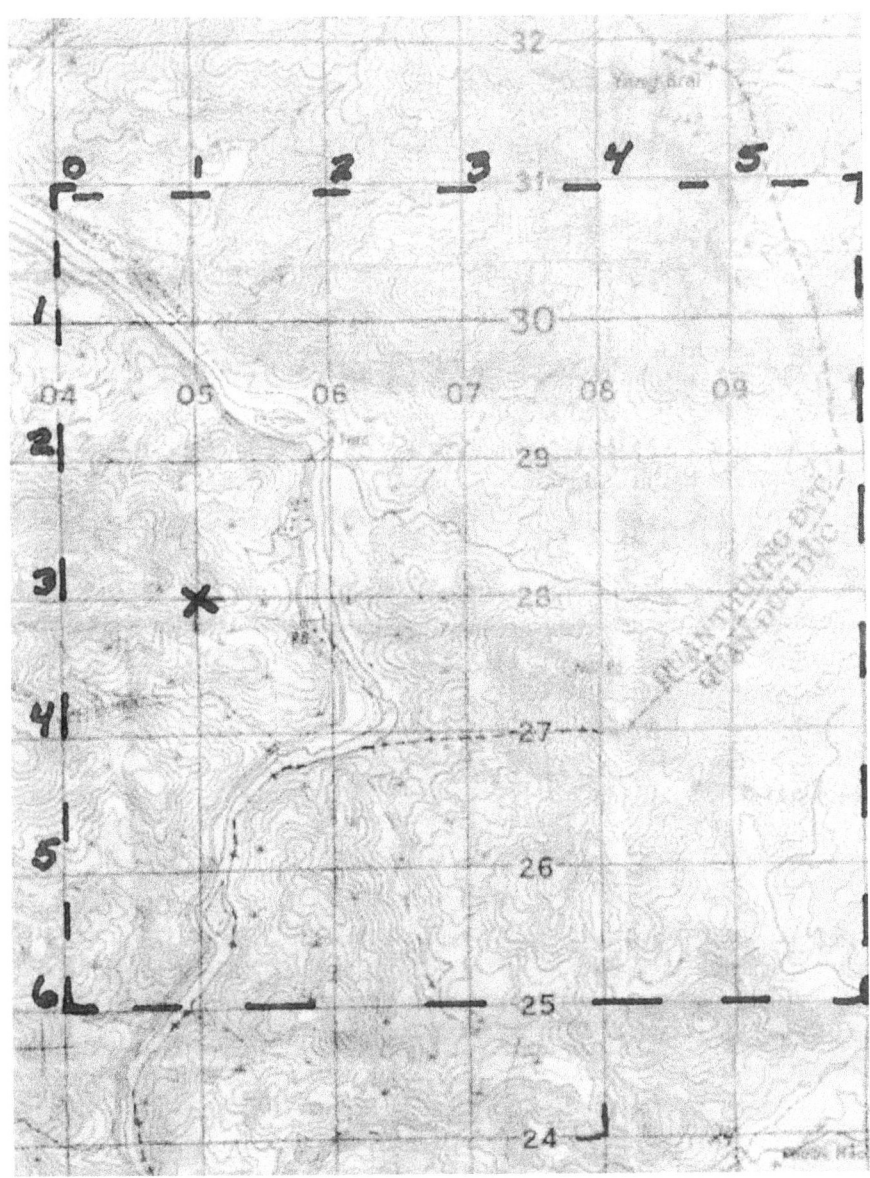

The "Grid"

"Twenty."

He shook his head.

"No more than eighteen rounds. You put in the full clip and the springs on these little bastards will jam," he told me as he tapped the end of the magazine against his leg to be certain that the rounds were well seated.

He filled one of my cartridge pouches with four magazines and laid a fifth cross-ways on top of the others, forcing the flap of the canvas pouch down until it clipped into place. "If you carry four pouches you'll have twenty magazines, three hundred sixty rounds.

"Some guys haul around extra magazines in their pack. Not gonna help 'em much in there. Here's what I use." He went over to his bunk and pulled out a cloth bandolier holding eight magazines. He looped it over my head and tied it snugly to my chest.

"Now you're starting to fit into the platoon." Fernandez nodded approvingly. "You're beginning to look like Pancho Villa."

"Each of us carries only half a Claymore on patrol," Chief continued.

"Half?"

"Yea, we cut 'em in two. Each side has a blasting cap, and cutting 'em in two makes them easier to carry and nearly as effective," he explained in the slightly pedantic voice of a high school math teacher talking to a dim student."

Fernandez reached under his cot and pulled an intact Claymore from its carrying case. He unsheathed his Ka-Bar and began slicing through the mine's thin plastic housing with no more concern than if he were cutting a slice of bread. In a few seconds, the mine split into two parts. He gouged out a small piece of the plastic explosive with his finger and looked at it thoughtfully.

"Some guys say it's good for a toothache. I've even heard of it being used to get high. Never tried it myself."

"Why not? You've tried just about everything else," Chief joked wryly.

Fernandez didn't take the bait. He rolled a small pellet of the plastic explosive in his hand. It reminded me of taffy candy.

"We use it to heat up our rations. It burns hot and without smoke. Not in the bush of course," he added.

"What do you use in the field?" I asked.

"We don't use anything; we eat our food cold."

"Give me your knife," Chief interrupted.

"I wasn't issued one," I replied.

"Shit, man … didn't they give you anything? You'd think the mothers were paying for the equipment themselves the way they hold on to it."

"Give 'em a break; they've got to have something to sell in Da Nang." Fernandez laughed.

Chief rummaged around his footlocker and came up with a Ka-Bar knife and a leather sheath. "Take this one," he offered, throwing it down on the cot.

The Ka-Bar was the same design the Marine Raiders had used in World War II. I drew the blade out of its sheath. It was a wicked weapon. The blade was covered in a dull black finish and razor-sharp.

"Ya got to have something to dig a shit hole with," Fernandez remarked, picking it up and holding it in his hand.

Chief grabbed more things out of his footlocker and handed me a stick of camouflage paint, a small plastic bottle of insect repellent, a compass, a set of small pencil flares, and a small metal signaling mirror. I put the things he gave me on my shelf so that I wouldn't forget anything tomorrow morning.

I shrugged into my web gear and Chief adjusted the straps until he was satisfied. He taped the clasps closed so the straps wouldn't loosen. I had put two canteens on my web gear; he added two more and moved all of them farther back and the ammunition pouches forward. My equipment felt much better each time he adjusted it, tighter and more balanced.

"This is the way I like my gear to hang," he said, stepping back and inspecting his work with satisfaction. He placed my rifle under my arm and showed me how the barrel would rest against the top of my cartridge packs.

He taped the sheath of the Ka-Bar upside down to the left shoulder strap of my web gear. A quick pull and it would be in my hand. He opened a new box of grenades and took out the baseball-shaped device. He cut off strips of green tape and wound them once around the pin. "This way the pin won't catch on a vine and blow up," he said in a matter-of-fact voice. He spaced a grenade carefully between each of my magazine pouches and hung two more on clips at chest level. He taped a cylindrical red smoke grenade to my right shoulder strap and told me to put on my pack.

I bent down cautiously and struggled into my pack. He helped me adjust it and told me to jump up and down. As I did so a faint ringing sound came from where a loose buckle met the end of a strap. Chief took another strip of tape and silenced it. I walked around and this time the gear was quiet. He stepped back and circled me like a tailor, tightening straps and pulling on equipment to be sure that everything was secure. With gear and ammo I must have been carrying over eighty pounds and I didn't even have water in my canteens.

"How does it feel?"

"Feels like it weighs a ton," I replied honestly, trying to walk around.

"That's nothin'," Garcia said as he watched me stumble around under the load. "When we were with the grunts we lived out of our packs for months on end. Tents, stoves, shovels, mortars, fuel, man, we humped everything into the bush."

"What are you griping about? I'm the one that got stuck with the radio. That mother weighs at least another twenty-five pounds." Fernandez complained.

Chief helped me strip off my equipment and hang it on the large nails over my cot. "Careful with those grenades; I don't trust the damn things," he warned.

Chief made a soft clicking sound with his tongue. It sounded like the command a horseback rider would make to urge his mount forward: *click click*.[2]

I pressed my tongue against the top of my mouth and tried to duplicate what I had just heard—*click click ... click click*.

Chief nodded. "When you're in the bush and you see anything—and I mean anything!—make that double click."

"If you hear that sound, freeze and wait for the hand signal. Here's the most important one," he said, drawing the second finger of his right hand across his throat in a slow slashing motion.

He repeated the gesture. "You see this, you freeze and get down, because someone's seen Charlie, and the shit is gonna hit the fan."

He bent his right arm and raised a closed fist. "You see *this* and you freeze! Not another fuckin' step!"

Fernandez held up his index finger. "You see this, and you punch the other guy right in the mouth!"

"You are really such a jerk; can't you take anything seriously?" Chief asked him, shaking his head.

"Plenty of time to be serious after I'm dead," Fernandez answered quietly.

9. Morning

There will be time. There will be time
To prepare a face to meet the faces that you meet.
—T.S. Eliot, "The Love Song of J. Alfred Prufrock"

It was still dark when the men started moving around in the hooch and I headed to the latrine and showers. As I sat there in the damp outhouse, I couldn't help but think that this might very well be the last time I made such a trip. It wasn't a comforting thought.

I came back to the hooch, grabbed a towel and was heading for the shower with my soap and razor when Garcia stopped me at the door and shook his head.

"Charlie can smell soap a mile away, besides…" he continued, rubbing the stubble on his chin, "the camouflage paint sticks better when it's got something to hang on to."

Dawn was just breaking as we got dressed. It was a lovely morning. The clouds lining the horizon to the east lit up with the first rays of the sun and turned pink and gold. To the west, the moon was fading, ringed by fading stars and the more brilliant Venus. I had woken to many dawns before, but the thought of this being the last one I might ever see made it all the more beautiful.

The men around me were also was getting dressed for the bush, pulling on the old gear that they had worn when they first came in from their last patrol, the utilities stained and still covered in dried dirt. I saw Garcia pulling on a pair of dirty pants and I kidded him about being too lazy to wash them.

"They blend in better with the jungle that way," he replied seriously.

I later took his advice and kept a set of ragged "bush utilities," separate from my other utilities. They were faded and muddy, but blended into the bush much better than the starched utilities I kept aside for inspections.

Sergeant Blaze entered the hooch to check on how we were doing. He wore a set of tiger-striped utilities that he had probably gotten from someone in Special Forces. The rest of the men were still wearing the standard green Marine Corps utilities we wore back in the States. We didn't get the new lightweight camouflaged utilities until several months later, although it was rumored that the Marine Corps Band had already received them. It was only proper; the band needed to impress the generals more than we needed the new equipment in the field.

The men took their time putting on their camouflage paint, holding up small signal mirrors to look at themselves, as intently as ladies putting on makeup. The happy-go-lucky group of men I bunked with had transformed themselves into grim-faced warriors whose faces I scarcely recognized. Chief told me that his Navaho ancestors painted their bodies for the same reasons we did, to provide camouflage, instill fear in the enemy, and indicate their role in the war party. He told me that the Navaho used black paint to indicate death and red to signify blood. We used black, brown and green colors for more practical reasons.

We had our choice of two kinds of paint. The newer type came out of tubes and produced vivid green and black colors, that produced a vivid glossy look. The other kind was a thick crayon held in a small metal tube, which opened on both ends. One end of the tube held black pigment, the other green. This type gave a duller look, which Chief said he preferred because it lasted longer in the rain.

Each man put on his paint as he pleased, there was no standard pattern. Some favored irregular blobs of color, others rather ornate designs. I was interested in seeing how, as an Indian, Chief would paint himself. I was expecting some flamboyant design, but practical as always, he simply painted one side of his face black and the other green. He told me that the simple design allowed him to put on his camouflage without a mirror. I fiddled around and finally came with a complicated design that Fernandez said made me look like Spiderman. Peering at myself in the mirror I thought I looked very cool. What a jerk I was.

The men thoroughly checked and rechecked their gear, re-taping clasps and buckles, checking their weapons. They carefully placed pens, small notebooks, maps and assorted smaller items in plastic bags, which they taped shut and dropped into their side jacket pockets. The other men seemed to be watching me with a critical eye, and they didn't hesitate to offer advice.

"Don't forget the backs of your hands and arms, and close your eyes and put some green shit on your eyelids. They look like spotlights every time you blink." Garcia advised.

"You don't have any paint on the backs of your ears," Fernandez noticed as he passed me.

"Tuck your jacket into your pants so the leeches don't crawl up your back," Chief warned, noticing that I was walking around the hooch with the jacket over my belt. As I started to pull on my boots, he threw me a small plastic bottle of insect repellent. "Spray your boots and cuffs and then tape your pants to the top of your boots. Otherwise the leeches will crawl up and make themselves at home on your balls." The pungent odor filled the room as I squeezed a thin stream of the bug juice onto my boots, sprayed a little on my hand and wiped my face.

"Shoulda done that before you put your paint on," Fernandez criticized. "Now your camo is going to be all smeared up."

I started to put the bottle of insect repellent in my side pocket with my map.

"No, not there!" he objected. "That shit will eat right through plastic. Put it in your top pocket with your paint so you can get to it easily when we take a break, and put your map in the your other pocket."

I reached for the small items that Chief had given me the night before and began putting the small pencil flares in the pants.

This time it was Garcia who stopped me. "No, not there!" he protested. "You don't want to sit on 'em, and if you start putting stuff in your pants you'll find yourself pulling them up every hundred yards."

I put on the only piece of new clothing that the supply sergeant had given me, a camouflaged wide-brimmed hat and proudly glanced at my reflection in the mirror."

Garcia took one look me, grabbed the hat off my head and kicked it out the door. "Goddamn parade ground piece of shit! Those things are no dammed good, won't even stay on your head in the bush."

He pulled a ratty green cap off his head and patted it affectionately. It looked like a sailor's hat with the brim pulled down. I remembered the camouflaged beret left at the bottom of my footlocker. Garcia reluctantly nodded in approval, but I hesitated to put it on.

"I feel sort of funny wearing a dead man's cap," I objected.

He shrugged his shoulders dismissively, "Up to you, man, but half my gear came from guys who don't need it anymore. Me … I kind of like the idea. Shit used by the old guys has a good feel to it."

I slipped the beret on my head. It fit perfectly.

"Tell me about Mariner," I asked sitting down on my cot, thinking about the Marine whose foot locker I had been given.

Chief and Garcia looked at each other.

"Johnny? It was an accident," Chief replied softly.

"No, it wasn't," Garcia objected. "Tell him the truth."

"There's not a lot to tell. We were on a prisoner snatch and found a heavily used trail. Blaze decided to pull back and set up the ambush the next morning, but before we withdrew he had Johnny set a booby trap on the trail."

"Johnny always liked fucking around with those damn things anyway" Garcia interrupted, shaking his head.

"Next morning, before it got light, he went out to retrieve it…"

"We told him to just leave it," Garcia added.

"Yeah, well … either he tripped the wire or for some other reason it went off."

"We told him to just leave it," Garcia repeated more softly.

10. Mount Up

There is no hunting like the hunting of men. And those who have hunted armed men long enough and liked it, never care for anything else thereafter.—Ernest Hemingway

When everyone was ready, Sergeant Blaze joined us to test-fire our weapons. I joined the other men as he led us down the hill toward the LZ. With my old bush hat, camouflaged face and other gear I may have looked like a Recon Marine from the outside, but inside I knew better. I watched the others and tried to blend in.

The sergeant stopped in front of a wall of sandbags that blocked a small cleft in the hillside. Chief was at the head of the line. Without waiting for an order, he turned to the hill, pulled back the bolt and fired his rifle into the embankment, a few single shots at first, then a few short bursts, and finally the entire magazine as he switched to full automatic.

"Mine works," he said, satisfied, lowering his weapon and checking to see that it was clear. "How about yours?" he asked, turning to me.

I braced the barrel of my M-16 on top of the sandbag and fired off a few bursts as Sergeant Blaze looked on. He put down the M-14 he was holding and held out his hand

10. Mount Up

to take my weapon. He loaded a new magazine and fired off a volley of rounds so quickly that they sounded like the rifle was set to full automatic, but he was pulling the trigger for each shot. He didn't say anything but nodded approvingly as he handed it back to me.

"Now don't fuck things up by cleaning that thing now that you know it works," Chief advised me as the other men took turns firing their weapons. He took some more camo tape and wound it around the handgrip of my rifle. When he was finished, he cut off a small piece and, moistening it with his tongue to keep it from sticking too much, pressed it lightly against the end of the barrel. "This will keep dirt out of the barrel until you need to use it, and it will then blow off with the first shot. Don't put on any more than this small piece or it will smoke and give away your position."

Garcia gazed reflectively into the small cave made by the rounds smashing into the hillside. "Someday, someone is going to dig around down here and come up with hundreds of pounds of bullets. I wonder what the hell they will think was going on?"

Blaze looked at his watch and told us that if we hurried we would have enough time for breakfast. We walked down to the mess tent and grabbed some ham and eggs. The men were quiet, each man thinking his own thoughts. The other Marines saw our war paint and avoided us. We ate quickly as a group and then walked back together to get our gear.

The sky was brightening as we made our way down the hill to the LZ. The men tried to relax, sitting down on the ground propped up against their huge packs like overturned turtles. Some talked or smoked, but most tried to get a few extra minutes of sleep. Fernandez checked in on the radio from time to time with our command post, trying to get an update for the sergeant on where the "birds" were.

The air was hot, but occasionally a cooler breeze swept off the paddies. I leaned against my pack, absorbed in my own thoughts. Part of me wanted the clouds to lift so we could get going, and part of me didn't, but it wasn't long before we heard the distinctive *clop-clop-clop* of a CH-46's rotor blades To this day that sound still brings goose bumps to my arms.

"Mount up!" Blaze shouted over the noise of the incoming aircraft. We rolled over onto our hands and knees and painfully straightened up, using our rifles to help support the weight of our packs and other equipment. Chief gave me a hand getting to my feet and gave me some last minute advice.

"When we go out, you stick close to me and watch Sergeant Blaze. Keep your eyes open and don't fuck up!" Chief emphasized his last words by punching me lightly in the shoulder.

The chopper came fast, flaring out a few feet above the LZ, its huge turbine engines screaming, I was hit with a sudden blast of hot air and blown sand from its rotor blades and had to turn my face away. The rear hatch was dropping even before the wheels hit the ground. We clambered aboard, ducking low and holding on to our hats against the hot downdraft.

Once on the ramp we were somewhat protected from the prop blast, but inside the helicopter the high-pitched scream of the turbines seemed even louder. The body of the chopper was bare except for a row of canvas and aluminum seats that extended along both sides. The chopper's crew chief in a green aviation helmet motioned us to move forward. Another helmeted Marine manned one of the two 50 caliber machine guns that extended from each side of the aircraft.

Our bulging packs and other gear took up most of the bench area and we had to sit sideways, nearly falling off the edges of the narrow aluminum and fabric seats. When everyone was aboard, the crew chief gave the go-ahead to the pilot. The tempo of the blades increased and suddenly we were airborne, leaving the ground in a roaring whoosh, skimming the rice paddies no more than a few hundred feet above the ground. As we flew over, I saw the Vietnamese farmers bending over the rice stalks they were planting in the mud. They were so used to helicopters flying over them that they didn't even bother to look up.

The ramp was still nearly all the way down, leaving the back of the chopper wide open. I worried that if the rear engine lost power and the aircraft pitched up we'd drop out the back hatch like peas falling out of a can, but no one else seemed concerned and the pilot left the back ramp down until we were high in the air.

I had been in old Marine choppers during training, but this one was truly a wreck. The windows were broken out and air blew freely through the craft. Candy wrappers and other trash blew around on the floor. Spent shell casings rolled from one end of the chopper to the other as we banked. I expected them to roll down the ramp and fall out the open tailgate, but they never did.

White clouds scudded by the aircraft. I couldn't help but think that these might be the last clouds I would ever see. I looked out at the sky and the lofty mountains realized that I stood a very good chance of never seeing them again and as I looked out at the clouds passing below me the words "How beautiful..." formed in my mind.

"How beautiful.... How beautiful," I repeated over and over to myself, and for some reason the phrase calmed me. These few words eventually became a protective mantra that I repeated on every mission. I know that talking about a "protective mantra" sounds foolish now, but at the time I didn't think it was silly at all.

The men sat facing one another on the narrow pull-down aluminum and canvas benches, their rifles cradled between their knees. I looked down at the faces painted in brown and green camouflage and wondered what they were thinking. Fernandez nervously rubbed his eyes, as if trying to avoid looking around. Garcia took out his crucifix from his neck and kissed it. Chief watched him and then, looking deliberately at me, put the barrel of his rifle to his lips and kissed it. I could see where he was putting his faith.

Only Sergeant Blaze seemed unmoved, slowly chewing a piece of gum and staring down impassively at the jungle passing beneath him. He reminded me more of a commuter taking the train to his job than someone about to risk his life in combat.

The air turned cold as we gained altitude. The chopper struggled to climb above the mountains that appeared in front of us. From a distance, they were a light blue, but as we got closer they turned a deep green. Tufts of white mist collected in the valleys. Rivers wound through the mountain ranges and at one point a waterfall plunged hundreds of feet into the jungle.

The crew chief motioned Sergeant Blaze who got up and moved to the cockpit where I saw him glancing at his map, nudging the pilot and then pointing his finger downward. He and Chief, who was running assistant patrol leader, had flown over the area the

10. Mount Up

previous day on an overflight and both were familiar with the landing site. We passed over a river and the sounds of the blades changed as we began dropping.

The crew chief pulled back the bolt on the 50 caliber machine gun mounted near the door, another gunner did the same on the other side of the aircraft. The site hadn't been strafed by Hueys[1] beforehand and they didn't fire. The pilot was going in "soft," hoping to insert us quietly. With any luck, the enemy wouldn't even know we had landed.

"Lock and load!" Blaze yelled back to us over the noise of the turbines.

Eight bolts slammed home as the springs holding them back released and the weapons armed. Sergeant Blaze moved back to his seat, somehow keeping his balance as the chopper started to descend in a tight circle. The men slid around on their seats and faced outward, their rifles pointing through the portholes. My head snapped as the CH-46 banked and sank with a sudden rush toward a small clearing in the trees below us.

Two Huey gunships shot from behind us. They must have been with us all the time, but I hadn't seen them. The gunships dove toward the ground, intentionally trying to draw enemy fire before our larger craft touched down. When I turned around, everyone except me was kneeling on the benches with their weapons pointed out through the open portholes. Now I knew how all the windows had gotten smashed out.

Our chopper banked sharply and in a few seconds we were hovering a few feet above the ground. Sergeant Blaze was standing facing the ramp as we struggled to our feet and prepared to exit. We felt the tires bump once on the ground and the aircraft settled down.

Suddenly there was a loud *bang*! It sounded as if someone had thrown a brick against the side of a bus. The machine gunner on the right side of the aircraft immediately started firing.

"Take this, you bastards!" he shouted, spraying the hillside with his M2 machine gun.

The other men swung around in their seats and opened fire as well. The entire chopper shook like something alive as the pilot applied full power and we lurched into the air.

Kneeling down next to Garcia I saw flashes of light coming from the tree line a few hundred yards away. Trying to keep my balance on the seat, I joined the rest of the team firing out the windows at the flashes I saw coming from the tree line. In a few seconds, my magazine was empty. I was fumbling around for another when I heard the whoosh of rockets as the Huey gunships came in on a strafing run. When I looked up, the entire hillside was on fire.

We were gaining altitude and pulling away, the chopper banking steeply and lurching from side to side in evasive maneuvers. We continued to fire through the portholes as we left the ground, firing until we were far out of range, shooting even after Sergeant Blaze yelled at us to cease-fire.

Suddenly everyone was laughing, shouting, giving one another the high five. The crew chief was so pumped he was jumping up and down and slapping the gunner on the back. The pilot looked back at us, a big grin on his face. This was my first taste of combat and, God help me, I enjoyed it. The adrenaline rush that I got from risking my life was a potent drug, perhaps the most potent of all.

We flew back to our compound. When we landed, the pilot and crew went carefully around the aircraft with a Magic Marker while we waited on the landing zone. They found three bullet holes through the cabin and two more through the right fuel tank, just below where I had been sitting.

Looking at the aluminum skin on the aircraft, some faint lettering under the paint caught my eye, and peering closer I could just make out the word *Budweiser*. Someone had cut a circular piece of aluminum from a beer can, sprayed it over with green paint, and riveted it to the side of the chopper. The aircraft was liberally pockmarked with these ad-hoc repairs.

As the insane rush of my first experience in combat began to fade, I found myself immensely tired. I figured that the day was over and I was looking forward to going back to the hooch, but the men still sat around the LZ. Sergeant Blaze was crouched down next to Fernandez and talking with someone on the radio. Within a few minutes another CH-46 landed.

Chief and the other men were refilling their magazines from boxes of ammo on the LZ and I asked him what was going on.

He looked up at me with surprise. "We're getting ready to go out."

"Out again?" I asked in a shocked voice. "We just got into a firefight!" I could hardly believe what he was telling me.

"Shit, man … that weren't no firefight; we just got shot out of an LZ, that's all," he told me with a dismissive laugh.

He opened up another box of M-16 bullets, carefully examining each round before sliding it against the magazine spring and pushing it in. When he had finished reloading, he pushed the box of ammo over to me.

"Better get loaded up, bro."

11. Alone on the LZ

Ah, it is hard to speak of what it was
That savage forest, dense and difficult
Which even in recall renews my fear
—Dante's Inferno

We reloaded our weapons and once again walked up the ramp. Once more, the chopper took off in a heaving lurch. Once more, the clouds passed under us and I repeated my mantra. Once again, we locked and loaded and felt the cool air turn hot and moist as the chopper descended.

The rounds coming through the fuel tank just under my feet had really sobered me up, and the excitement that I felt earlier in the day had been replaced by the hope that I wouldn't do anything stupid and let my teammates down. There is nothing like being shot at to knock some of the silliness out of you.

This time the pilot decided to try to sneak in alone, and dropped us into an abandoned rice paddy about five miles from our first location. As the chopper hovered about six feet above the ground Blaze ran down the ramp and leaped off. The rest of the team quickly following him. When I reached the end of the ramp, I hesitated. I couldn't even see the ground. Below my feet was just a sea of grass rolling like ocean waves from the rotor blast. Someone pushed me from behind and I fell forward, sinking to my knees in soft mud, smelling the pungent, rotten sweetness of the Vietnam jungle for the first time.

With a screaming whoosh and a blast of swirling air, the CH-46 climbed back into the cool safety of the clouds. After the high-pitched whining of the turbines and the clopping of the rotor blades, the silence seemed absolute. I looked around and found myself standing completely alone in the center of the clearing. I couldn't imagine what had happened. Had my teammates somehow gotten back on the helicopter and were even now miles away, or had they just taken off running as soon as they hit the ground and left me behind?

As I stood there helplessly, not knowing what to do, I suddenly heard a soft double-clicking noise and saw Sergeant Blaze rising to his feet only a few yards in front of me. Camouflaged by his paint and tiger-striped utilities, the sergeant had simply disappeared into the grass. If he hadn't moved I wouldn't have seen him. One by one, as if surfacing from a green sea, the rest of the team reappeared. After exiting the aircraft, they had fanned out in a large circle around the chopper to provide protection until it took off.

Following the sergeant's signal, slowly, quietly, single file, each man rose and took his place in a long column that snaked into the jungle. Chief led the way as point man, then Sergeant Blaze. Fernandez followed with the radio. I was next. Garcia, in the position of tail-end Charlie, was the last in line.

Chief had told me to watch how Blaze moved in the bush, but this was easier said than done. The sergeant seemed to flow through the jungle with an ease and quietness I could admire but not imitate. I stumbled awkwardly along behind him. Every piece of my gear seemed to catch on something, often a slender loop of vine no thicker than a pencil lead. I pushed myself forward expecting the vine to snap, but it stopped me in my tracks. Looking down, I noticed barbed teeth angled like fishhooks every few inches along the vine's entire length. The vine had entwined itself like a piece of barbed wire around my leg and I couldn't pull free. Fernandez saw me struggling, came over and cut the vine with a small throwing knife he had fastened to his web gear.

"Wait-a-minute vine," he whispered, giving me an encouraging smile and rejoining the column.

The trees growing hundreds of feet above our heads blocked out much of the light. The air was hot and humid and smelled like freshly turned earth. The team moved slowly, taking only a step or two at a time, twenty feet between each man, their entire attention focused on the surrounding jungle. Their rifles swung slowly from side to side—step, look, listen, wait, another step.

We paused for a few minutes while the sergeant studied his map. The men crouched down in a rough semicircle, facing out and alert to any sound. I glanced at my map, but despite all my training in navigation, without any landmarks, I was lost. In the thick jungle, I was only able to see a few yards in front of me. I knew from my compass that we were heading in a general westerly direction, but that was all.

The sergeant gave a hand signal that looked like someone putting a cup to his lips. One by one each of the men in turn drank a little water. I carried four canteens hooked into my web belt. Some of the men had six, and Fernandez, the radio operator, was carrying at least an extra gallon in a large plastic bottle he had strapped to the outside of his knapsack. I wished I had brought more, but Chief had advised against it, warning me that the more water I carried the thirstier I would get. Instead of taking a drink, Chief broke off a piece of grass and sucked on it. I would have liked to follow his example, but I lacked his willpower and drank nearly an entire canteen.

Even during the break, my muscles were so tense that they hurt. We had been moving less than an hour, but already my fatigues were soaked in sweat. I imagined an enemy soldier behind every tree. My right arm was aching from holding my rifle in a death grip. Watching the other men, I noticed that they rested their weapons on their cartridge belts, their right hands gripping the stocks, their fingers on the triggers. With the weapons held in this way the men were able easily guide them with one hand. I adjusted my cartridge belt so I could do the same and felt the muscles in my arm relax.

Blaze signaled and all too soon we began moving again. I glanced back and saw Garcia covering our rear, walking backward nearly as easily as the others moved forward. No one spoke. Occasionally Chief, running point, would hold up a closed fist and everyone would freeze expectantly. Each time he did this my heart would begin to pound, but in a few minutes, we would move on. From time to time, the sergeant would glance at his map and indicate a particular direction, but that was all. We kept moving around the base of the mountain, gradually climbing higher.

The almost impenetrable low undergrowth surrounding the immediate area of the LZ had given way to huge trees that towered above the jungle floor. They shut out the sun, but not the heat. Moisture dripped off the leaves above and fell as a light mist from high above us. We moved through a secondary growth that came up to our hips, and became waders in a green sea. The trees had trunks nearly eight feet across, with roots extending for yards around their base. Shafts of light pierced the top canopy in various directions, giving the entire area the feel of a huge cathedral. I imagined how tiny we would look from the tops of these gigantic trees. We would appear to be no more than a thin line of ants.

The adrenaline-fueled rush that I had felt when we first landed had now ebbed, and to a certain extent that was a good thing. It was impossible to stay keyed up so tightly for any amount of time. I began to notice the sounds of the jungle, birds and insects, and the wind flowing through the trees. My body began to sense a rhythm to my teammates' movements and gradually I became part of it. Every hour or so we would stop for a breather, form up our defensive circle and listen for any sign of pursuit. I began to relax and feel more at home in the jungle. At the next break I pulled out my map and thought I finally knew approximately where we were.

After a short rest we continued climbing upward, Chief skirting open areas, choosing the route that gave us the most cover. Suddenly I heard the soft clicking noise again. Chief looked back and slowly passed his right hand across his throat in a slitting motion. My heart started to pump faster. I slowly crouched down in the grass behind an old rotten tree stump. The men in front had disappeared into the ground. I suddenly felt a sharp sting on my leg. Looking down, I saw hundreds of red ants pouring out of the rotten stump I was leaning against. I gritted my teeth and tried not to move as they climbed up my leg and started to bite.

Finally, Chief signaled for us to move up; He had come across a well-used trail. We moved cautiously across the trail to the higher ground on the other side. Garcia caught my eye after we had crossed the path and pointed up and down the trail, indicating that he wanted me to watch both directions as he took a branch and carefully smoothed out the ground over which we had passed, erasing all traces of our crossing.

The sergeant glanced at his map again and we turned to our right heading directly up the slope. With every step, the slope got steeper and Blaze moved faster, climbing effortlessly upward. Everyone else was pulling themselves up using the shrubs growing out of the mountainside. I was forced to do the same, but every time I grabbed hold of anything I got either pricked or cut. I now noticed ruefully that other men were wearing light leather gloves. They had cut the fingers off the gloves so they could easily trigger their weapons, but the leather at least protected their palms. There was a pair of Mariner's gloves in my footlocker, but I hadn't seen the need for them and had left them behind.

Even with the new grooved jungle boots I had finally gotten from the supply sergeant my feet slipped constantly on the wet ground. For every two steps I managed to take forward it seemed I lost one. My pack seemed to pull me backward, and I pictured myself losing my balance and cartwheeling backwards down the slope. Fernandez moved up behind me. He was carrying the same amount of gear as the rest of us and had the additional weight of the PRC-25 radio. He looked completely exhausted. I gave him my hand as he struggled upward. He gained his footing and, stopped beside me for a moment to catch his breath, and as he did so he whispered a warning.

"Watch yourself. Every time we get a new guy in the team Blaze tries to break him."

We must have been close to the top of the mountain, but every time I made it up one slope another took its place. Finally, I felt a cool breeze and, looking up, saw a batch of blue sky ahead. The air flowing up from the valley below and blowing off the summit was like a splash of cool water on my face.

"Give my soul water," I thought to myself as we climbed the last few feet. I had no idea where the words came from; they just seemed to form themselves in my mind. The sun was going down in the west and from our vantage point blue mountain ranges stretched to the horizon. Clouds were forming in the valley below us. It was a majestic sight.

The team stopped as the sergeant and Chief checked out the area. I braced my feet against a low tree and leaned back against the slope. It was so steep that I was nearly in a standing position. Garcia straddled a log with both legs, leaned back and took a big drink from his canteen.

Chief signaled for us to move up and we finally reached the top of the hill. A well-used path snaked along the ridgeline. Sergeant Blaze scanned the terrain with his binoculars. He nodded with satisfaction and called Fernandez over to radio our position back to headquarters. It was here that we would set up our observation post.

Blaze led us back down the slope, leaving Garcia and Fernandez on the trail above us to warn us of any movement. About fifty yards down the hill there was a small clump of heavy brush. One by one, we followed the sergeant as he tunneled into the bushes.

The men kept their gear on and slumped to the ground waiting for darkness. It was on this nearly vertical slope that we would spend the night.

A light rain had begun to fall and water was running down the hill. Now that we had stopped, my legs started to itch terribly from the ant bites. Every move that I made to try to get comfortable, no matter how slow and careful, drew annoyed looks from the rest of the men who stoically sat quietly in the rain.

Finally, Blaze crawled over to me. I braced myself for what I knew was coming.

"What the hell is the matter with you? Can't you sit still?" he whispered angrily.

Without speaking, I pulled up my trouser leg to show him the ant bites, each of which was now a red circle the size of a dime. As if that weren't bad enough, three fat leeches had somehow found their way up my pants and had attached themselves to my calf. The sergeant reached into his pocket, pulled out a plastic bottle of bug juice and squirted them. They immediately shriveled up and dropped off.

Blaze shook his head and in an annoyed voice whispered to me, "Next time, make sure your pant legs are always tucked into your boots, and then tape 'em up. Otherwise you're just a meal for the bugs around here."

Chief had told me the same thing, but in the excitement of getting ready I had forgotten to do what he had told me. It was one mistake I wouldn't make again.

Each man had picked a spot where he thought he had the best chance of not sliding down the cliff. Most straddled small trees, their packs between their legs. I noticed that they had carefully arranged their web gear so that they could easily slip their arms into the straps. Their rifles were at their sides, facing upward, and they had stuck their knives into the ground by their sides. Everything they needed was right in front of them and could easily be found, even in the dark. I found a small bush that looked like it was well rooted into the cliff face, arranged my gear like the rest of the other men and wedged myself into position. I found that once I settled into position I was reasonably comfortable and I began to hope that I might even be able to get a little rest.

Sergeant Blaze gave the signal to eat. The men took turns, only one person eating at any time. I watched as Chief quietly removed a can of beanies and weenies from his pack. Taking the tiny P-38 can opener from the lanyard around his neck, he slipped the tiny blade over the lip of the can and pushed down, muffling the cut with his fingers. It took time, but there was no noise at all. When he finished eating, Chief wiped the can clean, wrapped it back in the sock he had taken it out of, and replaced it in his pack. I remembered that he had told me that the team never left leaving anything behind. A pebble rolled down the slope near me and I saw the sergeant climbing down toward Chief and me.

"You two take the next watch; you'll be relieved at midnight by Fernandez and Garcia. Put out the Claymores, but don't use them unless you're spotted. Maybe we can do a prisoner snatch," Blaze whispered, a trace of excitement in his voice.

Chief nodded, but I could tell he was less than enthusiastic about the sergeant's idea.

The sergeant tapped his watch. "Radio check on the hour; three clicks… Mayfly." With that enigmatic phrase, which Chief apparently understood, he disappeared into the jungle.

Chief unhooked a canvas pouch containing the Claymore kit from his web gear and began climbing upward to the ridgeline. I followed him. I thought we had climbed without a sound, but when we reached the ridgeline Garcia and Fernandez, the two men Blaze had ordered to guard the trail, had their rifles pointed straight as us. They motioned to a small boulder off the side of the trail where they had stashed the radio. When I looked again, they had both disappeared down the slope. We crawled over to the boulder and crouched down behind it. From this position we were able to see hundreds of yards down the trail.

"Cover me," Chief ordered. He opened up the canvas satchel he had brought with him and took out half of a Claymore mine. I watched from a distance as he carefully extended the wire prongs and fastened the mine upright in the ground a few feet off the trail. He covered the device with grass and leaves to hide it from view. He carefully inserted a blasting cap and, crawling backward, reeled the ignition wire back to where we sat behind the rock. Finally, he inserted the wires into the detonator. One squeeze would set off the mine, sending a wall of steel screaming down the trail.

"You do the next one," he whispered, handing me the second mine and giving me a tight smile. "On-the-job training."

I set up the Claymore at the other end of the trail and crawled back to the boulder. Night was quickly falling. The sun set behind the mountains leaving only a faint red glow. To the east, the first stars appeared in the sky and a full moon began to rise. The air was clear, and from where we sat we could see for miles. Garcia nudged me out of my reverie and with an annoyed look motioned me to direct my attention to my side of

On-the-Job Training (Wikimedia Commons)

the trail. His weapon remained trained on the other end. The bush was no place for daydreaming.

I glanced at my watch; it was almost time for the radio check. Garcia handed me the handset, obviously thinking that I knew what do with it, but I didn't. I put the handset to my ear and heard only static for a few seconds but then heard faint words through the headset.

"Mayfly, Mayfly, Mayfly radio check…"

I tapped Chief and pointed to the handset. He must have guessed my question and moved his thumb up and down three times. "Ah…" I clicked the handset's send button three times, sending the pre-arranged signal that meant all was well.

"Mayfly, acknowledged," the phantom voice replied as the static returned.

We were relieved a few minutes after midnight by Fernandez and Sergeant Blaze. Chief somehow remembered where we had climbed up. I wouldn't have been able to find my way back in the dark alone, but he slid down the slope directly to his pack. I knew I had left my gear close to his and stumbled across it in the dark, nearly pitching myself down the slope as I did so. I once again straddled my pack with my legs, pulled the silk blanket out of my pack and laid it underneath me.

In the darkness, the jungle turned into a fairyland. Every leaf and twig glowed with a silver phosphorescent fire. I turned over a small branch in my hand and marveled at the silvery pattern. Only the dark shapes of the Marines seemed immune from the icy magic, their shapes darker even than the shadows.

The rain woke me before dawn, at first a slight drizzle and then a steady downpour. I tried to ignore it by covering my face with my arm and then by pulling my beret over my face, but it was no use. In a few minutes, I was soaked. The rain continued to pour down, a chilling rain that made my teeth chatter. Surrounded by an impenetrable blackness, I could do nothing except wait miserably for the dawn. Daylight finally arrived, and with it a swarm of small biting insects. I rubbed repellent on my face and neck, but it soon washed off and the insects came back with a vengeance. Blaze seemed to stoically ignore the bugs, not even bothering to wipe them away from his face.

The insects bothered me, but even worse was a terrible itching inside my pants and down my legs. It was driving me crazy! I squirmed and fidgeted until Chief came over and in an annoyed whisper told me to stay still.

"I must have a rash from the ants,"

He reached in his pocket and handed me a tube of ointment, but as I undid my belt he saw what my problem was. "We don't wear underwear in the bush. Cut those shorts off and you'll feel better."

I sliced through the cotton fabric and stuffed the sodden cloth into my pack. The relief was immediate. Although my camouflage pants were wet, they didn't hold the water the way the way that cotton did. I wondered why they hadn't they taught us these simple things in training?

We took our turn guarding the ridgeline both night and day in the hope of capturing a prisoner. Blaze set up an observation post on the far side of the hill and spent hours scanning the forest below looking for signs of enemy activity, but the vegetation in the valleys was so thick that even binoculars couldn't pierce the jungle canopy. An entire NVA division could have passed beneath that cover without being seen. We spent three days on that miserable hill, baking in the heat of the day, soaked and freezing at night, setting out our Claymores, peering through binoculars at the hills around us and the valley below. We didn't see a thing.

The third night, I awoke to a soft whistling noise, close to me ... very close. I held my breath and heard it again. Suddenly I heard a muffled thump and a gasp as Sergeant Blaze grabbed Fernandez by the neck and with his hand over his mouth was shaking him.

"You either stay awake, you little bastard, or stop snoring," he whispered furiously. "If I hear you again—you're going to be wearing a gas mask."

I don't know if Fernandez stayed awake or not, but the rest of the night passed in utter silence.

12. Sniper

*And when I get to heaven and St. Peter rings the bell
One more Marine reporting, sir, I've served my
time in hell.*—Marine Running Cadence

The next morning Sergeant Blaze decided to leave our unproductive observation post and move closer to our extraction point, a valley to our east which had been bombed in a B-52 raid several months earlier. We woke before dawn and for the last time Chief and I climbed up to the ridgeline to retrieve our Claymores. The rest of the team spread leaves over our sleeping area to cover any sign that we had been there and then joined us on top of the hill.

Chief was once again the point man and led us along trail that traversed the mountain ridges. Another valley opened up in front of us and we could now see the devastation from the Arc Light bombing.[1] During our briefing we had been told that the strike had been "limited," but from a distance the valley floor looked like the craters of the moon. The blasts had ripped away the jungle canopy and huge circular holes pockmarked a bomb run that stretched for at least half a mile. Our choppers wouldn't have any problem at all finding a place to land there.

The sergeant got out his field glass and carefully studied the area.

"Any movement?" Chief asked softly. Blaze shook his head and motioned us forward.

We left the trail and started moving down into the valley itself. As we moved forward even the insects seemed to become still. The explosions had thrown a wall of earth and broken trees in front of us, forcing us to dig our way through the debris field. When we emerged on the other side, we saw a scene of utter destruction. Perfectly circular holes twenty feet across had ripped into the earth. The bomb craters were evenly spaced every few hundred yards across the valley floor. The holes must have been at least ten feet deep and in the weeks since the attack they had filled up with muddy water on top which a light green scum of algae floated.

Even though months had passed since the bombing entire area still smelled like an old latrine, a nauseating smell of cordite and rot that only got worse as we moved closer. The ground was muddy and the earth had a strange sponginess to it, It may have been my imagination but I felt as though the mud was covering something unwholesome under the ground, and perhaps it was.

The bombs had torn away the jungle cover, leaving only stumps and a few shattered trees, which were now stripped of their limbs and bark, but the jungle had already begun to reclaim the area. Grass and the shoots of bushes were beginning to emerge from the ground. Without the high jungle cover however, the heat was stifling, We slowly walked forward, keeping well separated and trying to stay as low as possible as we began to check out the area.

Chief suddenly dropped to the ground. We froze behind him as he slashed his finger across his throat and crawled slowly backward. "There's movement in a tree ahead of us," I heard him whisper.

Blaze crouched down, took out his binoculars and scanned the tree line in front of us. He shook his head and whispered, "There's something out there, but I can't make it out.." He shrugged out of his pack but then seemed to change his mind and motioned me over.

"You go with Chief," he told me, tapping the me on the shoulder and handing me his M-14. "If it's a sniper take him out."

I wasn't ready for this—it was only my first patrol for Christ's sake! Why hadn't the sergeant given the job to one of the more experienced men? Then I remembered that Fernandez had told me about Blaze always testing the new guys.

The M-14 he had handed me was the rifle we had trained with during basic, and I knew it well. The weapon in my hands was armed and ready, but I certainly wasn't, Chief had taken the binoculars and was already moving forward. There was nothing I could do except follow him as the rest of the team formed a defensive position behind us.

Keeping under cover and staying low, Chief and I gradually moved closer to our target. God, it was hot, and close to the ground the stench seemed worse than ever. We were still in a tangle of debris, but a short distance ahead of us there was no cover at all. We couldn't get any closer without exposing ourselves, if we went farther, the sniper would have a clear shot at us.

Chief stopped behind a stump and peered through his binoculars. I laid down in the mud and adjusted the sights on the rifle for the distance. Ahead of us I could see something moving in the branches of a shattered tree, but still couldn't make out what it was.

Chief suddenly laid his hand on my shoulder, "Relax ... it's only a piece of cloth."

We crawled closer and now I could clearly see a piece of canvas or something hanging from the crook of the tree. Chief stood up and moved forward, but I stayed where I was and kept my rifle trained on it. It was only when I heard the rest of the team move up from behind that I cautiously got to my feet. Chief continued moving ahead, eventually reaching the base of the shattered tree and motioned the rest of us forward.

12. Sniper

The author. "If it's a sniper take him out."

Forty feet up in a blasted tree, a poncho sized piece of canvas blanket hung down and waved feebly in the air. Whether it had been thrown into the tree by an explosion or simply had been blown there by the wind was impossible to say.

I handed the heavy M-14 back to Blaze with a huge sense of relief. He took it and handed me my M-16 without comment.

Following the bomb path, we came upon what may once have been a small village, now nearly buried by the force of the explosions. Wooden pillars that at one time would have supported walls and roofs were now pushed over, the splintered beams leaning away from the blasts. Fire had swept through the area and the ground was littered in clumps of charcoal and burnt wood.

We searched through the craters for bodies, uniforms, weapons, ammunition, anything else that might be useful to Intelligence but found nothing of value. If the village had been an enemy base camp at one time, it had been abandoned after the arc-light attack. Whatever evidence might have remained was now covered by the tons of earth thrown up by the bombs. We would need a bulldozer to know anything more.

We reached the end of the bomb run and climbed to the top of a ten-foot mound of debris. I looked back at the long bombing path and tried to imagine what it might have been like if anyone was on the ground. The B-52s flew so high that they wouldn't have even been seen. Like a hellish rain, the bombs would have fallen from the sky without warning, the explosions moving so swiftly that no one could have found cover before being obliterated.

The sergeant joined me on top of the mound. He took a long drink from his canteen and looked meditatively over the bomb run. "Awful lot of ordnance to blow up a few VC."

We cut our way back out of the mass of tangled vegetation ringing the bombed-out area and once again entered the shade of the jungle. Sergeant Blaze pressed on. I was sure he was hoping to come across equipment caches or graves from the bombing, but we found nothing.

More than anything else I wanted to get out of my utilities, which now were covered in mud and carried the stink of cordite and rot on them. I yearned for the shower that would wash the stink from me, but I was beginning to doubt whether there was enough water on earth to do that job. The smell was as much in my mind as it was on my clothes.

We continued moving away from the bombed out area, finding cover that night in a small jungle clearing where a massive jungle tree had fallen. We set up a defensive perimeter, and I found myself a good sleeping spot on a mossy bank near the tree's upturned roots. As darkness fell, I wrapped myself in my camouflaged silk blanket and, leaning back against my pack watched as stars filled the evening sky. Compared with our previous bivouac on the side of the hill, this mossy spot was a soft as a feather bed and it was such a relief to finally stretch out. If only the leaves would stop falling. I hadn't noticed them when I was putting down my pack, but every few minutes I would feel them fluttering down on my blanket. I gave up trying to brush them aside, pulled the blanket further over my head and drifted into sleep.

I awoke with the other men at first light and started rolling up my bedroll. As soon as I did so, a long line of hairy brown spiders began climbing out of their holes. All night long I must have been sleeping on top of a spider colony! The "falling leaves" that I had so casually brushed aside were the spiders trying to get in or get out of their homes.

Finally, almost reluctantly, Blaze led us back to the site of the arc-light bombing and we returned to the bombed out village and called our base to have us extracted. We grabbed our gear and set up a 360-degree defensive perimeter. After about an hour we heard the choppers heading toward us, a single CH-46 and two Huey gunships. The two blades on the 46 sounded a low *clop-clop-clop;* the gunships made a faster *whup-whup-whup* sound.

"Throw red smoke," Blaze ordered.

Garcia took a smoke grenade off his web gear, popped the pin, and threw it downwind a few yards away. It made a small pop, and a dense red cloud poured out.

"I see red smoke," the pilot radioed.

On the radio Fernandez confirmed the color with the pilot, and the aircraft began to descend. The Cong had a nasty habit of luring choppers into ambushes by also setting off a smoke grenade of their own. It was only until the pilot verified the color with us that he would land. The chopper's blades sucked up the smoke and then forced it downward, swirling it around us like giant red wings.

We ran up the ramp in no particular order, whoever was closest. The crew chief smiled as we entered. He knew that we had covered the area and hadn't found any enemy activity. As soon as the bird got up to altitude, everyone relaxed and started kidding around and talking about the patrol. The atmosphere was completely different from the tense trip outbound. We had done our job and no one had gotten hurt.

We flew low over the same rice paddies that we had flown over on the way out. The farmers were still tending their fields and living out their lives, oblivious to our passing. The water reflected the clouds and sky. Green tufts of new rice shoots poked their heads of green above the surface of the water.

"How beautiful, how beautiful," I thought to myself once again.

As soon as we landed, another team passed us, taking our place on the chopper. We were now safe, but the pilots and the airmen who had extracted us would be going back in again and again.

We made our way up the hill to the hooch. It was only a few hundred feet to the top, but after a long patrol it always felt much steeper and higher than it actually was. When we reached our hooch everyone dropped their packs and web gear with sighs of relief. The best part for me was taking off my boots and feeling my feet suddenly light and weightless. I grabbed a towel and headed for the shower with the rest of the team. The day was bright, we were young, my only worry had been about staying alive, and now that our patrol was over I didn't have to worry about that either.

13. Leaving Battalion

*Every man thinks meanly of himself
for not having been a soldier.* —Samuel Johnson

Nearly eight weeks had passed since I first joined Battalion Recon, and I had gone on two more relatively uneventful patrols. With the help of the other men in the team, I was gradually learning my deadly craft, but Blaze never gave me a word of encouragement. One evening at the club, I mentioned to Chief that I didn't think that he liked me very much.

"He don't like anyone very much … probably not even himself." Chief replied dismissively.

A few days later, we found a few members of First Force Recon joining us at the chow line. They had just moved down from some godforsaken firebase to the north and were setting up their compound next to ours. There were two Force Recon units in Nam: First Force Recon, which was now based next to us at Camp Reasoner, and Third Force, which was stationed near the North and South Vietnam border, an area known as the demilitarized zone or DMZ. The name was really a sick joke, because the DMZ was probably one of the most militarized places on the planet.

Force Recon Marines traced their lineage back to the Marine Raiders of World War II. Battalion Recon stayed reasonably close to the major Marine units protecting Da Nang. Force Recon conducted long-range reconnaissance patrols that went out much farther, some said all the way out to the Ho Chi Minh Trail on the border of Laos and Cambodia. There were even rumors that they ran covert missions over the borders, raiding, capturing prisoners, and gathering intelligence. No one really knew for sure.

We would see a group of them passing through the gate or joining us in the chow line, because both units ate in the same mess hall. It was easy to spot them. Their hair was so short that their heads looked shaved. Gold or silver jump wings were pinned to their chests. They ate by themselves and avoided mingling with the rest of us. After a few days, their general swaggering attitude started to piss us off.

After coming back from a long mission we resented seeing this bunch of cowboys in what we considered to be our area, The fact that they were not yet running patrols didn't help our attitude towards them. We knew what we had experienced in the bush. We didn't have a clue as to what they were up to, and they weren't telling. They kept to themselves and avoided questions.

On my last patrol, Sergeant Blaze had let me run point for a few hours, taking over from Chief. This was the most dangerous position, but I relished the trust that Blaze had placed in me. The very next morning, however, he pulled me aside after formation and in his blunt manner told me that I was going to be transferred to First Force Recon.

"If it's all right with you, sergeant, I'd rather stay in your team," I protested, remembering what Chief had said to me about Blaze getting rid of anyone who didn't measure up. I worried that I had somehow screwed up running point on our last patrol.

Blaze shook his head. "Not your choice. Force has first dibs on anyone Airborne, SCUBA, or sniper qualified. You're jump qualified and should have been sent up to Force when you first got in-country, but the captain knew that they would be moving down here, and…"

I finished up his thought for him, "You needed another man in your team."

"Yeah" he admitted frankly. He started to turn away but then stepped back and unexpectedly held out his hand.

"You did a good job for us. You'll make a good bush Marine."

These simple words and his handshake coming from someone I truly respected meant more to me than anything anyone else could have said to me.

That night the team got together at the hooch with me for the last time. By making multiple trips down to the club, they had accumulated more than enough beer to keep everyone happy. Garcia shared a bottle of Jose Cuervo and Chief put a tape on his fancy stereo. By the end of the night Garcia and Fernandez were singing in Spanish and I swore I was able to understand every word.

14. Welcome to Force

The mission of FORCE RECON is to conduct amphibious reconnaissance, deep ground reconnaissance, surveillance, battle space shaping, and raids. —Force Recon Mission Statement

The next morning, I gathered my gear together. After the going-away party the previous night my head felt like it was going to leave my body but I managed to make it to the mess hall and after a light breakfast felt a little better. The hooch was empty when I returned. The other men were either all on work details or off to Freedom Hill. I packed up my gear, but decided to go over to Force and sign in first and then come back for it later. I hoped I'd feel a little better by then.

Force Recon's compound was located next to Battalion but separated physically from it by a small stream that flowed down from the hill overlooking the base. To the east was a level open area they used for formations. Their command shack faced the parade ground and the Stars and Stripes flew from a small flagpole beside it. A red circular sign with the Force Recon emblem painted on it hung from a plywood board next to the command shack.

A group of Force Recon Marines jogged passed me as I entered the compound. They had stripped down to shorts and boots and were singing a running song as they passed by and headed for the road. They were lean and fit and looked like they were enjoying the morning run. They started another running chant as they picked up the pace and left the compound.

First Force Recon

> I wanna be a Recon Ranger
> I wanna live a life of danger
> I'm gonna go to Vietnam
> I'm gonna kill some Vietcong

I entered their command hut and handed my papers to the corporal behind the desk. He glanced at them and asked me to wait. He walked around the corner of the room and down a hallway, taking my papers with him. I heard some muffled words but couldn't make them out. He came back after a few seconds and told me to follow him, saying that the first sergeant wanted to meet me.

The first sergeant was a colossus of a man, well over six feet tall and weighing at least two hundred fifty pounds—perhaps more, his body a combination of fat and muscle but more muscle than fat. The sleeves of his pressed utilities were rolled up and his biceps strained against the jacket. His head was either naturally bald or completely shaven. A set of polished golden jump wings was pinned to his starched camouflaged utilities. He came over from behind his desk holding my personnel folder in his left hand. He stopped a few feet away from me and looked at me with cold blue eyes.

He extended his hand for what I assumed would be a friendly handshake. As he did so I saw a crude tattoo of a meat hook skewering a piece of flesh inked on his forearm. Drops of red tattooed blood snaked down from the meat almost to his wrist as he gripped my hand. The hook on his forearm bulged as his fingers suddenly tightened, his meaty hand enveloping mine with fierce pressure.

This was no friendly handshake; the bastard was doing his best to break my bones! I kept my face impassive and squeezed back just as hard. After a few seconds, he finally released his grip. I must have passed his test, because he nodded slightly and turned his attention to my paperwork.

"Where did you go through recon training?" he asked.

"I went through RIP[1] at Lejeune. I was first in my class," I told him proudly.

"RIP," he snorted dismissively. "Fuckin' waste of time. How many patrols did you do with those crap heads at Battalion?"

"Three, first sergeant," I replied, annoyed by the way he had dismissed my former teammates.

He snorted again and looked down at the folder he was holding. "I'm assigning you to First Platoon, Team Foresight."

He stood up and moved closer to me, bloodshot eyes boring into mine. "I'll just say this once, boy. You do your duty and we'll get along just fine. You fuck up or try to screw with me and I'll be over you like fleas on a dog!"

Over time, I began to hold the first sergeant in mild contempt. Despite his imposing physical presence, he never ran patrols with us and seemed to spend most of his time either drinking with his pals at the NCO club or lifting weights in a shed he had gotten the men to build for him.

I found myself outside in the blinding sunlight with my hand aching. The runners were returning, covered with sweat but still chanting as they ran down the road toward me.

> If I die in a combat zone
> Box me up and ship me home

14. Welcome to Force

> Pin gold wings upon my chest
> Tell my mom I did my best

I had passed the First Platoon's hooch on my way up. It was the topmost shack on the hill and built on pilings so that water from the nearby stream could run right underneath it. I climbed the steps, gave a knock on the screen door and stepped inside. Two Marines were inside sitting on their bunks. They turned toward me as I entered.

"First Platoon?" I asked awkwardly.

The nearest Marine nodded.

"I'm assigned to you guys."

"Ain't we the lucky ones," came a sarcastic comment from the man behind me.

The first man I spoke with got up from his bunk and came over. "Don't mind him. They call me Feo," he said, holding out his hand. I hesitated for a second thinking of the first sergeant's handshake, but this one was friendly. He pointed to the other Marine, who sat up and stretched.

"That ball buster over there is the Polack, but he won't be around much longer— Thank God."

"Polanski to you," the other man answered mildly. He got up from his bunk, pulled down a short-timer calendar from the wall and made a show of examining it. Most of the dates on the strange figure peering furtively out from under a helmet had been filled in. Only a few dates remained empty. Polanski counted them up. "Hmm ... five weeks, two days, and then, man ... I'm outta here!"

"The Polack's our tail-end Charlie," Feo told me, continuing to use the slur. "He never knows where he's going but always knows where he's been."

Polanski didn't even bother smiling at the stale joke he had probably heard hundreds of times before. I later learned that he had been on more patrols than anyone in the outfit except for a Marine they referred to as "Uncle." He was also the platoon's machine gunner. I was also trained as a machine gunner and that was probably the reason that I had been assigned to take Polanski's place on the team.

I remembered how one day near the end of boot camp our drill instructor had lined us up to give us our new Marine Corps assignments. He strode to the center of the barracks, holding a paper

"Five weeks, two days, and I'm outta here!"

in his hands. We stood at attention in two lines facing each other. The drill instructor glanced at the paper in his hand and with a wave of his arm settled our futures.

"Everybody on the left—Machine Gunners."

"Everyone on the right—Mortar Men."

I didn't care which line I was on, I just wanted to see action, but I saw the shocked expressions on the men across the room from me as they realized that the jobs their recruiters had promised them were just bullshit. Instead of going to school to learn jet engine repair or radio technology they were going to have to spend their tour humping mortar rounds through the boonies.

One poor fool made the mistake of going up to the drill instructor and complaining that he had been promised a job as a photographer with the "Star's and Stripes," the military's newspaper. The DI's grabbed him before he could even finish his complaint and frog-marched him out of the barracks. After two days in the "Motivational Platoon," he returned, covered head-to-toe in Parris Island mud, and "motivated" nearly out of his mind. He never mentioned the "Stars and Stripes" again.

As I looked around my new home, Feo told me that Polanski wasn't the only short-timer in the team. More than half of the men in the platoon would be rotating out in the next few months. Feo told me he himself had only a few months left in-country. Their places in the platoon would filled by new guys like myself.

"Here comes the Sergeant, Tom," Feo mentioned in a casual way, looking out the door.

I braced myself, but the man coming through the door couldn't have been more different from my former team leader at Battalion. He came right over to me and holding out his hand introduced himself with a smile.

Sergeant Tom seemed completely relaxed, without a trace of the restless edginess that marked Blaze. I liked him at once. He had a square, compact body, light brown hair and blue eyes. His friendly, open face seemed to hold a faintly quizzical expression, as if he was waiting for an answer to some important question.

"You came over to us from Battalion Recon?" he asked. I nodded and prepared myself for a disparaging remark.

"Good unit. You should feel right at home with us. We both do most of the same thing; we just run most of our patrols further out."

"A lot further out," Polanski interrupted from his bunk

"Yeah ... well sure," Tom admitted. "But don't worry. You'll fit right in."

He asked me where my gear was and then offered to help me carry it back. I settled my footlocker under one of the empty bunks and hung up my gear. While I was putting things away, he told me a little about himself. He told me that he really liked the Marine Corps and confided that he hoped to make a career in the military.

"Want to see my girl?" he asked hopefully.

He pulled a photograph out of his wallet and showed me a photograph of a pretty young girl standing by a red Corvette. "Got married and bought the Vette the same day. Can't make up my mind which one I want to get back to the most," he joked, mentioning that he only had a few months left on his second tour.

After Sergeant Tom left I remembered that the first sergeant had ordered me to get a haircut and Feo walked with me over to where an old Vietnamese papa-san was sitting in the shade behind one of SCUBA shed. Feo took off his cover[2] and pointed to his head. "High and tight."

The old man got up from his chair and with a courtly flourish he waved me into his seat. He folded an old poncho around my neck and started up an electric razor.

As the barber cut away, Feo explained to me that Force Recon's distinctive haircut originated with the D-Day paratroopers, who had their hair shaved like Mohawk Indians before jumping into France because they had been told that the Germans were terrified of being scalped.

"Will it work on Charlie?" I joked.

Feo shrugged. "I doubt it, but I never let him get close enough for me to find out."

"Hi-tite ... hi-tite," the barber repeated over and over as he clipped and shaved the hair from my head. He finally handed me a mirror and I peered for the first time at the thin ribbon of short hair running down the top of my head.

"One dolla ... one dolla," the barber interrupted impatiently, holding out his hand.

When we got back to the hooch several other Marines had returned. Feo introduced me to the team's Navy corpsman, Tony, whom everybody called Doc. Unlike the Army, which trained their own combat medics, the Marine Corps depended on Navy personnel who had volunteered to serve with the Marines. Once accepted into the program, our Navy corpsmen went through an extensive training program back in the States. Most of them eventually became capable soldiers. The problem was that there were never enough of them to go around.

Tony was a tough Italian kid from Brooklyn. He had jet-black hair and dark eyes set deep in a tanned face. He had just returned from R & R in Hawaii and was complaining to Polanski about his experiences.

"When I checked into the hotel I was wearing flip-flops and they told me that I had to wear shoes!" he told him indignantly. "I tried to explain that I had just gotten out of Nam and my feet needed to dry out, but they wouldn't listen. My feet were so swollen with jungle rot that I wasn't even able to wear sneakers. When I told 'em to stuff it, the manager called their chickenshit police, who threw me and my woman out of the hotel!"

"What did you do?" Polanski asked from his cot, rolling over on his stomach.

"We spent the rest of the week in a rented trailer a quarter mile from the beach. It wasn't that bad at all. We wouldn't have spent all that much time at the beach anyway," he smirked.

Frenchy, a young Cajun from the bayou country around New Orleans, sat on his bunk cleaning his rifle and listening intently to Tony's story. His dark eyes sparkled with interest.

"I'm going to Hong Kong for R & R," he broke in enthusiastically. "I've been saving my money and I'm going to get myself a rack of custom-made silk suits. The best tailors in the world are in Hong Kong," he told us knowledgeably, nodding his head.

"You're gonna go on R & R and spend your money on suits?" Doc asked in disbelief.

Frenchy nodded seriously. "Sure I am. When I get back to New Orleans, I'm gonna get myself a white Caddy and dress up in my new suits and..."

"Get yourself arrested," Feo interrupted, laughing at him. "You're going to look like a pimp."

"No way, man! I'll look like a businessman," Frenchy objected indignantly. "The cops, they don't mess with businessmen, and anyway, I'll have enough money saved by then to pay 'em off. I'm not gonna get screwed again," he told us in a determined voice, explaining that a Louisiana judge had given him the choice of joining the Marine Corps or going to jail. At the time I didn't know whether to believe Frenchy's story or not, but I was later told the same thing from other men who had been offered the same choice.

Another member of the team came through the door of the hooch carrying freshly laundered utilities and a package of sugared donuts, which he freely shared with the rest of the men. Feo took a donut, motioned me over and introduced me to Mac, the team's point man who had just returned from the PX at Freedom Hill. Mac was short, with a slim, wiry body. His eyes were set deep in a thin, hawk-like face and they seemed to hold a furtive wariness that I was later to see in my own. He shook my hand and seemed friendly enough but didn't say anything more.

A short fireplug of a man wearing a white apron and the ridiculous paper hat that they made you wear on mess duty entered the hooch. He gave me a strong handshake and in a deep, gravelly voice introduced himself as simply "Bo." He took off his apron and threw it with distaste on his cot, explaining that as soon as he had gotten to Nam he was assigned to the kitchen. I laughed and told him that the first thing I had done in Nam was saw up a big log for firewood.

Bo told me that had grown up in a small steel town in western Pennsylvania. He was working as an apprentice machinist at the local steel mill when he got his draft notice and decided to join the Marines rather than be drafted into the Army. He pulled out a photo of his girl and showed it to me, the two of them standing on the front steps of a modest house. He told me that he was planning to get married as soon as he got out. His dreams were simple: a job, a wife and a family.

Frenchy overheard what Bo said to me and told him that working for a steel mill he probably would have been able to get out on a deferment.

"How could I do that when everyone around me was being drafted?" he asked, genuinely puzzled.

"I would have taken the deferment in a heartbeat, man. In a heartbeat," Frenchy continued.

As I got to know him better, Bo's answer seemed completely in character. He was frank and honest to a fault, always willing to do his share and then some.

While we were talking another Marine entered, carrying a footlocker, which he set down by his cot. Relieved of his load, he put his arms over his head and stretched like a cat, the muscles in his forearms rippling.

Bo introduced us. "This here is Truman. We arrived here together, but somehow he managed to get out of mess duty."

"That's because they needed a straight-shootin' cowboy to protect their asses," Truman joked from his cot.

I found out later that he really was a cowboy, or at least a ranch hand. He came from Arizona, where his family made a hardscrabble living running a small herd of cattle. Truman turned out to be one wild guy.

I woke up at 0500 when a scratchy recording of a bugle played through the loudspeakers over at the HQ. I knew from the others that inspection was at 0700 and I wanted to make a good first impression. Sergeant Tom came in while we were getting ready, and asked if anyone needed anything. I shook my head and continued polishing my boots.

"We're sure gonna miss Tom when he rotates," Feo remarked meditatively after the sergeant left.

Feo put away his cleaning rod and checked his rifle one more time. He had told me that the major was a stickler for spit and polish, and I wanted to make a good first impression.

There were about fifty men in the formation, arranged by platoons with a sergeant or in a few cases a lieutenant in front of each platoon. Major Simbul stood facing us with Captain Bilger, his second in command, standing next to him.

Physically the major was everything I would have expected from a Marine Recon officer. He was of medium height and moved with the assurance of a natural athlete. His broad chest filled out his starched and pressed uniform. He was about thirty years old, his face bronzed by the sun. He made a good first impression on me. He seemed someone you could count on.

Captain Bilger was also a big man, but unlike the major, his body was running more to fat than muscle. The major moved quickly on the balls of his feet; Bilger padded behind. Both men wore golden jump wings on their chests. The first sergeant called us to attention as an honor guard raised the flags. The Stars and Stripes at the top of the flagpole, the Marine Corps flag beneath it. I was glad to be an American, proud to be a Marine, and honored to be a member of such an elite unit.

The major strutted down the inspection line with the captain and first sergeant in tow. The group made their way slowly down the line, carefully inspecting each of the men and finally stopping in front of me. The major looked me in the eye and grabbed my rifle for inspection. I released it instantly. He looked down the barrel of my M-16.

"Didn't they teach you how to clean your weapon at Battalion?" the major asked me ominously.

"He just joined us from Battalion, sir," Sergeant Tom broke in, sticking up for me.

"Well, this weapon's filthy; what have you got to say for yourself?" the major asked, ignoring Tom. I knew my rifle was reasonably clean, but I also knew the only acceptable answer to this question,

"No excuse, sir."

"I'll mark him down for his utilities too," Bilger added, smirking at me and writing something in a little book he carried with him. The major nodded approvingly.

Feo joined me as I walked despondently back to the hooch, after being told that I would be assigned to a work party for having a dirty rifle.

"Don't let it get you down, man," he advised. "If it wasn't your rifle, it would have been something else. Coming from Battalion, they were gonna fuck with you one way or another."

"I wanted to get started off on the right foot," I protested.

"Left foot … right foot … bullshit! I'm telling you, man, it don't mean nothing," he said in an irritated voice, seemingly as anxious to convince himself as much as me.

There were six of us assigned the job of repainting the officers' club. After we had finished, I returned to our hooch, grabbed my cleaning kit and set to work on my rifle. Sergeant Tom came over and sat down on the cot next to me watching me run my cleaning rod ineffectually down the barrel of my weapon. He suddenly reached over and laid his hand on my arm.

"It was my fault. I shouldn't have put you in the formation until you had a chance to get everything squared away."

His remark surprised me. He didn't have to say anything to me.

He held out his hand for my rifle. After checking to see that it was clear of any live rounds he looked down the barrel.

"There is a bit of gunk around the bottom of the chamber; it can really harden in down there. The armorer has some solvent that will get it squeaky clean in no time," he told me confidently, taking my weapon with him when he left.

"Nice guy," I remarked to Doc, stretched out on his cot next to me.

Tony nodded in agreement, hesitated for a moment and then remarked, "Maybe too nice."

A few days later a huge black Marine entered the hooch as I was getting ready to leave.

"First Platoon?" he asked in a deep voice. I nodded as he swung a huge duffel bag through the door with one hand and set it on the floor with a heavy thump.

Truman looked up as he entered. "Jeez, who's this big moose?"

From that moment on, it didn't matter what his real name was, everyone called him Moose. He told us he was a radioman and had been transferred into Force after spending his first months in Nam running patrols with a company of grunts. He was older than most of us and added a calming influence to our unit. He took the bunk next to mine, and over time we became good friends.

15. The Firing Range

This is my rifle [holding rifle]
This is my gun [holding crotch]
One is for killing
The other's for fun
—boot camp doggerel

One of Force Recon's secondary missions was field-testing new equipment, and this mandate often included the testing of new weapons. After formation Sergeant Tom told us that our platoon would be heading off to the firing range. The men smiled at one another; one thing Marines love to do is fire guns.

Two new Marines arrived just before we were setting out for the range. They barely had time to drop their duffel bags on the floor and grab their rifles before we headed out the gate. Mac, the Marine next to me, had a thick Maine accent that made his name sound

15. The Firing Range

like "Ma." He tried to correct us, but the other men laughed and from then on that's what we called him. The other new Marine told us his name was Ghant, but bouncing around in the back of a truck we didn't have time to do more than shake hands before reaching the firing range a few miles outside of our compound.

Our truck bumped down a barely maintained dirt road and stopped by a level open field. A long trench extended in front of us and targets of various kinds were set up in the distance. We jumped down and began unloading our lethal toys. The first thing we did was sight in[1] our M-16 rifles. I saw Mac zeroing in on the closest target and I asked him why he was adjusting his sights for so short a range. He explained that it was nearly impossible to see more than a couple of hundred feet in the jungle, and advised me to set my sights for no more than that distance.

Polanski and Mac got into a friendly argument about the best way to load the magazines on the M-16.

"You'll have another magazine ready if you tape them together," Mac advised, showing Polanski what he meant. He took two magazines and taped one upside down to the other. "After one is empty you can switch to the other by flipping them around ... only takes a second." With a fast twisting motion, he demonstrated what he meant.

"I don't like the way the rifle balances when you do that, and it's too easy for dirt to get into the second magazine and jam it up," Polanski objected.

"Well, you've got to do something," Mac responded defensively. He reached into a duffel bag that he had brought along and brought out an AK-47, which he told me later that he had taken during a prisoner snatch. He rummaged around in his bag and brought out a large curved magazine that he clicked it into place.

"The banana clip on Charlie's AK holds nearly thirty rounds, more than three times the number in the M-16 magazine, and it fires nice and slow." He pressed the trigger and fired off a few rounds on full automatic. The weapon bucked in his hands: Bam ... bam ... bam ... bam. He put down the AK and picked up his M-16 and fired for the same amount of time; the weapon sounded more like a buzz saw than a rifle, *zzzzIT* as the rounds screamed downrange, but after only a few seconds his magazine was empty.

"Now I'm standing here empty and Charlie still has at least ten to twenty rounds left. What you gonna do then?"

"At least the M-16 round spins and that gives it a lot more stopping power," I broke in. The two men turned around at my interruption and looked at me like I hadn't a brain in my head.

"Shit, boy, you sound just like a recruiting sergeant." Polanski laughed mockingly. "You still believe everything they told you in boot camp?"

He removed an M-16 round from one of his magazines and threw it over to me. "Sure, this little itty-bitty .22 bullet spins when it hits something. It will start spinning when it hits a twig in the jungle and once it starts tumbling who the hell knows where it will go."

He ejected a round from the AK's magazine and put it in my hand. I could easily feel that it was far heavier. "The AK's fires this 7.62 round, nearly the same as our M-14s. It will punch right through the tree you're hiding behind and waste you with no problem at all," he told me in an assured voice.

When I told them that my former sergeant in Battalion always carried an M-14, they nodded in approval, but said that it weighed too much.

"Oh, I like the M-16. It's OK, I guess," Polanski finally reluctantly acknowledged. "They finally got us stainless-steel barrels, and that fixed the problem with it jamming. Of course, that didn't help the poor bastards that were issued the original version. Those guys were stuck sitting there with a jammed gun and their dicks hanging out."

"At least they got the safety right," Mac added, holding up both weapons. "On the 16 it's right by your thumb. On the AK, the safety is on the left side. Charlie either has to either take his hand off the trigger or reach over with his other hand to release it. That gives us a second or so to grease 'em."

"If you really want some firepower try this," Polanski suggested, reaching into the truck and bringing out a weapon that I barely recognized. "How do you like this baby?" he asked, stroking it lovingly.

Polanski had taken an M-60 machine gun and removed the tripod, carrying handle and sights. Stripped down like that, the machine gun looked like some sort of bizarre rifle.

"Here's something I'll bet they never showed you in the States," he told me, taking a can of beanies and weenies from the box of C rations we had unloaded from the truck. He turned the can sideways and showed me how it clipped perfectly into the breech of the M-60. He took the weapon in his big hands and slung it over his shoulder. He smiled, showing me how it nicely it rested on his cartridge belt.

"Bring me that ammo box," he ordered, rummaging around the pile of ordnance and coming up with the Claymore mine in its canvas bag. Removing the mine, he took the bandolier of machine-gun rounds and stuffed it inside, leaving about a foot hanging from the top. Strapping the satchel around his leg, he fed the belt over the top of the beanies-and-weenies can and he closed the feed cover.

"Time to rock and roll!" he shouted, pulling back the lever and firing off a long stream of rounds.

"Here ... you try it," he told me, unloading the gun and refilling the ammo pouch. He slipped the M-60 over my head and adjusted the sling.

"Lay the belt over your forearm and keep your finger on the trigger," he advised. "You don't need anyone to help you feed the rounds."

I fired a short burst and then a long stream, the tracer rounds shooting out like liquid fire. "My God, this thing rocks!" I exclaimed.

"I knew you'd like it." Polanski smiled, satisfied by my approval and obviously in his element, his normally morose demeanor replaced with a contagious enthusiasm. I could see that he was enjoying himself. He took the machine gun from my hands and walked forward. firing from his hip, leaning against the recoil. He kept his finger on the trigger until he ran out of ammunition, the bullets tearing his downrange target to shreds.

The other men came over and eagerly lined up to fire the weapon. They took pictures of one another looking like bad-asses, blowing the targets, trees, and everything else within range to smithereens. The noise was deafening and after a few minutes my ears started ringing. I asked Truman for one of his cigarettes; broke off the filters, I stuffed it in my ears to at least block some of the noise.

Sergeant Tom brought out a CAR-15. It looked like a squeezed-down version of the M-16. The barrel was nearly five inches less than our M-16's and it had a folding stock that compressed it even more. Like the AK, it came with a long banana clip that held thirty rounds.

15. The Firing Range

We all loved it. The shorter barrel seemed perfectly suited for our type of operations. Tom told us that the Army's LRRP[2] units were issued the CAR and that we would probably be getting them shortly. As long as I was in Nam we never did.

"Take a look at this," the sergeant told us proudly, opening up a short black case. He brought out a target-grade .22-caliber pistol and screwed a long silencer onto the barrel. Each of us took turns firing the weapon. The silencer deadened the crack of the bullet and the pistol was extremely accurate. Tom told us that he planning to take the pistol along on our next prisoner snatch.

Officers, radiomen and NCOs usually were the only members of the team who carried handguns on patrol, but all of us were required to be familiar with a variety of side arms. During boot camp, we were required to field-strip the .45-caliber pistol blindfolded and put it back together in less than a minute. The .45 was a rugged weapon whose huge bullets packed a terrific punch, but in terms of accuracy it left a lot to be desired. After firing at a target less than a hundred feet away and hitting it only a few times Truman joked that he'd be better off throwing the damned thing at the enemy instead of shooting it. Sergeant Tom let us try the .38-caliber revolver that he carried in a shoulder harness. It was much more accurate, and the recoil didn't break your wrist every time you pulled the trigger.

We took turns firing a grenade launcher that Mac had gotten the armorer to modify. The standard Marine-issue M79 was nearly thirty inches long. It came with a standard rifle stock, a fourteen-inch barrel and fold-up sights. Mac had gotten the armorer to remove the sights and cut the barrel in half. The armorer replaced the standard shoulder stock with a small pistol grip, which Mac wrapped in camouflage tape. The finished weapon looked like a sawed-off shotgun. It weighed only half as much as the original weapon and in experienced hands was nearly as accurate. Mac had crudely written the word *Thumper* on what remained of the stock.

That afternoon we practiced setting up booby traps. We used smoke grenades so we wouldn't blow ourselves up. The simplest booby trap was simply a stretched wire secured to the pin of a grenade. When the wire tripped, the pin pulled and the grenade detonated. We also practiced with spring-loaded mines that detonated when pressure was released.

Sergeant Tom showed us some new anti-personnel mines that he had been issued and would be carrying on our next mission. These were small devices the size of a tuna fish can, but they were filled with enough explosive to take the legs off anyone unlucky enough to step on them. Tom thought that they would discourage pursuit, and he was probably right.

We finished the day blowing huge holes in the nearer targets with automatic and pump shotguns loaded with fléchette rounds.[3] Each shotgun shell contained twenty small steel darts that would shred anything within their short range. Mac told me that they usually carried at least one shotgun for extra fire power on prisoner snatches.

16. Mortar

When we are near we must make the enemy believe we are far away.—Sun Tzu, The Art of War

My first mission with First Force Recon ended before it really began. Our mission was to set up an observation post in Happy Valley, nearly twenty miles northwest of Da Dang. This was much farther out than I had ever gone with Battalion, but it was apparently a normal patrol for Force Recon teams.

We were making our way across the parade ground toward the LZ where we would wait for the birds to take us out. There were eight of us on the patrol, Mac, Polanski, Sgt. Tom, Frenchy, Feo, Doc, Ma and myself. Within four months, there would only be three of us left from the original team.

It had just stopped raining and there was a light mist hugging the ground, but you could tell that it was going to be a hot day. I was still experimenting with my gear and had added a small fanny pack to the equipment I carried. I thought that the small pack would hold my blanket and some small stuff, but it kept bouncing up and down with every step I took. I had stopped for a moment to adjust the straps when suddenly there was a flash and a small puff of white smoke appeared a hundred feet in front of me. I stood there dumbstruck, stupidly looking at the smoke billowing toward me. There was no sound for a moment, then a concussive *boom*. Someone screamed, "*Incoming!*" and everyone dove for cover.

I jumped into the shallow ditch made by the stream running through the compound as a second round slammed into a Jeep parked next to the HQ. As if in slow motion, the Jeep rose six feet into the air and then came down hard on its side, bursting into flames. A stream of thick oily black smoke blew over our heads. Jumping into the ditch had ripped the straps of my fanny pack open and my blanket was now trailing ridiculously behind me in the water. As we crouched there in the gully I was worried more about my equipment falling out all over the place than I was about being killed by a mortar round.

Marines were racing to their posts around the compound as the camp's warning siren blared away, as if belatedly trying to make up for its previous silence. Our team stayed where we were, crouched down behind the muddy embankment as cold water from the stream poured over our legs. All we could do was wait and hope that the next set of rounds didn't land on top of us, but nothing further happened and after about half an hour we were ordered to stand down.

"Where the hell did those rounds come from? We're only a few miles outside of Da Nang," Frenchy asked incredulously.

I shook my head. I sure as hell didn't know. This was our home base; if we were safe anywhere in Nam, it should have been here.

The mortar rounds had hit nearly in the center of the compound, a few yards from each other. The second shell had turned the Jeep into a mangled, burnt-out wreck. Whoever had fired the rounds knew what he was doing, but had mistimed the attack. If the rounds had come in a half an hour earlier the entire company would have been lined up in neat rows standing for inspection. For that matter, if I hadn't stopped to adjust the straps on my fanny pack I would have been killed when the first mortar round had hit.

The mortar must have been fired from somewhere on the steep hill looming over our camp, but we didn't know the exact position. A unit of RVN Rangers swept the mountainside a few hours later, but by that time the enemy was long gone.

The choppers wouldn't land until the LZ was secured and our mission was temporarily cancelled. Sergeant Tom took advantage of the extra time to continue our training. We went off to a corner of the compound where he assigned each of the more experienced men to work with the new guys.

As a radioman, Moose partnered with Feo. Ghant was matched up with Polanski, who would show him what he knew about running the tail-end-Charlie position. Sergeant Tom must have noticed something about Bo that impressed him, because he joined Mac, the team's point man.

Tony, our Navy corpsman, was getting short, and since there was no word whether or not we would get a replacement so I was assigned to work with him. Doc opened up his Unit 1[1] medical pack and went through its contents with me, taking out surgical scissors, compression bandages and medicines and explaining how to use things. Calling Ma over to act as a patient, he showed me different ways of bandaging and how to splint broken bones using whatever was at hand. Ma was a good-natured patient and let me wrap him up like a mummy, but when Doc brought out a hypodermic needle he made himself scarce. I had had basic first-aid training in training, but knew I had a lot to learn and Doc suggested that I spend as much time in the Aid shack as I could to get more experience.

With the new replacements, we now had eleven men in the platoon, three over the number normally assigned to a team, but that number was quickly dropping. Polanski got his orders and began packing up his things and getting ready to go back to the world. As his time grew shorter, he almost seemed reluctant to leave.

"What ya gonna do when you get back?" I asked him.

"Don't know," he replied almost sadly.

He reached down and pulled his Ka-Bar from his web gear. "I want you to have this," he said solemnly, handing it to me. "It was given to me by one of the short-timers when I first joined Force. He said it would bring me luck. Maybe it will do the same for you."

"Thanks," I told him, surprised and touched by his unexpected gift. "I'll pass it on."

I touched the blade with my finger. It was razor-sharp. "Keep it that way," Polanski advised. "A lot of men don't, but you never know when you're going to need it." He finished packing his gear and shuffled out of the hooch and out of our lives forever.

I meant to keep the promise I made to him about passing along the knife, but it was not to be. On my last parachute jump in Vietnam, one of my riser lines caught the knife handle when the chute opened, and my knife was ripped out its sheath. I watched it flash through the air, falling a thousand feet into the jungle below, but by then it had done its job in bringing me luck.

We were getting ready for another mission when Mac was called away to see the major. When Mac returned he immediately began packing up his duffel bag. He told us that his brother, who had been serving in another unit as a grunt, had died and that he was returning to the States for the funeral.

"I knew that he was hit, but I was told that he was going to be OK," Mac told us bitterly, his eyes filling with tears as he stuffed things into the bag. We looked away. None of us knew what to say.

"You have any other brothers?" Frenchy asked innocently.

"No," Mac replied.

"Well then, you're a sole surviving son. You can get out of Nam, maybe even get a discharge," he explained.

Mac stopped packing and gave Frenchy a cold stare.

"Don't worry; I'll be back," Mac replied resentfully, picking up the rest of his gear and leaving.

He never returned.

---

17. Contact

The first time you blow someone away is not an insignificant event.—General James Mattis

After a few days of training our Happy Valley patrol was reactivated. As before, our mission would be to set up an observation post and monitor the area for enemy activity. Sergeant Tom also believed that there was a good chance for a prisoner snatch. Bo replaced Mac, running point for the first time, and Truman joined the patrol.

We inserted onto a mountaintop a few miles from our planned observation point. As usual, we found a trail running along the ridgeline. The path was only about a yard wide and sloped away steeply for hundreds of feet on two sides. As we followed it, the entire country seemed to open up beneath us. Wisps of clouds floated above a river in the valley far below. The scene changed from minute to minute as the trail wound along the top of the mountain line. I felt like a giant striding over his mountain domain, the entire world flowing beneath my feet.

The ridgeline was bare, and we were moving in the open, but I felt reasonably safe. We were able to see a long way down the trail in both directions. No one could climb the steep slopes that fell away on each side of the trail. We didn't have to worry about ambushes, and were in a good defensive position even if we were attacked. We followed the ridgeline trails for several miles, Tom finally choosing the ones that descended toward the river. The bare mountain rock turned to grass, then to scrub brush, and finally almost imperceptibly to deep forest. We set up a defensive perimeter for the night and in the morning again moved cautiously toward the river.

We heard the sound of water ahead of us and came to a fast-running stream cascading down from the mountain above.

17. Contact

The water tumbled over a boulder into a small pool and we stopped to fill our canteens. We had iodine tablets with us and Doc encouraged us to use them. I followed his advice and so did Sergeant Tom, but none of the other men did. They probably figured that if sweet mountain water wasn't pure then probably no water on earth was. On my last patrol with Battalion Fernandez had come down with dysentery and I had seen how utterly miserable it had made him, I just wasn't willing to take the chance.

It was a beautiful spot; giant hardwood trees stretched upward and scattered the sunlight, leaving only enough for lush grasses to wave back and forth in the breeze. It reminded me of a park. We rested for a while in the shade and then continued along. The trail split and then split again, and each time it did Sergeant Tom grew more nervous.

"Something's keeping these trails open," he whispered nervously, leading us off the path and motioning for us to spread out more.

Doc had told me that Sargent Tom could "smell" gooks. He wasn't talking about smelling the pungent fermented fish sauce that the Cong used on their rice, but about a sixth sense that flared up even when they couldn't put their finger on the reason. Tom must have been feeling something like that now.

We usually kept about twenty feet from one another, slightly closer when the undergrowth was thick, slightly farther away when we moved through cleared areas. Next to the point man, perhaps the next most important position in the team was tail-end Charlie. The person who brought up the rear had to make sure that no one was following us. He spent most of his time walking backward, constantly scanning the jungle we had just passed through. Ghant had taken Polanski's place in this position. I was next to him in line, protecting his back as he protected mine. Our team was now spread out slightly more than normal, the men in front entering the tree line in front of us as we pushed through a patch of waist high grass.

Ghant and I, the last two members of the team were still in the open when I suddenly saw a flash of motion off to my right side. It disappeared for a second and then I saw it again. I froze and softly "clicked" twice. Ghant spun around as I slowly passed a finger across my throat. Without taking my eye off the spot where I had seen the movement, I crouched down slightly and pointed toward the trail we had just left. I risked a quick glance toward the rest of the team, but they had moved into the undergrowth and hadn't heard my warning.

An NVA soldier suddenly appeared on the trail we had just crossed. His head was down and his eyes were fixed on the trail ahead of him. He held an AK-47 loosely in his left hand and two Chi-Com[1] grenades hung loosely from straps around his chest. He carried a small canvas backpack and wore a sort of pith helmet on his head. Behind him, I saw more soldiers moving down the trail toward us.

I froze in position, my rifle held at my hip. Out of the corner of my eye I saw Ghant slowly raise his weapon to his shoulder. "No … don't move!" I silently willed. If we kept perfectly still the enemy column might walk right by us.

I heard a soft click as Ghant released the safety on his rifle. It was such a tiny noise, hardly anything at all, but at the sound the soldier in front of us paused and looked up. As if waking from a daydream, he focused his eyes on me and I saw the surprised expression on his face. As his rifle swung towards me I instinctively fired a full magazine on full automatic. I dove to the ground and reloaded as a fierce firefight erupted around us.

"Close up! Close up!" Sergeant Tom shouted from his position a few hundred yards away.

Ghant and I tried to move toward him, but the incoming fire was far too intense. For the first time I heard the sharp snapping sound of bullets as they passed close to my head, the longer, lower buzzing *hummm* they made as they passed farther away and a hollow *pop* as they hit the ground in front of my face.

I pulled a grenade from my belt and threw it toward the trailhead. It exploded and showered us with debris. As I reloaded Ghant took a white phosphorus grenade from his web gear. He pulled the pin and threw the gray cylinder down the trail. It exploded in a burst of fire, releasing a thick cloud of white smoke. The enemy troops screamed in agony as the phosphorous ignited in the air and burned into their skin.

Whether Ghant had planned it or not, the dense cloud smoke covered our movements for a few seconds. We were able to get to our feet and run toward the rest of the team as bullets flew around us. I saw Frenchy firing from behind a tree in front of me and made my way toward him. Ghant followed, turning around every few yards to fire another burst.

As soon as we reached the tree line, the team pulled back. Sergeant Tom led us down a streambed whose steep banks protected us from the enemy fire. We came across another larger stream, which grew deeper as we ran along it, slipping and sliding on the slimy rocks. We could hear AK fire coming from behind us, but there were no sounds of pursuit. We stopped for a moment while Sergeant Tom took a quick look at his map. He grabbed the radio and reported to base that we were in contact and needed an immediate extraction.

We needed to get out of the gully, if we were ambushed down here we wouldn't have a chance. Bo crawled up the embankment, poked his head over the top and gave the hand signal for "hold." He climbed down and then motioned us to follow him up the opposite bank. When I reached the top and turned back, I saw a small hut built over the side of the stream. It was made of bamboo and grasses and blended in perfectly with its surroundings. Normally we would have checked it out, but now our only wish was to get as far away from it as possible.

We ran for another hour, gradually making our way toward the top of a small hill where Tom thought a chopper might be able to land. Random automatic weapons fire was coming from the valley below us. The enemy may have been hoping that we would reveal our position by firing back, but we ignored the bait and just continued moving. We got to the top of the hill, but found a large tree that would prevent a chopper from landing. The sergeant threw down his pack, reached inside, handed me a detonator and a half Claymore and ordered me to blow it. The other men set up a 360-degree defensive perimeter around the top of the hill.

I taped the Claymore to the tree trunk, positioning the explosive so that the tree would fall down the slope. I ran the detonator cord back and got down behind a rock. I squeezed the detonator and a savage blast shook the ground. The tree shook and then slowly fell away from us exactly as I had planned. I felt quite proud of myself.

The CH-46 descended, but there still wasn't a large enough spot on the hilltop for it to land. The pilot lowered the back ramp and hovered, the front of the aircraft hanging in mid-air off the side of the hill as the end of the ramp bounced wildly around on the steep slope. Suddenly I heard a *bang!* and saw Truman flung into the air. A fraction of a second later something slammed into my back, knocking the wind out of me.

"I'm hit!" I called out weakly, trying to get my breath, but over the noise of the hovering chopper no one heard me.

I gingerly rubbed my hand against my back and felt something wet running down my jacket. My back and shoulder ached, but I got my breath back and I was still able to move. I slid down the slope toward Truman, who was lying a few yards below me. His web gear hanging in tatters around him. I rolled him over, dreading what I'd find. To my amazement his eyes opened and tried to sit up.

"Are you OK?" I screamed into his face over the noise of the rotor blast.

He nodded, reached down toward his leg and pulled at his cartridge belt, which fell apart, in his hands. One of his canteens slipped to the ground and I saw that it had been raggedly sliced nearly in half.

Truman must have been running town the hill toward the ramp as the chopper bounced around on the slope. One of the chopper's rotor blades had hit him a glancing blow, the impact tossing him aside and spraying me with chunks of his web gear. By all rights he should have been cut in two! A few months later another scout from Third Force Recon was struck in the head by the rotor of a CH-46 during the same kind of incline extraction and died a few hours later.[2] Truman wasn't even scratched!

We helped each other climb back up to the ramp and the crew chief pulled us in. The gunners were firing their twin 50-caliber machine guns into the valley below us. Ghant was already shooting from one of the windows and I joined him. Sergeant Tom was still on the ground a few yards away, kneeling down with Feo and talking calmly to the pilot on the radio. He waited until the last man was onboard before finally climbing onto the ramp himself. The chopper lurched into the air, banking away from the muzzle flashes coming toward us from the valley below.

The mood in the helicopter was wild as the men relived the action, everyone whooping and laughing. Once the initial euphoria of combat had passed, however, I once again felt my mind and body sink into a deep fatigue, and it seemed that at least some of the other men felt that way also.

"I'm getting way too short for this shit," Sergeant Tom muttered to himself as he removed the magazine from his still-smoking M-16 and stared out the window.

Later, sitting on my cot in the safety of our hooch, I thought about what I had done. During the firefight there hadn't been time to think. After months of Marine training, squeezing the trigger was more of a reaction than anything else. If I hadn't fired, the soldier in front of me certainly would have.

I looked over at Ghant sleeping peacefully at the end of the hooch. There was no trace of tension on his face—nothing to indicate that he had even a trace of remorse, and yet only a few hours ago he had either shot or burned alive several enemy soldiers, By doing so, he had probably saved not only his life but mine as well.

Why did I expect Ghant to do anything but sleep peacefully? He was only doing his job, a job that America had entrusted to him. A fisherman doesn't have nightmares about cleaning and gutting his still-squirming catch, Veterinarians inject poison into trembling puppies and go home to lunch. Killing is easy, people do it all the time.

Ghant and I didn't do anything to be proud of in the firefight, but we had nothing to be especially ashamed of either. If there was a sin it was not in the act of killing itself, but in our enjoyment and celebration of it. Reliving the firefight on the way back to our base all of us reveled in the part each of us had played. At the briefing after we had landed Captain Bilger told Ghant that he would be put up for a decoration for his "gallantry." His actions in throwing the Willie Peter grenade were not only condoned, they would be rewarded.

18. Golden Wings

Women and children can afford to be careless, but not men...
—Don Vito Corleone, *The Godfather*

With a few exceptions for men with special qualifications such as Moose, most of the men in Force Recon were either Airborne or SCUBA qualified. Many of the scouts were both. Force Recon paratroopers conducted three combat jumps in Nam. These were the only combat jumps made by Marines in the history of the Corps and, to my knowledge, the only jumps made by any unit during the Vietnam War.

Whether these operations were truly necessary or performed to enhance someone's military career is not for me to say. There were certainly advantages to clandestine parachute insertions. The drops are silent and at night jumpers are nearly invisible, but parachuting is extremely dangerous even in the best of conditions, and the jungles of Nam were an unforgiving drop zone.

In June 1966, a team of eight Force Recon Marines was dropped more than thirty miles west of Chu Lai, a staging area used by Charlie for years. Their mission was to observe the activity of three NVA regiments known to be in the area. They jumped at night from only eight hundred feet and landed undetected on a small hilltop. The following day the unit reported intense enemy activity and called in air and artillery strikes. That evening, however, enemy patrols stumbled across their hidden parachutes, and the team was pulled out under fire.

The following year a Force Recon team parachuted at night into Happy Valley, another hotbed of enemy activity. Their mission was to search out and destroy enemy ammunition bunkers. When they exited the aircraft, however, the team found themselves blown out of their expecting drop zone by strong winds and the jumpers were swept into the surrounding jungle. The team was scattered, and several of the men were seriously injured. The body of the team's Navy Hospital corpsman was never found.

The final Marine combat jump of the war occurred in 1968. Like the others, it was a night jump into a coastal area heavily defended by enemy. This time the jump went well. The team completed the mission and successfully returned to base.

18. Golden Wings

When I first got into Force, I welcomed the chance to jump. I loved the adrenaline rush of falling through space. After completing Army jump school at Fort Benning, I was entitled to wear the silver wings of a paratrooper on my fatigues and I wore them with a great deal of pride. I was looking forward to completing the five additional jumps I needed in order to qualify for the golden wings of a master Marine paratrooper.

My first in-country jump was at Red Beach, just south of Da Nang. As usual, we were loaded with over a hundred pounds of gear, a main and a spare parachute, weapons and other equipment. If we sat down we needed to help one another to get to our feet again.

As part of my Airborne training at Fort Benning, I had jumped out of a variety of aircraft ranging from the old C-114 Flying Boxcar to a jet. All of my jumps in Nam, however, were from helicopters, usually the ubiquitous CH-46 Sea Knight. Parachuting from a helicopter was a nice jump. Instead of having to force yourself out against the powerful slipstream created by an airplane's engines, you just dove off the back ramp.

We flew in over the water at fifteen hundred feet. I was the first man in the string to jump. I felt the tug as my chute blossomed and I began to drift toward our LZ on the beach. The wind was pushing me toward the shore, but not fast enough. The jumpmaster must have misjudged the wind speed and it looked like I would land in the water. I pulled down on my risers to increase my forward speed, but from hundreds of feet in the air it still looked like I was still going to miss the beach.

I had a desperate choice to make and I didn't have a lot of time to make it. I could either continue to pull down on my risers and hope that I would make the shore or decide to ditch in the water. If I was going to ditch I needed to drop my weapons and cut away my other gear or I would drown when I hit the water and was pulled under by their weight. I could do one or the other but not both. I was dropping fast and had only a few seconds to make a choice.

I decided to try to reach the beach. I reached up as high as I could and pulled down hard on the risers. That speeded up my forward momentum, but it still didn't seem to be enough. I suddenly remembered being told in jump school that we could pull a pin that would "pop the risers." The Army instructors had told us that doing this would unbundle the individual lines controlling the chute and give you more control. I reached up and felt the pin, but at the last minute a sudden gust of wind carried me over the beach and I landed on the sand a few feet away from the water. One of the riggers came over to help me gather up my chute.

"For a minute there I thought I'd have to pop my risers," I told him shakily as he helped me with the billowing silk.

He looked at me with a puzzled expression on his face. "You drew one of our new Navy chutes." He pointed to the risers. "These here are quick release pins, you pull them and the entire chute detaches so you're not dragged along the ground."

He took hold of the both pins and pulled them. The silken parachute instantly freed itself from the harness and sailed off down the beach. I could just picture myself falling through the air, wondering in the few seconds I had left on earth what in the hell had happened.

A month earlier, another replacement had joined our platoon, a tall, soft-spoken black guy we nicknamed Slim. Like myself, he had been transferred from Battalion Recon to Force because he was jump qualified. Slim had also been trained as a sniper and we all expected that he would fit in well with the other members of the team. Slim and I would often pair up together on parachute jumps, inspecting each other's equipment to be sure that straps were tight and that the rip cord ran free. We joked about the ritual, comparing it to monkeys preening each other, but checking out each other before a jump was really no joke. A mistake could cost you your life. I trusted Slim and hoped that he trusted me.

As we boarded the helicopter for our next jump, I asked Slim why there were so few black paratroopers.

"Too much sense," he replied wryly.

"What does that say about you?" I kidded him.

"Not enough sense," he told me, shrugging his shoulders ruefully.

This jump would be a static line jump from a CH-46. On static line jumps, we clipped our ripcords onto a steel cable running down the middle of the chopper. Our rip cords would be automatically pulled after we had fallen about thirty feet, but it would take another hundred feet before the chute fully extended itself.

"Stand up!" the jumpmaster yelled over his shoulder.

"Clip on!" he shouted as we clipped our ripcord to the cable.

"Get ready!"

Slim was the first man in the stack. I was next in line. We were trained to shuffle forward as a unit so that each person jumps out only a few seconds after the man in front of him. Jumping out so close together gave us the best chance of landing in as small a group as possible in the drop zone. We crowded together awkwardly. The first position in the jump string was the worst place to be if your nerves weren't steady. Standing with your feet a few inches from a thousand-foot drop is not for the fainthearted. It gives you too much time to look at the ground and contemplate your sins.

Slim had gotten a letter from home a week or so ago and since then seemed tense and worried. Back in the hooch, he kept staring at the pictures of his wife and baby daughter and I wondered if he was having family problems, but he was a private person and I didn't want to intrude.

"Go!" the jumpmaster yelled, slapping Slim on the leg, but Slim froze for a moment in the doorway.

"Go!" the jumpmaster screamed again.

The men behind me heard the command and pushed forward. As Slim hesitated for a moment in the doorway, I bumped heavily against him. I tried to catch my balance but couldn't stop myself, and we both tumbled out of the aircraft nearly at the same time. Slim's chute opened beneath me, causing my parachute to be caught in the dead air immediately above his and only partially inflate. I landed on top of Slim's canopy, sinking to my knees into what felt like an extremely soft bed.

Slim looked up to check his chute and saw my feet sinking into the top of his parachute and starting to collapse it.

"Get off me!" he yelled, knowing that in a few seconds his chute would collapse from my weight, and that we would probably both become entangled.

"I'm trying!" I shouted desperately.

I bounced across the top of his chute like it was a trampoline, and with a giant step I walked off the edge, falling through space past him.

18. Golden Wings

As soon as I stepped off, both of our chutes ballooned out and separated, but we we were now coming down far from our intended drop zone. I landed in a field about a quarter mile from where we had expected to come down. I could only watch as Slim crashed against the thatched roof of a Vietnamese hut at the far end of the field and tumbled to the ground. Before he could get to his feet a very angry mama-san rushed out of the door with a broom and swatted at him. He managed to push her away and was packing up his chute when the family water buffalo came around the corner of the hut. It lowered its massive head and walked menacingly toward him. Slim forgot about packing up and took off running, his chute billowing out behind him.

Night jumps were even more dangerous. On a daylight jump, we knew which direction the wind was blowing from our path over the ground. To some extent, we were also to pick out the best landing spot. Our chutes had a slot in them that would allow them to spill air. This gave us a forward speed of about ten miles per hour. If the wind was blowing from the north, for example, at fifteen miles per hour and you turned the chute to the south, you could land at only five miles per hour. On a night jump, you can't see what direction the wind is coming from. If you made the wrong decision and went with the wind, you would be moving over the ground at twenty-five miles per hour and dropping at fifteen, an excellent way to break your bones.

On one night jump, we were told that we would be landing in an open field. In the darkness however, the jumpmaster must have mistaken our position. It was only as I got within a hundred feet of the ground that I realized that I was coming down not into a clear field, but into a jumble of boulders on a hillside. More by luck than skill, I somehow landed between two of them. The men following me out the door weren't as lucky.

They jumped just as the chopper passed over the peak of an eleven-hundred-feet hill. Since the jump was made at fifteen-hundred feet, this left only three hundred feet for the chute to deploy—the bare minimum. Slim later told me that he felt his chute pop open and almost immediately hit the ground. None of us had any idea where we were, and had to wait until daylight before being located.

Major Simbul seemed to love to parachute and often joined us, offering a case of beer to the first team to radio in that they were on the ground. The Third Platoon always seemed to win, but on the next jump I was determined that our platoon would call in first.

The radio was too heavy and awkward to land with it. After his chute inflated, the radioman would lower it on a fifty-foot line so that it would hit the ground before he landed.

On the next jump, I volunteered to carry the team's radio. I asked a guy I knew in the Com shack for a couple of handset extension cords and plugged them together until I had about fifty feet of wire. I attached one end of my extended cable into handset and taped the handset into my jacket pocket. After we jumped, I let down the radio and then immediately called in that our team was on the ground, even though we were actually a few hundred feet in the air. We won the major's carton of beer, but that night at the club I "fessed up" and shared the beer with the other jump teams. They loved my joke but watched me so closely in the future that I couldn't pull the same stunt again.

Once we had reached twenty-five jumps, we were entitled to wear the gold jump wings of a Marine paratrooper. Slim, and I and a few others had now reached that goal. After we had rolled up our chutes and put our gear in a waiting truck we were ordered to join a small group of men standing at attention on the other side of the jump zone. Men who had already earned their gold jump wings were assembled facing us.

The major stepped forward holding a small cardboard box in his hand. Calling us to attention, he began talking about the history of Force Recon and our unit's commitment to our country and one another. The speech was short but sincere. At the end of it he congratulated us once again. Reaching down into the box he was holding, he held up the golden insignia. It glowed in his hand.

"Men, I'm going to continue an old Force Recon tradition. Take off your jackets."

"Eyes front!" the first sergeant bellowed as he and the major approached the first man in line.

I heard a hollow thump and a muffled gasp.

"Eyes front!" the sergeant ordered again as the major moved in front of me.

The first sergeant took another set of jump wings from the box and unscrewed the clasps from the end so that the sharp pins meant to push through the cloth of a uniform were free. There were two of them, one at each end, each nearly half an inch long. The major took them from the sergeant and placed the insignia on my bare chest, the points digging into my muscles. With a sharp blow of his fist he drove them in.

"Congratulations." He reached his hand out and I shook it as blood streamed down my chest.

He moved down the line while I tried to get my breath back from the major's punch. The golden insignia hung down heavily from my chest, held in place by the two prongs that dug deep into my flesh. The ceremony concluded with the major telling us that he was proud of us and expected each of us would continue the traditions of First Force Recon and bring honor to our unit.

"Dismissed," he finally ordered.

We grouped up and began a five-mile run down the beach chanting an Airborne song as we jogged along.

> C-130 rolling down the strip
> Airborne troopers gonna take a little trip
> Stand up, hook up, shuffle to the door
> Jump right out and count to four
> If my chute don't blossom wide
> I've got another one by my side
> And if that chute don't blossom round
> I'll be the first one on the ground

When the run was over, I gingerly pulled the bloody prongs out of my chest and pinned the golden wings on my utility jacket. They were one of the few emblems authorized by the Marines to be worn on utility uniforms, and I was immensely proud of myself for having earned them. The puncture marks on my chest remained for weeks and the entire area turned black-and-blue from the blow. I didn't care. I knew that the bruises would eventually fade. I was proud to be a member of Force Recon and especially proud to finally wear the golden wings of a Marine paratrooper.

When I reflect on it now, how foolish I had been to have risked my life for a small insignia and an extra fifty dollars a month in hazardous duty pay, but I was only a young kid, and jumping out of an aircraft was one hell of an amusement ride! I have an old photograph of Slim and me horsing around with the other new Marine paratroopers under the brilliant Asian sun following the golden wings ceremony. I still remember what a good time we had that day, sitting in the sun, drinking some beer and playing with a volleyball someone had brought along. We were proud of what we had accomplished, and I was thrilled to be part of the elite fraternity of Marine paratroopers. Many of the men happily playing ball with me that sunny afternoon never made it out of Nam alive.

19. Toothpaste

Any life is made up of a single moment,
the moment in which a man finds out, once
and for all, who he is.—Jorge Luis Borges

The makeup of our team was changing. Feo had less than a month left before his tour ended and Sergeant Tom pulled him out of the bush. As the time for his rotation back to the States neared, Feo, like Polanski before him, seemed to withdraw into himself. When he wasn't on a work detail, he spent his last days smoking grass with some other heads[1] behind the club. When we returned from our next patrol, we found that he had gotten his orders and was gone. He was a good friend of mine and I hadn't even had a chance to say good-bye to him.

A lance corporal named Stout took his place in our team, transferring over from the Second Platoon. He moved his gear into our hooch, stretched out on his cot and promptly fell asleep. Stout had a pale furrowed brow, and with his moonlike face peeking out from under his blanket he reminded me of a little pig. He slept more than anyone I ever knew and I began to suspect that the Second Platoon had wanted to get rid of him and had somehow foisted him on us. I couldn't imagine how he had gotten into Recon in the first place.

When he wasn't sleeping, Stout spent most of his time in the company of some southern rednecks who had also recently come in as replacements. I didn't know them very well and really had no desire to get to get to know them better. A few days earlier I was walking with Moose over to the mess hall. Moose had just entered the building when one of Stout's friends poked me in the back. As I turned he sneered at me.

"Why don't you stick with your own?"

"Why don't you fuckin' mind your own business?" I responded angrily, turning my back on him and stepping inside.

"Nigger lover!" I overheard another one of the new replacements call out behind my back.

This was the first time that I had heard anything like that in Force Recon and it woke me up to the racial discrimination that now seemed to be beginning to take hold even in our unit. Perhaps race hatred had always been there, but being white, I had never been affected by it. I'm certainly no paragon of virtue, but I never gave a shit about the color of a person's skin or anything else except whether they were a good person at heart. I didn't like Stout because I didn't trust him, and I didn't like his new group of friends because I didn't have to.

We were now running patrols into the dense jungle along the Laotian border and it was becoming increasingly difficult to find places for choppers to land. In the area around Da Nang abandoned rice paddies extended deep into the foothills, but the jungle in the mountainous regions to the northwest was nearly impenetrable. We might be able to rappel in, but then we faced the problem of how to get ourselves out again.

A few weeks ago, one of our teams had captured a high-ranking NVA officer. Encouraged by the success, the major had decided to send a double team on another prisoner snatch. Our platoon would be paired with Stout's old unit, the Second Platoon. The plan was for our team to do the snatch while the Second Platoon provided cover.

These double patrols were Captain Bilger's pet idea. He argued that by doubling the size of the team we would double our firepower. This was true, but the more men in the team, the more difficult it was to remain undetected. A bigger problem was that teams were not used to working together. Aside from the occasional friendship that grew out of a chance meeting in the chow line or club, we barely knew one another.

Our next mission would be led by Lieutenant Dean, the Second Platoon's new officer. Dean was a short guy with glasses, rather soft-spoken. He seemed to be cut from a different cloth than most of the other officers I had come across. While we were waiting for the birds, he came around and introduced himself to each member of our team. He had only been in-country for a few months, but the guys in the Second Platoon said he was getting to know the bush and was a decent guy. I was certainly willing to give him the benefit of the doubt.

We flew into a valley about four clicks from the proposed ambush site. The pilot found an open area on top of a ridgeline and the insertion was uneventful, but the jungle was as dense as any I had seen. It took us two days to climb down from our insertion point, cross a valley and reach our planned observation point. Once there, we found ourselves a good position overlooking the river valley and we soon spotted movement along the riverbank.

Dean passed around his binoculars. From our high location I saw small groups of soldiers carrying supplies across a shallow part of the river. In less than an hour we counted more than fifty NVA soldiers. Some were carrying huge packs; others pushed bicycles loaded with what looked like sacks of rice.

Moose radioed in our position and the lieutenant gave headquarters a whispered situation report and we were told to keep observing. We formed ourselves into our standard defensive circle with everyone facing out. With a smaller team, only a few yards would have separated us and we would have been able to see everyone in the group. With the extra eight men, the circle was too large for everyone to see one another.

Dean made his way around the around the perimeter checking on each man. He stopped where I was sitting and in a whisper told me that he had spoken to the major and that the prisoner snatch was still on. Tomorrow morning we would move closer to the river and set up the ambush.

The men shucked their gear, got out their sleeping blanket and took turns eating. The lieutenant opened up a can of crackers and began talking to me in a low voice as he ate, asking me where I was from and how long I had been in Vietnam. None of the other officers had ever shown any personal interest at all in me at all, but his questions made me feel uncomfortable. The bush really wasn't the place to get to know one another, and I wasn't used to anyone talking when we were on a mission. I kept my concerns to myself. He was an officer, and it wasn't my place to tell him anything.

Darkness was coming on and I heard the lieutenant move over to Stout and tell him to set out two Claymores at the top of the hill.

I could see Stout fumbling with his equipment and crawled over to check on him as he pulled the mine out of his pack and started to move up the hill.

"Detonator?" I asked.

"Oops … nearly forgot." He smiled in his foolish way, rummaging around his pack and pulling out the igniters and wire.

I took the Claymore out of his hands and pointed to the bulge on one side. "This goes away from us," I reminded him.

"I know… I know." He nodded earnestly.

Bo told me that he was on sentry duty with Stout a few weeks earlier. Stout had put out the Claymores, but the following morning when Bo went out to take them in, he found that they were all facing in the wrong direction—toward the the bunker instead of away from it. The men inside would have blown themselves to kingdom-come if they were attacked and triggered the mines! Stout swore that "Charlie" must have turned them around, but no one believed him.

We settled in for the night, quietly eating our cold rations and trying to sleep. It was a long night. We woke before dawn and everyone got their gear ready for the ambush. Stout crawled back up the hill to bring in the Claymores he had set out the previous night. The word was passed around our defensive circle that we had a man above us on the hillside bringing in the mines.

I was just shrugging into my pack when I heard a warning *click click* from Ghant, who was crouched down next to me. He pointed to a movement in a cluster of bushes a hundred feet below us. The bushes below us rustled and in the dim light a figured emerged from the dense underbrush.

Ghant fired a single round, but to his horror, instead of an enemy soldier, Stout stumbled forward, dropping the Claymore he was carrying and clutching his chest.

The corpsman from the Second Platoon was by his side in seconds. He cut away Stout's web gear and ripped open his jacket. Ghant's bullet had hit Stout on the right side of his chest. If it had hit him on the left, he would have been killed instantly, but he was still in bad shape. Bloody foam emerged from the small puckered blue hole in his chest with every breath that he took.

The corpsman worked swiftly, opening up the Unit 1 and pulling out a plastic patch that he taped across the wound to make an airtight seal. Stout moaned again as the medic turned him over onto his right side so that his good lung wouldn't drown him in his own blood.

Lieutenant Dean scrambled over, aghast at what had happened. "Didn't you get the word that he was coming back in?" he yelled frantically at Ghant.

"Not from below us," Ghant protested miserably, shaking his head.

Stout must have gotten confused and circled around to come back in from a completely different direction than he went out. I was right next to Ghant and seeing the movement had nearly fired myself. My finger was on the trigger, God only knows why I didn't shoot.

"We've got to get him out of here, sir," the corpsman told the lieutenant as he continued bandaging.

Dean called in for an emergency medevac. As dawn broke, we made out the characteristic *clop-clop-clop* of a CH-46 descending. It wasn't a dedicated medevac chopper, but we didn't care, and Stout sure as hell didn't either. He was gasping for air with every breath and it didn't look like he was going to make it. We popped a smoke grenade, and the pilot confirmed its color. The jungle cover was so thick that we didn't spot the descending aircraft until it was nearly directly overhead. The pilot radioed that there was no place for him to land, but if we could clear him an opening in the jungle he thought he would drop a litter.

I took a roll of det cord[2] and moved down the mountain. I found a place where the cover was slightly less dense, but there was a huge dead tree poking up from the forest floor that I had to blow. I secured the mine to the tree with tape, attached the detonator and backed away. I crouched down behind a large rock and squeezed the igniter. The tree fell just the way I had expected, making a small opening in the canopy.

The pilot hovered over the opening I had made and lowered down a metal litter. The corpsman strapped Stout into it and he was winched off the ground. The cable caught on a small tree as Stout was being pulled up, but the pilot added power and yanked it completely out of the ground. The basket was winched into the chopper and the aircrew cut the tree loose. In a few seconds Stout was gone and the jungle suddenly became very quiet. We all knew that Ghant's rifle shot followed by the explosion would have alerted every enemy soldier in the area to our presence.

"Lieutenant," Moose whispered, holding the radio handset. "The pilot radioed that they were fired upon when they left the area. We're going to have visitors!"

We huddled together in a tight group while the lieutenant studied his map looking for a way out. There didn't seem to be any clearings nearby and we didn't have enough explosives to blow a larger LZ. We had to find another solution. A CH-46 on a routine supply flight was the closest chopper to us and diverted to our location. The pilot radioed that they had a jungle penetrator onboard and suggested using it to extract us. The lieutenant agreed; we really didn't have any choice.

The jungle penetrator was a torpedo-like tube with three small fins that extended out from the bottom. It was designed to rescue pilots who had bailed out of their planes. We hadn't trained on it, but now it seemed like our only hope.

We heard the CH-46 dive through the clouds above us and hover. The door on the bottom of the chopper opened, and the penetrator dropped toward us. It came down near Bo and we both tried to grab it as it bounced crazily along the ground. The dammed

19. Toothpaste

thing seemed alive! Just as we nearly got to it, the cable would jerk and it would slither away. Bo finally tackled it and managed to pull out the three small metal seats that folded into the torpedo-shaped body.

We climbed onto the seats and hung on as the cable tightened and we were jerked violently into the air. We crashed through the treetop canopy, trying to hang on as the branches tore at us. As soon as we cleared the trees, the damned thing began spinning, and it was all I could do to hold on as we were winched upward.

As we got closer to the bottom door of the hovering chopper, the spinning slowed somewhat, but I could tell that the opening in the floor of the craft wasn't big enough for both Bo and me to fit through at the same time. The crew chief was standing inside the aircraft holding on to the device that controlled the winch. He had his flight helmet on and with his dark visor down it was impossible to see his face. I motioned to him to slow down the winch, but he didn't.

"Stop!" I screamed as my head slammed into the bottom of the aircraft.

The line dropped a few feet. The chief was holding on to the cable with a gloved hand and trying to center it over the opening. I saw him press the electric switch with the other hand, and once again we were pulled upward. This time my head went through, but the back of my pack caught on the edge of the door and I felt myself pulled backward off the cable. The pressure was enormous.

"You're pulling us off!" Bo yelled as his shoulders smashed against the opening.

Over the noise of the twin turbines, the crew chief wasn't able to hear us at all. I saw him reach over to push the button to start up the winch once again. I desperately struggled to pull myself up, standing on Bo's legs and then on his shoulders so that we might go through the opening one person at a time.

The winch started again, and Bo and I were pulled inexorably through the small opening like toothpaste in a tube. My muscles couldn't resist the fierce force of the hydraulic winch and I felt myself losing my grip on the cable. Suddenly one of the straps on my web gear snapped under the strain. My pack ripped away from my shoulders and I was able to squeeze through the hole in the belly of the chopper. Bo followed a few seconds later.

The crew chief was leaning out the side door and lowering the penetrator back to the ground for another pickup. I grabbed his shoulder and spun him around.

"You asshole! You nearly crushed us!" I screamed, hitting him across the side of his helmet with my open hand. The dark visor covering his face popped up, revealing the face of a scared little kid who looked like he should have been in grade school.

"Can you run that thing through the side door?" I yelled at him over the noise of the engines.

The boy nodded and, flipping down his visor, spoke through his microphone to the pilot. The penetrator's cable was attached to some kind of sliding arm, and in a few seconds he had moved the contraption over to the side door and was sending it down again. Everything worked better, much better. The men came up two or three at a time and Bo and I helped pull them in. As soon as they were inside, they took up firing positions by the windows. Soon only the lieutenant and Moose were left on the ground. The crew chief sent the penetrator through the canopy one last time.

From my position by the side door I saw the lieutenant grab the winch line and hold it as Moose straddled the tube. Nearly at the same time, flashes of ground fire appeared on the hillside and our door gunner opened fire. The turbines screamed in protest as the pilot applied full power and banked sharply away. I watched as Moose and the lieutenant were jerked violently off the ground.

The crew chief kept his finger on the winch and continued reeling in the cable. I looked down and saw that the two men were now only a dozen yards from the door, but as the chopper gained forward speed the cable was pulled back at a steep angle. I heard the screech of metal against metal as the heavy steel wire cut into the thin aluminum of the doorframe. As the pilot banked violently to get away from the incoming rounds, the penetrator began spinning, the cable swinging wildly underneath us, but the two men were now less than fifty feet from safety.

The crew chief kept reeling the line in and we finally pulled Moose and the lieutenant inside. Moose refused to let go of the cable and we had to pry his fingers away. He sank to the floor, his head down, his eyes closed. We tried to help him sit up, but he feebly waved us off. The lieutenant wasn't in much better shape, both of the men still so dizzy that we had to practically carry them up from the LZ. When we finally managed to drag Moose onto his cot he pulled a towel over his head and for several hours refused to move or respond to anything we said to him.

20. Hospital Visit

Wild men who caught and sang the sun in flight
And learn, too late, they grieved it on its way,
Do not go gentle into that good night.
—Dylan Thomas, "Do not go gentle into that good night"

We tried to tell Ghant that it wasn't his fault he shot Stout, but it didn't do any good. When he found out that Stout was still in the hospital at Cam Ranh Bay he desperately wanted to see him.

"I need to apologize," Ghant insisted.

"It wasn't your fault, it was an accident."

"No, I need to apologize," Ghant repeated stubbornly.

I didn't want to go. Stout wasn't a close friend of mine, but Sergeant Tom didn't want Ghant to go the hospital alone and talked me into accompanying him.

We caught a Huey that happened to be flying into the hospital compound at Cam Ranh Bay. We flew over white sand and blue water, the hospital a small Quonset hut city unto itself. Ghant didn't say much, once we landed, he just bit his lip and followed me around as I tried to find out where we should go.

The white buildings of the main hospital sat near the beach and runways, and a sentry

20. Hospital Visit

pointed out the red-tiled administration building.to us. A white-suited corpsman sat behind a desk looking at a TV screen across the room from him.

"Let's see," he said, pulling out a clipboard. "Stout ... ah, here it is... Lance Corporal Stout, Hut Three D across the Quad third building on the right. Lucky you came today; he's being moved tomorrow, back to the States," he told us, turning back to the TV.

We found Hut 3D and opened the door. The room was white, the sheets were white, and a white-suited nurse sat at a small stainless-steel table off to the side. She looked up inquiringly. The air-conditioning was on full blast.

"We came to visit a patient, Lance Corporal Stout," I told her.

"You can't have your weapons in here; leave them outside," she ordered in a severe voice. "Only one of you can see him at a time." She glanced down at our muddy boots with distaste. "The other will have to wait outside." Feeling like schoolchildren, we stacked our weapons by the door and re-entered.

"You go first," I told Ghant. "I'll wait outside."

He came back after only a few minutes.

"How is he?" I asked when he returned.

He shook his head sadly, "Not good, man ... not good at all."

The nurse was at the door holding it open and impatiently motioning me inside.

"We keep it closed for the air-conditioning," she told me.

"How's he doing?" I whispered to the nurse as we walked along the corridor.

"I really don't know. I was just assigned to this wing." She pulled a clipboard from behind her desk and glanced at Stout's chart. "Looks like they had to remove a lung."

The nurse pushed open the door to a room at the end of the hallway. The light was dim, and my eyes took a moment to adjust from the brightness outside. A small figure lay extended on the bed. A bottle of saline solution was slowly dripping fluid into the tube attached to his right arm and a bag of urine hung down from his hospital bed. Monitors beeped quietly from instruments pulled up on carts around him. Some kind of breathing apparatus beeped at the bedside, the tube ending on a plastic mask that covered his mouth and nose.

"You have another visitor," the nurse chirped cheerfully. Stout's mild blue eyes opened and focused on me.

"Hey, man, how ya doin'?" I asked with forced gusto. The masked head moved slightly.

If it weren't for his straw-colored hair, I wouldn't have known it was Stout at all. Crisp white sheets were pulled up tightly against his chin, leaving only his head and one freckled arm free. The head nodded slightly again, and the throat swallowed. The heart monitor by his bedside beeped slightly faster.

"He still has breathing tubes in and can't talk yet," the nurse told me, "but we'll fix that when he gets back to the States, won't we?" she said, speaking to him as if he were a baby.

"Don't be too long," she whispered to me before she turned and left.

Stout's eyes followed her and then swung back to my face.

"I hear you're going back to the States. You're a lucky bastard. Wish I were goin' with you." I prattled on for a few minutes with forced gusto, feeling like a fool.

Stout's eyes watched me anxiously. He seemed to be desperately struggling to say something to me, but perhaps he was just struggling for breath. His right arm, connected to tubes and bottles, rose and fell, thumping against the sheets. He became even more agitated and started pulling at the sheets that encased his body. I looked around for the nurse, but she had left the room and was talking to someone in the hallway. Stout's hand finally fell back against the bed and he lay still. His eyes closed and the beeping of the monitor slowed.

I stood up and patted his hand. "Well, I've got to get back, I just stopped in to say hello."

All of the resentment and ill feelings that I had at one time harbored toward Stout completely left me, and I felt enormously sorry for him. I hadn't liked him very much, but he didn't deserve this. I had only been with him for a few minutes, but I couldn't bear to sit there and watch him suffer.

As I turned and started to walk away Stout's arm once more started pumping up and down and he once again started clawing at the sheets that encased him. I called for the nurse, who broke off her conversation and hurried over to soothe him. I continued walking, despising myself for being the coward that I knew myself to be.

21. The Coop

There was a ladder set up on the earth
And the top of it reached to heaven and behold
The angels of God were ascending and descending on it!
—Genesis 28:10–19

Grunts occasionally brought back a prisoner from one of their ambushes, but that didn't happen very often. Their ambushes were set up to kill. When they did manage to capture a prisoner, their fire would alert the enemy to the Marines' presence and they would usually leave the area. This made any information that a prisoner might provide much less useful.

Our methods were completely different. If our prisoner snatch was successful, the enemy wouldn't even know that one of their soldiers had been captured. Our technique was simple but brutally effective. We would conceal ourselves close to a likely trail and wait until we saw a single soldier pass. Predatory animals always prefer to attack stragglers, and we were no different. We hunted in areas that the NVA considered safe and there always seemed to be individuals separated from their comrades, and it was these we went after.

Two or three men would grab the prisoner and subdue him while others provided cover by blocking the bottom and top of the trail. If everything went well, the whole operation would take less than a minute and the enemy would remain unaware of our

21. The Coop

presence. We spent a lot of time training for these types of missions, but they seldom worked out the way they were planned.

In an ideal situation we would carry the prisoner to an open area where a helicopter could land and extract us, but in the dense jungle these open LZs were rare. For our next prisoner snatch we were planning to use the "ladder" for the first time. This was a cut-down steel-cabled net originally used to transport heavy equipment and other supplies by helicopter. For our use the net had been cut down until it resembled a two rung ladder. The chopper would hover, the net would be released, and we would climb up and attach ourselves using a short rope and a carabiner. Once we were on the ladder the helicopter would carry us a short distance through the air until it found a safe place to land. We had practiced with the system for weeks and were confident that it would work in the field.

Intelligence believed that the enemy was assembling for a major offensive and our next mission was the capture of an officer. Enlisted men like ourselves rarely knew much and I assume that it was no different in the enemy camp. The problem was knowing which of the NVA were officers because they dressed and looked almost the same as their lower ranking soldiers. In the field we also looked alike.

We had been inserted without incident into an old hillside rice paddy in an area the grunts, had named Mortar Valley, for obvious reasons. After a few days without any sign of the enemy Sergeant Tom decided to move down into the Valley itself.

We followed a creek bed downward. It had been raining heavily all day and water was pouring from the hillside. The ground leveled off, and we found a trail leading up from the stream. The first trail we were following intersected with another and then a third. There was a tall jungle canopy overhead but, aside from waist-high grass, little ground cover. I knew I didn't like the looks of this place at all. We moved forward searching for a good place to set up an ambush, but the farther we traveled, the less cover we found. We reached a large swamp fed by the stream and had to turn around when Bo, suddenly froze and moved his finger across his throat. Two soldiers were walking away from us. They were holding a green plastic sheet over their heads to protect themselves from the pouring rain and weren't carrying weapons. Their thoughts must have been on getting somewhere warm and dry. Huddled under their improvised rain gear, they passed by without even looking in our direction. We would have been able to grab both of them, but our instructions were to capture an officer, and it was unlikely that an officer would be chummy enough with a subordinate to hold their hand. We circled away from the trail.

Bo once again raised his hand, in the closed-fist signal that meant "don't move." We froze in place and saw a small structure built out of brush and small trees. In front of it was a cleared area enclosed by poles lashed together and set into the ground. Smaller sticks were woven through the poles to make a make a wattle fence. I heard a soft clucking sound and realized that we were looking at a chicken coop.

A hundred feet behind the coop was a large pile of brush and debris that had probably been left behind when the ground was cleared for the coop. It seemed to be the only decent cover around. Tom motioned us forward, and we burrowed into the pile. After a few indignant squawks when we first approached, the chickens ignored us and devoted their attention to scratching the earth for grubs. Occasionally one would cock her head and look at us with strange golden eyes, fluff her feathers and cackle. It was a strangely soothing sound.

It was strange how quickly our bodies could go from the adrenaline-fueled rush of the first sighting to feeling almost relaxed. The brush pile made a good hideout, and we were able to see anyone approaching. From our hidden position we watched one or two soldiers meander down the path. They passed only a few hundred yards from us, completely unaware of our presence.

Sergeant Tom was still hoping to find an officer to take prisoner. As dusk fell and the heavy rain continued, he ordered Truman and myself to move forward and scout out the area. The two of us left the brush pile and circled around the path. We could smell smoke from cooking fires in the air. We crawled up a low embankment and peered over the edge. Ahead of us was a small NVA base camp, complete with the North Vietnamese flag hanging from a tree limb. There were four small huts built of bamboo and leaves and a larger open structure with benches and a covered roof. Everything blended perfectly into the landscape. From the air, the entire camp would have been invisible.

As we watched, a woman came out of one of the huts and put a cooking pot on the fire. She wore black pajamas and had a woven cone-shaped hat on her head to keep off the rain. She called out in a demanding voice to someone inside the shack and eventually an old man reluctantly came out of the hut and began breaking up some firewood for her. The wood was wet and smoked as he threw it on the fire. From the far end of the compound, two other soldiers appeared to take down the flag.

"Boy, wouldn't you like to bring back that flag?" Truman whispered to me eagerly as we watched them. I'm sure he would have loved to, it was just the kind of crazy stunt he would relish.

The camp had a relaxed, homelike feeling about it. I thought about how NVA soldiers lived in the jungle for years at a time. They didn't get to rotate back after their tour was over. They were in it for the long haul.

Truman suddenly tapped me softly and slowly pointed. High above the stream was an observation post built into the crook of a huge banyan tree. A heavy machine gun, still manned by the two soldiers who had passed us earlier in the day, stood on the ground beneath it. The two sentries were huddled down under their poncho trying to avoid the rain and were looking away from us. We crawled backward and made our way back to our brush pile to report what we had seen.

"Did you spot any officers?" Sergeant Tom asked hopefully.

I shook my head.

"Well, where the hell are the rest of them?" Ghant asked irritably. The camp was large enough for fifty men, but we had seen only a handful.

"Sleeping in their tents, trying to keep dry, same as we would," Truman replied miserably, shivering in the cold rain.

"The main force must be somewhere nearby; they'll be back," Tom assured him.

He ordered Ma to set out Claymores and radioed back to headquarters for instructions. We were ordered to stay in place and continue to observe. The prisoner snatch was still on. As darkness fell, we could smell food cooking and the sweet scent of the Muc Luc sauce that the Vietnamese loved to put on their rice drifted toward us. The smell of the food made us hungry, and we opened up our cans and began eating our cold rations.

20. Hospital Visit

Our movements had packed down the leaves and the pile of debris was beginning to feel like home.

As darkness fell, the two sentries returned to the compound, walking hand in hand in the same friendly way that our RVN scouts walked together with their male friends. One of them stopped to take a piss only a few feet away from where Ma had placed one of our mines.

As night fell, the chickens followed one another back inside their coop to roost. Their clucking slowed and they eventually went to sleep. The rain stopped around midnight and a full moon rose. A few hours later we got our gear on and moved out of the brush pile, hoping to get our ambush set up before dawn broke. We were gathered in a tight group a hundred yards from the chicken coop when we heard laughter and the clanking of equipment. We crouched down in the grass as thirty NVA soldiers came down the trail and entered the village. Shouts of welcome and laughter greeted them as they entered their camp.

We had missed our chance, but perhaps that was probably a good thing. If anything had gone wrong in the snatch we would have found ourselves outgunned, the hunted rather than the hunters. We began to move back toward our hiding place.

Suddenly the chickens start to squawk and scuffle around and we saw a young boy holding a basket and walking sleepily along the path that led to the coop. He had obviously arrived to collect eggs for the returning men and the chickens weren't too happy about it. Truman was carrying a silenced .22-caliber pistol for the prisoner snatch, and slowly withdrew it from his holster, but Sergeant Tom put a hand on his shoulder and stopped him.

"He's only a kid for Christ sake," he whispered.

We heard the boy rummaging around inside the coop for eggs, and we could hear the chickens flapping and scuffling around inside. The boy came around the front of the coop holding his basket of eggs in one hand and clutching a chicken tenderly under his other arm. He was looking down trying to pet and soothe the bird in his arms and for a moment I thought he would walk right by us when the bird suddenly escaped from his clutches. Flapping her wings furiously, the chicken ran around in front of the coop. The boy followed, and saw us crouching in the grass. With a startled look he dropped his basket and ran down the trail screaming, "Eee... Eee... Eeeee!," with every leaping step.

We ran away just as fast in the opposite direction, away from the shouts we could now hear coming from the compound. I could hear Sergeant Tom calling for an immediate extraction as we ran.

We knew the birds were on call, waiting for our prisoners, but it would still take them some time to reach us. The swamp was ahead of us and we ran into it, splashing through the knee-deep water, slipping and sliding on the submerged slime-covered logs. We forced our way deeper into the swamp, the water gradually rising until we were forced to hold our rifles over our heads. If Charlie caught up with us we would have been trapped and unable to defend ourselves.

Behind us, we heard machine-gun fire from the compound, followed almost immediately by a loud *swooch* and the sound of explosions as one of our gunships unleashed its rockets.

I heard the sound of a CH-46 in the distance. As it drew closer I saw the ladder hanging unfurled from the ramp. Truman threw a smoke grenade to guide the helicopter to our position and the pilot descended into the swamp with the lower rungs of the net trailing through the water. Bo and Truman were the first to reach the ladder. They climbed up as high as they could until there was enough room for the rest of us to hook on below.

When all of us were attached, the chopper surged upward, lifting us into the sky. Tracers from the gook's machine gun arced up at us through the jungle canopy. We hung from the rungs of the ladder as we flew through the air, firing our rifles at the tracer rounds and muzzle flashes we could see coming from below us, continuing to fire even when we knew the camp was far out of range.

22. Jonah

The sailors mark him; more and more certain grow their suspicions of him.—Herman Melville, *Moby-Dick*

We were returning from another routine patrol. We had humped the hills for over two weeks without seeing a thing. All of us were beat and looking forward to a shower and a cold beer. We were surprised to find Gunny Barker was waiting for us when we stepped down the ramp of the chopper. Barker was a short roly-poly guy, much older than the rest of us and, of course, a lifer. He held the rank of gunnery sergeant[1] and was in charge of the company's administrative workload, keeping records up-to-date, ordering supplies, that kind of stuff. Of course he didn't do any pencil pushing himself; he had a small crew of pogues[2] to do it for him. Barker was one of the guys you will find in any organization. He had found a comfortable niche for himself and was perfectly content to just roll along with the flow until something better came along.

Barker was waiting for us with bad news. Eight days ago, the Fourth Platoon was returning from patrol. They had exited the helicopter and were walking off the ramp when a grenade accidentally exploded. Three men were killed, and the rest of the team seriously wounded.

"It happened right where you're standing," the gunny told us, pointing out the exact spot with a certain grim relish.

I wasn't particularly surprised by what Barker had just told us. I had seen exhausted men coming back from a three-week patrol unhook their grenades and casually toss them like so many softballs into a box with twenty others. I had seen them with a sighs of relief shuck their web gear as soon as they reached their cots, dropping mines, flares and ammunition onto the floor of the hooch without giving a second thought to what they were doing. It was all too easy for me to imagine how the accident had happened

"From now on the armorers will remove all your ordnance on the LZ. Major's orders," Barker told us.

22. Jonah

We formed a line by the side of the LZ and stood with our hands extended out from our sides while an armorer carefully stripped off our grenades and other explosives. We couldn't leave the LZ until after we had been patted down a second time. I understood the reason for the major's decision, but it was still a humiliating experience. It was plain that they didn't trust us to look after ourselves, and after the last accident perhaps they were right.

In Nam, it wasn't enough for you to know your stuff; you had to depend on everyone around you to act professionally as well. A mistake on the part of another would take your life as easily as an enemy bullet. After months in the bush I now understood why Sergeant Blaze had tested me so rigorously when I first joined his team. He needed to know if there were any weak links in his unit, but it is always difficult to really know what is inside a person.

I remembered Paul, another Marine who had joined our team as a replacement a few months earlier. He was putting his gear away when a bunch of us got back from a morning trip to Freedom Hill. Paul had been transferred over, as I had, from Recon Battalion. He was tall and very thin, with mild blue eyes and light blond hair. He spoke in a soft southern accent, not Deep South, maybe the hills of Appalachia.

I asked him whether he knew Chief and the other guys from my original team. He shrugged his shoulders and said that he had only been over there a few weeks and didn't really know anybody. I found this a little strange but didn't press him.

Bo asked if he had ever been on any patrols and he shook his head and returned to putting his gear away. When he had arranged everything neatly and had his bunk made up, he carefully took a Bible out of his footlocker and, turning his back on the rest of us, began reading. Bo raised his eyebrows at me and I shrugged, but I could tell the other guys didn't like the way Paul was acting. It was lunchtime, and we grabbed our mess gear and headed for the mess tent. Ma asked Paul to come along, but he simply shook his head and resumed his reading.

Paul didn't even make an attempt to fit in. He didn't leave the compound or go to the club. If asked, he simply shook his head. He spent nearly all of his free time sitting on his bunk reading the Bible. He had a pocket version that he even took with him on work details or guard duty. He hardly talked to anyone at all. I think that was what annoyed the rest of the guys more than anything else. He acted like we were beneath his notice.

"Hey, man," Truman kidded him once, "what you reading that all the time for? You got to keep your eyes open in Nam, not stuck in a book."

Paul looked annoyed. "It's not just a book; it's the Bible," he replied.

"Yeah, man, sure, the Bible ... but like I said, you don't want to be readin' that all the time out here. Get yourself killed you don't keep a sharp eye out."

"Don't you believe in God?" Paul asked, looking up at him.

"Sure," Truman answered, "but I believe that you got to look out for yourself as well."

"Don't you believe that God is all-powerful and created each of us?"

"That's what the nuns taught me," Truman replied, taking a long drag on his cigarette.

"Do you believe that he has a plan for each of us?" Paul asked relentlessly.

"I guess so," Truman answered reluctantly.

"Well, if he is all-powerful, and has a plan for each of us, then we can't do anything except follow his will. By reading his word I am doing just that."

"Yeah, man, but you're in the Green Machine[3] now; you're in Nam!"

"He put me here," Paul replied impassively.

"Look, man, all I'm sayin' is that you better put that book away and get your shit together before we go out," Truman warned, turning away in frustration and ending the conversation.

Paul didn't bother to answer, but didn't put his Bible away either. Truman and I walked outside to where some other men were throwing knives into a rotten tree stump at the back of our hooch. It was one of the few ways we had to release tension and beat boredom.

"We've got to get rid of that guy," Truman said to me suddenly as he waited for his turn to throw.

"What do you mean?" I asked, pulling my knife out of the stump.

"You know damn well what I mean," Truman replied, pointing a finger back at the hooch. "That new guy is bad news."

"He just got here; give him a chance," I argued.

"No way," Truman responded, tossing his cigarette to the ground and grinding it out with the heel of his boot. "He's bad news … we got to get rid of him." He backed up another twenty feet and threw his blade. It spun end over end and bit deep into the stump.

I didn't spend a lot of time thinking about Paul's argument. The concept of an all-powerful God controlling our every action was too morbid for me. If true it would mean that the damned burning in hell forever delighted him every bit as much as angels singing his praises in heaven.

I pushed these thoughts out of my mind. I was not a theologian but a Marine—and a thirsty Marine at that. I joined Bo and the rest of the guys at the club. After a couple of beers, I had forgotten all about Paul's vengeful God and was lustily singing filthy songs along with the rest of the men at the bar.

> Oh, my name is Sammy Small
> Fuck 'em all, fuck ' em all
> Oh, my name is Sammy Small
> And I've only got one ball
> But it's better than none at all
> So fuck 'em all, fuck 'em all

A few days later we were assigned another mission. Not a single person in the team wanted to go out with Paul, not even Bo. Finding a way to get rid of him became the main focus of conversation in the hooch. Truman half seriously suggested that they break his leg, but they finally decided to just bring their concerns to Sergeant Tom. They asked me to come along but I told them Paul was just a new guy and that they needed to cut him some slack. They ignored what I said and met with Tom without me. I don't know what they told him, but that same day Paul was taken out of our team and assigned temporary work in the armory. When we got back from our next patrol we found that he had been transferred out of Recon and assigned to some grunt outfit guarding the airfield at Da Nang.

"Thank God!" Truman remarked rather ironically.

Less than a month later Ma, told us he had learned that Paul had shot another Marine and then killed himself. At first, I didn't believe it, but Sergeant Tom confirmed the story later in the day.

Paul had been assigned to guard duty and was in a bunker with another man when they apparently got into an argument. The other Marine was found dead a few steps outside the bunker. He had been shot in the back, apparently killed trying to run away. They found Paul's body inside, a single bullet hole through his head. His small Bible was found still open underneath his body.

"You see?" Truman nodded smugly when he was told about Paul. "I told you he was bad news."

What could I say? They were right, and I was wrong. I was the only one in the platoon who had stuck up for him. My willingness to give him the benefit of the doubt had put not only put myself but also my friends in danger. The other guys had him pegged from the very beginning and spat him out like the Jonah he was.

---

23. The *New Jersey*

We will cut our enemies down in droves.
Our fires will be the substance of their nightmares.
We will protect our brothers.
The fields of the dead shall serve as evidence of our passing.
—Machine Gunners Creed

We relied on silence, camouflage and our small numbers to remain undetected. Our defensive tactics were simple. If discovered, we briefly engaged the enemy to get their heads down and then ran to the nearest LZ. It wasn't very heroic, but we simply didn't have the firepower to fight off a large force.

Over time, the North Vietnamese learned both our strengths and our weaknesses. They knew that once we had landed and disappeared into the jungle their chance of finding us was slim, so they tried to stop us from ever getting on the ground. They set up machine-gun nests above LZs that they thought we might use. We were shot out of so many insertions that for a while it almost seemed to be normal. The birds would try one LZ, receive fire, and fly us directly to an alternate site. Sometimes it took two or even three tries before the pilots were finally able to get us on the ground.

Reports then started coming in that the enemy was booby-trapping likely LZs. The gooks would place a string of grenades on tall bamboo poles, tying the pins to one another with fish line, which was nearly impossible to see from the air. The blades on the landing chopper would pull the pins and set off the grenades just as the helicopter was setting down. After losing several choppers the pilots insisted that the LZs be rocketed before they landed. The explosions set off any booby traps but also alerted the enemy to our presence.

Sometimes it seemed that the enemy would intentionally let a team land and then ambush them as they made their way out of the LZ.

A few weeks earlier a team lost three men in just such an ambush. Everyone would have been killed if it hadn't been for the bravery of the aircrew who came back in under fire to extract the rest of the team.

The remaining men in the platoon returned to the same area a few weeks later looking for revenge. They set up their own ambush not far from where their friends had been killed. The mission was supposed to be a prisoner snatch, but the team returned without any prisoners. The men had taken their own brutal revenge, walking off the ramp displaying bloody knives and the severed ears of four North Vietnamese soldiers. I'm sure that at least the officers must have been aware of the mutilations but chose to turn a blind eye.

One can't expect a group of vengeful Marines to act like a bunch of choirboys, but I was revolted by watching them wave around their gruesome trophies. I didn't think there was any excuse for this kind of deliberate savagery, but perhaps it wasn't my place to judge them. I hadn't seen my friends shot to pieces in front of me.

To the best of my knowledge the enemy never took a Force Recon Marine prisoner. The NVA hated us and we were told when we volunteered for Recon that if we were captured we would be tortured and then executed. None of us of us ever expected to get caught of course. Suckled from infancy on a steady diet of World War II movies and cowboy TV shows, we were confident that we would always prevail. If we were wounded, it would only be a scratch to the arm. If captured, we would escape. We would emerge from the toughest situation with a wisecrack and a wave to the girls.

I guess there is nothing wrong with these delusions. We wouldn't have done half of the things that we did if we had thought seriously of what could happen to us. Few teenagers think about the consequences of their actions, and for all of our swagger and hard words, that's what we were. I never heard of anyone in the company worrying about ending up in a wheelchair, losing his sight or being shot in the face, yet these things, and worse, were the inevitable consequences of combat.

We saw ourselves as hunters, not the hunted, but that was about to change. Rumors now began to circulate that the NVA had set up special hunter killer teams that specialized in tracking down and destroying recon patrols. We never knew whether these elite enemy units really existed, and we really didn't spend a lot of time thinking about them. When you are running through the jungle being chased by fifty regular soldiers or being flushed out of your hiding places by a specialized hunter killer team, it really didn't seem to matter. Our options were still the same, fight, run or die.

In the past, a successful mission was one in which the enemy never even knew we were there. We were the ghosts of the jungle, appearing and disappearing without a trace.

We weren't an infantry unit and didn't have the firepower to engage heavily armed NVA forces in an extended firefight. The only thing that we had going for us was the element of surprise, but some officers decided that it was time for Force Recon to change our tactics. Instead of setting up concealed observation posts and calling in artillery or air strikes as we had done in the past, more teams were now aggressively walking the trails, looking for trouble.

23. The New Jersey

I began thinking about whether it would be possible to carry Polanski's stripped-down machine gun on patrol. It had just been sitting in our hooch since he left. Everyone I asked told me that the M-60 would be too heavy to carry on an actual mission, but Sergeant Tom encouraged me to give it a try. He was just as anxious to get as much firepower in the team as I was.

I attached a sling to the M-60 and found that if I rested the barrel on my cartridge belt it balanced very well. My web gear took most of the extra weight. Polanski had shown me how a C ration would feed rounds right into the chamber and a demolitions pack strapped to my thigh would give me a few hundred rounds. Not a lot, but enough. I knew I couldn't carry both the machine gun and my M-16, but Mac's cut-down M79 grenade launcher balanced nicely in a sling across my other shoulder and I could strap a bandolier of explosive M79 shells across my chest. If I could have found a way to strap a LAW to my shoulders I probably would have carried that along as well!

The more aggressive tactics seemed to be successful, at least at first. Several patrols were able to surprise small enemy units on their home territory and destroy them. On their next patrol the men of Killer Kane wounded and captured a high-level NVA officer. Buoyed by these successes, Captain Bilger sent Foresight back into the jungle around Charlie Ridge.

The name spoke for itself. Charlie Ridge was a high plateau overlooking a large valley west of Da Nang. The grunts had gone in several times to secure the area, but each time the NVA seemed to come back stronger than before. On our next mission we were to check out the area to see if there was any new activity.

We were flying along the ridge about a quarter mile from our LZ when we started receiving fire from the top of the ridge. The slow flash, flash, flash from tracer shells arced up toward us. The pilot dove and swerved away from the fire as we returned it, the chopper's .50-caliber machine guns clattering away as we fired our M-16s through the broken-out portholes. Everyone in our team knew that we were wasting our ammunition. The heavy anti-aircraft gun was well beyond the range of our small arms fire, but it made us feel better to snarl back. The pilot landed at a remote firebase so the crew chief could check out the aircraft for damage. Four holes were found high on the fuselage, but the crew decided that the aircraft was safe to fly and within a half hour we were in the air again.

This time we landed without incident, but our new location was outside the range of supporting artillery. Once again we would be on our own. As the bird left we heard a distant rifle shot. We ran along the ridgeline, moving quickly away from the LZ and hoping that the shot was just an isolated hunter. When we stopped about an hour later, however, we heard another shot, this one on the opposite side from us. I felt like a deer being flushed from its hiding place by a line of hunters and I know that Sergeant Tom was thinking the same thing. He decided to cut the patrol short and head directly toward a small valley about five miles ahead of us where our map showed a possible extraction point.

We moved quickly and after a few hours neared our hoped-for LZ. Sergeant Tom led us down a sandy path that led to a small valley. Moose kept trying to establish radio contact with our base, but the hills around our position prevented the signal from getting through. He reset the antenna, fiddled with the dials of his radio and shook his head in frustration. We were just too far out.

The valley floor must have been formed from an old riverbed, because as we made our way down from the hills the ground changed from dark jungle earth to pure white sand. The trees thinned out and the somber jungle canopy opened up, allowing us to see the brilliant blue sky again. The jungle trees were now completely replaced by thick brush that we were barely able to move through. Eventually we were forced to push through on our hands and knees, unable to raise our heads above the interlocking branches, scuttling like crabs through the small tunnel made by the men in front of us. My web gear seemed to catch on every branch, and despite my best efforts, the M-60 that had balanced so nicely from a sling across my shoulders when I walked upright now hung awkwardly from my chest and dragged along the ground.

The sun beat down mercilessly and the white sand reflected the heat. The tunnel we made through the underbrush was turning into a nightmare. I lost all sense of direction and just followed Truman's backside as we squirmed through ahead of me. The ground was sloping steadily downward and I knew that meant we had to be moving toward our extraction point, but it felt like we had been crawling for miles. When we finally emerged from the undergrowth, we found ourselves on a sandy embankment overlooking a large field of razor grass.

Now that we were able to look around, I glanced at my map and realized that we had come out at the wrong end of the valley. We must have gotten turned around when we crawled our way through the thick undergrowth. The LZ we had been moving toward was at the other end, but this wasn't a problem; the field in front of us was just as suitable. Sergeant Tom decided that we would stay where we were and have the chopper come to us.

We moved back to stay out of sight and spread out. Moose fiddled with his radio and was finally able to establish contact with our base, but he was told that the weather was deteriorating and it would probably be quite a while before the birds could get to us. We settled in for a long wait. At least we hadn't heard any more rifle shots since we moved into the valley.

It looked like we had made it through another patrol and I started to relax. I shrugged out of my pack, leaned against a small sapling and settled into the white sand. If I closed my eyes I could almost imagine that I was home again. The air was hot and still; even the insects were quiet as a light rain began to fall. I checked my canteens and drank my water, which was warm as blood. I checked out my weapons. The M-60 and its ammo belt were both covered in fine sand and I was worried that it might jam if I tried to fire it.

I just wanted to lie back like the other guys and rest, but Marine training runs deep, and I couldn't relax until I cleaned my weapons. I pulled my poncho liner from my pack and started field-stripping the machine gun, carefully laying out each part on the liner and cleaning it as best I could with an old bandanna. The fine white sand had gotten into everything. I carefully cleaned off the bolt and wiped down the belts of machine gun ammo. I had cleaned the M-60 so many times my fingers worked away without conscious thought.

Bo's soft *click click* shocked me back to reality.

I looked up to see him looking toward us and slowly drawing his finger across his throat and pointing through the bushes at the far end of the valley. Heat waves shimmered in the still air and it was difficult to see clearly, but peering through the leaves I suddenly saw a tiny figure emerge from the far bank. First one soldier, then three and then suddenly a dozen more.

"Shit … there must be fifty of them at least," Tom muttered, peering through his binoculars and turning to look back at us.

"Shit" was right! My M-60 was lying on the ground in twenty pieces.

The rest of the team took up defensive positions. I heard someone behind me on the radio, but my mind was focused on putting my weapon together. Where the hell was the firing pin! After a few seconds of panic I found it on the corner of the blanket and snapped the final pieces into place.

Sergeant Tom crawled over to me and pointed to a driftwood log about twenty feet away. "Set up the M-60 over there and dig in. Bo can help you."

Keeping low, Bo and I crawled over to the log and carefully cleared away the undergrowth until we had a clear field of fire. Using my Ka-Bar, I chopped off a Y-shaped branch, drove it deep in the sandy ground and laid the barrel of the machine gun in the groove formed by the two branches. It would have to serve as a makeshift tripod.

I had carried a belt of machine gun ammo in a Claymore bag and a couple belts more in my pack. A few hundred rounds at best. That might be enough for a few quick bursts and would give us some covering fire, but it wasn't nearly enough for an extended firefight. Bo spread out his silk blanket on the ground to my right side to keep the rounds out of the sand and carefully laid out what ammunition we had in folded rows. I draped the belt of machine-gun shells over a beanies-and-weenies can, carefully placing the first round into the breech and firmly closing the cover. I was as ready as I could be.

Placing the weapon on my shoulder, I sighted down the valley at the soldiers moving along the dry riverbank. At the moment they were well out of range.

The thought occurred to me that in all the war movies I had ever seen the machine-gun nest was always overrun. My mind pictured Bo and me flying through the air after a grenade attack. I looked down at the silk tarp we were lying on. Bo and I stood an excellent chance of dying in this sandy little hole.

Bo passed me the small binoculars he sometimes carried. The soldiers hadn't yet moved down into the field, but I easily picked out several dozen sitting on the embankment on their side of the valley. They had gathered together in small groups, taking advantage of the break, leaning back against their packs the same way that we did.

I focused the binoculars on one man standing alone along the opposite bank. He was dressed in a green uniform and had a tan helmet on his head. He didn't seem to be carrying nearly as much gear as the other men. Perhaps he was an officer. As I watched, he took off his helmet and wiped his hand across his brow and took a long drink from his canteen. He was probably just as hot and thirsty as we were.

"They don't know we're here," Bo whispered hopefully. "If they did they wouldn't be just sitting there."

I remembered the shots that had dogged us since we landed and wondered if they knew that we were coming and were going to set up an ambush for the choppers. Perhaps we had just moved a little faster than they expected.

I handed the binoculars back to Bo. I didn't need them; I could see the entire scene in my mind. It would only be a matter of time until they grouped up and began moving toward us. We had nowhere left to go and would have to try to fight them off. They would engage us with rifles and grenades. We would kill as many as possible, but they were a superior force and we would run out of ammunition. Once that happened we would be overrun, and it would be all over. A kind of glum resignation settled over me.

Sergeant Tom was still on the radio, studying his map and softly giving map coordinates for a fire mission, but I couldn't imagine who he was talking to. I knew that we were beyond artillery support and the lowering clouds would prevent air strikes.

"Better do something quick!" Bo urged, looking through his binoculars.

A small group of enemy soldiers had started moving in our direction, the main body getting ready to follow. Sergeant Tom was looking at them through his binoculars. He crawled over next to us. "I've got the *New Jersey* online, but I need more time. If they come close can you slow them down?"

I remembered reading in the "*Stars and Stripes*," that the battleship *New Jersey* had been retrofitted for duty in Vietnam, and I read that that it was capable of firing a shell weighing two and a half tons over twenty miles. This was far beyond the capacity of any artillery piece we had ever called in before.

"Feed me, Bo," I ordered, putting the stock of the M-60 to my shoulder, clicking off the safety, and getting ready to fire if they turned in our direction.

Suddenly an enormous screaming roar shredded the sky over our heads. I was used to the sound of artillery rounds, but this was something completely different. It sounded as if some giant had picked up a boxcar and hurled it through the air. The round exploded into the woods on the far side of the valley, tearing up the jungle well beyond the field.

We watched as the NVA soldiers dove down the embankment and tried to find safety. A second round screamed in, and the far edge of the field erupted in smoke and flame. The enemy soldiers were scattering, most running for their lives along the embankment but some trying to find cover in the field. A small group was running directly toward us, pushing their way desperately through the grass in a futile attempt to outrun the explosions moving quickly toward them.

I could hear Sergeant Tom speaking calmly into the radio, "Right five hundred, down five hundred," and finally, "Fire for effect!"

When I was a small boy I had watched in horrified fascination as my father poured boiling water on an anthill in our driveway. The NVA soldiers caught in the barrage behaved like those ants. Caught between the shells and our small arms fire their ranks dissolved in confusion, some of the soldiers running back into the jungle, others hugging the ground, as others, not knowing which way to turn, stood frozen in place, seemingly resigned to their fate.

Another series of rounds from the *New Jersey* came over and we had to duck down and cover our heads. Round after round, the shells from the ship screamed through the air and pounded the field. Clouds of dirt and smoke were thrown hundreds of feet into the air and sand and debris rained down on top of us. The ground itself jumped and shook beneath our bodies.

"Cease fire!" Tom shouted into the radio.

The barrage had lasted only a few minutes, but that was all that was needed. Fires were burning on the other side of the valley and the enemy had disappeared as though they had never been there. We had no desire to draw attention to ourselves by leaving our position and stayed where we were. The rain showers had passed, and Sergeant Tom called in again to have us extracted.

In less than an hour we heard the welcome sounds of the choppers. The gunships came in first, fast and low, spraying the field with rockets and machine guns. There was no return fire. A few minutes later four lumbering CH-46s landed and a company of wild-eyed grunts ran into the field and set up a defensive perimeter. We got our gear together, ran for the nearest bird and took their places. A few minutes later we were in the air, flying low over the area toward where fires were still burning. The prop wash from the chopper's rotors flattened the grass in the field and we saw bodies sprawled below us.

The mood inside the chopper was subdued. All of us realized that we were very lucky to have survived. If we had been spotted, or caught in the open as we were being extracted the odds would not have been in our favor. As soon as we landed Bo and I made a detour to the club and grabbed a couple of beers before heading back to our hooch to drop off the rest of our gear.

We were later told at our debriefing that the *New Jersey*'s shelling had killed twenty-four NVA soldiers. I wondered if the man whom I had watched through the binoculars had gotten away or was lying below us in the field. At least he enjoyed a cool drink of water before his world exploded around him.

24. Sic 'Em

Evil lies deeper in human beings than our socialist-physicians suppose, and no social structure will eliminate evil because abnormality and sin arise from the soul itself.—Fyodor Dostoyevsky, *A Writer's Diary*

Bo and I had just come back from patrol and were heading to the mess hall to get some hot food for the first time in nearly two weeks. There was a long line as men waited to plunge their mess gear into the buckets of boiling water that were used to sterilize our plates and utensils. We found ourselves waiting behind Uncle in the chow line.

I had heard that Uncle had been busted and reassigned to the motor pool, but didn't know the reason, but I was shocked by how much he had changed. The rumpled figure in dirty utilities standing in front of me with a cigarette hanging out of his mouth bore little resemblance to the squared-away Marine I had known when I first joined Force. He still had his natural ability to lead, but the men he now attracted into his orbit were now the outcasts of the company.

Bo nodded to him in a friendly way as we shuffled forward in the line. Uncle grunted, turned away and then looked back and asked us if we wanted to go into Da Nang City. He explained that he had been assigned to get supplies from the Special Forces base near the river and needed two men to go along with him to provide security.

Bo and I would have joined the devil himself for a chance to get out of the compound for the day. We finished breakfast, grabbed ammunition and were waiting by the outer sentry post when Uncle pulled up in a truck. A beefy Special Forces sergeant sat on the passenger side of the cab. As we approached the truck a mongrel dog jumped up, bared his teeth and snarled at us. The Green Beret laughed and slapped the dog away from the window. Uncle motioned us to get in the back and put the truck into gear.

It was a beautiful day. The air was sweet and the sun felt warm on our shoulders. The rice in the paddies was just coming up and the water reflected the sky like a giant mirror. As we approached the city, we passed the gaudy stalls of the local vendors and I was once again struck by the quantity of goods that they had for sale. If you had money, you could buy anything from a bottle of high-end Scotch whisky to an oil painting of Ho Chi Minh.

We moved slowly; the road was jammed with military trucks, motorbikes, carts of all sizes, and foot traffic. We finally reached the Da Nang River and watched as medevac Hueys landed on a sandy spit of land in the middle of the river. As soon as they touched down a gang of Vietnamese cleaners swarmed over the choppers with buckets of river water, washing away the blood and gore while the pilots and their crew sat under an umbrella drinking beer. It was a risk that I wouldn't have taken. I would have worried about one of cleaners setting up a booby trap in my aircraft while I sat in the shade enjoying a cool drink.

If you wanted to stay alive in Nam, you couldn't be too careful. One of our motor pool drivers had nearly died after buying a cold soda from one of these same street vendors. When the ice cubes in his drink melted they released rat poison.

We had nearly reached the Da Nang Bridge when we finally came to a complete stop.

"See what's holding things up!" Uncle called back in an irritated voice.

Bo scrunched down in the seat and pulled his bush hat over his eyes. "I'll stay here," he said lazily. "Lookin' ain't gonna make things go any faster."

I told Uncle that I'd go and hopped down from the bed of the truck.

As I walked toward the bridge I saw the end of a Korean convoy blocking the road in front of us. I had read a gushing article in the *Stars and Stripes*[1] that described the Korean forces as stone-hard killers whose presence struck fear into the North Vietnamese. The word in the field was that the Koreans spent most of their time traveling up and down the main highways in long convoys looking for equipment to steal. Like army ants they took in whatever fell across their path. It was rumored that they could grab an unattended Jeep sitting on the side of the road and have it repainted and added to end of their column in less than twenty minutes.

As I got closer, I noticed that one of the Korean trucks had hit and overturned a farmer's cart on the narrow bridge ahead of us. Half a dozen Korean soldiers had left their vehicles and were grabbing the melons that had spilled onto the roadway. The farmer ran over to one of the soldiers and raised his hands imploringly, but the soldier just laughed and tossed a melon to another man. While this game was going on other Koreans were busy stealing the rest of his crop. When the cart was completely empty, they carried it over to the side of the bridge and, still laughing, pushed it over the rail into the river. The farmer sat down on the side of the road and buried his face in his hands.

24. Sic 'Em

A group of Vietnamese school children were waiting their turn to cross the bridge. The boys and their teacher were all dressed in dark slacks and white short-sleeved shirts, the girls in white blouses and black skirts. The students had been patiently waiting in two lines to cross the bridge, the girls on one side and the boys on another. When the Koreans pushed the farmer's cart into the water the young boys had surged forward, but their teacher ordered them back into line.

I was suddenly startled by Uncle blasting the truck's horn behind us. The Special Forces sergeant stuck his head out the window and yelled down at the teacher, who urged his students to move to the side of the road.

"C'mon ... Move it! Move it, I said!" the sergeant bellowed, waving his arms and shouting as Uncle continued to blare the horn.

The teacher looked back and hesitantly shrugged his shoulders. There was no place that they were able to go, the bridge was still blocked. His gesture seemed to infuriate the sergeant. He opened the truck door and jumped to the ground. His mongrel dog followed him out the door, running to the front wheel of the truck and lifting his leg.

"Get over heah!" the sergeant ordered. The dog ran to his feet and crouched down expectantly.

"Sic 'em!" the sergeant hissed, pointing to the children on the bridge.

The dog took off like a shot. Their teacher saw the animal coming and spreading his arms he stepped in front of his students trying to protect them, and the dog went for him, burying teeth in his leg as he tried desperately to pull away. The sergeant watched with a satisfied smile on his face as the dog bit again and again.

"Get over heah!" he finally ordered. The animal immediately let go and ran back to his master, crouching down and panting from the run.

The teacher was helped to his feet by his students. The girls were holding their hands to their faces and crying, the boys glaring at us with hate-filled eyes. The teacher hobbled to his feet, looked at the sergeant, nodded subserviently and tried to smile. Urging his students across the bridge, he hobbled off as fast as possible, his pants in bloody shreds.

The sergeant turned toward me and smiled.

"Ya see that yellow bastard run?" He laughed.

"You asshole!" I responded hotly.

The sergeant smirked, walked back to the truck and hoisted his bulk into the cab. His dog followed closely at his heels, wagging his tail happily.

I continued standing there by the bridge, half-hoping the sergeant would sic his dog on me. I would have gladly shot the little beast, but it wasn't the dog's fault. He had been trained and commanded to attack by his master. The animal had simply done what he was ordered to do, but what about the sergeant? He had no such excuse.

I looked back again at the teacher and his students as they crossed the bridge and moved down the road. I wished there were something I could do or say to him, but it was too late. I imagined how I would feel if I were put in his place. Hundreds of Vietnamese had witnessed the attack. The story would be told and retold, fanning the fires of resentment into hatred against us. It was at that moment that I realized that America would never win this war. It was all over; we might as well just cut our losses and leave right now.

The line of vehicles started moving again. Uncle pulled up and opened the side door as the sergeant and his dog jumped back into the cab. From the back of the truck I could hear the two men laughing.

Bo sat up as I climbed onto the truck bed.

"Everything OK?" he asked sleepily.

"Just great," I muttered as the truck inched forward.

---

25. River Rat

Believe me, my young friend; there is nothing—absolutely nothing—half so much worth doing as simply messing about in boats. —Kenneth Grahame, *The Wind in the Willows*

We stopped for a moment at the checkpoint just before one of the bridges spanning the Da Nang River when Bo spotted someone he knew crossing the road in front us.

"Hey, Mackie!" he called out.

The Marine he had yelled at waved and jogged over to the truck. Bo introduced us and told me that he and Mackie had both gone through SCUBA school together at Subic Bay in the Philippines. Mackie nodded and smiled, obviously happy to see his friend again.

"What are you doing in Da Nang?" Bo asked him.

"River patrol, bro, right here by the bridge. Why don't you come over?"

Uncle had heard us, "Go on. I'll pick you guys up when I come back through late this afternoon!" he yelled back from the driver's seat.

"Yeah, on our way back from the whorehouse." The Army sergeant laughed crudely.

Mackie led us down a path paved with sand and cracked clamshells to the river. Ahead of us was a thatched hut built on stilts over the water. An American flag flew from a small flagpole and a white Boston Whaler was tied up at a dock next to the hut. He pushed the door open, and we stepped through into a large open room. There was a huge stereo set at one end and a refrigerator at the other. A full-sized bed took up the other wall. SCUBA tanks and assorted underwater gear were carefully stacked near the door. Mackie opened up the refrigerator, which was full of beer, and opened up two ice-cold cans.

We walked outside and sat down in the shade of a porch that wrapped around the hut on the river side. In the distance Vietnamese fisherman were swinging their wide nets into the water. A cool breeze blew over the river and I felt the habitual tension that I had carried for so many months slowly ebb away.

"So what's with this river patrol stuff?" Bo asked.

"The brass think that one of these days NVA sappers are going to float down the river and mine the bridge, so my job is to dive down a couple of times a day and check things out," Mackie explained. "They even promoted me to sergeant," he bragged.

Bo shook his head in admiration. "No shit? We're still lance corporals."

Mackie grinned. "It's a tough job, but somebody's got to do it."

"You're a lucky bastard," Bo told him enviously.

That's just the way things were in Nam and you had to accept it. Some guys like Mackie got a plush assignment and spent their tour in a riverside paradise while others became grunts and spent their days slogging away in the mud of the trenches. Some men were awarded medals while others ended up in the brig. Some made it home to tell their war stories; others were shipped back in a body bag.

Bo said that it was all luck, but I was beginning to believe more in fate. I had no idea which one of us was right or even if there was any real difference between the two. I just tried to keep myself together and hope for the best.

A sudden a burst of automatic rifle file drove away my thoughts and sent Bo and me diving for the ground.

Mackie didn't move from his chair. "Whoa ... easy now," he said soothingly as we picked ourselves up off the floor. "That's just the RVN firing. They shoot at logs or anything floating down the river that the gooks might use to sneak up on the bridge. When they're bored they'll fire at just about anything."

"Let's take the boat out and get some dinner."

Mackie led us down to the river where a new Boston Whaler with two 100 horsepower Mercury outboards sat tied to the pilings. He threw in a case of beer, his diving gear and a spear gun and hit the ignition. The engines caught on the first try and we soon found ourselves roaring up the river. It was impossible for Bo and me to keep the smiles off our faces. Now this was the life! Mack ran up the center of the river for a few miles and then cut the engines and allowed the boat to drift.

"How about a nice fat fish for dinner?" he asked, picking up the spear and slipping on a mask and fins. "There's extra gear in the boat," he told us before jumping overboard. "Come in if you like."

Bo grabbed another beer, put his feet up on the deck and sat back. "You go ahead. I'll just stay here and soak up the sun."

I stripped off my shirt, grabbed an extra mask and flippers and dove into the water. It was warm and crystal clear. I saw Mackie free diving about thirty feet away and swam over to him. He pointed down with his spear gun and I made out a school of large fish swimming lazily against the current. He took a deep breath and dove, but he missed his first shot and the fish instantly scattered. He came up shaking his head ruefully.

"I haven't missed in quite a while.... Oh well, we'll just have to try something else."

We swam back to the boat and climbed back on board. Mackie put the spear gun away and rummaged around the boat's locker and came back with a grenade in each hand.

"What are you gonna do with those?" Bo asked, sitting up nervously.

"Get dinner," Mackie explained, pulling the pin on one of the grenades and casually tossing it into the water. It sank and then exploded with a dull thud, throwing spray high into the air. Large numbers of stunned fish rose to the surface. Mackie was ready. He had a net secured to the end of a long pole and scooped them up.

Looking around, I saw the boats of the Vietnamese fisherman converging toward us from all over the river. They threw their nets out as soon as they got close to us and scooped up the dead and dying fish. Smiling and shouting, they urged Mackie to throw more grenades.

"Not a bad way to win hearts and minds," Mackie joked, making fun of the slogan that was repeated over and over again on Armed Forces Radio.

Another explosion shook the water. A huge black fish floated to the surface on my side of the boat and I reached down to grab him. I almost had him into the boat when he began to struggle, and I felt a sharp pain as his dorsal fin went into my finger. Damn, I dropped him back into the water and he disappeared.

Mackie fired up the engine and we left the Vietnamese to net the hundreds of smaller stunned and dying fish. We had more than enough for our own dinner. As the twin Mercury engines started up we heard arguments breaking out among the Vietnamese as they fought over the last fish.

When we finally got back to the dock, it was early afternoon. In no time Mackie had the fish cleaned and a charcoal fire started in a small grill on the deck. He even had lemons in the fridge. He sprinkled pepper over the fish and dribbled melted butter over them before placing them on the grill, skin side down. After a few minutes on the charcoal the fish were cooked to perfection. Leaning back against the wall, tired from the swim, eating fresh fish, drinking the cold beer, listening to the stereo, I could hardly remember that we were in a combat zone.

There was Vietnam, and then there was "the Nam." Serving in this war ran the full spectrum, from the hell world of the Marine grunt who lived most of his tour like a rat in a hole to the world of a Saigon pencil pusher who rarely left his office except to visit the nearest whorehouse. Sure, it was possible to get killed anywhere in Nam and helicopter crews and patrol boat units suffered high casualties. But at least in the Air Force or Navy you died clean. Even in the Marine Corps there were plush assignments to be had, and Mackie certainly seemed to have fallen into one.

For bush Marines like Bo and me, life in Nam bounced from one extreme to another. One day we were deep in the jungle, out of food and running for our lives. The next day we were sitting on a veranda eating fresh fish and drinking ice-cold beers, taking life as it came. The bad times made the good days even more vibrant and precious. Looking out at the clouds passing overhead and the fishermen throwing their nets into the blue waters of the river, I had to admit that life couldn't get much better than this.

My thoughts, however, went back to what had happened earlier in the day and I began to feel less than comfortable with myself. I remembered the Vietnamese teacher hobbling away across the bridge as he tried to protect his students. I remembered the look on the farmer's face as he pleaded with the Koreans to stop and give him his melons back.

I wasn't a particularly religious person, but I had been brought up to believe that anyone who knows the good that he should do and doesn't do anything is just as guilty as the person who commits the act, but could I really have done anything at all? The Koreans wouldn't have listened to me any more than the sergeant's dog. I took another drink of beer, but memories of what had happened that morning left a sour taste in my mouth.

26. The Red Corvette

*To forget the dead would be akin to killing
them a second time.*—Elie Wiesel,
Night

A few weeks passed and one day after formation Bo and I asked for permission to go to pick up our pay at Freedom Hill. We asked Sergeant Tom if he wanted to come along with us, but he begged off, explaining that he was scheduled to rotate back to the States in a few weeks and needed to get his gear packed up.

Freedom Hill was located only a few miles down the road from Reasoner. We hitched a ride, picked up our pay, and spent most of it getting haircuts, our utilities cleaned and starched, and having a leisurely lunch of fried chicken at the cafeteria they had there. There was no point in hurrying back and it was nearly dark when we finally hopped a truck and returned to base.

Frenchy was waiting for us on the steps of the hooch when we got back. He turned his head away from us as we approached. In a choked voice suddenly blurted out: "Sergeant Tom's been killed."

I felt a coldness run through my body. I found it difficult to believe what I had just been told. Only this morning he had stood in front of us at morning formation. We had spoken to him only a few hours ago.

Frenchy shook his head miserably and told us all he knew. The Third Platoon had a new lieutenant assigned to them and Tom had been asked to go to help him get squared away. It was going to be a short patrol, run less than five miles from our base, more of a training mission than anything else. We referred to these as "snap-in" patrols because the new officer was being trained to snap into a new team and instantly take command. I always hated the term. It was absurd to think that someone whose only qualification was a few months in Officer Candidate School could "snap-in" and replace an experienced sergeant who had worked his way up through the ranks and usually had years of combat experience.

The team had been inserted into an open rice paddy at the base of a mountain that we could see from the club. As was his custom, Sergeant Tom led the way out of the chopper. The other men began following him down the ramp, spreading out in our normal defensive circle. The chopper was still on the ground when it received a short burst of small arms fire from a nearby hillside. The men on the ground collapsed the circle and ran back up the ramp as the men still inside the chopper provided covering fire.

Sergeant Tom waited until the rest of the men were safely inside before turning and running back himself. He was only a few feet from the ramp when there was a sharp explosion and he was blown backward. No one knew if he had stepped on a mine, set off a booby trap, been hit by a mortar, or what had happened.

"It don't really matter now, does it?" Frenchy told us sadly.

Tom was the best bush Marine in Force Recon. If a scout as good in the bush as Sergeant Tom had been killed a few miles from our base, how would I survive? I hated myself for the selfishness of my thoughts but couldn't help but recognize their truth.

There was a small building used for a chapel at Camp Reasoner, and a few days later I joined other men for the service that was being held for our sergeant. The officers sat on one side, the enlisted men on the other. A Marine captain from the Chaplain Corps came over from Da Nang to conduct the service. We sang a hymn; the minister led us in a prayer and then turned the service over to Captain Bilger. He explained that during the attack an enemy's round had hit one of the Sergeant Tom's grenades, which exploded, killing him instantly.

Major Simbul stood up behind the podium and gave a short eulogy. He told us what a good Marine Sergeant Tom had been, how much the unit would miss his leadership and how difficult it would be to find a replacement. The major's very words, "unit," "replacement," "snap-in," brought home to me just how expendable we were. The Marine Corps' "Green Machine" could chew us up and spit us out without missing a beat.

For me, the words of the two officers were cold and empty. Sergeant Tom belonged to us, and always would. We knew him far better than the two officers standing in front of us did, but we were not given any chance to participate in the service. Denied any opportunity to grieve, we were forced to sit silently like the dumb animals we were.

My thoughts went back to Tom's wife and the new Corvette that he was so looking forward to driving again. We sang a final hymn, and the service ended. The chaplain briskly packed away the cross and other religious tokens in a canvas carrying case and he and the other officers left the chapel. The enlisted men followed. I'm not a particularly religious person, but I sat for a few minutes and said a final prayer for the soul of my mentor and friend. As I walked out of the chapel I noticed a red cross inscribed in the tiles of the white linoleum floor.

It was covered in mud from our boots.

27. An Hoa

This just goes to show you again—this whole aerial warfare business isn't quite perfected.—last French radio transmission from Dien Bien Phu before the base was overrun by Viet Minh forces

A few weeks later, Major Simbul told us that Force Recon would be moving out of Camp Reasoner to a remote airstrip known as An Hoa. Our new base would be about thirty miles southwest of Da Nang. Closer to the Laotian/Cambodian border where we would be running many of our future missions.

"Where we are going, what we will be doing is Top Secret," he warned us. "If anyone asks you what outfit you are with tell them you're the First Laundry Company."

We all started laughing, thinking he was joking, but he sternly cut us short.

"I'm serious," he admonished, "no jump wings, no jump boots, nothing."

27. An Hoa

What he was proposing was just short of absurd. Anyone seeing our haircuts and equipment would know that we weren't the "First Laundry Company," if indeed there ever was such a unit. I also thought it likely that there were more than a few Communist sympathizers among the Vietnamese workers who entered our compound every morning to take our trash, cut our hair, and cook our food. It was naïve to think that they wouldn't know that we were leaving Reasoner, and they probably knew where we were going before we did. In any case, we followed the major's orders, removed the insignias we had previously worn with such pride, and joked with each other about our new unit, the First Laundry Company.

A few days later we found ourselves flown out to a barren plain surrounded by mountains. There was an airstrip down the middle, a few scattered tents and not much else. A sign by the airfield welcomed us to An Hoa.

"Why would they set up an air base here?" I complained to Moose as we pounded stakes into the ground and strung the razor wire around the perimeter of our new home.

"The gooks will be looking right down our throats; this place is just like Dien Bien Phu," I told him, looking up at the surrounding mountains.

"Dien Bien who?" Moose asked chuckling.

I explained to him that Dien Bien Phu was where the French had suffered their final defeat in the last Indochina war. I told him how the French had moved thirteen thousand troops into a barren airfield surrounded by high mountains. The French believed that their air force would keep the enemy at bay, but the Viet Minh army led by General Giap moved heavy artillery into the mountains above the air base and surrounded it. After a long and bloody siege, the French were forced to surrender and forced out of Vietnam forever. A few years later the first Americans began arriving to take their place.

"No use worrying about it," Moose replied in a resigned voice as he picked up another stake. "There isn't a damn thing you and I can do about it, except dig in deeper."

And dig in we did. As soon the wire was laid we began digging trenches. The Seabees came in and built some plywood platforms while we set up tents that looked like they had been left over from World War II. The Seabees laid down metal platforms for our new LZ and in only a few days we began sending teams out into the surrounding mountains. Almost immediately the patrols made contact. It seemed the mountains around An Hoa were swarming with enemy troops.

An artillery company was brought in and set up camp next to us. The cannon cockers, as we called them, worked stripped to their shorts in the blistering sun, firing round after round into the surrounding hills. The Air Force put up additional hangars at the opposite end of the airstrip and soon we heard the buzzing sound of Puff's mini-guns as they strafed the mountainsides.

Our team was assigned to man one of the bunkers the Seabees had built around our compound. We arrived to find ourselves in a chest-high hole in the ground surrounded by a double row of stacked sandbags. Curved steel plates kept the ground from caving in around the hole. A ¾-inch steel plate set on 4 × 4 posts formed the roof. Truman rolled over the sandbagged wall and found himself standing in four inches of water that had collected on the floor. He swore and stomped off with a determined look on his face. He returned half an hour later dragging a wooden pallet. Which he threw on the floor to keep our feet dry. Truman was good at scrounging things like that.

Before nightfall we placed half a dozen Claymore mines around the bunker, carefully running the wires back to the bunker and placing the black plastic detonators on top of the sandbags. Each igniter had a trigger mechanism that generated an electric current when the grip was squeezed. The electricity from the igniter set off blasting caps, which in turn detonated the C-4 explosive. The front of the Claymore was a wire mesh containing hundreds of small steel pellets. Driven by the C-4, these pellets fanned out in a deadly hail of steel. They were our last line of defense.

I set up our M-60 machine gun and braced the tripod with sandbags. Bo laid out the long belts of machine-gun ammo beside them, covering the rounds with a silk blanket to keep them clean and dry. I took the starlight scope out of its case and laid it next to the M-60. This battery-operated scope enhanced the natural light and gave us the ability to literally see in the dark. Unfortunately, the starlight scope gave me a blinding headache if I stared at the green images that it produced for more than a few minutes. I preferred using a standard pair of binoculars, which were nearly as good at gathering light.

The long, flat plain of An Hoa stretched up the mountains three or four miles away. There was an old aluminum storage shed outside our perimeter a few hundred yards to our right and a strange Vietnamese farmhouse about a quarter of a mile to our left. It was strange to see it there because everything else in the area had been bulldozed flat when they built the air base. What was even stranger was that a Vietnamese family still lived there. Buffeted by helicopters, subjected to the noise of our artillery, this poor family was often also tormented by bored Marines who would try to hit the house with illumination flares.

There was a large storage shed close to our position that also worried us because it blocked our view. NVA sappers could keep the shed between us and them until they were almost on us. For all we knew it could be holding a few hundred NVA soldiers at this very moment!

Frenchy lit up a cigarette and looked out at the mountains in the distance. The sun was behind them and they glowed purple red. "Sure is pretty here," he murmured softly.

"Why don't you raise your head a little more?" Truman kidded. "Sniper nick your ear and you're out of here." Frenchy had been slightly wounded twice before. If he got a third Purple Heart he'd be able to apply for a job in the rear, maybe even get transferred out of Nam.

"I'm considering it," Frenchy responded thoughtfully. "But you never know… I was talking to a grunt the other day and he said that his friend needed one more Purple Heart so in the middle of a firefight he raised his hand, waved it around and got a neat one right through his arm. He was loaded onto a medevac chopper, but as it was taking off an RPG[1] hit the aircraft and everyone aboard was killed."

"If it's your turn to go … ya jes' gotta go," Truman remarked.

"Ain't that the truth." Frenchy nodded. "Take Sergeant Tom, two tours in Nam, twenty-four Recon missions, two weeks left to go in-country and he goes home in a body bag."

"And that only half-full," Truman added grimly.

I told him the story about a corporal in one of our teams who was getting short and had asked his officer to take him out of the bush. He told him that he had heard the voice of God warning him that if he went out again into the jungle he would die. The

27. An Hoa

corporal only had a few weeks left on his tour and his officer listened to his request and assigned to work the radio relay outpost Force maintained on Hill 452. Although this post was later nearly overrun by NVA sappers, at the time it was thought to be a safe assignment. The first night on the hill, however, a severe thunderstorm ripped through the area. A bolt of lightning struck and set off his grenades, instantly killing him and the Marine standing next to him.

Truman unexpectedly started to laugh.

"How can you laugh at something like that?" I asked him, shaking my head.

"Why not? I'm sure God did," Truman replied, still chuckling to himself.

"Heads up ... we've got company," Bo warned, glancing out toward the perimeter.

A stocky figure was working his way along the wire toward us. It was Gunny Barker. He reached our position and peered into the darkness of our bunker. "Keep your eyes open tonight, fellas; the grunts have been reporting movement all around their perimeter; they might come after us next." he warned, moving along to the next bunker.

After he left we talked for a while as the moon and stars came out. Moonlight lit up the distant mountains in a silvery sheen, and the stars twinkled like blue diamonds in the clear air. Perhaps the stars in the night sky in the States were equally as beautiful, but in Nam I had all the time in the world to admire them. Bo took up the first watch, and the rest of us spread out our ponchos and tried to get some sleep.

Our world exploded at midnight. Bo had just reached over to shake me awake for my watch when a tremendous blast shook the ground. Everything danced dizzily in front of my eyes, a crazy pattern of red and black. I dove for the floor as shrapnel and debris rained down around us. I heard and felt the solid jolts of metal fragments embedding themselves in our sandbags. In front of us we saw the storage shed topple over. It had taken a direct hit from a rocket. Something inside was burning furiously and thick black smoke drifted over our position, stinging my eyes and making me cough.

Truman was yelling something, but I couldn't hear anything other than a hollow ringing in my ears. In the distance I saw ghostly figures moving through the smoke in front of us. I grabbed the M-60 and started firing. Truman and Bo joined in. Flares were now going off all along the perimeter and another machine gun opened up from the tower, their tracers merging with my own. As my hearing returned I heard a siren wailing in the distance.

With a roaring whoosh, another rocket screamed over our heads. I hit the ground again and was immediately buried by the other men falling on top of me, each of us trying to be the one deepest in the hole. Two or three bodies piled on top of you would stop shrapnel almost as well as a sandbag. The rocket blew up behind us, and we all scrambled up again to defend our position. Flares and illumination rounds lit up the base for hundreds of yards around the perimeter. A cargo plane sitting near the end of the runway had gotten a direct hit and was engulfed in flames, adding its own light to the hellish scene. The radio crackled as the positions around us reported in.

Major Simbul was on the radio trying unsuccessfully to get fire coordinates from the men in the tower. We heard the frustration in his voice as he tried unsuccessfully to establish radio contact with them. Whoever was on the radio must have been holding their talk button down and couldn't hear incoming transmissions. If things weren't so serious it would have been funny.

"Here comes one now!" a laconic voice would call out. A few seconds later another rocket would roar overhead and explode in the distance.

"What are the co-coordinates?" the major implored.

"Here comes another one," the phantom voice responded.

"Where are they being launched from?"

"Here comes another one…"

Despite the intermittent incoming fire, it was soon apparent to us that our section was not the direct target of the attack. The first few volleys had been short, but the gooks adjusted their aim and now the rockets were passing well over our heads, hitting the far end of the runway where the cargo planes were parked. After about ten minutes the attack slowed and then stopped completely. Maybe the enemy ran out of rockets, or Marine artillery fire drove them away. It didn't matter to us. We stayed at our posts, the ground in front of us lit up by the fires from the burning storage shed.

When dawn broke we were relieved of guard duty by men from the Fourth Platoon. They told us that the enemy had tried to storm the far end of the base where aircraft were housed. The grunts defending the hangars had stopped them in the wire. The attack on our section had only been a diversion. We later learned that the enemy's 122mm rocket barrage destroyed or damaged several aircraft and killed or wounded five men.

As we left the bunker we suddenly heard someone in front of us yelling frantically for a corpsman. We ran toward to find several Marines crouched over a naked figure lying on the ground next to the showers. It was one of the drivers from the motor pool. He was covered in a soapy froth of blood and dirt, his body covered with small shrapnel holes. A bar of soap was still clutched in his fingers. He must have been taking a shower when the attack began and ran out to find cover. He had probably been killed in the first few minutes of the attack and had been lying there all night. The medics arrived, but they couldn't do anything except take his body away. We couldn't do anything to help him either, and continued on to the mess hall. It may sound callous now, but we were hungry.

We got our food and sat down at a table where one of the men in the motor pool soon was telling everyone who would listen that a mortar round had landed directly on top of his bunker without exploding. He said that the spent round had punched through the sandbagged roof and hit him in the leg. He limped around the mess hall pulling up his pant leg at every opportunity and showing off a livid bruise, which he said matched the red star insignia forged into the top of the shell. His story was a bit too much for me to swallow, but he said that anyone who didn't believe him could come over to his tent and check out the unexploded mortar for himself.

A little later that morning a truck passed by our compound carrying the mangled bodies of a dozen enemy soldiers killed in their attempt to storm the perimeter. The pile of corpses bounced up and down on the rough road as the truck rumbled along. Two grunts sat on the tailgate, every once in a while pushing the bodies back with their rifle butts to keep them from rolling out.

We were kept busy reinforcing the wire and digging in deeper. Scattered through the compound were chunks of shrapnel from the rocket attack. I had always thought of rockets as light, rather elegant things. There was nothing elegant about the rusty pieces of metal that littered the ground. These rockets looked like they had been constructed out of heavy steel piping. They must have been over ten feet long.

The Seabees arrived with their heavy equipment and demolished what remained of the storage shed. Now we had a straight field of fire for a thousand yards in front of us. They also dropped off a dozen concrete drainage pipes. We rolled these into place on either side of the tents. We closed off their ends with sandbags, leaving only enough room to squeeze in. The culverts were intended to be used as quick shelters in the case of another rocket attack. They wouldn't stop a direct hit, but they were certainly better than nothing.

The next day a half dozen Army Slicks touched down just outside our perimeter. The fast and nimble small choppers would have been far better suited to our types of missions than the clunky CH-46s, but we never got to use them.

"Get a load of these hotshots," Bo muttered, nodding toward a group of Special Forces soldiers who were now busily setting up their tents directly in front of our fire zone. Their spit-shined boots, green berets and spiffy tiger-striped utilities were a far cry from the muddy helmets and flak jackets we were wearing. Small Army Slicks[2] kept arriving all morning and by noontime the tents of a Special Forces camp stood just outside our wire. Rumors spread that they were going to be running patrols with us as part of a joint Army/Marine recon force.

We believed the scuttlebutt. It was just the kind of half-baked publicity stunt that the top brass would relish. There was soon a brisk trade going on across the wire. Marines trading Ka-Bar knives for tiger-striped utilities, bush hats for berets, captured AKs for revolvers. If the officers on both sides hadn't stopped the brisk business I am sure it wouldn't have been long before we would have been trading our trucks for their helicopters.

An Hoa with the concrete culverts next to our tents.

I'll say this for the Army guys: they had their priorities straight. The first thing the Special Forces guys did was set up a bar. They stretched camouflaged netting across some poles to block the sun and brought out folding tables and chairs. Sitting in our foxholes and bunkers, we listened to their music and watched them drinking their beer a few hundred yards away. Enlisted men weren't invited over, but our officers crossed the wire to visit our new neighbors. captain Bilger returned with a green beret on his head and a half-plastered expression on his face.

"Excuse me, sir," Bo asked respectfully from our foxhole as he passed, "are those guys going to be here for long?"

The captain glanced back over his shoulder at the new camp. "Far as I know," he responded curtly, turning to leave.

"But sir," Bo persisted. "There're right in front of our fire zone. They don't even have any wire up. Come nightfall they're going to be a perfect target."

The captain looked blearily back at the Army post and shrugged. "Not your problem, Marine."

"What a grade-A asshole," I muttered as he turned away.

"What the hell are we supposed to do, fire right into their base?" Bo asked in disgust.

I had to shake my head. It was ironic that Bilger was our company's intelligence officer. To me he seemed to show as much intelligence as a mole.

That night the far side of the base was attacked again by rockets and mortar fire. Nothing as intense as the previous day's shelling, but enough to make the Army guys reconsider An Hoa as their new home. In the morning the Army guys folded up their tents, got back in their Hueys and took off for a quieter location. We didn't have a chance to run any patrols with them, and that was probably just as well.

There was a huge steel tower on our compound that must have been left from before the war. It was nearly a hundred feet tall and was connected to some kind of conveyor apparatus. From the top of the tower you could you could see for miles over the flat plain of An Hoa. Bored Marines would sit up there for hours with binoculars searching for "targets of opportunity." We carried up some sandbags and mounted a special .50-caliber machine gun on top. The armorer had mounted a powerful telescopic sight on the gun and by doing so, had turned it into a superb weapon for sniping. When set to fire on semi-automatic the heavy .50-caliber round was able to reach out and kill from incredibly long distances.

During the Civil War the painter Winslow Homer had looked through the cross hairs of a sniper's scope and remarked that sniping was "the closest thing to murder" that he could imagine. Nothing had changed in the years that had passed since that time. A sniper had the power of life and death, the power of God himself, in their hands, and that power was intoxicating.

We would focus the cross hairs of the scope on the farmers tending their fields and make jokes about how easy it would be to "waste 'em." All it would take would be the slightest pressure of our finger on the firing paddle and they would die. During the day, however, our true enemies remained hidden in the mountains above us, emerging only under the cover of darkness to fire their rockets and probe our defenses.

We continued to work on improving our fortifications. We added sandbags around our tent and the Seabees came back and built a squat sandbagged building that would hold a dozen men. Every night some of us were selected to man this new bunker. In the event of an attack we were supposed to run out of the bunker fully equipped and ready to fight.

Each evening we would enter through the small doorway, dragging our flak jackets, helmets and weapons in with us. In the crowded, airless room sleep was nearly impossible. As soon as I crawled through the door I felt that I was suffocating. The earth-floored room reminded me of a crypt and once inside I found it difficult to breath. I decided that I had better chances in the bush than I did waiting for a random rocket to hit our bunker, and like many of the other scouts I began volunteering for extra missions. I felt I had a better chance of surviving in the jungle.

28. Buzzard Bait

No comment, no warnings, no complaints, no protests ...
not one thing to be said to anyone.—Nixon's instructions
to Kissinger prior to bombing Cambodia

After Sergeant Tom was killed, our team went out with a number of temporary patrol leaders. These were all experienced sergeants borrowed from other platoons. I continued to be assigned the role of assistant patrol leader, making sure our team was ready and going out on overflights to select good insertion points. These flights were very useful because from the air we were able to get a good feel for the terrain we would be dropped into.

It was early December and Force Recon was now running patrols within Laos and Cambodia as part of America's "Secret War." The Air Force and the CIA were trying desperately to interdict traffic along the Ho Chi Minh Trail, the network of hidden roads and trails that the enemy used to move soldiers and supplies from North Vietnam through Laos and Cambodia into South Vietnam. The dense jungle canopy made most of the trail nearly impossible to see from the air and Intelligence relied on our patrols to give them the information they needed.

We had to laugh as we returned from these missions to hear President Nixon solemnly assure the American public that the United States had no ground forces in either country. The administration was trying to keep even the massive Cambodian bombings off the record and to a large extent was succeeding. Our ground missions over the border were also classified as *Top Secret*. As a practical matter, Tricky Dickie's subterfuge really didn't mean all that much to us. In the mountains and jungles borders were invisible, known only by different-colored lines on our maps. We crossed back and forth across the paper borders with impunity.

Our teams had been observing a portion of the Laotian portion of the Ho Chi Minh trail for several months, collecting information about the location of enemy base camps and calling in air strikes on targets of opportunity. Teams came back with reports of hundreds of soldiers moving along the trail, some of them combat units, others supply troops carrying food and equipment into South Vietnam. The North Vietnamese had spent years expanding, fortifying and camouflaging their supply highway. American air strikes didn't seem to be making much progress at stopping the flow of men and material.

An earlier team had moved in at night and planted CIA-designed electronic motion detectors near a heavily used section of the trail, but the signals from the sensors were never received. Intelligence believed that the detectors were operating because aircraft flying over the area could receive the signals, but that the mountainous terrain was probably preventing the transmissions from reaching further. Our mission was to set up a radio relay high above the valley where the sensors had been placed.

After we had installed this equipment we were to proceed in closer to the trail to evaluate the effects of a recent airstrike on a critical river crossing. The Air Force had been pounding this area for weeks, confident that they had finally cut it.

Truman and I would be joining Sergeant Davis and men from the Third Platoon. I had gone on patrols with him before and knew him to be a good man in the bush. It wasn't unusual for members of one team to go out with another. Sometimes teams needed specific capabilities such as a corpsman or radio operators, in other cases they were undermanned through combat losses or disease.

At our briefing Captain Bilger introduced us to a "Mr. Jones," who was supposedly a civilian "communications expert." Jones was a rather portly middle-aged man in black trousers and a white short-sleeved shirt. From the way he was sweating I could tell that he hadn't been that long in Nam, and I also questioned whether Jones was even his real name.

He laid a canvas pack on the table and removed a green metal box much smaller than our PRC-25, but it only took a glance for us to know that this baby wasn't standard Marine Corps issue. The radios we normally carried held a variety of switches, dials, and attachments for handsets, and other peripheral equipment. The unit sitting on the table in front of us had only a recessed sliding on/off switch and a jack to plug in an antenna. The unit was completely plain, no writing, not even a serial number.

"All you need to do is run the antenna down from a tree, plug it in and turn the unit on," Mr. Jones explained in a brisk manner, pulling a thin wire antenna out of the satchel and showing us where it attached. He pointed to the sliding on/off switch. "Just one thing," he warned. "Once you turn this switch on don't move the unit again."

"Why's that?" Truman asked innocently.

"There's a motion detector inside and enough C-4 inside the box to blow itself and anything around it to bits," Jones explained calmly.

"How do we retrieve it then?" one of the other men asked.

"You don't," Jones answered, "The device will self-destruct when the battery dies."

"When will that be, sir?" Truman asked with a worried look.

"That information is classified," Captain Bilger interrupted.

"Not for quite a while," Mr. Jones finally answered for him.

"Just great," Truman turned to me and muttered as we left the briefing. "Now we're carrying around a fuckin' time bomb with us."

We decided to draw straws to see who would carry "The Box," as we now called it, and I drew the short straw. The others seemed relieved, but I actually preferred to handle the unit myself. I didn't want someone like Truman forgetting what he was carrying and dropping the damn thing on the ground next to me.

We were inserted quietly into an old field about two miles from the trail. Another team was waiting for us on the LZ and they rushed aboard the aircraft as soon as we exited. We called this maneuver piggybacking and it usually worked well. The pilots liked piggybacks because they thought that the LZ would be safe. We liked it for the same reason.

Once the chopper had dropped us off we started climbing upward toward higher ground to set up the radio. The monsoon had ended, but the weather was still cold and wet. The terrain was steep, but we had climbed worse. We reached the top just before dusk. None of us wanted to stay around the box any longer than we had to, so while the others set up a defensive perimeter Sergeant Davis and myself looked for a place to set it up.

Near the top of the hill was a dead tree whose trunk had been partially hollowed out. Davis gave me a boost, and I managed to climb to the top. In the distance I saw the river that marked the Laotian border and knew that just beyond that was the trail itself. If the box was going to work anywhere, it would work from here.

I secured the antenna to one of the branches and then dropped it down to the ground. Even up close it looked like just another vine. We set the box firmly inside the tree trunk, plugged in the antenna and covered the opening with twigs and leaves. Sergeant Davis waved us away, took a deep breath and switched the unit on. We had no indication whether it was working or not.

We pulled back several hundred meters and set up for the night. A light rain had begun to fall, and a chilling wind blew up from the valley. We wrapped ourselves in our thin silk ponchos and tried to sleep. It started raining heavily around midnight. When dawn broke, we moved cautiously down the mountainside toward the trailhead. Our orders were to avoid contact at all costs, and it took us nearly a day to move into position. We found a good spot in a swamp bordering the river to conceal ourselves, but a heavy fog had moved in and the other side of the river was hidden from view. Fog is funny stuff; sometimes it will mask nearby sounds and occasionally amplify those from far away.

As soon as it got dark, we heard the sound of a diesel engine. The noise increased and then faded away, as if something was going forward and then backing up. We couldn't see a thing, and eventually the sound stopped.

We decided to stay where we were until there was enough light enough to see what was going on. At dawn the rain stopped and the fog began to lift and once again we heard the sound of an engine moving toward us. Sergeant Davis looked through his binoculars and then silently handed them to me.

A large open truck overflowing with supplies was moving slowly down the road followed by a long line of soldiers. At one point the truck slid off the road, but soldiers ran up and pushed. The drivers shifted gears, revved his engine and everyone forged ahead.

The Air Force's bombing raids had obviously failed. If anything, the explosions had opened up the jungle and made it even easier for the NVA to expand their network of roads.

As dawn turned into day silence fell over the trail. After a couple of hours without seeing anything we cautiously pulled back. When we finally left the swamp, I looked down at my legs and saw that that my pants were covered in fat black leeches that stubbornly hung on when I tried to pull them off. While I was wading through the murky water I hadn't felt a thing. These leeches were much larger than the pale gray-colored ones that attached themselves to us in the jungle. Blood dripped from their suction marks when I pulled them off, but I hit them with bug juice and they shriveled up and let go as they died.

We established radio contact, sent in a SITREP,[1] describing what we had seen, and pulled back from the border. Our patrol had now lasted nearly two weeks, and we were running low on rations. We were tired, wet, cold and hungry when we finally reached the overgrown rice paddy that was to be our extraction point. We called in for the birds but weren't at all surprised to be told that the cloud cover prevented them from reaching us. Rain was coming down hard and hillsides around us were shrouded in mist, their peaks disappearing into the clouds. If the pilots weren't able to even see the ground, we couldn't expect them to pick us up.

At first none of us particularly cared. We had traveled many miles from the Ho Chi Minh Trail and felt that we were now out of danger. We just had to wait until the weather cleared. We waited and waited, but every day it seemed the rains came down harder than the day before.

We all preferred to carry extra ammunition to extra food. To keep down the weight, we usually took no more than a can or two of C rations per day and provisioned ourselves for a two-week mission. When we realized that our patrol would be extended we had tried to ration ourselves, but now we were out of food. Truman found an overlooked can of beanies and weenies at the bottom of his pack. He cheerfully ate the sausages himself, cruelly showing each one to us before popping it with exaggerated satisfaction into his face. He then offered to sell the remaining beans to the highest bidder. Frenchy offered to trade a carton of cigarettes for a spoonful of beans, but he was outbid by Sergeant Davis, who promised Truman a two-day pass.

I took out my notebook and drew pictures of hamburgers and hot dogs, tearing out the pages and doling them out one page at a time to the other men. The men ate the paper drawings with relish and smacked their lips in imagined delight. Soon they were placing orders for steaks, pizza and beer. I filled as many of the orders as I could but eventually used up all of the pages in my notebook.

As soon as I closed my eyes my imagination conjured up elaborate feasts. I dreamed of huge tables groaning under the weight of fat, crispy chickens, rare steaks and glazed hams. Hours upon hours were passed in these reveries as we sat huddled under our skimpy blankets in the rain.

In the hope of taking our minds off food we even resorted to playing with the ever-present leeches. Each of us would select the largest bloodsucker that we could find and put it on our arm. Once the buggers latched on we'd hold out our arms and bet on which leech would hold on the longest. We watched them get bigger and bigger as they sucked away. Usually they would bloat up and fall off after about ten minutes, but Truman had one enormous black leech that he must have attached itself to him back in the swamp. The creature was so engorged that it looked like a small balloon. Of course, we all knew that the game we were playing was a very stupid thing to do. The last thing we needed was these obscene creatures draining our blood, but we needed something to keep our minds off the thought of food.

During recon training we had been taught how to live off the land, but we couldn't use the techniques we had been taught without drawing the attention of the enemy to our location. We searched around the immediate area for edible plants, but the only things we found were a few pale mushrooms that we couldn't identify, and no one wanted to risk eating. We set out a number of simple snares, but there didn't seem to be any sign of animal life in this part of the jungle. We couldn't draw attention to ourselves by hunting and there weren't any lakes or streams to fish in. All we could do was wait.

We began to suffer the initial stages of starvation. At first I was ravenously hungry, but as the days passed that feeling diminished and I became extremely weak and very tired. Just getting to my feet and walking a few steps left me dizzy. My teammates were in equally bad shape. Day after day we sat in the mud and the rain hoping the clouds would clear. A fine fungus started growing over our boots and web gear. Even our clothes started rotting. The jungle itself was getting ready to devour us.

One afternoon I looked up and saw an enormous black bird perched on a tree limb just over my head. The branch was as thick as my arm, but it bent under the bird's weight. At first I thought I was hallucinating, because it seemed impossible for anything capable of flying to be that large. I raised myself into a sitting position and we observed each other. He had a large yellow beak and looked at me with alert black eyes. He was completely black except for a slight white ring around his neck. The strangest thing about him was his head, which looked like that of a turkey and had no feathers on it at all. He sat absolutely still, gripping the branch with powerful claws. With a sudden chill I recognized the bird was a huge vulture and that he was patiently waiting for us all to die.

I nudged Truman, who was sitting half-asleep next to me. He took one look at the bird and then jumped to his feet and waved his arms. The bird pushed off from the branch and almost lazily spread his wings and glided silently away.

"Goddamn buzzard." Truman shook his head angrily. "Comes back here I'm gonna kill and eat him."

"Yea we could have too, if you hadn't scared him away!" I hissed back angrily. I could almost taste a nice buzzard stew.

The next day we received word that the choppers were going to make one more try at getting to us, but we were warned not to get our hopes up. The weather was still bad and projected to get worse. Shortly after daybreak we heard the welcome *clop-clop-clop* of a CH-46 hovering in the clouds above us. We popped smoke, to mark our position, but I doubted that the pilot would be able to see it. The sergeant tried to guide the bird in by radio using the sound of its engine. The pilot descended slowly, coming down almost vertically through the overcast. The aircraft finally broke through the clouds only a hundred feet above our heads and landed in the overgrown rice paddy.

As soon as I stood up I realized how weak I had become. I was barely able to walk the few hundred feet to where the chopper was waiting. Several of the other men were even in worse shape than I was. They were unable to lift their packs to their shoulders and were forced to drag them along the ground.

When we got into the chopper, we realized that our rescuers were the same flight crew who had extracted us several months earlier with the jungle penetrator. After they had returned us to our base, I had given the pilot a Ka-Bar and inscribed with the name of our team on its sheath. They had done an incredible job of flying, descending blind through thick clouds, guided only by our radio. I never knew their names and they didn't know mine, but they had willingly risked their lives to rescue us.

"When we got the word that some of the men from Force needed help we all volunteered to get you," the baby-faced crew chief told me as he helped us climb up the ramp. Once in the air he brought out a garbage bag filled with candy. He told us that everyone at the base knew that we had run out of food, and had chipped in to buy the candy for us. We attacked it greedily, tearing aside the paper like animals and stuffing one candy bar after another into our mouths. We seemed unable to control ourselves. By the time we landed, all of us were sick as dogs and could barely drag ourselves back to our hooch.

Despite our woozy condition, we were debriefed shortly after we got back. An Air Force major joined Captain Bilger and the enigmatic Mr. Jones at the debriefing. They heard the bad news about the effectiveness of his bombing campaign without comment, shaking their heads in disbelief when we told him about the truck we had seen.

We showed Mr. Jones on the map exactly where we had placed the electronic device and told him how we had camouflaged it.

"Is it working?" Truman asked.

"Sorry, that's classified information," Bilger replied automatically.

"When do we need to replace it?" I asked, shifting the question slightly.

Mr. Jones understood perfectly well what I was trying to get at. "Not for quite a while," he responded, smiling.

"Well, all right!" Truman crowed, giving me a high five.

---

29. A Christmas Carol

Jingle bells, Mortar shells
VC in the grass
Take your Merry Christmas
And shove it up your ass!
—a Vietnam Christmas carol

Looking back, I find it amazing how quickly youthful bodies can recover from such an ordeal. When we first returned from the mission I was barely able to walk, but in a few days I had recovered most of my strength, if not my weight. I was still famished and we gorged ourselves on the chow line, finishing up one helping and going back for seconds or even thirds. Truman had a case of C rations by his cot and would open the cans one after another and eat the revolting stuff cold.

I began to have a powerful craving for a pizza. No matter how I tried to put the image of a nice big cheese pizza out of my mind, it came back a minute later stronger than ever. I began to think about making one myself. Truman was still so hungry that he had volunteered for mess duty, where he scarfed down everything within reach and brought back leftovers to the hutch. I told him my ideas for the pizza and told him all I needed was some bread dough, cheese and tomato sauce. I knew if anyone would be able to get the ingredients Truman was the man, and he didn't disappoint. He returned later that afternoon with not only what I had asked for, but a can of mushrooms and a jar of olive oil as well.

I found a steel garbage can by the mess hall that I appropriated for the project. I cleaned it until it sparkled and punched a few holes in the bottom with my Ka-Bar so that air could escape. I got some bricks and made a bed for the can to rest on upside down. Truman contributed a metal tray from the mess hall. I was now ready for the pie itself. I took the bread dough, spread it out and added the tomato sauce, the cheese and the mushrooms. When we were finished, we had something that certainly looked like a pizza.

I sprinkled olive oil lightly over the top and carefully set the garbage can upside down on top of the tray. Truman inserted a large plug of C-4 at the bottom of our makeshift oven and lit it off. The C-4 burned furiously and soon we smelled the pizza cooking. We piled a couple of sandbags on the outside of the garbage can to keep the heat in. After about fifteen minutes we figured it was done and took off the can. I've had a lot of pizza pies since then, but none have tasted as good as the one that Truman and I cooked that day in a garbage can with C-4. It was simply superb.

We had returned to An Hoa a few days before Christmas. When I went to pick up my mail I was surprised to find a package from my high school buddies waiting for me. The other guys crowded around to see what was in them.

Frenchy pawed aside the paper and without asking grabbed a *Playboy* magazine out of the box. Truman followed his example and came up with a hot rod magazine. I grabbed what was left of my gift and huddled over the carton, slapping away the hands of the other men who were pawing playfully at the box. There were two coffee cans stacked together in the middle of the box. Each held a small bottle of bourbon. I stuck one bottle under my pillow and passed the other around so that everyone would share my good fortune. I took a big swig and holding up the bottle wished everyone a "Merry Christmas" as they passed the other bottle around the hooch. The box of magazines and booze seemed like a gift from another planet.

The rain finally stopped on Christmas Eve, and the stars came out. Bo and I found ourselves together on guard duty. Once in a while the artillery post next to us would send a barrage into some faraway target. Along the perimeter pop flares would arc upward, illuminating the ground in brilliant white light. We huddled down in our ponchos, peered through our starlight scopes at the ghostly green landscape surrounding us and thought about Christmas at home.

At midnight Bo nudged me awake. I faintly heard someone in another bunker on the other side of our compound softly singing the opening words of the hymn "Silent

Merry Christmas!

Night." Some other Marines came out of the tents and foxholes and joined in the singing. Soon a vast chorus filled the air as hundreds of voices joined in from all around the base. All was quiet for a minute or so after the final stanza was sung, but then, all too soon, the artillery started firing again.

30. A Close Shave

You will not be punished for your anger
You will be punished by your anger.
—Buddha

30. A Close Shave

A crop of three new lieutenants had arrived at Force Recon headquarters while we were out on our last patrol, and the major had begun assigning them to the various teams. At formation the next morning we were told that one of the new officers, a First Lieutenant Lord, would be taking charge of our platoon. As we stood at rigid attention, the new officer took Sergeant Tom's place in front of us.

Lieutenant Lord was probably in his middle twenties, a lean, rawboned man. Everything about him looked new, from his spit-shined boots to his crisply starched camouflaged utilities. His hair had been cut so short that his head looked nearly bald. Unlike most of the other officers however, he wasn't wearing jump wings, and I wondered if he had even gone through recon training. I learned later that he hadn't, and in fact had simply been transferred over to Force Recon after completing OCS.[1]

The major and captain moved down the line inspecting the men. When they reached our platoon, the major motioned our new lieutenant over to join the inspection group. The officers made their way down the line of troops and eventually came to me. I clicked back the bolt of my M-16 and smartly presented arms for inspection.

Ever since my first Force Recon inspection I had taken extra care to present myself well at formation. I had learned from the more experienced men the trick of keeping an extra set of starched utilities and a pair of spit-shined boots set aside just for the daily formation. I kept my "cover" or Marine field cap, freshly sprayed in starch and molded into the iconic Marine style. Thanks to Sergeant Tom the armorer had returned my rifle to me in spotless condition and I kept it that way. I thought of myself as one squared-away Marine. Looking good and keeping my equipment in good condition was something I prided myself on.

Lieutenant Lord looked me over without comment and the officers moved on to Bo, who was next to me in the formation line. He also passed his weapon inspection, but the major marked him down for not having shaved close enough. Bo's beard had always been his nemesis. It was blue-black and extremely coarse. No matter how much he scraped away, he would often get written up for not shaving close enough. At one point he had irritated the skin on his face so much that Doc gave him a medical waiver exempting him from shaving until his skin had healed.

After we were dismissed, the lieutenant ordered us to meet him back at our hooch in ten minutes. I thought that he was going to tell us more about himself and get to know us better. Instead he made us stand outside at attention and gave us a stern lecture on how he was going to turn us into the best team in Force Recon. Men from the other platoons smirked at us as they walked past and saw us standing at attention being berated. We were humiliated and confused. We thought we already were the best team in the company.

If Lord wanted to lecture us, he should have done it somewhere private, not out in the open where the entire company could hear what he was saying. He went on to tell us how disappointed he was in having someone in our platoon get written up at inspection and that he wasn't going to stand for it. He seemed to regard Bo's stubble as a personal affront, and the longer he talked the more worked-up he became.

"In the future I expect each of you to be squared away, and that includes being clean shaven," he told us sternly, pulling Bo out of the line and having him stand in front of us. He pulled a safety razor out of his pocket and handed it to me.

"Show him how it's done," he ordered.

"What do you mean, sir?" I asked stupidly, holding the razor in my hand.

"Dry-shave him," he ordered.

"Go ahead; do it," Bo told me in a resigned voice.

"No, sir." I shook my head and tried to hand the razor back to him.

"I'm giving you an order," the lieutenant warned, his gray eyes boring into mine.

I shook my head again but didn't say anything. I was going to tell him that I didn't think he was giving me a lawful order, but I didn't want to find out if I was right or wrong at a court-martial. In the military the penalties for disobeying a direct order were severe and the chance of being convicted nearly a certainty.

Glaring at me, Lord grabbed the razor out of my hand and handed it to Truman, who obviously thought the whole thing was nothing more than a big joke. He cheerfully scraped away at Bo's chin for a few seconds before the lieutenant told him to stop. We were dismissed and went back inside our hooch.

"What a prick!" I exploded as soon as we were inside.

"Ah … it don't mean nothin'," Bo replied dismissively, rubbing his reddened chin.

It may not have meant that much to Bo, but it meant a great deal to me. Dry shaving someone in public was humiliating, something I couldn't imagine any decent officer would have even thought of doing. Lord hadn't even gotten to know us yet!

With that one order Lord had shown his soul to me. He had ordered a degrading act against a member of his own team, simply to assert his authority. He didn't need to do another thing for me to dislike him. He was a bully, and I had always hated bullies.

I understood the need for a command structure. No army can be effective without effective leadership, and I had always respected and worked well with my military superiors. The sergeants who had led us on previous patrols were experienced, seasoned veterans and I would have followed them anywhere. Now however, it seemed that we were to be led by a new lieutenant who, I suspected, had a chip on his shoulder but no combat experience at all!

31. Hell's Half Acre

I walked in a desert.
And I cried,
"Ah, God, take me from this place!"
A voice said, "It is no desert."
I cried, "Well, But—
The sand, the heat, the vacant horizon."
A voice said, "It is no desert."
—Stephen Crane, "I Walked in a Desert"

For a few weeks our new lieutenant left us alone, and I gradually began to think that he had forgotten about the shaving incident. Perhaps he was embarrassed by it; more likely he was just busy getting settled in. He stood in front of us during formation and disappeared as soon as we were dismissed. We passed the time getting our gear together and trying to catch up on sleep. In the bush no one slept that well.

After several weeks had passed we were told to report to the intelligence shack to be briefed on a new mission. Lieutenant Lord was standing with Captain Bilger at the front of the room when we entered. We saluted and were ordered to sit down as the captain told us that our next patrol would be an Arc Light assessment. I heard Moose groan softly behind me.

Arc Light was the code name given to a B-52 strike against targets without significant anti-aircraft defenses. The bombers would drop hundreds of five hundred pound bombs from 35,000 feet, carpet-bombing an entire valley and obliterating everything in their path. We would be required to go in afterward with plastic bags and collect whatever remained of military interest and try to determine the number of enemy killed by the raid. This usually meant pawing through body parts.

I don't think that anyone who has ever seen the slaughterhouse that resulted from a carpet-bombing run or smelled the stench of such an attack could ever be the same afterward, but Lieutenant Lord nodded his head enthusiastically as Captain Bilger described the mission. It seemed that our new lieutenant couldn't wait to get started.

For me, the Arc Light bombings fell into the same category as the Agent Orange[1] defoliations. They may have been effective, but there was something obscene about them. If killing had to be done I preferred it up close and personal where the enemy soldier had just as much of a chance of killing me as I did him. Dropping bombs from thirty thousand feet with no real risk just didn't fit my mental picture of what it meant to be a warrior.

For a long time I had kept these thoughts to myself, but one time I made the mistake of sharing them with Moose. He listened silently for only a moment and then shook his head and glared almost angrily at me.

"What kind of bullshit you talkin'? I thought you had a good head on your shoulders and now you soundin' like a damned fool. You think if Charlie had aircraft they wouldn't be usin' 'em? They have their kids out every night planting booby traps to blow the legs off any Marine that trips them. Where's your precious honor in that? I don't care if the little brown bastards are shot, blown up or buried alive and you shouldn't either!"

I didn't have an answer for him then and I don't have one now. I realized that his words had a lot of truth in them, but I was stung by them and from then on kept my thoughts to myself.

The captain turned the briefing over to Lieutenant Lord, who described the details of the mission as if he were a coach prepping his football team for the big game. He wrote our individual assignments on the blackboard with circles and arrows as though he were outlining a play. As usual Bo would run point and I was assigned to shadow him. Moose was to carry the radio and a corpsman from the Second Platoon would be joining us. When we reached our objective three of us would go in to do the actual assessment while the others provided security. The lieutenant assigned Ma to take over my usual role of assistant patrol leader.

"Payback for the dry shave," I couldn't help thinking to myself.

After the briefing I felt like I had been demoted and bitterly shared my feelings with Truman. He just laughed and reminded me that I had never been promoted in the first place. Assistant patrol leader was only a position, he reminded me, not a military rank.

"You had extra responsibility but no real authority and no extra money either. You're better off just takin' care of your own ass," he told me cheerfully.

The next day we met the lieutenant at the LZ. Compared with the rest of us he sure looked sharp, with a new set of camouflaged utilities and gear that looked like it came right out of the box. He wore a .45 in a shoulder holster and carried a new M-16. Despite the heat on the LZ, he strode up and down in front of us talking loudly into the radio. Moose, carrying the heavy set was tethered to him by the radio cable, and forced like a dog on a leash to follow him.

"What's with that guy?" I asked Moose as the lieutenant finally sat down and Moose was able to get away from him.

Moose leaned back gratefully against his pack, lit up a cigarette and considered my question.

"He's starring in his own movie," Moose finally responded.

"Well, we're not in a movie and we're not in his cast."

"Maybe not," Moose answered, snubbing out his cigarette, "but he don't know that yet. I learned in the grunts that sometimes the enemy isn't only Charlie sitting under a banana tree; it's just as likely to be a green officer standing right in front of you at formation."

The birds were coming in and the lieutenant stood up and motioned for us to get to our feet.

Moose threw away his cigarette. "Just watch yourself with him and don't be no fool."

Lord and Ma had selected an LZ that may have been ideal for the pilots, but it certainly wasn't that great for us. The open field they chose was easy for the choppers to land on, but there was little cover. We dropped down on a high plateau while gunships fired rockets into the hillside next to us as diversion.

Without tree cover we were totally exposed to the heat of the sun, and within a few minutes of running with our heavy packs all of us were soaked with sweat. The terrain changed slowly from low bushes, to scrub grass, to finally nearly barren rock. We could see the low hill that was our objective in the distance, but to reach it we would need to cross miles of open ground. I was beginning to think that the entire area had been defoliated a long time ago by Agent Orange. It wasn't natural to find such a barren area this high in the mountains.

After moving a few miles Lord called us together and radioed in a SITREP back to HQ. I noticed that his face and neck were bright red from the sun and I started to worry about him. It usually took several months for new guys to get accustomed to the heat and humidity of Nam. Some men never seemed able to adjust.

The corpsman dug into the Unit 1 and handed out salt tablets. At the time the thinking was that if you sweated too much your electrolyte balance would get out of whack and your muscles would cramp up. Lieutenant Lord swallowed his without comment and without water. The rest of the crew pulled out their canteens, popped the small pills and took long drinks. Lord called Moose over and called back another SITREP to base. I poured some water over my bush hat and felt the momentary delicious coolness as I put it back on my head. Lord handed the handset back to Moose and, motioning us closer, brought out his map and pointed to the hills ahead of us.

"That's our objective, men," he gestured expansively, telling us what everyone already knew.

At first it seemed that the lieutenant was determined to push on, but Ma argued that the best thing to do would be wait until night, when we would be able to move without being seen. Somewhat to my surprise, the lieutenant agreed. We had only been moving for a few hours, but already Lord looked tired and he stumbled slightly as he got to his feet.

A few hundred yards ahead of us was a cluster of small boulders that would give us at least some cover. We moved up and settled in among them, trying to stay low and out of sight. It was still early in the morning, but already the heat was radiating off of the rocks. We spread out and tried to find shade. I spotted a small shrub a few feet ahead of me. It was no more than eighteen inches high, but at least it threw a shadow.

There was no movement to the air at all, and as the hours passed and the sun rose higher in the sky the temperature continued to rise. Even after the sun reached its zenith at noon the temperature seemed like it was still climbing.

The dark volcanic rocks around us had absorbed the sun's rays from earlier in the day and were now radiating them back out. I felt like I was a biscuit being baked in an oven. I poked up my head and looked around to see the barren landscape around us shimmering with heat waves. I hugged my bush, doing my best to keep my head in the small triangle of shade. The sun traveled with agonizing slowness across the horizon. The sandy ground seemed a little cooler a few inches down and I tried to burrow into it. My heart was pounding against my chest and I felt my entire body shake with every beat.

I heard a scuffling motion behind me and saw the lieutenant trying to sit up. His face and neck were beet red and thick blue veins were bulging from his forehead. I crawled over to him.

"Are you OK, sir?"

"Got a headache, that's all," he responded irritably, pushing me roughly aside,

"Here, drink some more water," I advised, handing him my canteen, but he shook his head and stretched his long body on the sand. Unlike me, he didn't seem to be sweating at all, and this worried me as much as anything. I took my canteen and without asking dribbled some water over his shaven head. Annoyed, he pushed my hand away.

"What the hell do you think you're doing?" he protested irritably.

"Sir, we've got to get you cooled down," I insisted.

He pushed me away again.

I crawled over to where our corpsman was sitting. His eyes were closed and he reacted with a start when I touched his shoulder.

"Doc, I think the lieutenant is in trouble," I told him. "He looks like crap, and I don't think he's drinking enough water."

He crawled back with me to where Lord was sprawled out on the ground, Doc took one look and without comment wet a bandanna with water and placed the wet compress on Lord's forehead. This time the lieutenant didn't object. In the few minutes since I had left him Lord's face had turned from bright red to a pasty paleness. The lieutenant groaned slightly as the medic poured more water over his head, but didn't open his eyes.

Doc motioned Ma over.

"The lieutenant's got heatstroke; you gotta call in a medevac."

"Can't he wait until dark?" Ma objected. "We call in a chopper now and we'll give away our position. The mission will be compromised."

"If we don't medevac him now, he's gonna die," Doc replied bluntly.

Ma still hesitated. He moved over to where the lieutenant was lying and touched his shoulder.

"How do you feel, sir? Do you want us to get you a medevac?"

The lieutenant shook his head slightly, but his eyes remained tightly closed. I didn't know if he was answering Ma's first question and telling us he was feeling really bad or was protesting getting taken out of the field. He turned his head away and both of us watched a wet stain spread between his legs as his bladder let go.

That did it for Ma; he didn't waste any more time. He got on the radio while the corpsman and I did our best to cool the lieutenant down. I took off his utility jacket and continued to pour water over his body as Doc sat him up and finally got him to drink a little water. Moose reached HQ and reported our situation and position. Major Simbul approved the medevac, but we were told that our mission would continue.

Less than an hour later, we heard the sound of a Huey coming in fast and low. There was no need to pop smoke; we were in plain sight. The chopper landed on its skids and we helped the lieutenant to his feet and half-carried, half-dragged him to the doorway. His head bobbed around as if he were drunk. Two medics pulled him inside and immediately laid him on a cot and threw bags of ice on top of him.

"Got any water?" Truman shouted eagerly to the crew chief as he spotted the ice bags. No one heard him over the whine of the engines. The chopper took off, leaving us to the heat and the silence.

32. Wounded

If such be the will of God, let it be.—Socrates

The medevac had given away our position, but we decided to stay where we were until it got dark so that we could move without being seen. I crawled back under my little tree. I hoped the lieutenant would be all right and decided I should cut him some slack. As a new officer he was just falling back on whatever bullshit they had filled his head with at OCS. He could spot a Marine who hadn't shaved closely enough, but he hadn't a clue about how to pace himself in the bush.

The day wore on and the heat gradually diminished. As dusk fell we gathered our gear together and began moving toward the higher ground. Night fell without a moon and the darkness was absolute as we followed a compass bearing toward our objective. As we climbed higher we had to climb more rugged terrain. We somehow moved through a field of large boulders, stumbling forward, climbing the larger rocks, sometimes pushing our way through the tightly packed brush that had grown up between them. It would have been difficult to cross this rocky landscape even during the day, how we ever managed to traverse such terrain at night still eludes me, but we pressed on.

I had just climbed to the top of a large boulder when I heard a warning click from Bo. Suddenly the night lit up with the flash of an explosion and I was blown backwards. One moment I was looking around for a place to put my feet, and the next I was flying through the air. I landed on my back, my head smashing against the side of a boulder. I heard the sounds of rifle fire on my left, but my pack was wedged between the rocks and I couldn't see what was going on. I struggled to twist myself around, but my body didn't seem to want to obey.

"I'm hit!" I shouted once, the effort draining me.

The firing got farther away, and I sensed that the team was moving away from me.

"Don't leave me behind; I'm hit," I pleaded in a weak voice.

A dark shadow passed against the night sky. In a reflexive move I swung my rifle around and pointed it at the figure looming above me.

"C'mon, man ... let's get out of here," Bo's familiar voice urged, jumping down beside me and helping me to my feet. I tried to walk but as soon as I tried to put weight on my leg a sharp pain radiated up for my left knee. I felt curiously detached from the firefight that was erupting around me. My ears were ringing from the blast, my head was aching, and the pain in my leg was excruciating.

The rest of the team had broken off contact to avoid giving away our position. I later suspected that we had surprised a small enemy unit in the darkness and that they were now trying to get away just as fast as we were.

There was a small hill just ahead and Truman helped Bo drag me up the slope. The force of the blast had torn open the demolition pouch that I had strapped to my leg. It contained a dozen M79 rounds. I saw the shells falling out of the shredded canvas bag and rolling down the slope.

"Get the rounds," I remember muttering weakly, but they ignored me.

We reached the top of the hill and Doc cut open my pant leg. He gave me an injection of morphine and I felt a warm numbness spreading through my body. I stopped worrying about my leg and drifted off into a narcotic bliss, oblivious to the frantic activity going on around me.

Ma had called in for air support and a Puff gunship was sent out. Throughout the long night the aircraft circled our position firing its mini-guns in a huge circle. Each of the aircraft's three guns could fire at up to a hundred rounds per second. Puff could put a bullet or glowing red tracer (every fifth round) into every square yard of a football field–sized target in less than ten seconds. Frenchy held a strobe light in his hand all night long to mark our position. The rest of the team dug in around the top of the hill, but Puff's tremendous firepower kept any possible attackers at bay.

Stupefied by the morphine, I watched the stream of white fire in bemusement as Puff circled our position and thousands of rounds pounded the ground around us, and remarked how beautiful they looked. I remember seeing the men beside lying down beside me in a protective circle, and feeling completely safe. I thought of the pilot and aircrew flying thousands of feet above me, doing everything they could to protect me and remember feeling both enormously grateful and at the same time completely unworthy of such attention. The morphine peaked, and I lost consciousness.

When I woke it was morning and someone was pulling me into a sitting position. A CH-46 had landed to extract our entire team. Bo and Truman half-carried me into the chopper while the rest of the men took up their defensive positions by each window. The medic on the bird bent over me and with a sudden sickening tug pulled away the dressing that Doc had placed over my leg with such care. The morphine had worn off and I screamed at the sharp stabbing pain.

Immediately Doc was bending over me, pushing the other man aside. "What the hell do you think you're doing?" he shouted angrily. "Let him alone! He'll be OK till we get to the hospital."

"Suit yourself, man," the medic responded, shrugging his shoulders and turning away.

The sudden pain and the motion of the chopper made me dizzy and I turned my head toward the bulkhead to avoid being sick. Looking down through the floor grate, I saw a trail of my own blood.

Doc wiped my forehead "You OK, man?" he asked.

"No," I answered truthfully.

"Hang on, we're almost there."

---

33. Cam Rahn Bay

In bitter safety I awake, unfriended;
And while the dawn begins with slashing rain
I think of the Battalion in the mud.
When are you going out to them again?
Are they not still your brothers through our blood?
—Siegfried Sassoon, "Sick Leave"

I was flown directly to the hospital complex at Cam Ranh Bay. The chopper landed, and I was carried out on a litter by two aids. In my half-drugged state it seemed like another world, white light, white sand, white concrete walkways, white buildings, doctors and nurses in white. I tried to sit up to see where they were taking me, but my neck and back hurt and I finally lay back and let myself be carried. I heard the sound of laughter and looked over to see a group of doctors and nurses playing volleyball. I would have been quite a sight in my dirty jungle utilities, camouflage paint, and the letter M[1] written in bold on my forehead, but the bright young things were engaged in their game and didn't even look over as I was carried past.

We passed through the entranceway to a large concrete building. On the ceiling overhead someone had painted a slogan: *Through these halls are carried the best men in the world*. Only someone flat on their back could have easily read the words. The orderlies took me into a waiting area where a medic cut away what was left of my clothes and snipped away at the field dressing that Doc had applied. A nurse washed the camouflage paint from my face and arms with alcohol. A doctor appeared, roughly probed my knee and then ordered X-rays.

"Doesn't look too bad," he remarked confidently as he slapped my shoulder, and walked out.

"Easy for him to say," I thought ungraciously, "not his leg."

The nurse wheeled a portable X-ray machine into place above me and took X-rays of my knee and leg. A few minutes later the same doctor came back with two other doctors looking more concerned.

"Well, you have a few pieces of shrapnel in the muscle of your left leg, no problem. But one fragment is lodged behind your kneecap. We'll have to get it out."

He didn't look at me directly but spoke over my head to the small group of nurses and medics around me. I felt like a piece of meat lying there on the examining table. I realized at that point that I had completely lost control of my body. They were going to do whatever they wanted to me.

"Prep him for a spinal," the doctor ordered as he turned and left the room.

The nurse took away the sheet that had covered me and swabbed my back with alcohol and left me lying naked on the table. The rapid change from the humid heat of the jungle to the cold air-conditioned environment of the hospital had already made me feel chilled. As the alcohol evaporated I felt like I was freezing. My teeth began to chatter from the cold and for the first time since I was wounded I felt the sudden chill of fear.

The doctor arrived again. Under his directions the nurse bent me over until my head nearly touched my knees. I suddenly felt sick to my stomach and tried to sit back up.

"Do you want to end up paralyzed!" the doctor yelled roughly pushing me over again, "Keep still!"

No, I certainly didn't want to end up paralyzed. His words scared the hell out of me and I tried to stay as quiet as possible as he injected something into my spine. My lower body turned warm and numb and I lost all sensation in my legs. The doors to the room swung open, and I heard a small boy asking his mother something. I was still bent over and couldn't see anything except my feet, but I wondered what the child was in the hospital for. The doctor finished up whatever he was doing to my back and a nurse helped me straighten up.

I looked around and saw another Marine being wheeled rapidly across the room. Blood was dripping from his gurney and leaving a red trail on the floor. As he passed he looked up with a vacant stare at one of the nurses pushing the gurney and in a weak voice called out again for his mother.

I was given another shot, which put me out completely. I awoke to hear someone near me moaning. In the far distance under a light someone dressed in white was moving around. I tried to focus my eyes as the figure approached, but everything was a blur.

"Quiet!" the nurse ordered in an annoyed voice, "The other patients are trying to sleep."

I heartily agreed with her. "Can't someone shut that bastard up?"

I suddenly realized that she was speaking to me. I had been the one moaning and keeping everyone awake. I suddenly had a tremendous headache. My stomach rolled over, and I vomited into my bedding and promptly passed out again.

When I awoke it was morning. Sunlight streamed in from the high windows and the hallway was filled with sounds of cheerful voices and the metallic clang of food carts being pushed along. Everything looked very bright and clean except for my bed, which was still stained from last night. I folded the top of the sheet over so it wouldn't show.

My leg was wrapped in bandages from my toes to my upper thigh. As long as I remained still it only ached, but the minute I tried to move a sharp burning pain radiated through the entire left side of my body. When I touched the exposed skin of my leg it felt hot. I turned to the left and saw the outline of a patient next to me. His head was bandaged, and he seemed to be sleeping. The bed on my right was occupied with a young Vietnamese soldier with a stomach wound.

I looked up to see a pretty nurse looking down at me with a smile on her face. "How are you doing, Marine?"

"OK," I mumbled hoarsely through dry lips.

"That's good." She turned away toward the man on my left.

The nurse's delicious bottom bending toward her patient aroused familiar although, considering my condition, impractical thoughts. She rearranged his pillow and turning back to me noticed my soiled bedding.

I felt embarrassed but couldn't think of anything to say.

"Let's get that cleaned up," she said brightly, and in short order it was done.

"Now, let's get you something to eat," she told me cheerfully.

I was still dizzy and somewhat sick to my stomach and shook my head no, but she ignored me. A few minutes later a breakfast cart was wheeled in the door by two male orderlies dressed in spotless white medical garb.

The nurse returned and propped me up in bed. "Try to eat something," she urged. "It will make you feel better."

I picked at some fruit and then pushed the tray aside. I still felt too sick to eat.

A young doctor entered, accompanied by a aide holding surgical tools on an enameled tray. He reminded me of an acolyte assisting a priest at the sacrament. The doctor barely glanced at my face but turned his entire attention to my leg. I felt a sharp jab in my foot. "Feel this?" I nodded. "This?" An even sharper one. I winced and nodded. He grabbed my foot and began slowly twisting it from side to side and then without warning bent my knee upward. I gasped at the sudden pain.

"Looking pretty good," he told me with satisfaction, "but of course we couldn't get all the pieces out."

"What do you mean?" I asked.

"Well, there were some small fragments behind the kneecap that you'll just have to live with."

"You try living with them," I thought resentfully.

The doctor turned away, leaving me to my thoughts. As he walked out the door he issued a final order to the nurse. "Let's get that knee in traction … ten pounds should do it."

This began a new torture, even before I had recovered from the old ones. Two muscular orderlies came in and rigged up some kind of pulley system to my bed and attached it with hooks to the bandages around my calf. They wired a ten-pound sandbag to the contraption to put tension on my leg. At first my muscles fought the weight, but they soon tired and the sandbag pulled inexorably at the bones in my knee.

I felt shackled to the bed, and it was impossible for me to sleep with my leg constantly under tension. After the first day, I tied a small knot in the cord and by wedging the knot against one of the supports managed to take the pressure off. When the doctors or nurses came by I reached under the sheets and unhooked the cord. In my mind I knew it was a stupid thing to do, but I found it impossible to tolerate the weight constantly pulling on my leg.

After a few days I was able to sit up in bed and hang my feet over the side. My left leg was still swollen, but I was given a wheelchair and was now able to get to the bathroom at the end of the hall. This was such an important thing for me; I had felt so embarrassed asking for a bedpan. After another week they gave me a pair of crutches and I was able to hobble outside and sit in the sun.

I was scheduled for physical therapy the following week. I was wheeled down the hall to a small air-conditioned room where I was put on a series of exercise machines. The worst was some kind of leg lift. A nurse adjusted weights on a lever, which I was supposed to be able to lift up and down. Whenever time I tried to move my left leg, however, a sharp pain in my knee stopped me. The nurse nodded at me encouragingly. "The more you do the easier it will get." She reduced the weight slightly, and I tried once more.

"Does it hurt?" she asked.

"Sure does," I answered, the sweat breaking out on my face.

My leg not only hurt, but it also felt swollen and stiff. Every time I tried to move my knee it felt like something was grating against the bone. Small slivers of metal were also starting to make their way through the skin on my calf and upper leg as if trying to escape from my body. I would feel them start to poke through my skin and pull them out with my fingers. I put them in a saucer on the side on the little table at the side of my bed. I had quite a little pile accumulated and was planning on saving them. I thought perhaps I could melt them down and make a ring out of them, but one of the orderlies dumped them out when I wasn't looking.

For some reason there were only a few patients in the ward that I was assigned to, and most of these were moved out to other areas within a few weeks. The more seriously wounded men would be flown to Japan or back to the States as soon as possible. Occasionally I would talk to one of the other patients, but there was surprisingly little interaction between us. Everyone was focused on themselves, and I guess I was the same way. The man in the bed next to me was a young ARVN soldier who had been shot in the stomach. He spent most of his time studying a fat mathematical textbook and told me that he hoped to get out of the Army and go to college, but after a few days he developed a high fever and was taken away to another ward.

One day after physical therapy I decided to hobble around a little bit more and explore the wing attached to ours. I made my way down the hall, pushed my way through the door separating our wards and found myself by another ward. There was no one at the nurses' station and the lights were turned down very low. The room was half-filled with men sitting around or lying on their bunks.

"Who's there?" one of the men asked, turning his bandaged face to me.

I began to shake my head before realizing that they couldn't see my gesture.

"Sorry, I'm in the wrong place," I answered awkwardly as more bandaged faces turned toward my voice.

"So are we..." the nearest patient responded in a sad, resigned voice.

I pushed my way back out the door and made my way back to my hut. I never wandered the halls of the Cam Ranh Bay Hospital again.

My leg gradually got stronger, but my knee still hurt whenever I tried to put weight on it. I was surprised to feel how weak my leg muscles had grown in just a short time without activity. At first, I was unable to lift more than a few pounds, but at the end of a week, I had worked up to ten pounds and was able to hobble around if someone supported me. Soon I was able to walk up an inclined ramp by holding on to side rails.

The medical staff was good to me, but there was an unbridgeable gap between us. I had been in combat and they hadn't. It didn't make me feel exactly superior, but it did create a barrier between us, at least in my mind. One part of me wanted to talk to them about what I had gone through, but I knew they really didn't want to know. I saw their bright smiles and listened to their bantering voices and wanted to just shake them out of their world and plunge them into mine. Of course, I didn't do anything of the sort. Even if they had wanted to listen, I wouldn't have known what to say.

The nurse told me that I would probably be in the hospital for at least another month. At first this sounded fine to me; every day that passed was another day to enjoy my life, another day to cross off my short-timer calendar. I still had six months left in-country. More than enough time to get myself killed. It was such a gift to be spoken to with respect and even kindness. What a joy it was to listen to a soft female voice.

Forced by my injury into stillness, I was content just to be. I felt myself being healed just as much by the white light streaming through the large window over my bed as from the medical care. As the bandages came off I somehow felt like a better me was gradually being released from the rigid military shell in which I had been encased.

The longer I was away from my unit, however, the more I started to worry about my teammates. I didn't want to think of myself as a shirker and I felt guilty sleeping in a clean hospital bed when they were out risking their lives humping the bush. I worried that without me watching out for them they would miss the thin trip wire that would take them out. At the same time whenever I thought about going back to the bush I felt a hollow feeling of fear in the pit of my stomach. It felt like the first second when an elevator descends. It was so easy to get killed out there.

As I got stronger, however, I knew that I had to go back to my team. I started pushing myself in the physical therapy sessions and telling the doctors who came to examine my leg that I felt better than I really did. I was soon able to hobble around on a pair of crutches.

In my head I knew that my behavior was completely unreasonable. Logically I should have been trying to stay in the hospital as long as I could. Every day I spent in my bed was one less day I had to spend in in the bush, but my heart was with my buddies. I felt that I needed to get back to them. They needed me!

33. Cam Rahn Bay

I impressed the doctors with my progress and was told that I'd probably be able to return to my unit and limited duty in two or three weeks. My return actually took place sooner than they had expected.

I was walking slowly around the hospital compound with a cane when I came across a poster nailed to one of the columns. It described a patient barbeque that was going to be held at the beach that weekend. Boy, that sure sounded good to me.

The head nurse was sitting at her desk at the end of the hallway. We didn't see much of her, but the younger nurses referred to her in less than flattering terms. I limped up to her desk and asked her for a pass to the party. She looked at me and shook her head dismissively.

"No, you're not ambulatory, you really should still be on crutches," she said looking at my cane with disapproval and turning back to her paperwork.

"Lady, I'd walk through burning coals for a beer right now," I joked.

"'Captain' to you," she responded angrily, tapping the insignia on her shoulder with a manicured fingernail and turning away once again.

"Well, we'll see about that," I stubbornly thought to myself.

An hour before the picnic bus departed on Saturday I wrapped my leg up tightly in an ACE bandage and grabbed my cane. I didn't know what I'd do if they checked for a pass, but when the bus arrived I melted in with a group of other pajama-clothed patients, hauled myself up the steps and plopped down into a seat at the front of the bus.

The driver took us directly to the beach. We were let off in a paved parking lot. In the far distance a party was in full swing down by the water. A tent had been set up on the beach and there must have been a hundred doctors, nurses and orderlies milling around. Everyone was having a great time swimming, playing volleyball, and partying. There was no way that the broken men on the bus would be able to walk the quarter mile to the water to join them. We realized that the event was more for the medical staff than patients.

We made the best of what we had. There was a roofed-in patio overlooking the beach with some picnic tables and chairs and we set up our own little party there. One of the orderlies brought us a couple of cases of beer, and around noon they sent us grilled steaks from the fire pit. We had a good time in our own way and didn't get back to the hospital until it was nearly dark.

The witch in white was waiting for me when I tried to sneak past her and get into my bed.

"I should write you up!" she threatened, eyeing me with distaste.

I took a final swig from the can of beer I had hoped to drink in my bed, crushed the can I was holding in my hand and smiled at her without saying anything. This seemed to infuriate her even more.

"If you're well enough to party on the beach you're good enough to go back to your unit," she told me angrily.

"Fuckin' A!" I drunkenly responded as I limped over to my bed.

I received my hospital discharge orders the following day and hobbled out of the compound.

I was told that since I had gotten wounded Force Recon had moved out of An Hoa and was now stationed at a firebase about twenty miles south of Da Nang. I caught rides on a couple of trucks and arrived late in the afternoon. The entire team gathered around me when I got back. It sure felt good to be back among them.

Bo slapped me on the back. "We missed you, man, didn't think you were coming back."

"Well, how did you guys make out, run many patrols?" I asked when everyone had quieted down.

"Not a single one," Truman answered. "With you and the lieutenant gone we were pulled out of the bush. Since you were hit we've just been training. Rubber boat at China Beach, a few jumps, Bo attended SCUBA school, we didn't go out once!"

I looked from one to another as they beamed at one another and nodded happily.

"Not a single one," Bo confirmed.

"Shit…" I muttered.

34. Gassed

But soon early Dawn appeared, the rosy-fingered, and gathered the folk about the pyre of glorious Hector.—Homer, *Iliad* xxiv.776

Lieutenant Lord was back on active duty. He never mentioned getting heatstroke and we never asked him about it. My knee gradually regained its strength and after a few more weeks of rest I was also able to return to the team.

Three days earlier, a grunt platoon had run into an NVA ambush. The platoon's sergeant had been shot in the head and killed instantly; two other Marines were wounded. Under heavy fire, the grunts were forced to retreat. Leaving the body of their sergeant behind.

In ancient Athens when young men were inducted into the army each warrior took an oath never to leave their comrades behind. The same concept is enshrined in the Marine Corps slogan "nemo resideo."[1] During the Korean War, fighting their way back from the Chosin Reservoir Marines lashed the frozen bodies of their dead to the turrets of their tanks rather than leave them behind. One of the secondary missions of Force Recon was combat search and rescue. We hoped to find the living, but more often we returned with the dead.

At our briefing Captain Bilger told us that the Air Force had sprayed the ambush site with Agent Orange to eliminate any cover. The entire area was then bombarded with shells filled with tear gas crystals. Bilger explained that the combination of these two chemicals would make it impossible for any enemy troops to remain, or so he believed.

"Any questions?" the captain asked.

Truman raised his hand.

34. Gassed

"What is it?" Bilger asked in a resigned voice.

"Begging your pardon, sir, but why don't the grunts send in their own men?"

"They tried to, but they got shot out of the only LZ in the area; you guys are going to have to rappel in."

The captain pointed to a strapping young Marine who stood at the back of the room. "Corporal Luchini here was on the patrol and volunteered to go out with you. He can lead you to exactly where the ambush took place."

We all turned and looked back. Luchini was a big guy with thick black hair and bronzed skin. He looked like he had been in-country for quite a while and knew how to take care of himself.

The captain described how we would need to wear gas masks so the tear gas wouldn't affect us. Once we found and retrieved the sergeant's body we'd blow ourselves an LZ and be extracted. That was Bilger's plan anyway.

The search team would consist of the lieutenant, Truman, Bo, Corporal Luchini, and myself. Moose had gone on R & R and a radioman from Third Platoon would take his place.

"Speed is of the essence, men," Captain Bilger had told us. "You have to get the sergeant's body out of there before the gas wears off and the NVA decide to come back."

We were scheduled to leave in two days, not a lot of time to even get ourselves ready, much less get Luchini up to speed as well. After the briefing we walked over and introduced ourselves. He was quiet but friendly enough. He told us that he had been in-country for eight months and was trained as a machine gunner. He told us about the ambush without being asked.

"He was hit by one of the first rounds. I was so close that I had to wipe his brains from my shirt. We couldn't get back to him; there was just too much fire."

"Don't worry; we'll get your friend back," Bo reassured him.

Luchini nodded but looked far from convinced.

The first thing we needed to do was teach him how to rappel. After the briefing we took him aside and showed him how to knot a Swiss harness[2] out of heavy line. We attached a couple of "D" clamps in the front of the harness and gave him a pair of heavy leather gloves to protect his hands from rope burns. He had never rappelled before and we told him how much fun it was.

"You just have to relax and get used to it," I told him as he followed us up the ladder to the small platform on top of our rappelling tower. I hooked on to the line and showed Luchini how the carabiners[3] worked together to apply friction and brake the fall. I moved to the end of the platform and leaned back, holding the rope in my right hand behind my back and lightly gripping the line in my left. I told him how throwing your right hand out would loosen the friction while bringing your hand to the small of your back would tighten the carabiners and stop the fall.

Luchini peered over the edge of the platform and looked at me dubiously as I sprang backward and slid through the air. I dropped about ten feet and caught myself. He seemed to be listening to me as I stopped myself several more times and then finally slid to the ground. I unhooked myself from the rope and climbed back to the top of the tower.

I had always liked to rappel and considered myself good at it. We would have contests, betting beers on who could make it down with the fewest number of stops. I found that if I pushed off strongly from the parapet and let myself free-fall I was able to make it to the ground in one bound without braking. It was a lot of fun but rather risky. If you broke too soon, the momentum of such a stunt would crash you against the steel struts of the tower. If you broke too late or didn't take into account the stretch of the line, the landing could break your legs. It was a fine sport.

Luchini only needed to learn the basics. I watched as Bo double-checked his line and positioned him on the edge of the platform. The big Marine was clearly petrified and pulled back from the edge.

"I'm scared of heights," he finally admitted, looking down at the hundred-foot drop.

"Just lean back and relax, man," Bo instructed in an encouraging voice.

Luchini moved once more to the edge of the tower, but instead of letting the harness take his weight he held on to the line with a death grip and instead of springing off kept his feet pressed up against the steel girder. As the line slipped through his hands and his body dropped, his feet lost their purchase and he started to fall headfirst through the air. For a tense moment I was sure he was going to hit the ground upside down and break his neck!

"Brake!" Bo yelled frantically.

At the last moment Luchini pulled his right hand back and the 'biners bit into the rope, stopping him abruptly. He was now hanging upside down forty feet in the air. I threw down another rope and jumped after him. When I got to his level I stopped myself and by pushing down on his feet got him turned right side up again.

"That went pretty well for the first time," I joked, "but you're supposed to go down feet first."

Luchini didn't say a word. He just looked at me with a terrified expression on his face.

"Don't grip so hard with your left hand; just use it for balance," I advised. "Use your right hand to control your speed. If you throw it out to your side you will go faster; bring it in to behind your back and you'll slow down or even stop."

With my encouragement he dropped down foot by foot until he finally touched the ground.

"Good job," I congratulated him.

"My back." He grimaced, reaching back to pull up his jacket. The rope had cut an angry red welt across the lower part of his back.

"Yeah, that happens all the time," I commiserated.

Most trainees would come back from their first rappelling experience with ugly rope burns across the lower part of their backs. These took weeks to heal and often left permanent scars. It took newbies quite a while before they got to the point where they trusted their equipment and could let go of the rope. Unfortunately for Luchini, we didn't have a lot of time.

"You did really well," I told him encouragingly. "Let's give it another try."

He followed me up the ladder, but when we got on top he looked down at the ground and stepped back from the edge of the platform.

"No way!" he objected, shaking his head. "I didn't volunteer for this shit."

Nothing we could say would convince him to try again. Every time we nudged him to the edge of the platform he would freeze and refuse to push off. Eventually we were forced to give up. If Luchini wouldn't even jump off the tower there was no way that he was going to rappel hundreds of feet out of a hovering chopper.

Bo and I came up with a different idea. Our team would rappel in and secure the LZ. Once we were on the ground Luchini could be attached to a harness and lowered down using the chopper's rescue winch. After we had retrieved the body we would blow an LZ for the chopper to land and extract us.

Lieutenant Lord approved our idea. If he wanted to salvage the mission he didn't have any choice.

In addition to gas masks and our normal rappelling gear we carried a body bag. It was a thick rubberized sack shaped like a sleeping bag. A long zipper ran down the front and thick canvas carrying straps were stitched along the sides. When we opened it up a moist rubbery smell filled the hooch. It gave me a chill just to look at the damn thing.

The operation didn't start out well. When Lieutenant Lord saw that Truman was carrying his Swedish "K," he sent him back to the hooch to get his M-16, warning that if he didn't get his ass back to the LZ in five minutes he'd be written up.

Truman was pissed and stormed off in a huff.

The Swedish K was a stubby little "grease gun" that was ideal for close combat operations. It was designed to be a fully automatic weapon, but you could fire single bursts by rapidly releasing the trigger. The weapon was really nothing more than a heavy sliding bolt that compressed a spring. The force of an exploding round pushed the bolt back and loaded another round. The magazine held thirty-six rounds.

Although I didn't think Lord's threat was necessary, I did agree with his decision. The K wasn't in standard use, and if we got into a firefight we would have a problem getting ammunition for it. I also knew how much we depended on the sounds of weapons to determine friend from foe. The firing of an AK sounded completely different from that of an M-16. I wasn't used to the sound of Truman's weapon and didn't want to mistake him for one of the enemy.

I was carrying "THUMPER," Mac's cut-down M-79 strapped across one shoulder, and my stripped-down M-60 hanging from the other. It sure gave me a warm and fuzzy feeling to have that machine gun in my hand. I had found that it balanced so well that there was no problem at all rappelling with it.

As we waited for the birds to arrive and Truman to return, Bo tried talking to Luchini, but the big Marine barely responded. We gave him the benefit of the doubt—maybe he was just normally somber before a mission; maybe he was thinking of his friend.

My own mood improved somewhat when instead of Huey gunships, two new helicopters screamed into the LZ and landed. They were the Cobra attack helicopters that were just being deployed by the Marine Corps, sleek, mean-looking machines, loaded with cannons and external rocket pods, so narrow that the co-pilot sat behind the pilot instead of next to him. Shark teeth were painted in white over the bulbous forward gun ports, giving the choppers a fearsome aspect. I had never seen these new choppers before, and Force Recon may have been one of the first units to get them for close air support. At the time I was glad to have them with us.

The Cobras took off with a roar, and another beat up CH-46 landed. It was only a short flight to the area where the grunts had been ambushed. There was no sign of the enemy, but the Cobras rocketed the hillside with repeated barrages before the CH-46 dropped in. We adjusted our gear and put on our gas masks. The moment I put on my mask I felt claustrophobic. The tiny windows on the mask made it difficult to see as well as breathe.

The aircrew got Luchini into a harness to be lowered out of the side door on a cable while the lieutenant, Bo and Frenchy rappelled through the opening at the bottom of the chopper and spread out below us. I waited for the radioman to go ahead of me, but for some reason he had his pack off and was frantically rummaging through it.

Finally he raised his gas mask and blurted out, "I've lost my gloves."

Rappelling gloves were made of thick leather and protected our hands from rope burns. When we were rappelling and dropping fast the leather gloves would actually smoke from the friction of the rope. Not having that hand protection was a serious problem.

Looking down, I saw Luchini being lowered out the door. Now there would be four men on the ground without a radio.

"C'mon, get going!" the crew chief, unaware of the problem, urged him nervously.

Before I could stop him, the radioman wrapped his bush hat around his right hand, grabbed hold of the rope with his left and jumped through the door. I adjusted my gas mask and followed him down. I detached from my line and looked over to see him getting to his feet. I followed him down and landed next to him.

The radioman was shaking his hands in the air like he was trying to cool them. Despite the bush hat, the rappelling rope sliding through his hands had ripped the skin completely off his palms and fingers. I couldn't see his face under the gas mask, but the pain must have been excruciating.

The lieutenant was already starting to move the team out when I ran over and grabbed his shoulder.

"We've got a problem, sir!" I yelled through the thick rubber of the mask.

I pointing to the radioman who was crouching down, his arms crossed in front of him, holding his hands under his armpits as though he were trying to keep them warm. As we approached, he held them up to the lieutenant. They looked like two bright red gloves. It was obvious that there was no way this guy could work the radio. He couldn't even hold his rifle.

Lord put his head close to mine and pointing at the radio shouted through his mask, "See if you can call our choppers back!"

I took the handset and called for a medevac.

I heard the pilot, but with my gas mask muffling my voice the pilot couldn't understand what I was saying. I took a deep breath, pulled my mask off and blurted out the lieutenant's message. My eyes immediately started to tear up from gas crystals that littered the ground, but I managed to get the pilot to understand what we needed. He swung back and lowered the harness that Luchini had used only a few minutes earlier. We slipped it over the radio operator's shoulders and he was hoisted to safety. I grabbed the radio and we set off.

The chopper's rotors had churned up the ground and released more tear gas. I put on my mask, but the air inside of it was now contaminated. Every time I took a breath I felt like I was drowning. My eyes were streaming and my throat felt like I was breathing through burning coals. I could barely see through the small oval windows, and what I saw looked like a vision from hell. Agent Orange had killed every piece of vegetation in the area. Black smoke from the rocket attack swirled around the dead trees and bushes. Every step we took through the dead grasses released tiny puffs of tear gas from the crystals that littered the ground. The lieutenant gathered us together in a small circle so we could hear one another.

"Is this where you were ambushed?" Lord asked Luchini, holding out his map.

"I'm not sure. It all looks different. I think it's down this way," he replied in an uncertain muffled voice.

The rest of us followed him down the hill. There was no cover at all. The dead branches on the bushes we walked through broke with ominous snapping sounds as we brushed against them. There seemed to be smoke swirling around us in the air, but at first I thought it was tear gas crystals turning into gas as we moved through the area.

"This is it!" Luchini suddenly called out in an excited voice. "They hit us right down there."

We came to a small gully and saw the evidence of a fierce firefight. The ground was littered with shell casings. If the grunts had been ambushed here it was a wonder that any of them made it out alive. We moved toward the spot he indicated, but there was nothing there except more spent rounds. Luchini and I continued searching down the gully while the other men carefully searched both sides of the hill. We didn't find the body.

"The bastards must have dragged him away," Luchini muttered bitterly.

We were preparing to continue looking farther down the hill when we got a call on the radio from one of the Cobra pilots. He told us that fires from their rocket attacks had ignited the dead brush and the flames were spreading rapidly toward us.

"You need to get out of there now!" the pilot warned tersely.

We started moving back the way we came but ran into a wall of flame and couldn't proceed. We tried another direction but again ran into heavy smoke and fire. It seemed that whatever direction we tried was blocked. I suddenly realized that unlike the Hueys or the CH-46s, the Cobras didn't have any way of taking us off. Their cockpits were only big enough for the pilot and the weapons officer who sat behind him. The Cobra was a killing machine pure and simple. If the Hueys or a CH-46 were nearby we could have blown an LZ and they could have landed and taken us aboard, but the Cobras didn't have any room for passengers.

"Now we're screwed," I thought to myself. Without waiting for Lord's orders I requested a CH-46 extraction.

The pilot of the chopper that had taken our radioman came back online. "We're heading back to you. Get to the top of the hill and we'll drop the SPIE[4] rig to you."

We had practiced being extracted with the clumsy jungle penetrator. We found that it balanced better if we took off our packs and put them on the seats before climbing onto the tubular seat. The riggers sewed up a special harness for us using parachute straps. With a short rope and two 'biners we were able to hook on to the jungle penetrator's cable and the extraction harness would support us if we lost our grip. With our hands free it was even possible to fire our weapons. The jungle penetrator, however, was never an ideal solution. It was cumbersome and was capable of holding only one or at the most two men at a time. All too often, the penetrator was let down through the hatch in the bottom of the CH-46 instead of the side doors. I was still having nightmares of being squeezed like toothpaste through the narrow floor opening. Freud would probably say that I was reliving my birth, but I know exactly where the dream comes from.

The SPIE solution was simpler, but it worked even better. A rappelling rope with multiple "D" rings or heavy straps knotted on every ten feet or so. When a hovering chopper dropped the extraction line all we needed to do was clip on to it to be jerked into the air. At first, we used the same simple Swiss seat we had used for rappelling; later each of us carried a short length of rope, which attached to the modified extraction harness that the riggers had made up for us. The other end of the short rope held a heavy carabiner. The technique was eventually named "SPIE" for Special Insertion and Extraction. At the time we simply called it "the rope."

We pushed our way upward, forcing a path through the dead underbrush, gasping as we desperately tried to pull air through the filters on our masks. Smoke swirled around us and we heard trees crackle and pop as they exploded into flame behind us.

"We got to get out of here!" I heard Luchini scream frantically through his mask.

"Well, no shit," Truman responded, giving him a push that sent him stumbling forward.

The flames were only a few hundred yards away when we finally reached the summit. The CH-46 swooped down and hovered fifty feet above our heads. Two extraction ropes were hanging down I grabbed the nearest line, spun Luchini around and hooked him on to a loop in the line with one of my spare carabiners.

"What the hell are you doing?" he shouted angrily as he reached back with his hands to see what was holding him. I ignored him and latched on to the ring above him. We were lifted into the air together as the chopper pulled away from the hilltop. As soon as we were away from the hill I ripped off my gas mask and took a deep breath. How wonderful it felt to simply breathe fresh air again. As we pulled away, the fire reached the top of the hill. Fanned by the rotor blast of our departing helicopter the flames suddenly surged upward hundreds of feet into the air. We had gotten out of there just in time. The hilltop where we were standing only a few minutes before was now a giant torch.

As soon as the helicopter gained forward speed, we stretched out in a long line under it. It was the closest thing to flying that I ever experienced. If I stretched out my arms I felt that l that was soaring through the air like Superman. Unlike the cumbersome steel-cabled cargo net where everyone sat or stood around you, attached to the SPIE system I felt like I was alone in the sky. Of course, unlike the multi-stranded cargo net, a single bullet could sever the rope line and I really would end up really flying through the air. Luchini, hanging below me, certainly wasn't relaxing and enjoying the ride. Instead of letting his harness take his weight, he clung to the rope with both hands, as if trying to climb it.

Our pilot hovered over a remote artillery base and slowly descended, dropping us to the ground. As soon as my feet touched the earth I released myself and then unhooked Luchini. The CH-46 landed a short distance away and we climbed aboard. The radioman was on the floor leaning against one of the seats, holding his red hands out in front of him and grimacing with pain. Luchini was slumped over next to him, his face in his hands.

Bo moved over and sat next to him and put his arm around his shoulders. "Don't worry; we'll get your buddy. Just wait until the fire dies down and we'll try again."

"Not with me you won't," he told Bo firmly, turning away from him. "You guys are crazy!"

As we took off we saw the entire hilltop we had just left burning fiercely. A ball of flame suddenly shot up from the summit as we pulled away. As we gained altitude and I couldn't help but think to myself that this fiery pyre was a far better tribute to a fallen warrior than the thick rubber body bag we were planning to put him in.

35. The Pit

The black slit ... opened on a pit, a window into nothing.
—J.R. Tolkien, *The Lord of the Rings*

Once more we were sent into the mountains northwest of Happy Valley. We had been there so many times that the area was becoming like a second home to us. Captain Bilger told us that Intelligence believed that the NVA's Third Northern Brigade was building up their forces in the area and we were ordered to find out where.

"This could be really important stuff," Captain Bilger told us rubbing his hands together enthusiastically.

"How many soldiers are in a brigade, sir?" Truman asked in an innocent voice.

"Well, of course, it's not their entire brigade," the captain backtracked, "probably no more than four or five hundred men."

"Thank you, sir," Truman replied, turning around and rolling his eyes at me.

Lieutenant Lord continued the briefing. Bo as usual would be running point. I would be second in line covering him, followed by the lieutenant. Ma would be our assistant patrol leader and Frenchy would run tail-end Charlie. Moose would be our primary radio operator, but the lieutenant ordered Truman to carry an extra radio in case, as he put it, we needed to "split up." I wasn't sure what he meant by his offhand remark. We had never split up before. In my opinion there were too few of us as it was.

We were also taking a new Navy Hospital corpsman with us. He was a fresh-faced kid who looked like he would have been more at home in a high school band. He had tough shoes to fill. Tony, our team's previous medic, was as good in the bush as any scout in the company. He had made it through his tour without a scratch and had rotated back to the States a few weeks ago. We had laughed as he promised to "party like a big ass," whatever that meant, when he got back to the States. The new man inherited Tony's Unit 1 medical kit and the title "Doc." I hoped that he had inherited Tony's luck as well.

We inserted without detection on a barren hillside and found a wide trail cut through the jungle. The entire area had been defoliated with Agent Orange and the trail was covered in dead brown leaves, which crackled under our feet.

The lieutenant decided that instead of avoiding the trail as we usually did, we should stay on the road and get through the defoliated area as quickly as possible. We all hated these areas. There was something ghastly about Agent Orange. It killed everything, not only the vegetation. Nothing moved; even the insects were gone. The chemical may have eliminated Charlie's cover, but it did the same to us.

Bo was just ahead of me when something caught my attention a few feet ahead. I grabbed his arm and pulled him back just as he was about to take another step. He glanced back at me startled.

I raised my hand for him to stop and looked more closely at the ground in front of our feet. It seemed to me that there was something unnatural about the pattern in the leaves. If you asked me what, I couldn't have told you. There was just something about them that didn't look right to me; they had fallen too perfectly into place. I took my rifle butt and probed the ground ahead of us. The earth suddenly gave way and I pitched forward. My rifle barrel had gone completely through the thin covering of leaves. I had nearly fallen into a deep hole whose bottom was lined with sharpened wooden stakes.

The rest of the team set up a defensive perimeter as Bo and I began to carefully pull aside the leaf cover. In a few minutes we had exposed the edges of a ten-foot-deep pit. The top of the hole was covered in a light mat of split bamboo, which in turn was covered by the dry leaves. At the bottom of the pit wooden stakes were set firmly into the ground and lashed together by heavy vines to a sturdy bamboo frame. The vertical sides of the square hole were perfectly smooth. There were no signs of loose dirt or even shovel marks to mark the trap. Anyone or anything falling into the hole would be impaled on the stakes, which looked like they had been smeared in shit. It was a beautifully built killing machine, and we had nearly walked right into it.

Our patrols were run so far out into enemy-controlled territory that we rarely encountered the booby traps that caused so many casualties among the grunts and soldiers patrolling closer to their bases. We had never come across anything like this mantrap before. We eventually came out of the dead zone and found a concealed spot to spend the night. It was getting dark, and we set up a defensive perimeter and prepared to get some rest.

When Ma woke me around midnight for my radio watch the entire jungle was glowing with light. Every leaf, every blade of grass, sparkled with foxfire. When I moved my hand across the ground it glowed and shimmered. Even my jungle boots were covered in phosphorescence. I felt as though I had been somehow transported into a magical realm.

"How beautiful the world is," I thought to myself, looking at the sparkling leaves and repeating my mantra, "how beautiful."

We were on the move again at dawn, climbing slowly upward toward the hill we hoped to use as our observation point. We came to a bombed-out slash of hillside where there was no cover for nearly a quarter of a mile. Bo had begun leading the team back into the jungle to avoid exposing ourselves, but Lieutenant Lord signaled him to continue across the open area. Bo shook his head and stood where he was. Sergeant Tom never would have led us through such an exposed area, even if it meant that we had to slog for miles to get around it. The risks were just too great. If we were caught in such an open area the entire team could be wiped out.

I looked over at Lieutenant Lord and saw that once again his face was red and that he was sweating heavily. He had exchanged the bandanna that he had worn on his first patrol with us for a floppy bush hat, but he still looked exhausted. I realized that either he didn't recognize the danger of moving in the open or he was just too tired to care.

Bo suggested that he go across first to check out the other side before anyone else and Lord reluctantly agreed. I didn't like the idea at all, Bo could be caught in the open, or we could be observed from the surrounding hills as we made the crossing. There was nothing to be done, orders were orders. Bo shucked his pack and scrambled across the steep slope, staying as low as possible. He made it to the tree line without incident and disappeared into the jungle. After a few minutes he emerged and gave us the all-clear sign. We went across one at a time and regrouped on the other side. We were lucky, but everyone in the team knew the lieutenant had made a bad call.

We continued climbing and found a trail running across the top of the ridgeline. Ahead of us loomed a set of huge stone boulders set deep in the earth. They may have been some strange natural rock formation, but to me they looked like they had been erected a long time ago by men. In either case, they provided us a good defensive position, and we set up our perimeter around the largest one.

The next day dawned clear and hot. We had nearly reached the base of the hill that we hoped to use as our observation point, and I was really looking forward to a break. Suddenly Bo raised a clenched fist, and we stopped dead in our tracks. He moved forward cautiously, and I saw him carefully examining the ground in front of him. I followed his gaze and saw a black wire half-buried in the ground to the right of the trail. Bo moved to the left and carefully pushing aside a bush uncovered another section of the wire.

"Another booby trap," I thought, my heart pounding. One touch on the trip wire and it would blow us away. I looked around for cover, but there wasn't any nearby. Bo continued to probe around in the dirt and to my relief moved away.

"Communications line," he whispered softly to me as he passed.

Lieutenant Lord radioed HQ and eagerly told them what we had seen. A communications line was a rare find. We didn't have the equipment with us to tap it, but if another team could be sent in with the necessary gear, we could then eavesdrop on the enemy's communications and learn their plans. Instead of withdrawing from the area to protect our discovery, however, Lord ordered us to split up and follow the line to see where it led.

He ordered us to break into two groups, one part of the team following the line into the valley on our right, the other the valley on the left side of the ridgeline. Truman, the new medic and I would be in the first group and go to the left; Bo, Ma, Frenchy and the lieutenant would follow the wire to the right. We would keep in touch by radio and meet up by the stone pillars at nightfall.

We split apart, each unit moving slowly away from the other. There was a large open field of razor grass to the left of the trail and the three of us started moving carefully through it. Just before the grass closed over our heads there was a short burst of enemy fire. We dropped to the earth and crawled over to the cover of a large boulder.

"Try to make radio contact with the lieutenant," I whispered to Truman.

We crouched down in the grass as Truman tried to reach the other team. After a few minutes he shook his head with frustration. He slipped the radio from his shoulders and, laying it on the ground in front of him, checked the settings

Suddenly our new corpsman stood up and opened fire yelling, "I see 'em! I see 'em!"

"And now they see us too! Get down, you asshole!" Truman screamed, pulling at his jacket.

Almost immediately bullets began to chop up the razor grass all around us. Truman dropped the handset and dove for cover behind the rock, leaving the radio behind. When the fire stopped for a moment he tried once again to reach it, but was once again sprayed with automatic weapons fire and had to pull back behind the boulder.

"Leave it!" I ordered. It would have been suicide for Truman to continue to expose himself, and we didn't really need the radio, The other team carried another one.

The fire coming at us was intermittent. I began to hope that there were only a few enemy soldiers in front of us. We couldn't see anything in the tall grass, but as long as we kept our heads down Charlie wasn't able to see us either.

I motioned to Truman and Doc and they followed me as we hugged the ground and began crawling away. We eventually made it to the tree line without being spotted and made our way back to the rendezvous point by the stone pillars. Our teammates were already there. Bo and Frenchy were laying down Claymores at each end of the trail while Ma provided cover from atop one of the huge stones. Moose had a green towel over his head so his voice was muffled and was hunched over his radio trying to make contact with our base. When we arrived, Lieutenant Lord was climbing up the rock pillar toward Ma to get a better view of the situation.

I ran over to Moose.

"Are you OK, man? We tried to call you. I thought you were shot!"

"I'm OK, but the radio's toast," he answered disgustedly, removing the towel from around his head.

He pointed to a bullet hole that went straight through center of the radio set. The metal case had blocked the round and probably saved his life, but the radio was toast.

"Where's your radio?" he asked me, remembering the second one Truman had carried.

"We had to leave it."

"Oh shit," he swore softly, looking at me, his eyes wide.

That was an understatement, without a radio we wouldn't be able to call in for extraction. No one would even know that we had been in contact.

It was my decision that we had left it, and I knew it was my responsibility to get it back. I dropped my pack and ran back the way I had come, trying to stay under cover as much as possible. I finally reached the field of razor grass. From the high embankment I saw the boulder that had protected us in the center of the field. I didn't see any enemy movement.

Keeping under cover I shimmied down the embankment and once again began crawling slowly through the grass. The sun was blazing hot, and after a few hundred yards of pushing my way through the undergrowth I was exhausted. Once I entered the grass I wasn't able to see anything more than a few feet in front of me and could only hope that I was still moving in the right direction. I considered popping my head up to get a bearing on the rock, but I knew it wasn't a good idea. For all I knew, there was a sniper just waiting for me to show myself. At any moment I expected to hear the rattle of an automatic weapon, but except for the hum of the insects the field remained eerily quiet.

My imagination ran wild as I thought about what the enemy might be doing. Maybe they were setting up a machine gun or perhaps preparing to move in a line through the grass to flush us out. Perhaps they were sighting in a mortar or getting ready to light the entire field on fire. I tried to put everything out of my head and just concentrate on crawling forward in a straight line.

Just when I thought that I had misjudged my direction and had gone past the boulder. I found it. I cautiously looked around to the front and saw that the radio was still where Truman had dropped it. I cautiously reached around and slowly pulled it toward me around the back of the rock. I changed frequencies, grabbed the handset and immediately made contact with our base. I gave them our position and told them we needed air support and an immediate extraction.

"Wait one," the response came back.

"Yeah, fat chance of that!" I thought to myself.

I had told them everything they needed to know; now I had to get out of here. I rolled over, strapped the radio on my back without getting up and started crawling back the way I had come, following the tunnel I had made through the razor grass. I knew it was only a matter of time until the enemy returned in force. I had to get the radio back to my team and tried to crawl faster, but the heat had sapped my strength. There comes a time when you are so tired that exhaustion overcomes fear and even reason itself. I just could not crawl another foot through that damned grass.

"The hell with it," I said to myself, getting to my feet and walking the remaining distance to the tree line. It was such a foolish thing to do, but it is said that "God protects drunkards and fools," and I reached the tree line without getting shot. I crouched down behind a log to get my strength back and was reaching for the radio again when I saw a quick movement in front of me. I raised my rifle and sighted in the movement. I had nearly squeezed the trigger when our new corpsman stepped out from behind a tree.

"Man, I nearly wasted you!" I told him angrily, standing up and startling him.

"I thought you needed help, so I followed you," he replied in a plaintive voice.

"You've helped enough already. If it wasn't for you, they wouldn't have even known we were there."

He dropped his eyes and I immediately regretted my outburst. This was his first patrol. I shouldn't have expected him to know what he was doing. Following me was a foolish act that had nearly gotten him killed, but it was also a brave and selfless one.

"C'mon, let's get out of here," I said more softly, taking his shoulder and turning him around.

We made it back to the stone pillars. I handed the radio to Moose, who took it with a sigh of relief and immediately re-established contact with our base. Lieutenant Lord climbed down from the top of the stone pillar, took the handset and crouched over his map. I don't even think that he knew I had been gone. A few minutes later, he gave us the signal for us to gather together.

"Are we going to get extracted, sir?" Truman whispered hopefully.

Lord shook his head and told us that our mission had changed. We were ordered to join up with a Marine infantry company and lead them back to where we had first made contact.

Bo pulled up the Claymores that had been protecting our flank and ran back down the trail, moving through the night to put in as much distance as possible before the NVA got their act together and came after us. At the time, we thought that the sooner we joined forces with the grunts the safer we would be, but we were mistaken.

36. Grunts

Prince Henry: I did never see such pitiful rascals.
Falstaff: Tut, tut; good enough to toss;
food for powder, food for powder;
they'll fill a pit as well as better ...
—Shakespeare's *Henry IV*

We traveled without stopping all night, trying to put as much distance behind us as possible and not stopping until we reached our rendezvous point with the grunts shortly before dawn. Exhausted, we finally settled down just off the trail to wait for them. Less than an hour later we heard the grunts coming toward us, clanking gear, low talking, an occasional laugh, a muffled curse. As they got closer, we could smell cigarette smoke and then sweat.

"We gave them the coordinates, why don't we just get out of here," Truman whispered to no one in particular.

I couldn't help but agree with him. It didn't make much sense to me either. We had never worked closely with a large infantry unit before, and I was worried. The gooks would certainly know that we had found their sanctuary and would either be moving out or digging in, and I feared the latter.

Moose had been in constant contact with their radio operator and had let them know we were waiting for them just off the trail, but their point man and two or three other Marines walked right by us as we crouched in the underbrush. When we stood up and stepped silently onto the trail and into their column, one of the Marines who had just passed us swung around with his rifle at the ready.

"Shit! Where did you guys come from?" he shouted in a shocked voice as he lowered his weapon. We were just as surprised by his outburst as he was by our sudden appearance. We seldom spoke above a whisper in the bush.

The column halted as Lieutenant Lord went back to meet with their commander, a young captain. As the two officers huddled together over maps our two groups sat down on the trail and studied each other. It was obvious that they weren't happy to see us and they didn't bother to hide their feelings. They knew that the only reason we were there was to lead them into a shitload of trouble.

We never found out where the grunts came from, but from the look of their mud-covered gear and haunted eyes it certainly wasn't from some R & R center in the rear. They had probably been called in from some remote firebase where they were shelled during the day and ran ambushes all night.

Each man carried an incredible amount of gear, their packs bulging with supplies. In addition to the weaponry that we carried they humped mortars, LAWs, machine guns and enough ammo for an extended firefight. They wore flak jackets and helmets emblazoned with symbols and slogans. The words *Don't Mean Nothin!* were written on the helmet of the big Marine who had spun around in front of us. He reminded me of a weary bouncer at the end of a long shift—not someone you wanted to fuck around with.

We were as nervous in the bush as deer, alert to every sound and quick to flee. We knew the enemy was near and expected the grunts to keep down the noise, move slower, ditch the cigarettes. They didn't seem to care. Dangerous steel-helmeted troglodytes, they carried themselves with an assured, almost insolent, "bring it on" attitude.

We took the lead, walking cautiously back up the trail we had run down a few hours before. I was sure we were going to be ambushed. If I was in Charlie's position that was what I would have done, but the path remained clear. I remembered Bilgers assessment of an NVA battalion in the area and worried that we were being led into an even bigger trap.

The officers set up a makeshift command center while our team formed a defensive perimeter around them. The captain called over his sergeants and gave orders for his men to move forward and take command of the high ground, a low hill that rose to our west. The grunts dropped their packs and joined up into fire teams. There was no bullshitting going on now.

The grunts moved up the hill in leapfrog maneuvers, each platoon covered the other with intersecting lines of fire and was clearly in their element. I recognized the tactics as those I had learned during advanced infantry training, but I had only dim memories of them now. To the grunts these maneuvers were second nature.

They had only gone a short distance when we heard the sound of a heavy automatic weapon. The grunts had made contact and their assault teams returned the fire. The noise of the firefight seemed to come in waves, intensifying, slowing and then increasing even more. The fast cracks of the M-16s, blending with the slower, heavier fire of the AK. The staccato fire of M-60s was matched by measured bursts of a heavier enemy machine gun higher on the hill.

The grunts attacked again and again, but the NVA solders were apparently well dug in and standing their ground. A steady stream of wounded men was now stumbling back down toward the makeshift medical station, and Lieutenant Lord ordered us to blow an LZ for the medevac helicopters. We weren't carrying enough explosives ourselves to do this, but the grunts were carrying a half-dozen Claymores and in a short time we had them at our disposal. They hadn't been cut in half and held the full amount of C-4, but the trees around us were massive. Even with the extra explosives I doubted that we could create an opening large enough for a chopper to set down.

Truman and I moved off about a hundred yards to a level area and began placing the charges. We taped the Claymores to the outside of the circle so that the trees would fall away from the center and, we hoped, leave a cleared circle at least big enough for a Huey to squeeze in.

"Fire in the hole!" I yelled, squeezing the detonator. No point in being quiet now.

A sudden explosion shook the ground. The charges cut the trees at their base and they crashed down exactly as we had planned, but I knew that the small clearing that we blasted still wasn't big enough for a chopper to land.

The medics were bringing over wounded. I looked up and saw a medevac Huey swooping down and hovering overhead. It dropped a stretcher basket and Truman and I helped strap a few of the more seriously injured men on to it. Some moaned in agony as their litter lifted into the air, but most gritted their teeth and were silent. It was a slow process, but eventually the Huey flew off with five men. I looked down and saw my pants were covered in their blood.

Truman and I returned to the command center. The captain looked back at the number of casualties being brought down the hill. He shook his head in frustration when Lord told him that the opening was too small for a larger helicopter to land. He grabbed the radio and crouching down began to speak urgently into it and a look of relief crossed his face.

"They've diverted a pallet of explosives to us; it should be here shortly."

A few minutes later we heard the hollow "clopping" sound of a CH-46. Swinging below it on a steel cable was a large wooden pallet covered in a tarp. A few seconds later it hit the ground. We detached the cable and the chopper banked away. We pulled off the tarp and saw hundreds of pounds of C-4 plastic explosive, each individual brick wrapped in black plastic. Someone with brains in his head had also stuffed in several spools of detonation cord and a box of fuses.

"Think we got enough?" Truman asked me sarcastically, looking at the huge mound of explosives in front of us.

"Enough to blow the entire mountain and ourselves with it to kingdom come, if we're not careful," I warned him as he grabbed the blocks.

I wished that Bo were with me; Truman would have loved to set off the entire pallet just for fun. We stuffed the plastic blocks of C-4 into our knapsacks and each of us put a roll of cord over his shoulder. We moved off a few hundred feet away from the pallet and began to clear a larger LZ. We used the det cord to secure small blocks of C-4 around the base of each tree and daisy-chained the cord to the next block of explosive. The initial charge would travel almost instantaneously along the cord, exploding the next block of C-4 as it went. We made a big spiral, placing the charges outward as we had done before.

Truman smiled in anticipation as I handed him one of the ignition units. These were shaped like fat pencils with a ring at one end. We backed off as far as we could and pulled the fuses at the same time. The lit off with soft pops and we immediately got up and started walking away. We now had thirty seconds to reach shelter before the C-4 detonated. There was an outcrop of rock about three hundred feet away that I hoped would protect us from the blast. I remembered the warning words of one of my explosives instructors: "Once you pull the fuse just walk away ... you run ... you fall ... you die."

The seconds were passing and I had to fight the urge to run for safety. We had just reached the rock and crouched down when an enormous explosion shook the hill. There was a sudden pressure and then sharp pain as debris from the blast began falling all around us. We emerged from behind the rock covered in dirt and debris, my ears ringing and my head cut and aching from a piece of flying wood that had grazed my head. Truman whooped and hollered.

We had blown a circular opening in the jungle at least a fifty feet in diameter. The trees had been blown off near their trunks, the stumps poking jaggedly upward, but their upper limbs were now in an incredible jumble, piled like pick-up sticks every which way. Truman and I wrapped the limbs with more det cord and set off smaller charges that quickly cut up the remaining trees. In a few minutes we had a space big enough for the birds to land. Truman joked that he was going to go into business as a logger when he got out of the service.

A CH-46 made a trial pass over the new LZ and then gingerly settled to the ground. It was immediately filled with wounded men.

37. The Quick and the Dead

Men do not fight for flag or country, for the Marine Corps or glory or any other abstraction, they fight for one another. —William Manchester

Truman was helping carry stretchers to the waiting CH-46, but I suddenly felt too sick and dizzy to join him. I put my hand to my head and it came away wet with blood. I left the LZ and made my way over to where the where the medics were working on the wounded, but they were far too busy to pay any attention to me. I sank down with my back against a tree, closed my eyes and hoped that my headache would go away.

I must have fallen asleep for a few minutes. Someone called out my name and I opened my eyes, confused in the way that sometimes happens when you fall asleep in a strange room. I saw our new corpsman running over to me and I sat up.

"You OK, man? You look like shit," Doc asked in a concerned voice.

He reached toward my forehead and pressed a bandage against my head. I felt a long gash along my hairline where a chunk of tree had hit it.

Another medic came over. "Ya shoulda worn your helmet," he admonished.

"Don't have one."

He looked at me queerly and handed me another pressure bandage. "Just hold this against your head for a few minutes and it will stop. Scalp wounds always bleed like hell."

Doc helped me to my feet. Standing up, I saw a long line of men laid out on the ground behind the tree I had been leaning against. They appeared to be sleeping, but it was a terribly still sleep. Flies and other insects drawn by the smell of death were swarming around the bodies and gorging themselves on the pools of rapidly coagulating blood.

They walked with impunity across the faces of our dead. As I looked down, one landed on the open eye of the Marine who I recognized as being on the hill with me. Caught in the finality of death, he couldn't even brush a fly aside.

Doc followed my gaze. "Lotta dead … lotta dead."

In death everything had been taken from the fallen Marines, even their names. They were grouped together and referred to simply as "the dead."

"Do you know where the rest of the team is?" I asked him, feeling a sudden need to get back to my friends, get back to the living.

He shook his head and turned back to his duties as more wounded were brought in.

I walked down the hill. A small knot of officers were gathered around their captain and I saw Lieutenant Lord among them. The two officers were hunched over a map and I overheard them say that they were planning to call in an artillery strike on the hilltop. The low cloud cover apparently prevented an airstrike.

On our missions we had often called in artillery from remote observation sites, but this was the first time I had been so close to the target. Normally we would be sitting on a hilltop with binoculars a thousand yards or more from the impact zone. The captain radioed up to his men on the hillside, warning them to keep their heads down as the artillery barrage began.

The rounds came whistling in over our heads, passing over the top of the mountain and detonating somewhere in the valley on the other side. The captain adjusted the fire, steadily walking the rounds closer. Suddenly the next set of shells exploded directly on top of the Marines on the hill! We heard our own men screaming as jagged shards of steel slammed into them, and the mocking laughter of the gooks.

"Cease fire; cease fire; for God's sake cease fire!" the captain shouted desperately into the radio.

The shelling stopped immediately. The captain put his head in his hands and rocked back and forth. No one seemed to know what had happened. Personally, I thought that shells had probably hit the tops of the huge trees growing on the side of the hill and exploded before they reached their intended target, but perhaps the coordinates were incorrect or the rounds were faulty. Whatever the reason, the result was catastrophic. The grunts were forced to withdraw, each fire team providing cover for the other as they leapfrogged down the hill, dragged their wounded behind them, as we provided covering fire.

I found myself nearly out of ammunition. The grunts made their way over to the medical area where the bodies of their friends were laid out in long rows. The Marines kneeled down and carefully stripped cartridge belts from the bodies of their comrades. I followed their example, reaching down and slipping two bandoliers of M-16 ammo from the shoulders of the blond Marine I had been sitting next to only a few hours ago. His body was already starting to stiffen. As I slipped the ammunition from his shoulders I realized they were covered in his blood. Smelling the salty sweet odor of death I hesitated.

"Bad karma, very bad…" I thought uneasily. The last guy who wore this equipment was going home in a body bag.

My fear of running out of ammunition however, proved stronger than the thought of taking what I needed from a dead man. I fastened the bandoliers around my chest and tied them down.

Looking up, I saw two Marines sliding down the hill toward me. One man had been shot in the leg and was being helped down the slope by his buddy. I ran over to help, but he waved me away.

"Some more wounded are still up there!"

"I'll get 'em," I shouted.

I ran up the hill following the bloody trail the two men had made coming down, but after a few hundred yards I lost it. I could hear rifle fire above me and climbing higher found a trail that curved around the side of the hill, but as I climbed higher the sounds of the battle seemed to be receding, and I stopped for a moment to get my bearings. I was totally alone for the first time in many months and in that solitude strange thoughts rose to the surface of my mind. I realized that there was a very good chance of my dying on this hill. For a moment I thought of just continuing to walk, away from the battle, away from the Marine Corps, away from everything, but I pushed the thought aside.

I had promised to bring in the wounded and by God I was going to do just that! I turned around and ran back the way I had come. The sounds of the fighting growing more intense. As I came around the bend of the trail, I saw a young Marine crouched down along the bank firing an M79. To my right the rest of his platoon were directing their fire at an enemy bunker dug into the hillside above us. I joined the fight, crouching down behind a stump and firing my rifle at the muzzle flashes coming from the top of the ridge. The other Marines were shouting as they fought, and I was suddenly also filled with the savage, irrational joy of combat.

"Bring it on, you bastards! Bring it on!" I yelled, firing my rifle like a madman.

I heard a soft plopping sound and turned to see the Marine next to me slide to the ground. The M79 fell from his hands and blood spurted from his chest with every beat of heart.

"Corpsman!" I yelled looking around frantically for help.

I dropped my rifle and tried to stanch the flow of blood by pressing my hand against his chest. I felt the pressure of his life's blood press against my palm for a few seconds, then the pressure eased and in a few seconds I felt nothing at all.

I grabbed the M79 that had fallen to the ground beside him and began firing round after round into the bunker. The feeling of insane exaltation had left me as suddenly as it had come, replaced with a cold hardness. I continued firing until I had used up all the M79 rounds. A corpsman finally crawled over to my position, took one look at the man lying next to me and moved on without saying a word. The men next to me were now nearly out of ammunition and we were forced to pull back down the hill dragging our dead and wounded with us. I made my way back to the command area hoping to find the rest of my team.

The grunt captain looked up as I passed. My utilities were covered in blood. With a dazed look on his face the officer called out to me as I passed.

"Who are you?"

I shook my head and continued walking; his simple question was a koan[1] riddle beyond my ability at the time to answer.

38. Blessed Sleep

> *We are such stuff*
> *As dreams are made on, and our little life*
> *Is rounded with a sleep.*
> —Shakespeare, "The Tempest"

I found the rest of my team digging in along the east side of the hill with the grunts. Night was falling and the grunts were digging foxholes and trenches, trying to get as deep into the ground as possible. Bo had a borrowed a shovel from the guys next to us and had gouged a shallow hole for us. I joined him using my knife to break up the earth for him. The ground was soft clay, and we were soon able prepare a fairly decent fighting position for ourselves.

Soldiers in the Roman legions would dig a protective trench up to the shoulders of the shortest man in their unit before they rested for the night. Here we were, burrowing into the ground like animals while back in the States astronauts were training for a flight to the moon. So it goes.

The grunts seemed to be at home in the earth. Each man carried his own entrenching tool and they knew how to use them. About sixty feet away we saw that a group of three of them had finished digging their trench and were rigging up a poncho over the hole to keep out the rain that had started to fall. They had started a small fire at one end and the scent of whatever they were cooking carried over to us. I guess they felt they had done everything they could do to prepare and now just wanted to eat before it got dark.

Moose had started a fire in his foxhole and Bo and I joined him. For the first time I ate hot food in the bush. I have to admit that it made all the difference. The canned rations tasted a whole lot better after they had been heated up. Lieutenant Lord came over to our positions. He warned us that we wouldn't be reinforced until morning and that there was a good chance that we'd be attacked before then.

He pointed to Bo and myself. "I told their captain that we would provide advanced warning of any attack and I want you two to go a few hundred yards beyond our perimeter with a walkie-talkie and report to us if you hear any movement."

Bo and I looked at each other. Did Lord have any conception about how dangerous a job he was sending us on? If the NVA did attack we'd be caught between them and the fire of own men. What he was asking us to do was suicidal, but he wasn't asking for volunteers; he was giving us a direct order. There wasn't any way Bo and I were going to get out of it.

"We'll be calling in illumination rounds as soon as it gets dark. They should enable you to see anything moving in front of us," the lieutenant continued, oblivious to the effect his words were having on us.

"And anything out there will be certain to see us as well," I thought to myself.

When night fell Bo and I left our foxhole and crawled out beyond our lines. Bo carried a short-range walkie-talkie; the other one was left with the grunts in their foxhole to our left. They promised to listen for our transmission but seemed more interested in setting up their M-60 to rake the ground in front of them. We moved out well beyond our perimeter. I found a pile of rocks with a large bush over the top and crawled under it. Bo kept moving a few hundred feet farther and disappeared under a low shrub.

The illumination rounds came in on schedule, lighting up everything with their weird yellow/white light. The flares made a popping noise as they, ignited in the air and floated down on a small parachute. They would light up the area underneath for two or three minutes. As soon as one died, after ten or fifteen seconds another one took its place. Bo and I had to stay quiet and concealed. In the light of the flares any movement that we made could easily be seen.

Since the patrol began I had hadn't had any sleep at all, and now we were facing another twelve hours on lookout. Lying prone on the warm earth, I struggled to keep my eyes open. If Bo and I could have stayed together, we would have been able to spell each other or at least keep each other awake, but there hadn't been enough cover in this open area for us to do that. The ground was warm and sandy and I burrowed into it like it was a soft feather bed.

I jerked myself awake.

"Go to sleep now and a VC will cut your throat for sure," I warned myself, but it was becoming more and more difficult to stay awake After more than thirty-six hours without sleep my body seemed to have a will of its own which could not be denied. I took out my Ka-Bar and jabbed the point in my leg hoping that the pain would keep me awake, but it was useless.

I awoke to a crack of thunder. I checked my watch, it was now nearly midnight, and I had been asleep for several hours.

Another illumination round popped, and I suddenly saw something move in the tree line in front of us. My heart started to pound, and I was suddenly wide awake. An NVA soldier was moving toward me. A second round went off, and the man froze in the light. He was carrying an AK but not a lot of other gear. Instead of a helmet, he had a piece of brown cloth tied around his head. As the light from the flare faded he began moving again, slowly, carefully, keeping to cover the way that we would. The light from the flare faded and I lost sight of him for a few seconds.

Another round went off and revealed him once again, a few yards farther, again frozen in place. He was slowly moving closer where Bo was hiding. I raised my rifle but I was afraid that if I fired, the trigger-happy grunts behind me would open up with their machine gun, but if I didn't stop him he might spot Bo.

When the next flare went off however, he had turned away from Bo's hiding spot and was moving into the jungle in front of us. Now I hoped that Bo wouldn't shoot, but I needn't have worried.

When I crawled over to Bo's hiding place I found him curled up in a little ball, fast asleep. I placed my hand on his shoulder. Startled by my touch, he woke instantly reaching for his knife.

"Give me the radio," I whispered hoarsely to him. "We're outta here." He didn't ask me any questions, just handed it to me.

Some lookouts we had turned out to be!

I called in to let the grunts know we were coming back through the lines and warn them not to shoot. I told them that we had heard movement and to keep alert.

We crawled back to our lines and had just made it into our foxhole when the NVA launched an attack on the grunt line to our immediate left. They must have circled around the hill and were hoping to surprise us, but the grunts were ready. They were holding the high ground, were well dug in, and had been warned. They answered the attack with machine gun and rifle fire. Crisscrossing lines of tracer rounds joined by the strobe-like effect of the illumination rounds created a hellish light show.

The rain which had held off while we were making our way back now started coming down in earnest, the raindrops flashing into steam as they hit the hot barrels of their machine guns. I fired mechanically at the muzzle flashes and the shadows flitting among the trees. When the grunts' 60mm mortar rounds began falling around them, the enemy soldiers broke contact and pulled back.

"Don't you just hate those little bastards," Truman muttered grimly, snapping another magazine into his still-smoking rifle.

I shook my head. No, I didn't hate them at all. I didn't need to hate them to kill them.

39. Rats

Our dried voices, when
We whisper together
Are quiet and meaningless
As wind in dry grass
Or rats' feet over broken glass
In our dry cellar
—T.S. Eliot, *The Waste Land*

The earth turned and it was once again morning. The cold, sick feeling that always seemed to remain with me after a firefight gradually receded as the sun cleared the treetops.

The grunts moved out of their trenches and took a body count of the enemy soldiers they had killed. They made two piles, one for weapons, the other for bodies, taking more care with the weapons than they did with the dead enemy soldiers. Two Marines would each take an arm and pull the corpse along the ground until they reached the body pile. One of the men would then take hold of the feet while the other lifted the arms. Swinging the body a few times back and forth to gain momentum, they would finally throw it on top of the mounting pile. I didn't stick around the watch.

Overhead I saw what seemed to be a squadron of Army Hueys bringing in wave after wave of Air Cavalry troops onto the LZ we had blown. The generals had ordered a major assault on the hilltop. Jumping out of the small choppers the Army guys sure looked sharp, their utilities and gear seemed new; even their choppers were freshly washed.

39. Rats

They set up a command post in the clearing where the dead Marines had been laid out the day before, and I saw Lieutenant Lord with the other officers poring over maps. For a moment I considered telling Lord about the NVA soldier we had seen, but decided against the idea. He might also ask what Bo had seen and knowing Bo, he would probably have admitted to falling asleep on watch and been court-martialed. It was better for me to just keep my mouth shut.

I walked back up the hill to where Truman and I were sharing a foxhole. I had just settled in with him when a small group of grunts came over to borrow some of our camouflage paint. The officers decided they needed fresh information before beginning the final assault, and these men were assigned to scout out the enemy positions.

"Need a hand?" Truman suddenly offered, getting to his feet and grabbing his rifle.

"Sure," their sergeant agreed, smearing more paint around his neck.

I looked over at Truman incredulously. What the hell was he thinking? It wasn't as though they had asked for our help.

Truman turned to me. "Want to come along?"

No, damn it! I didn't want to "come along," but I didn't want to let him go up there without me either. Why did he always have to be such a jerk? I got to my feet and resentfully joined the other men who were crawling up the steep hill toward the enemy bunker near the top of the hill.

The thick underbrush prevented us from seeing more than a few feet ahead of us, but no one wanted to be the first to poke up his head. We eventually made it up to where the grunts had been stopped the previous day. We crawled into the shallow trenches the men had hastily dug a hundred meters from the hilltop. The ground ahead of us had been burned and blasted by the fighting. Thousands, of shiny spent cartridges littered the ground around us. From our new position we could clearly see the earthen bunker at the top of the hill, but nothing moved.

I was still carrying the M79 grenade launcher that I had taken yesterday from the Marine who had been killed next to me.

Their sergeant turned to me. "Put a few rounds into that bunker."

I pushed one of the fat grenade cartridges into the weapon and snapped the barrel shut. With a soft *whump,* the round arced up and exploded directly on top of the earthen mound. There was no return fire. I reloaded and sent up another one. Again, there was no response. The sergeant scanned the trenches with his binoculars and then fired a quick burst from his M-16. There was no response.

"I think they're gone," he muttered.

"Could be a ruse," I warned him softly.

The sergeant sent one of his riflemen around to the right and another to the left. The two crept closer and closer to the bunker until they were finally only a few feet from it. One Marine tossed in a grenade into the bunker and there was a muffled explosion.

"It's empty!" he shouted back.

"Watch out for booby traps!" I yelled out to him as the rest of the fire team started moving toward the bunker. Not for the first time I wondered why I always seemed to be the one looking out for the other guys. When was someone going to start worrying about me?

I cautiously climbed up the hillside to join the rest of the men at the top of the hill.

The ground beneath our feet was also littered with enemy shell casings, this time those of the heavier cartridges the AK-47 fired. The sergeant radioed down to the captain to bring up support and in a few minutes another grunt platoon had joined us at the top of the hill. They jumped into the trenches and immediately started setting up their machine guns to protect us from a counterattack. In only a few minutes they had made themselves right at home.

The NVA had built an impressive defensive position into the hillside. It was no wonder that they had held out for so long. Their bunker was strongly built of earth and heavy logs. It was dug down about six feet and big enough to hold a few dozen soldiers. The bunker was connected and protected by two deep trenches extending out from each side. The sides of each trench were undercut, giving some degree of protection from the air, and the walls were reinforced by a lattice of tightly woven tree branches. Scattered around the top of the hill were more mats made of grass and brush. At one time these mats probably covered the trenches, concealing all enemy activity from the air. It was no wonder that the grunts had such difficulty taking the hilltop.

Charlie had retreated in good order. They hadn't left any equipment around and there were no signs of casualties. They had probably heard the waves of Army choppers landing and had prudently decided to withdraw before they were surrounded.

We were soon joined by the Marine captain, and then a large group of Army soldiers. Truman and I were following the grunt sergeant back down the path to get the gear we had left in our foxhole when the sergeant suddenly stopped in his tracks and looked intently at a dead shrub on the side of the hill. Keeping his weapon at the ready and calling out to one of his men to cover him, he carefully tugged at the bush. It came away in his hand, revealing a small perfectly square hole cut into the earth. He had spotted the entrance to a tunnel. Without speaking a word, the sergeant took a Willie Peter grenade from his belt, pulled the pin and casually dropped it down the hole.

As he did so, the captain called out from behind him, "Wait!—Prisoners!"

The grenade detonated deep in the ground. White smoke billowed out of the hole and seeped out through half a dozen other openings. The hillside seemed to be honeycombed with tunnels. The sergeant turned around slowly to face his commander.

"Sorry, sir, I didn't hear you in time," he told his captain impassively.

Turning to one of the men behind him, the sergeant asked almost politely, "corporal, you wanna go down there and see if you get the captain here a prisoner?"

A short Marine reminding me of a skinnier version of Bo immediately began stripping off his equipment. He took a .45 pistol from his shoulder holster and a flashlight that was clipped to his web gear. Taking a role of tape from his jacket, he tightly taped the pistol to the flashlight. He removed a gas mask from his pack, slipped it over his head and without hesitating squirmed into the hole, disappearing from sight.

"My God," Truman marveled. "Does that guy have balls!"

The sergeant looked at him with surprise. "He's our tunnel rat," he told us, as if that explained everything.

"He's crazy; that's what he is," Truman muttered softly under his breath.

I knew that it was unlikely that anyone would be left alive in the tunnel after the grenade had exploded. If the burning phosphorus didn't kill on contact, it would burn up all the oxygen in the hole and asphyxiate anyone down there, but to crawl through a tiny hole in the ground with nothing more than a pistol and a flashlight required bravery beyond my comprehension.

A few minutes later we heard a shuffling noise, and the corporal pulled himself out of the hole. "Opens up quite a bit once you get in, but it's empty now."

The sergeant turned to his captain. "Sorry about your prisoner, sir," he told him, his face blank.

It seemed like I wasn't the only enlisted man who had problems with authority figures.

Around noon, as Marines opened up cans of rations the Hueys returned with hot pizza pies for the Army guys. The soldiers looked on with amusement as we crowded around and begged them for slices. To them it was apparently no big deal. Didn't everybody in Nam get fresh pizza delivered by helicopter?

We always carefully crushed and carried out our any cans or extra rations so that the enemy wouldn't know where we had been. The grunts and Army guys simply tossed their cans and other garbage down the hill.

That night the rats came out to feast. At first there was only the clink of metal and the soft rustle of paper as the rodents found the cans and pizza boxes. Occasionally a squeal, as the vermin fought one another for a particularly good piece of leftover cheese. The sounds got louder as they finished off the bottom boxes and started working their way up the slope. Finally they reached our trenches.

I was exhausted, and I pulled my blanket over my head and tried desperately to get to sleep despite the rats, but it was impossible. I squirmed frantically and kicked out whenever I felt the touch of soft paws running over my body. They seemed to be tugging at my blanket, trying to get at me.

Suffocating under the wet blanket, I sat up and stuck my head up just as an illumination round went off above us. I looked down at my feet to see a huge rat frozen by the sudden light sitting on my boot. Behind it the slope was crawling with scores more. It was a scene from a nightmare.

Where had they come from? How could there possibly be so many of them? It seemed as though every rat in Vietnam were moving toward us. All around me I could hear muttered curses as the grunts kicked and writhed under their own tarps. I spent the rest of the night gritting my teeth and devising rattraps. In my mind they fell by the hundreds into vat of boiling oil, were blown to bits by Claymores, or were crushed beneath tank treads. That night madness seemed very, very close.

The rats departed at dawn and so did we. The lieutenant, bless him, somehow wrangled us a lift back to our base in one of the Army choppers. We climbed aboard, sitting in the open doorway, holding on to the edge of the door, our feet on the metal skids. The small craft lifted lightly above the tree line and we flew over the enemy bunker, a tiny swatch of brown against the deep green of the surrounding forest. The Marines were getting ready to move out and were in the process of destroying the enemy complex with explosives. Most of the Army soldiers had already left. As we flew away I wondered how this tiny section of earth could have been worth the lives of the men who had fought for it. We were in control of the hill, but what did that mean? Had we even won the battle? I wasn't at all sure.

As soon as we got back to base our team's new corpsman requested a transfer and to my surprise his request was approved. I never did find out what our new "Doc" told them to get moved out so fast, but he left the following week for the hospital at Cam Ranh Bay. Good for him. There is nothing like watching men die next to you to shatter your illusions and bring you face-to-face with reality. I bumped into him a few months later. He told me that he had stopped telling anyone about his only mission with First Force Recon because no one believed his stories.

40. Sink or Swim

Water, I ask a favor. Through this indolent
Arrangement of measured words, I speak to you
Remember your friend who swam in you
Be present to my lips in my last moment
—Jorge Luis Borges, "Poem to the Fourth Element"

Force Recon Marines were expected to be qualified in both Airborne and SCUBA, but the war had disrupted the training program and most of the scouts were now either one or the other. To get as many men dive qualified as possible Force would send men over to Subic Bay in the Philippines to take a basic two-week SCUBA course. Bo was chosen to attend the course and returned to our team tanned and relaxed, telling us stories about diving for lobsters and swimming through the warm and crystal-clear waters of Subic Bay.

Bo told us that their dive master had given them the "opportunity" to practice exiting from a submerged submarine. Bo explained that the sub went down about fifty feet and the divers were loaded into one of the escape hatches. The hatch was then nearly filled with water, leaving them just enough of an air pocket for them to take one last deep breath. The outside hatch was then opened and the sea flooded the chamber. The trainees were expected to inflate their life preservers and ascend to the surface.

"You had to continuously exhale as you surfaced. If you didn't your lungs would explode," Bo told me in a matter-of-fact voice.

I laughed and told him that this reminded me of the time we were given the "opportunity" to jump out of a jet at the conclusion of our paratrooper training at Fort Benning.

The divers had a small shack where they kept their equipment and rubber boats. Every week or so if not on patrol, they would go off base to a small nearby lake to dive and one day Bo invited me to come along. The divers loaded their gear into a truck and we set off. It was a beautiful day. The small lake was clear and warm. I had always loved to swim and the minute I entered the water my body relaxed in happy pleasure. I floated on my back slowly swimming along and looking at the deep blue sky and towering white clouds.

A path circled the lake and two girls in formal Vietnamese dresses were walking along it. Their dresses were made of pink silk, and each had a small white parasol to keep off the sun. The exotic beauty of the scene filled my heart with pleasure, something that had been missing for many months.

Bo had his tanks on and was swimming through the water about ten feet below me. I dove and tapped him on the shoulder. He turned toward me and then unexpectedly slipped his mouthpiece off and held it out to me. He was offering to share his air with me. I had never used SCUBA gear before, but I inserted the mouthpiece and found that it was easy to breathe. We took turns sharing the mouthpiece. As Bo swam deeper I followed.

We hit an icy layer of water about thirty feet down, and I decided that I'd had enough. I tapped Bo on the shoulder, released the mouthpiece and headed toward the surface. I was deeper than I had ever been before, and the mirror of air on the surface seemed impossibly far away. As I swam upward I experienced a sudden pain in my chest, but I remembered what Bo had told me about needing to exhale as you surfaced. It was a long way up, but I never seemed to run out of air. When I finally reached the surface, I realized what a stupid thing I had done. I could have easily drowned in that small pool.

On another training session we practiced beach mapping. During World War II thousands of Marines had been killed assaulting the island of Pelu in the Philippines. The beaches surrounding Pelu were ringed by coral reefs that were covered at high tide but exposed at other times. When the assault was delayed, the landing craft ran aground on the offshore reefs. Over five thousand Marines were either killed by the murderous ground fire or drowned when they tried to swim ashore. Since that time, a detailed underwater survey was performed before every Marine landing.

Despite our being in a combat zone we continued training for these kinds of operations. A Navy high-speed patrol boat would drop us off and we would gradually swim into the beach. Each diver carried a weighted line marked off in feet. We would position ourselves in long rows and swim in together, measuring the depth of the water every twenty-five feet and recording it on a slate hung around our necks. From these measurements we would develop a contour map showing the water depth, bottom composition, and any obstacles.

In practice it was a far more exciting story. To avoid enemy fire, an inflatable rubber boat was strapped to the side of the patrol craft. These boats were capable of moving at nearly fifty miles per hour, although they slowed down for pickups. A dive master sat strapped in the bow of the rubber boat facing backward. Divers lined up along the railing of the patrol craft and waited for the signal to jump down into the rubber boat, which was bucking around like it was alive. Once in the boat, we would lie down across the inflated tube and at a signal from the dive master each roll off the side as the next person took his place. The dive master counted off the seconds between each man to ensure an even spacing as they were dropped off.

The first time I attempted this the shock of hitting the water drove my breath away. I somehow managed to hold on to my dive mask, fins, measuring line, slate and waterproof marker as I was tumbled around by the powerful wake. I rose to the surface and bobbed around trying desperately to catch my breath. A long line of men stretched away on either side of me, each man spaced evenly about a few hundred yards apart.

Using pre-arranged signals, we moved together toward the distant beach and began the survey, dropping our weighted measuring line to the bottom and recording the depth of the water as we swam forward. When we finally reached the shore we immediately turned around and swam back to where we were to be picked up. There was a strong current running, and I was forced to swim hard just to remain in place.

In the distance I heard the sound of the approaching patrol boat. It was running straight down the line of men, the rubber dinghy plunging manically alongside. The dive master was now holding a flexible rubber hoop. Treading water, each diver had his left arm with his elbow bent. If everything went well the hoop would hit the crotch of your arm, and you would be jerked aboard the boat like a hooked fish.

From the water it seemed like the river patrol boat was going to run right over my head. If anyone is interested in the experience, I would suggest lying down on the edge of a highway and watching as a tractor-trailer passes a few feet away. If you wanted to fully experience it, you might try rolling back and forth into the roadway to simulate the effect of currents.

We had to rely completely on the skills of the captain of the patrol boat. Too close and the craft would run right over us, too far away and we couldn't reach the hoop. But in my case the captain had his shit together and I was pulled aboard on the first run and was able to watch as my teammates were plucked from the water. At the end of the second run everyone was aboard except Truman, who had missed the loop on two occasions.

"We'll just slow down and bring him in," the captain finally suggested to our first sergeant, who was chewing on a fat cigar and watching the pickups from a seat in the bow of the boat.

He shook his head. "No! He comes aboard like everybody else or he stays in the water!"

We crowded around the rail and watched as the boat made another high-speed pass. This time Truman seemed to be in a better position. The loop caught his arm, but he was too tired to pull himself up and was dragged alongside. Refusing to let go, he caught hold of the dive master's arm and was hauled aboard stark naked, the force of the water had ripped his swimsuit completely off. I don't think that he could have stayed afloat much longer. When he was finally hauled aboard he was trembling with exhaustion.

The next day we did another beach survey, this time using our six-man inflatable rubber boat. We were dropped off by the patrol boat before dawn and paddled about a mile along the beach facing Da Nang's airstrip. We carefully recorded the depth of the water in twenty-five-foot intervals along the beach as we paddled in. The exercise was expected to take us most of the day, but by mid-morning we had completed the survey. The patrol boat wasn't scheduled to rendezvous with us for another three hours so decided to paddle to the beach. We landed our boat on the sand near the end of the runway. Looking across to the other side, we saw an enlisted men's club, and Truman and decided to pay it a visit.

We watched for any landing planes and seeing that the flight path was clear, started to run toward the club on the other side of the runway which was a hundred yards wide and made of interlocking steel plates. The center of the runway was covered in oil and streaks of rubber, which absorbed the heat and the farther we got from the edge the hotter the steel became. In our bare feet it felt like we were running on top of a greased frying pan, but we were more than halfway across and couldn't turn back. Desperately trying to keep our feet from the hot steel, we leaped across the runway like two demented gazelles. Tears of pain were streaming from our eyes before we finally reached the end of the runway and in a final bound collapsed into the cool sand on the other side.

The airmen and soldiers sitting around the tables of the club had watched us in astonishment as we ran toward them. We must have been quite a sight as we finally came over wearing nothing but swim shorts asking for beer.

"Where the hell did you blokes come from?" an Australian gunner sitting at one of the tables asked in a friendly manner.

"Out there," Truman replied, airily waving his arm at the ocean, "rubber boat."

"Man, you guys must really be thirsty," he replied, looking at the empty blue water surrounding the base. He took us inside the club, where an Air Force sergeant was putting away some glasses.

"Give my friends here some beer," the Australian told him.

"We were really hoping for a case or two," I corrected him.

The sergeant took one look at us and rubbed his fingers together. Neither of us had any money on us, but I was wearing my new dive watch. I had paid nearly two hundred dollars for it, but right now I wanted the beer more. I took it off my wrist and held it out to him.

"I'll trade it for two cases of beer."

The bartender examined my watch skeptically but finally went into the back room and returned with two cartons of Budweiser. He didn't care; it wasn't his beer.

"Wouldn't have a couple of old towels around, would you?" Truman asked, interrupting the bartender, who had strapped my watch on to his arm and was now admiring it. He came back with a few old rags. We tore them into strips, poured some beer over them and wound the cloth around our feet.

This time our feet were protected, but we were nearly hit by a cargo plane that was on final approach and came in for a landing just over our heads. It passed so closely that we were buffeted by the propeller blast! We finally made it back and dropped our cases of beer on the sand where the other men welcomed us as the heroes we were. Stupid heroes, but heroes all the same.

Bo had had his own adventure. He had spotted a giant clam in the water and had somehow pried it off the bottom and dragged it onto the beach. The shell was nearly three feet across and the clam weighed over fifty pounds. The rest of the team had propped the monster on its side and were in the process of prying open the shell with their knives. Bo cut off a piece of clam and handed it to me, but it was as tough as a rubber tire and tasted like it had been marinated in ammonia. I spit it out and rinsed my mouth out with beer. The clam was inedible, but the shell was beautiful, a deep creamy white with traces of pink. We put the bottom half of the shell into our rubber boat. Bo was planning on mounting it over the door of the dive shack.

Poor clam, attached for decades to a rock on the bottom of the sea. Encased in beautiful armor, impervious to any underwater threat but easily vanquished by an attack from another realm. I looked up at the aircraft circling overhead and the warships plying the surrounding waters. Are not all of God's creatures nothing more than predators or prey? And do we all not take turns playing our various roles? Poor deluded souls human beings are. Gazing into oblivion and pinning our hopes on salvation while the equally doomed creatures around us live their lives without hope but also without fear.

We got back in our raft and slowly paddled out to sea. It was almost time for us to be picked up again. I felt wonderful, the blue water, the sun, the beer. The only problem was that the heavy, barnacle-encrusted clamshell, rolling around, had made hundreds of tiny holes. By the time the Navy arrived to pick us up, our rubber craft was collapsing around us. The giant clam was taking its revenge.

We sank the few remaining cans in the clear waters of the South China Sea and got ready to be picked up. The patrol boat pulled up alongside and the sailors watched us with amusement as Truman struggled drunkenly to climb aboard. Their captain looked around at the slowly sinking boat and the empty water surrounding us.

"How the hell did you guys get plastered out here?" he asked in a bemused voice.

After watching Truman stagger around, the sailors left the rest of us in our slowly sinking craft. They passed down a line from the stern and slowly pulled us back up the river. When we finally neared the dock, they dumped Truman unceremoniously into our craft, threw off our line and left us to paddle the rest of the way back to the shore.

As the Navy captain backed his boat away, I saw him look back at us, shake his head and mutter, "Marines…"

41. Hot Water

The fire you kindle for your enemy often burns yourself more. —Chinese proverb

After the first rocket attack at An Hoa destroyed the storage shed, Major Simbul placed our entire company on high alert. When not on patrol we spent most of our time in the trenches. It seemed like our base was under nearly constant attack. Sometimes we'd be rocketed two or three times a night. We became used to the sound of rockets and shells falling on us from the surrounding mountains. We would hear an explosion, someone would shout, "Incoming!" and a few seconds later the sirens warning of an attack would belatedly go off. We'd roll out of our cots, grabbing our flak jackets, helmets, and weapons while still moving, and dive into the nearest trench. I was nearly always the fastest one to get under cover, and I didn't mind in the least when the other guys piled on top of me.

The military news media never seemed to mention An Hoa. I overheard in one our sergeants complaining to Truman about our lack of coverage from Armed Forces Radio.

"A year ago it was Khe Sanh this and Khe Sanh that," he complained. "Last night we got hit by ten rockets!" he continued, holding up fingers. "Ten!" he repeated for emphasis. "It just ain't right. You never hear a word about An Hoa on the radio. We're goin' through the same shit they were!"

"Maybe we need to get shelled more," Truman joked.

"Yeah, man," the sergeant agreed, missing the irony and nodding his head.

After a while we realized that it was far safer to be in one of the fortified bunkers around our perimeter than sleeping in our canvas tents, and we volunteered for guard duty when we weren't in the bush. Over time the bunkers had gotten to be fairly comfortable. As long as we weren't ordered to do so, we didn't mind slowly working away building up our defenses and making things more comfortable for ourselves.

It must be a part of the American spirit to delight in improving things. One of the platoons had leveled the ground in our bunker and added a layer of sandbags to the wooden pallet that Truman had put down so that our feet would be dry. Another team had encircled the bunker with a second layer of protective sandbags. When we took over the post again, we found some wood and built a sleeping platform for the guys not on watch. There was a large piece of sheet metal lying at the end of the runway that we carried back to replace the tarps we had originally strung up to keep the rain out. When we had finished we had a cozy little home that was reasonably secure and to some extent even comfortable. Once night had fallen none of the lifers came out to hassle us.

The sergeant would muster us up shortly before dusk. Teams were usually kept together, usually three or four men. This time I was joined by Truman and Frenchy. We picked up a case of C rations, extra ammo, a starlight scope, an M-60 machine gun, a box of grenades, a box of pop-up flares, a radio, and half a dozen Claymore mines. Before it got dark we carefully placed the mines into position in a semicircle around our perimeter and covered them in grass to conceal them. We ran the detonation wires back to the electrical detonators in the bunker. These were set in a long row on a makeshift shelf near the tops of the sandbags. We were careful to place each detonator in the same left-to-right order of the charges so that if we were attacked we could easily select which mine we wanted to detonate. We opened up a box of new grenades, attached a few to our web gear, and placed the others next to the Claymore fuses. We set up our M-60 machine gun and placed the ammo box with additional rounds next to it. We loaded the M-79 grenade launcher and placed it on the sandbags next to the machine gun. We were as ready as we could be for whatever came.

The razor wire in front of our position was laid out in a zigzag pattern. There was a path through the wire in front of each post so that we could maintain the wire, but this path was covered by overlapping patterns of machine-gun fire. Anyone trying to get to the bunker using the path would have a tough time getting through our defenses. Charlie of course knew this. When they attacked a base such as ours they used specially trained sappers who would slide Bangalore torpedoes[1] under the wire. These massive charges would cut the wire and might even explode our Claymores.

We opened up a box of rations and sit around eating and talking until the sun went down completely and it was time to settle in and get serious. We made a radio call into the command center and let them know that we were on active alert. We had divided up the watches so that each of us got a few hours of sleep.

Two or three times a night we would see flashes on the mountains surrounding us as Charlie fired his rockets. We would follow the paths of the rockets across the sky, but it was difficult to pinpoint the exact launching sites. It seemed to me that after launching one or two they would move, but our artillery would open up anyway and we would see explosions and fires erupting on the hills surrounding us. Most of the enemy rockets hit the airfield, but some fell short and exploded in our compound.

When the warning sirens wailed, we awoke instantly, grabbed our weapons and stared out at the illuminated ground in front of our position, hoping that our bunker wouldn't be the one attacked, hoping that we wouldn't hear the dreaded shout, "gooks in the wire!"

Time passed; the man on watch would wake up his replacement and go to sleep himself. Night faded and almost imperceptibly; the darkness would lift like a gauzy curtain slowly being drawn aside. At first we would be able to see the coils of wire in front of us, a few minutes later the line of trenches leading to the other bunkers. The blackness of the night sky slowly changed to a deep violet-blue. The silvery light of the moon, if there was one, faded as dawn approached, but Venus, the morning star, glowed even brighter on the horizon. The period just before dawn was the "witching hour," when ghosts and memories seemed to hold the strongest sway over me.

Civilians, lulled by sex and worry-free dreams, would never know the dawn the way that we did. They would have been long abed, waking only reluctantly to the full light of day. We cursed sentry duty but at the same time were blessed to see the beauty of the early morning.

I had drawn the last watch. Truman and Bo were sleeping quietly, but Frenchy had been tossing and turning all night long. He eventually pushed aside his blanket, and came over to me. We both stood behind the machine gun looking out over the sandbagged trenches in front of us.

Frenchy was as tough and street-smart as they come, but he had a quick, nervous temperament and having rockets dropping around him for weeks on end hadn't helped his mental state one bit.

He looked out at the barbed wire surrounding us and began to talk softly, almost to himself.

"Ya know, I've already got two Purple Hearts; if I got hit once more I'd be out of here. All I need is a slight wound." He picked up the heavy stapling gun we used to fasten down a plastic tarp and holding it in his hand speculatively. "I don't want to end up going home in a body bag."

None of us did, but I wasn't willing to get involved in anything like what he seemed to be suggesting. I wasn't even sure if he was really serious or just playing with my mind. With Frenchy you never really knew for sure. Whatever he might have been planning it was something he'd have to do without my help.

When I didn't say anything, he took that as answer enough, and put the stapler down. His other two wounds had been blighters,[2] serious enough to get him taken out of combat for a while but not bad enough to injure him permanently.

"I don't like the odds… I feel that my luck is running out."

I tried to reassure him, "The odds don't change, you got the same chance of being hit each time you go out."

"Maybe so, but if they keep sending me out on mission after mission the odds turn

41. Hot Water

against me," Frenchy replied. "Take a deck of cards. What are the odds of you being able to pick a particular card out of the deck?"

"One out of fifty-two ... unless you cheat like someone I know."

We all knew how Frenchy hustled the new men in the company in poker, returning to the hooch with their money filling his pockets.

"With the numb-nuts around here, I don't need to cheat." Frenchy answered dismissively.

"Anyway," he continued, "If you keep putting that same card back in the desk again and drawing over and over again it won't be long until you pick it."

I thought about what he said. We had all heard about rumors about the ridiculously low survival times of infantrymen once in combat. For a rifleman, survival time was measured in seconds. No, there was certainly nothing irrational in Frenchy's fear. He really did stand a pretty good chance of going home in a body bag.[3]

I saw in his argument however, the rare chance to mess with his mind the way that he had so often messed with mine.

"Well, if you feel that way, you should volunteer for more patrols," I told him wickedly,

He looked up at me like I had gone completely insane.

"Look at it this way," I persisted. "Don't you agree that the odds of being wounded in a firefight are much higher than the odds of getting killed, and the odds of being lightly wounded are much higher than being seriously hurt?"

Frenchy thought for a moment and then nodded hesitantly, unsure of where my argument was heading.

"Like you said, you only need a scratch to get your third Purple Heart and get out of here. The deck is stacked in your favor. If I were you I'd take the bet,"

French shook his head and turned away dejectedly, "No thanks... I'll pass."

I guess that even with the odds in his favor the stakes were too high for even him.

Dawn started breaking and the sky flamed red, the "rosy-fingered dawn" beloved by Ulysses and his Greek warriors so many centuries ago. The Myrmidons were our companions in arms. I knew exactly how they must have felt seeing the sky lit like fire. We had both survived the dreaded night and were given the gift of another day of fierce brightness.

Bo was snoring under a thick cocoon of poncho liners. I kicked gently at his feet, the only part of his body exposed. The snoring stopped and he pulled back his blankets and raised his head. He sat up, rubbing the thick blue-black stubble covering his face. He nudged Truman, and they began gathering up their gear.

When the night watch ended, the last sentry on duty was assigned the job of starting up the officers' hot-water heaters. Today it was my turn. I grabbed some matches out of my pack and walked down the hill toward the showers.

Water for both the officers and the enlisted men came from two large aircraft fuel tanks the Seabees had suspended on a rack over the showers. Each tank had a hole cut in the top for the water heaters. These were long enclosed tubes of sheet metal about six feet long. A firebox was made by welding a cap at one end and placing a perforated steel cylinder a few inches off the bottom. The other end was left open to serve as a chimney.

White fuel tanks held water for our showers.

The heaters used kerosene as a fuel. This was stored in a small can with a tiny spigot soldered to its end. The can was held against the side of the chimney by a simple bracket. A small hole cut in the side of the chimney allowed the fuel valve to be inserted through the side of the tube. Opening the valve allowed a tiny trickle of kerosene to drip into the combustion chamber to keep the fire going.

To start the heaters you dropped a match down through the fuel hole. Sometimes it would take a few tries for the droplet of fuel to get going, but once fired up it would stay burning until the kerosene in the fuel tank was exhausted. There was enough fuel for a few hours, plenty of time for the officers to take their showers. The heaters were turned off at night because the glow from the tubes attracted mortar and rocket fire. Enlisted men lit the heaters themselves; the officers simply assigned the duty to the men coming off watch. Today was my turn to get their hot water ready.

It was still quite dark when I stumbled half-asleep down to the shower area. Leaving my flak jacket and helmet on the ground, I climbed the ladder to the roof of the shower. I lit a match and tossed it down into the tube like I had done dozens of times before. This time, however, the heater exploded with a tremendous roar followed by a blast of fire that burned my arm! I threw myself backward to get away from the flames and rolled off the roof. I picked myself up off the ground to see a plume of smoke and fire shooting twenty feet in the air out of the heater's chimney pipe. It looked like an upside-down jet engine had somehow attached itself to the shower.

A faulty fuel valve on the heater must have been leaking kerosene into the combustion chamber for hours. I climbed up the ladder and cautiously looked at the roof. Flames were now lapping at the kerosene container itself. I ducked back down fearing that the fuel can could explode any moment, but I quickly realized that I couldn't let the fire just burn itself out. The flames from the heater were lighting up the entire compound and would give the enemy a perfect target for their rockets.

Fully expecting the fuel can to explode in my face at any second, I climbed back onto the roof and kicked the metal can as hard as I could. It flew off the platform and rolled to the ground. Without fuel the flames that had been blasting out of the stovepipe immediately subsided. I put out the small fires still burning the plywood on the roof of the shed and, shaken to the core, climbed down.

It was now daylight and Marines were beginning to move around in the compound. Everyone was talking about the rocket attack. As I walked away I saw several Marines pointing to the burn marks on the shower as proof of another hit.

Captain Bilger was heading toward the shower with a towel around his waist. He was coming from the officers' quarters and hadn't seen the fire damage on the opposite side of the shed. He entered the shower building, dropped his towel and turned on the water.

As I turned the corner, I heard a gasping curse.

"God damn it! The fuckin' water's cold!"

42. Elephants on the LZ

A river watering the garden flowed from Eden.—Genesis 2:10

We had been dropped off at the base of a mountain in an isolated mountainous area north west of Da Nang. Only a few teams had gone into this isolated area before us, and they had named it the "Garden of Eden."

We had planned to be inserted directly into the valley itself, but the further we flew the more the weather deteriorated and as we passed over the valley we could see it was covered in clouds. The peaks of the mountains surrounding it poked up out like islands emerging from a gray sea. There was no way the pilot could descend into the valley itself. There was however, a small opening in the cloud cover at the base of one of the hills and the pilot was able to circle down and insert our team.

We pushed on, leaving a swamp and gradually climbing higher. The terrain became steeper as we ascended. Eventually we were reduced to pulling ourselves up from tree to tree. Anyone stopping to rest found himself slipping backward down the rocky slope.

As usual Bowman was running point when suddenly we heard his warning *click click*.

Everyone froze, but after a few minutes we saw him crawling back and whispering something to Lieutenant Lord, who then gave us the word to move forward. When I pulled myself up the last few feet I was surprised to see that a narrow dirt road had been cut into the side of the hillside. It was overgrown in places but overall in remarkably good condition. Normally we avoided trails, let alone a road, but in this case we had no alternative, the slope had become too steep for us to ascend without special climbing equipment.

The road wound its way gradually upward, the underbrush gradually thinning out and the trees growing larger. Bo again stopped in his tracks and turning around pointed to a space between the trees. He made a strange waving motion with his hands, spreading his fingers apart as though measuring something. The signal seemed to be a warning of some sort, but it certainly wasn't one that we normally used. Bo backed up and then made a wide circle taking him well over to the outside of the road. Truman followed carefully in his footsteps, peering strangely at a space between the trees. From a distance I couldn't see anything, but as I approached the spot in the trail where Truman turned off I saw the reason for the detour.

A huge spider web spanned the entire roadway, and in the exact center was the mother of all spiders, a shiny black monster with a body that seemed as large as a dinner plate. The tips of each of her feet were bright red, as if dipped in fresh blood. As I approached, she scuttled a few inches forward on the web, the strands trembling and bending under the weight of her body. As I drew even closer, I noticed small black dots clustered around the center orb. Baby spiders, hundreds of them, each a perfect replica of the other, were clustered around their mother.

Keeping the nightmarish black creature in constant view, I moved carefully around her, afraid that she would suddenly spring at me, but she remained still. Suddenly the web began to tremble and more baby spiders ran down the strands toward the center of the web. I had been so focused on the mother that I hadn't see the rest of her babies until I had nearly walked into them! I had never heard about a spider as big and patterned as distinctively as this one, and wondered if it was an unknown species. For a foolish moment I thought about capturing one of the babies and sending it to a museum for identification. If it was an unknown species such discovery might make me famous!

With a swift aggressive crawl, the mother spider suddenly moved closer and I changed my mind about doing anything. Messing around with this family could prove to be a lethal mistake. Backing away, I turned around and passed along the same signal I had received to Moose, the next person in line. Big, I indicated, spreading my hands, as big as a dinner plate. Moose looked at me and shook his head, not understanding the signal. I pointed to the web and repeated what I had done. He drew slowly closer and his eyes widened as they focused on the web.

We continued moving carefully down the road. It didn't look like it had been used recently, but the ground was hard and it was impossible to tell. We were nearly at the top of the mountain and as the ground leveled out we came to a sagging iron gate set into two stone posts. At the side of the road just beyond the gate was a granite block with an iron ring embedded in its side. One look and I knew exactly what it was. The iron ring would hold a horse steady while a lady stood on the granite block to mount or dismount from a horse or carriage. It was a relic from a very long-ago time.

There was some sort of structure in the distance. We cautiously moved forward and saw the foundation of what had at one time had been a large mansion built in European style. Tall columns that at one point must have held up an overhanging roof lay in pieces on the ground. We spread out to check out the area but there was no sign of anyone having been here recently.

I walked up the stone steps to where the front door would have been and turned to face the road. I could see for miles. Forested peaks poked up from the clouds still covering the valley below us and a cool breeze flowed up the slope toward us. It was a magical place.

It was now getting dark, and we set up our gear in a sunken courtyard for the night. I had first watch. The sky was clearing, and a full moon rose from behind the hills. The silvery moonlight shining down on the courtyard seemed to erase the ravages of time. The cool wind carried the sweet smell of some distant flowering plant. I leaned against a stone pillar and I thought about the men and women who had lived out their lives here.

I knew the French had colonized Vietnam, Laos and much of what was now Cambodia as far back as the late 1800s. The area was then known as French Indochina. Was the house abandoned after the French defeat at Dien Bien Phu, or did the owners leave earlier for some other reason? How did they ever manage to build such a house on top of a mountain in Vietnam and why did they abandon it? The moon gave light but no answers.

I sank deeper in my reverie.

It must have been quite a change from everything they must have known in their far away homeland. Did the house echo with laughter and glow with candlelight? Did the families hold parties in the sunken garden where I was now sitting with my weapons spread around me? I felt like an intruder, a barbarian crouching in a roman villa.

My thoughts were broken by the sharp crackle of the radio. "Foresight, Foresight, radio check." I keyed the handset and silence once again descended over the hilltop. A few hours later Moose came over to relieve me. He spread out his gear and leaning back against one of the stone pillars made himself comfortable.

"Wonder who built this place?" I whispered.

Moose glanced around dismissively, "Probably fools like us."

"What do you mean?"

"Why can't you see this was a military outpost? They had men like us and a gang of coolies dragging everything up this hill so that they could lord it over the poor bastards who lived here.

I shook my head, unwilling to let go of my new dream so quickly, and told him I thought we were sitting in a sunken garden of an old French estate.

"Sunken garden my ass! We're sitting on a damn parade ground."

As I looked around and saw things through his eyes, I realized that he was probably right.

"What are you going to do when you get out of here?" I asked him to change the subject as he leaned back and stared at the sky.

He thought for a moment, "I'd like to give something back to my people, maybe become a teacher."

"I think you'd make a great teacher," I told him encouragingly.

"You think so?" he asked, obviously pleased.

"I'm sure of it."

I looked back at the lieutenant, sitting alone on the crumbling steps of the house staring into the distance.

"Wonder what the lieutenant will do when he gets out?"

Moose laughed mirthlessly. "He told me he was going to join a group of mercenaries and go fight in Africa."

I turned to him in astonishment.

"I shit you not. That's what he told me," Moose insisted.

"Fight for who?"

"I guess anyone who will pay him the most." Moose saw the look on my face and continued, "Don't you go blaming him now ... it's not his fault. He jes' ain't grown-up yet."

I wasn't blaming the lieutenant. It was such testosterone-fueled daydreams that had led me to enlist in the Marine Corps in the first place, but Lord's plans for his future worried me.

I had my share of high school military fantasies when I had first arrived in Nam, but after months in the bush they had been swept away by gritty reality of combat. The last thing I needed was to be led by an inexperienced officer whose head was still filled with absurd daydreams of military adventure.

We packed up and moved out at dawn. The road ended at the old mansion, but a path snaked down the valley side of the mountain and we followed it. The trail was less than a couple of feet wide and cut deeply into the north side of the mountain. When it was cut or by whom we didn't know. The ground under our feet was rocky and there was no way of knowing when it had last been used.

At first the path descended gradually, winding down in long loops from the summit. The farther it went, however, the steeper and narrower the trail became. Soon it was nothing more than a slit cut into the side of the cliff. We faced the wall, and shuffled slowly along, carefully moving our feet sideways one careful step at a time.

I heard the other men moving along in front of me, but the only thing I saw was the rock wall a few inches in front of my nose. I searched desperately for any handhold, a little root, a small projection, anything I was able grab on to, but these were few and far between. My web gear prevented me from pressing tightly against the side of the cliff and my pack felt like it was trying to pull me over backward. I was carrying the bulky Unit 1 medical pack clipped to my chest and this prevented me from pressing closely against the rock wall. Whomever had built this trail had certainly not designed it for bulky Americans in full combat gear. My legs started shaking with fear and exhaustion. I looked down at the void beneath my feet and nearly bumped into Truman, who had suddenly stopped moving.

Directly in front of him a small waterfall was falling down the cliff face from far above. The falling water had cut away a three-foot section of the trail and the rocks next to the opening were coated with algae. I looked down at the sheer hundred-foot drop beneath my feet and knew that I couldn't go any farther. I could just picture myself falling backward onto the boulders below. I thought that Truman had stopped because he was also paralyzed with fear.

"Could you get my canteen?" he suddenly asked me. "I can't reach it." He was holding on with one hand and pawing at a canteen attached to his pack with the other.

I couldn't believe it!

"You crazy motherfucker, are you completely nuts? We're hanging off a cliff and you want your canteen?"

"I'm thirsty." he replied petulantly.

"Why don't you just take a piss up here while you're at it," I responded angrily.

"Already did," he replied with a laugh, giving up the canteen idea and hopping nimbly over the gap.

"I swear to God, Truman, you crazy bastard, I'm gonna kick your ass!" Sudden anger replaced my fear and I jumped across the opening and scuttled after him. He laughed and easily stayed ahead of me, moving his hands and legs sideways with the agility of a rock ape, completely ignoring the sheer drop beneath his feet.

The trail finally leveled out and I heard sounds of relief ahead of us. Looking to my side, I saw Bo climbing off the trail onto a rocky ledge that overlooked the valley. Truman climbed up beside him, reached out his hand to me and pulled me up onto the ledge. My anger instantly evaporated.

I shook my head at him. "You crazy bastard!"

He smiled happily.

From our vantage point we could see for miles across a lush valley. A waterfall spilled down hundreds of feet into a blue river that ran down the valley between banks of white sand. Huge trees stood as protective sentinels around a field of tall grass. The air was soft and warm and carried the smell of fast-flowing river water up toward us. For the moment the war seemed very far away.

I could have stayed there for hours. We set up our normal defensive perimeter each man facing out. My shirt was soaked in sweat and my legs still felt shaky from the climb along the cliff. I was sitting down leaning against my pack, my feet stretched out in front of me. I had just taken a big drink of water from my canteen when I saw a slight movement in the grass a few yards in front of me and the head of a large brown snake rose up, the black slits of his eyes looking directly into mine. I froze.

During training we had been told that there were a hundred types of snakes in Vietnam. Our instructor had joked that ninety-nine were poisonous and the last one would squeeze you to death. We all laughed at the time, but I didn't laugh at the snake in front of me. He was nearly five feet long and had the characteristic blunt snout of a pit viper, a species known for aggressiveness.

I thought for a moment about my rifle, but I didn't want to jeopardize the mission by using it. I slowly freed my arms from my pack straps and eased my knife from its sheath. The snake was still about ten feet away from me, but in my sitting position its head was level with my own. I could almost feel his fangs sinking into my face. My feet were still extended out in front of me and I slowly pulled them back and sat up straighter. The snake suddenly dropped his head and slithered through he space between Truman and myself flowing over the ground so fast that he reached the other side of our defensive circle in seconds.

The reptile stopped a few feet from the lieutenant's back and again his head rose up. Lord was facing outward, looking intently through his binoculars at the valley below us.

I moved slowly toward it, my knife in my hand. I now wished that I had shot the damn thing, mission be damned. A knife wasn't the best thing to use, even a long stick would have been better, but my knife was all I had. The snake's red tongue flicked rapidly in and out as it tasted the air. Lord moved slightly and behind him the viper's head rose up as he got ready to strike.

The reptile suddenly sensed my approach and his head swiveled around toward me. I got ready to slash, but before I could move the head dropped down, and the snake wiggled over the lieutenant's pack and disappeared into the grass next to him. Lord hadn't noticed a thing and continued looking through his binoculars.

My mind flashed back to seventh grade and my favorite teacher, Mr. Fishelli. With the unconscious cruelty of children, we nicknamed him "Fish." When I knew him, he was a tall, thin, very quiet man with a dark, heavily lined face. He had three children and worked on the weekends at a clothing store to supplement his meager pay as a junior high school teacher. One day someone brought in a pet garter snake in an aquarium and we were all invited to hold it. Fish recoiled as the snake was offered to him to hold.

Almost in a trance, he told us that as a young Marine during World War II he had fought his way across the Solomon Islands. One night he woke up to find something heavy lying on his chest. When he opened his eyes, he saw the head of a huge green snake hanging from the mosquito netting a foot or so above his head, the rest of the snake's body curled on top of him. Fish paused, his mind frozen in time.

"What did you do?" one of my classmates asked impatiently.

"Well, I didn't do anything, we stared at each other for a few seconds and then it slithered away."

"Was it poisonous?" one of the girls asked breathlessly.

"Most of the snakes on the islands were."

"Why didn't you kill it?"

"I was afraid to move."

With that admission the boys started laughing.

Fish looked around the room and in a quiet, sad voice told them, "I just hope to God that none of you has to go through what we did."

Now here we were, Fish's seventh-grade jesters, all together in Nam, and things didn't seem that funny anymore.

We packed up and moved toward the floor of the valley, hearing the roar of rapids as we got closer to a river. In a few minutes we came to a fast-flowing river a few hundred feet wide. A quick check up and downstream eliminated any hope that the rapids would be any less in either direction. If anything, they looked even more dangerous.

"We'll have to try swimming across," Lord whispered as we reached the bank.

We started stripping off our gear, but Moose hesitated. "I don't think I can make it, sir. I can't swim."

"You can't swim?" the lieutenant asked incredulously. One of Recon's requirements was that everyone pass a rigid swimming test.

"In my town…" Moose looked down at his feet and hesitated as he paused for the right word. "Negroes weren't allowed in the pools," he finally blurted out.

"But you must have passed the swimming test to get into Recon," the lieutenant persisted.

"Never even took it. I guess they needed a radiomen and they transferred me in."

"We've got rope." I suggested, "I could swim across and secure a line to the far side."

The lieutenant looked at me skeptically. I hadn't volunteered for a thing since he first took over the platoon.

"OK, we'll cover you from this side," he finally replied, nodding in agreement. I a

42. Elephants on the LZ

piece of parachute cord and making a sling tied my rifle across my back. I wasn't going anywhere without it. Ma handed me the climbing rope he was carrying and tied one end to a tree on the riverbank. I carried the other end well upstream to adjust for the current, put my feet in icy water and began wading out.

The current was much stronger than I had anticipated. I was in water only up to my waist but barely able to hold my footing. I stumbled a few feet farther but then suddenly lost my balance and in seconds was swept downstream. I swam hard for the opposite bank, but I was held back by the rope dragging in the water behind me.

There was a large boulder in the middle of the river and with a desperate kick I managed to pull myself into the eddy behind it. I was safe for the moment. I hung on to a shrub growing out of the side of the rock and tried to get my breath back. The icy water was rapidly sapping my strength. I had hit my bad knee against a submerged rock and it was aching.

I found myself alone, and once again that strange temptation to just leave everything behind took hold of me. All I needed to do was let go of the rope and I could just drift away from the war, away from the Marine Corps. I looked back to the shore and saw my buddies lined up along the riverbank. The rest of the guys were depending on me, I might drift away, but what could I drift toward?

I took the end of the rope and passed it over the boulder and around the shrub I was holding on to. I pulled the line tight so that it was out of the water completely and wouldn't hold me back. I took the other end and set out once again for the far shore. I felt the current take me once again as I left the eddy, but I swam hard and finally pulled myself up onto a small sandy beach on the other side of the river. I crawled up the bank waited for a few minutes to get my breath back and to make sure that there was no enemy movement around me. I tied the line tightly to a tree on the other end pulled it tight. Using the rope for support the other men pulled themselves across one man at a time. Moose was the first one over.

We put our gear back on, regrouped and set out once again to explore the valley. With the river running through it, and the high hills on all sides it was a beautiful spot. We had traveled only a short distance however before Bo signaled us to stop. He motioned the Lieutenant Lord forward and they both disappeared into the tall grass. They reappeared after a few minutes and signaled us to move up. Ahead of us I saw a downed helicopter.

As we got closer it was obvious that the aircraft wasn't one of ours. It was a single-rotor helicopter similar in style to our old Sikorskys, but it had the bull's-eye insignia of the French Air Force painted on its side. The aircraft was riddled with machine-gun holes, and it looked like a fierce fire had swept through it. It was now nothing more than a burnt-out shell. Over the years the airframe had sunk deep into the earth. It was obvious that the chopper had been sitting there in the mud for a very long time. There were no armaments left, and to my great relief, no bodies either.

Looking over the old wreck, I couldn't help but think back over the decades that the Vietnamese had been fighting, first the Japanese, then the French and now the Americans. After thirteen months those of us still alive would go back to our former livers, but the enemy soldiers we were fighting would remain. Charlie was already home.

We moved away from the wreck and continued down the valley. We crossed several streams that flowed down to the river from the surrounding hills. The valley floor was covered in grass rather than the thick underbrush we typically had to force our way through. The area reminded me of a park and I was just starting to relax when I heard the soft *click click* of Bo's warning signal.

There was a jumble of rocks ahead of us and we slowly took cover as the lieutenant peered through his binoculars. After a few minutes he gave us the signal to move closer. We had stumbled across some kind of small stone building which looked liked a temple. Four upright columns that must have once supported the roof stood at each corner and the floor was paved with smooth oval stones that looked like they had been polished by the river. A large rectangular block of stone formed a primitive altar with strange swirling patterns carved into its base. As I examined them, they changed before my eyes like an optical illusion, one moment appearing as a flower, the next the image of a daemon. I tore my gaze away from the hypnotic effect.[1]

Truman, crouching down behind one of the front pillars, suddenly got up and walked forward. He had noticed the sunlight glancing off what looked like a ceramic plate. Brushing the grass aside, he found another darker one a few feet away from it. He called the lieutenant over and they both started digging with their knives, trying to expose more of whatever it was.

"Watch out for a booby trap," I whispered.

Truman immediately backed away from the hole, but Lord ignored me and continued digging. I crouched down behind one of the stone pillars. If someone was going to get blown up, it wasn't going to be me.

After a few minutes the lieutenant had uncovered the top of a large urn. It looked like it had been buried in the ground for a very long time. Roots had grown to encircle both the urn itself and the top cap that Truman had spotted. The lieutenant took his knife and slowly pried the cover loose as I braced myself for the explosion that never came. Lord reached inside and came up with a fistful of rice. The entire urn was filled with it. It was impossible to tell how long the rice had been buried or by whom. The rice grains could have been preserved in their stone container for decades, perhaps centuries.

The lieutenant thought the rice was left by the Vietcong and radioed in that information to headquarters. I thought it just as likely that it had been a food cache buried by Montagnards living in the valley or perhaps an offering to whatever obscure god lived in the stone temple, but who could tell?

Lord moved over to the next urn and again began digging with his knife.

I moved back behind my stone column and I noticed that the other men were also all behind cover.

The lid on the second urn was darker in color and looked like it had been cut from some kind of soft stone. Lord pried off the cover and peered inside.

"There's something inside; it's not rice… I can't see what it is … something," he whispered in an excited voice.

He reached in and managed to grab hold of the end of a piece of coarsely woven brown cloth. It unraveled and disintegrated in his hands as he pulled on it. Suddenly there was a loud thump as something fell back inside. I instinctively crouched down waiting for an explosion, but instead I heard a soft tinkling sound as the lieutenant continued to pull on the cloth and whatever was inside continued to fall out.

42. Elephants on the LZ

"I think it's a bandolier of ammo," Lord whispered in excitement as he squeezed the small piece of cloth he was holding through the opening. The old cloth started ripping again, but Lord quickly reached inside with his other hand and managed to grab it. He placed the small packet that he had retrieved on his leg and began to unroll the protective cloth only to pull back with a gasp as a dozen small bones fell to the ground.

I had to hand it to him, he didn't show any emotion. He simply shoved the burial shroud, bones and all, back into the pot and quickly dropped the cover back on. He stood up and wiped his hands on the ground.

"Move out," he ordered hoarsely.

We left the cover off the first urn in case it really was an enemy food cache. The first rain would destroy the rice inside.

Darkness was falling, and we needed to find a good place to hide so that we could clean our weapons and repack our soaked gear. My wounded knee was swollen from where I had smashed it swimming to the rock and. I was worried that if it got worse I wouldn't be able to keep up. We found a good spot in a grove of heavy bamboo a few hundred yards away from the downed French aircraft and buried ourselves deep within it. Some of the bamboo trees were six inches in diameter. It was difficult to move through them and even harder to find a place to lie down, but once inside the grove we were concealed and no one could sneak up on us without our hearing them. We were also close to our planned extraction point. There was a good sized clearing by the river where our choppers would have plenty of room to land. Moose called in our position and Lord asked to be extracted the following morning.

The day dawned bright and clear. Moose made contact with the pilot and we got ready to move. We heard the sound of a gunship making a pass across the valley and the CH-46 hovering overhead when Moose called the lieutenant over.

"They can't land," I overhead him say. "The pilots say we've got a small herd of elephants and some other animals on the LZ!"

Bo and I looked at one another, I knew from our map that the Garden of Eden was only a few miles from an area known as Elephant Valley, but I had never really thought about the reason for the name and had never heard of another patrol reporting that they had seen elephants.

Lord took the mike, spoke for a few minutes, and then came back to us.

"Keep your heads down; they're going to fire a few M79 rounds from the chopper to scare them off."

The CH-46 came in low and we heard the explosions as M79 rounds hit the far side of the valley. The explosions stopped, a few seconds passed, and then we heard the noise of something huge crashing through the jungle towards us! We didn't have time to do anything more than crouch down as the bamboo trees shattered around us as a small herd of elephants stampeded past our position! It was just sheer luck that we hadn't been trampled.

We grabbed our gear and got shakily to our feet. Concealed in the thick underbrush we hadn't seen the elephants charge by us, but there was no mistaking the broad trail they made as they stampeded through the jungle, a bulldozer couldn't have done a better job. We followed the wide trail they had made through the jungle to our extraction point.

It was obvious to me that someone on the helicopter had screwed up. Instead of the

M79 round landing between us and the elephants and scaring them away, it had exploded on the far side of the LZ, causing them to run toward instead of away from us.

We made our way to where the helicopter was now touching down. On the middle of the ramp was the Major Simbul with a movie camera in his hand, filming us as we ran inside. Truman had to push him aside to get in and take a defensive position in the window. Next to the major was the top sergeant, holding an M79 grenade launcher. I had never seen either one of these men on a patrol before.

Having the major and the top sergeant on board was strange enough, but to have the major taking motion pictures of us running into the chopper really blew my mind. I knew that we hadn't been in contact with the enemy and that the extraction was probably reasonably safe, but in Nam you could never tell what was going to happen. His place was back at the command center doing whatever the officers did back there, not taking motion pictures like some frigging war photographer.

Usually we would have taken off right away, but the sergeant said something to the crew chief, unsheathed his Ka-Bar knife and jumping off the ramp ran to the far side of the field.

"Now what?" I thought to myself as we pointed our rifles out the windows and waited impatiently to take off. "Let's get the hell out of here."

The sergeant returned dragging the severed head of a huge buck deer behind him by the antlers. With a grunt and a giant heave he threw the bloody thing on the ramp. He clambered aboard after it and the pilot immediately applied full power. The pilot and crew must have been just as anxious to get off the ground as we were. As we pulled away, the sergeant looked around proudly, obviously expecting us to congratulate him on his trophy. He seemed faintly discouraged to see everyone on the team was still nervously staring out of the ports and covering the LZ with their weapons.

As soon as I saw the first sergeant coming back with the deer head I realized what he had done. Instead of aiming to frighten the elephants away from the LZ, he had shot at the deer in order to get a trophy buck. For the rest of the trip back we had to watch the deer head roll around the back of the aircraft, coating the ramp with its blood.

---

43. Foresight…Foresight…

I will protect our men in Vietnam—unless Congress hamstrings me.—Richard Nixon, 1969

A few weeks earlier one of our teams had found an NVA base camp and captured a high-ranking North Vietnamese officer who provided particularly valuable information about troop strengths and enemy plans for the area. Our major got a lot of credit from his superiors for this intelligence, and we weren't surprised to learn that our next patrol would be a prisoner snatch. We were well aware how dangerous these missions were. If the enemy became aware of our presence, we could quickly find ourselves in a really bad situation. A prisoner snatch was all "up close and personal." The only thing we had going for us was the element of surprise.

Our methods were brutally simple. The trap would be sprung from each end. Two men would close off the top of the trail, two the bottom. Facing outward, they would close off the ambush area. Simultaneously the "snatch" group would subdue the prisoner, forcing him to the ground and binding him.

We would be running the prisoner snatch with a few men from the Third Platoon. Braun, one of their best scouts, would be joining us as well as their Navy Hospital corpsman. Sergeant Lear, the team leader from the Third Platoon, would be running the assistant patrol leader's position under Lieutenant Lord's command.

We had nearly a week to prepare and Lord had us spend the time training. We went down to the firing range to zero in our weapons and practice with some new ones.

Doc carried an air gun that fired a tranquilizing dart that he confidently told us would immobilize a horse. The sergeant carried a match-grade .22-caliber pistol with a silencer screwed on to the barrel, and Braun packed a pump-action shotgun loaded with fléchette rounds.

Lieutenant Lord brought along a crossbow of all things! It was an evil-looking weapon, the short steel bow mounted into a fiberglass stock. He inserted a crank into the stock of the crossbow and turned the handle that pulled back the wire string and flexed the metal bow. The crossbow had a mechanical sight and Lord trained the weapon on the center of an isolated outhouse about two hundred feet away. With a soft *twang* the arrow discharged, moving so fast that I couldn't even see it fly. There was a tearing sound as the bolt hit the thin plywood near the top of the shithouse door and tore through the other side.

Sergeant Lear asked to give it a try, but as Lord handed it over the outhouse door slowly opened and one of the drivers from the motor pool stuck his head out and peered furtively around. Seeing a group of men staring at him a few hundred yards away, he pulled up his pants and scurried away before anyone could stop him.

As we drew closer the sweet scent of marijuana hit us and we understood the reason for his sudden departure. Remote outhouses were often used by "heads" as safe places to get high. With the latch locked from the inside no one was able to get in, and they could always drop a roach into the shit-can if someone approached. The man probably never even noticed the arrow tearing through the wood a few inches above his head!

Watching the rapidly retreating figure, the sergeant started laughing. "Luckiest man in the outfit."

"I might have killed him," Lord replied, his voice shaking.

The next day we regrouped at a sandy field just outside the LZ. Sergeant Lear told us he had been a Marine unarmed combat instructor before coming over to Recon. He said that the lieutenant had asked him to teach us some hand-to-hand combat techniques that might prove useful to us on our next mission.

Lear was a lean sandy-haired man who wore glasses. He looked fit enough, but no one looking at him would have thought he was a tough-guy.

He told us to form a circle around him and asked for a volunteer.

"I'm your man," Truman responded smiling, getting to his feet.

"OK, slap your leg if you need me to release you," Lear told him.

Truman rolled his eyes at us and smirked.

With a lightning-quick motion Lear suddenly stepped behind Truman and with one hand around his neck locked his other arm behind his head and squeezed. Truman's body went suddenly went rigid and he desperately slapped his hand against his leg. Lear immediately released him and Truman fell to his knees. Lear ignored him and focused his attention on us.

"That hold is called the naked strangle. It's not really a stranglehold, the arm cuts off the blood supply to the brain by applying pressure to the carotid artery. If it is done correctly you can incapacitate an opponent in seconds without him being able to make a sound."

He turned to Truman and helped him up. "Could you call out?" he asked him.

"Call out … shit no. I thought I was going to die!" Truman answered hoarsely, rubbing his throat.

"Yeah, that hold can be lethal. Don't go showing off this stuff to your girlfriend," Lear warned. "One Marine accidentally snapped his woman's neck."

"I've got better things to practice with my gal," Truman joked, breaking the somber mood.

"Show the men something they can use to restrain the prisoner once we get him on the ground," Lord requested.

Moose was the biggest guy in our unit. Lear had him lie down on the ground and positioned Bo, the smallest guy in our unit above him, facing the opposite direction. He placed Bo's arm under Moose's neck and showed him how to lock it against his leg, explaining how the other arm could apply pressure. Despite his strength, Moose was unable to break free and grimaced in pain as Bo put force on his elbow joint. Moose tapped the ground and Bo instantly released him.

"That's enough for now," Lear advised. "You would have broken his arm if you continued."

We paired off and practiced the hold he had just shown us.

He asked if there were any more questions and Frenchy asked him about knife fighting. Lear took a dead stick from the ground and broke it in two, handing one to Frenchy and keeping the other.

"Attack me," he ordered.

Frenchy cautiously circled him and with a sudden move slashed at Lear's stomach. With a seemingly casual motion Lear flicked his stick at Frenchy's wrist and blocked the blow. Frenchy winced and backed away but suddenly flicked the knife to his other hand and again jabbed it at Lear's stomach. Once again, the thrust was blocked as Lear sliced upward at the extended arm. Lear put up his hand and called an end to the exercise.

"If these were real knives, you would have had both arms disabled and I could have killed you whenever I wanted, but better yet, don't even get into a knife fight in the first place." He spun Frenchy around and pulling back his head stabbed him low in the back with his stick. "Go in from behind, snap his head back and stab him in the kidneys. He'll be dead in seconds."

"I could have thrown the knife and gotten you," Frenchy objected, ruefully rubbing his sore wrist.

"I wouldn't try it in a real knife fight. You don't want to be left holding nothing but your dick in your hand," Lear advised.

Despite Lear's advice, we spent most of our lunch break throwing knives, bayonets, and tomahawks into a dead tree. There was something satisfying about seeing the heavy blades sinking into the wood. Lear was good with a throwing knife, but Frenchy was even better. The little Cajun was able to hit a six-inch target over thirty feet away nearly every time, the flashing blade spinning twice in the air before sinking deep into the tree.

The next day Lord had us practice the ambush over and over again. Truman was assigned to be point man. He would protect the top of the trail with Frenchy. I would cover the other end and Moose would watch my back. The lieutenant, Ma and Braun were assigned to be the grab team, the men responsible for subduing the prisoner. Their responsibility was to take down the prisoner without a sound, bind his mouth with duct tape and either tie his hands or put him in handcuffs. Doc would then come in and give him an injection which he assured us, would "put out an elephant."

We set up an ambush-training area just outside of our compound. Truman and I stretched a knotted cord between us and passed it to the main group clustered at the center of the grab zone. A double tug on the line alerted the team that a single enemy soldier was moving down the trail and the ambush was on. A single tug meant that we should hold off because there was more than one.

After doing mock drills Lieutenant Lord ordered Truman to play the role of Charlie "diddy-boppin'" down the trail. As he came into view I gave a quick double jerk on the line and Moose and I stepped onto the trail, blocking it from both directions. I heard nothing more than a slight scuffle as Truman was tackled and bound. In a few seconds the grab team had him cuffed and gagged with duct tape. The men strapped him into an extraction harness, moved quickly off the trail, and carried him away. Lord was pleased with the way the practice had gone. He wanted us to do it again and ordered me to take Truman's place. The other men gathered together with Lord for some last-minute instructions and then disappeared down the trail.

I walked down the path for a few hundred yards and then started back, passing the area where we had done the first snatch. Nothing happened, and I didn't see or hear anything. I continued walking and was just turning around to go back when the lieutenant blindsided me in a low tackle. A second later I felt a savage impact as Ma hit me high from the other side. I felt a sharp shooting pain in my ankle as it twisted under me from the double impact.

Before I could do more than groan, duct tape was wrapped around my mouth, and my hands bound behind me. I found myself being dragged along the ground. When they finally released my arms, I tore the tape from my mouth and grabbed Ma by the collar.

"What the hell were you trying to do, break my leg?" I asked, furiously shaking him.

"The lieutenant told us to hit harder," he answered when I let him go.

"Hit 'em hard … hit 'em hard," I mimicked cruelly. "You think we're in a fuckin' football game?"

Lord had turned away from us, but I knew that he was close enough to have heard what I said. I used my rifle to help me get to my feet, but it was obvious that my ankle was badly sprained. Doc took out his Unit 1 and wrapped my ankle in a compression bandage and told me to keep it iced up and elevated until the swelling went down.

Ghant had just returned from R & R and was putting away his things when I finally limped into our hooch. When I explained, he laughed and accused me of faking a injury to get out of the patrol, but the joke was on him because he ended up taking my place on the mission.

The day of the prisoner snatch arrived, but I was still unable to put full weight on my ankle. I watched the other men get ready and limped down to the LZ with the rest of the men. It felt strange to see them board the chopper and take off. In one way I was relieved not to go, but on the other hand, I didn't want to see them leave without me.

I don't know whether it was the pain in my ankle or the concern about the team that kept me awake that evening. I gave it up trying to sleep and hobbled down to the communications bunker. The COM shack was inside a squat sandbagged bunker in the middle of the compound. The Seabees had constructed the basic building when we first took over the area. They dug a square hole about forty feet wide and built walls and a roof out of massive timbers. Heavy steel plates were bolted to the roof. As soon as the wooden shell was completed, the first sergeant had work parties adding layer after layer of sandbags to the side and top of the building. I can see him now, stripped to the waist, a colossus of a man, his face bright red in the sun, standing on the top of the bunker yelling down to us at the top of his lungs, "More bags! More bags!"

This type of brute force work was right up his alley; it was the one place where he could show off his strength. I suspected that he was drunk, but it was difficult to tell because he acted like this all the time. As fast as we threw the sandbags up to the roof, he would throw them down along the sides so they formed an irregular mound three or four feet deep. It would have been easier for us to place them ourselves, but that wasn't what he wanted. After working us like dogs for nearly a week he had finally built up an ugly mound of sandbags. When monsoon rains began the entire structure began to sag and then collapsed completely. It would have been funny if we hadn't spent so much time and sweat on it.

Major Simbul must have learned his lesson, because he brought in a truckload of Vietnamese to clean up the mess. They completely removed the old and started over from scratch. They carefully molded each bag so that it interlocked with its neighbors and laid strings of barbed wire between each section to anchor everything tightly in place. In less than a week the bunker was completed. They did a beautiful job. The sandbagged walls leaned gracefully inward and supported those protecting the roof. When they finished it was the most heavily fortified building in the compound.

I remarked to Moose what a nice job the gooks had done compared to our crude efforts.

"What do you expect? They've got a lot of experience; they've been building bunkers for thirty years," he replied sourly.

The com bunker might not have been officially off-limits to enlisted men, but during the day none of us would go near it. It was the realm of officers and lifers. At night, however, the officers wouldn't be around, and I was hoping to find out about my team.

I entered the bunker through a narrow tunnel that led down to a large dimly lit room. The first thing I noticed was a large map of the An Hoa area that was taped to a moveable blackboard in the center of the room. Brightly colored pins and labels showed

43. Foresight…Foresight…

the location of the three teams, currently in the field. Team Foresight was indicated by a red sticker and I could see they were now on a hilltop overlooking Happy Valley.

The radio operator sat in a rather plush leather chair in the corner of the room. In front of him, a long table held a rack of communications equipment. His chair was on wheels and he could easily roll from one system to another. The room was lit only by the dials of the radio sets and a small lamp.

A young corporal was on duty. He was wearing a headset and sat hunched over his radio equipment, adjusting the dials and making notations in a large black notebook. I recognized his face but despite our being in the same unit had never spoken to him. The technicians, like riggers, motor-pool mechanics, and other support personnel, tended to stick to themselves and rarely mingled with bush Marines. Working closely with the officers and usually being given an NCO's rank upon completion of their training, they were exempt from much of the harassment and work parties that constantly made our lives miserable. Combat Marines held all these techs and office jocks in mild contempt. God knows what they thought of us. The corporal looked up at me questioningly as I entered.

"Any word from team Foresight?" I asked.

He clanked at the clock mounted over his desk. "They're due for another radio contact in about twenty minutes."

"Mind if I stick around?" I asked.

He shook his head, "Make yourself at home, I'll put it on speaker."

He turned a switch and static emerged from a speaker on the wall. He consulted a notebook and adjusted the dials on his equipment. I knew that every hour the base called out on an agreed frequency to get a SITREP from teams in the field.

"Spillway, Spillway, Spillway… SITREP."

Three distinct clicks came from the speaker. I pictured the man on watch carefully pressing the "Send" button three times and then peering once more into the darkness of the jungle.

"Affirmative, Spillway," the corporal confirmed the contact.

He looked at his book and adjusted the dials on his radio to a new frequency.

"Deerfly, Deerfly, Deerfly… SITREP," he radioed but only static came from the speaker. After trying three more times without receiving anything back, the corporal made a notation in his book and switched frequencies.

I looked at him questioningly. "They're not responding?"

"Happens all the time. They're probably out of radio range. I'll try them again in another hour."

I thought about the teams that had simply disappeared into the jungle never to be heard from again. How many times had the radio operators tried to reach them before giving up?

He glanced at the clock again and motioned me to come closer.

"Foresight … Foresight … Foresight … SITREP."

Two clicks came from the speaker.

"Affirmative, Foresight," the corporal answered.

I could easily imagine the team huddled together on some steep mountainside, the man on watch trying to stay dry, trying to stay awake, holding the receiver to his ear and listening to the radio transmission that was their only link to home.

Running through the radio frequencies, the corporal picked up other traffic, aircraft on bombing runs, grunts calling in artillery, Vietnamese voices.

"Lots of time we'll pick up a firefight," the corporal offered. "Want me to see if I can find one?" he asked eagerly.

The thought of eavesdropping while people on the ground were fighting and perhaps dying turned me off, but I knew he was only trying to be friendly and declined.

I woke at dawn and made my way over to the com bunker again. The corporal was still on duty and excitedly motioned me over.

"Foresight just called in and they've got a prisoner!"

He ran out of the bunker to alert the major. The news spread fast and there was quite a large group waiting at the LZ for the team to arrive. The major and a small group of officers drove up in a Jeep as two choppers appeared on the horizon. The first came in with Lieutenant Lord and most of the team hanging from the cargo net. It hovered over the LZ and gradually the net and men were lowered to the ground. The major ran over to the lieutenant, congratulating him on the successful mission.

The second chopper came in fast and low. As it got closer I saw Ma hanging from one rope and a figure in a brown NVA uniform hanging from the other, but something was wrong. Their extraction ropes were twisted together and I could see two men locked in a deadly struggle hundreds of feet in the air. The chopper came in in a screaming rush, and both of the men hit the ground at nearly the same time, Ma quickly detaching himself from his rope, the prisoner crumpled unconscious beside him.

The lieutenant ran over to the prisoner, turned him over and gasped. The soldier's face was a mess of raw flesh, his eyes were swollen shut, his teeth were broken, and his mouth and nose were streaming with blood. For a moment I thought that he had been shot in the head.

"For Christ sakes, Ma, I told you to soften him up, not beat him to death!" Lord shouted, staring down at the inert figure by his feet.

"He got one of his hands free and every time he swung into me he'd try to grab my grenades!" Ma responded angrily. "What the hell did you want me to do, let him blow me up?"

Ma's violent outburst startled the lieutenant. He was always the most self-controlled member of our team, and I had never even heard him raise his voice before.

"But the prisoner," the lieutenant muttered.

"Fuck the prisoner! He's still alive, ain't he?" Ma responded, grabbing his rifle and walking angrily away.

Lord re-taped the prisoner's hands and turned him over to Captain Bilger, our intelligence officer. He was put on a stretcher, carried over to a waiting helicopter, and in a few moments was gone from our sight. Bilger stood there looking at the departing chopper and I walked over to him.

"What will happen to him, sir?"

He turned to me in surprise. I had never spoken to him directly before. "Why, he'll be turned over to the RVN for interrogation of course," he replied taking a cigarette from his mouth and turning away from me.

I had hear rumors of RVN "interrogations" and their notorious prisons where captured enemy troops were locked up in cages so small that they could neither stand up nor lie down. After a few weeks they lost their ability to walk and were forced to scuttle across the ground like obscene crabs.

"But he's seriously injured," I protested. "He needs to go to the hospital."

"Not your problem, Marine," Bilger replied in an annoyed voice.

When I got back to our hooch, Ma was sitting on the steps with his hands over his face. His utilities splattered with blood, his knuckles swollen and raw.

"Better get those hands looked at."

He looked up at me and I could tell he had been crying. "What would you have done?" he asked miserably.

"The same as you, bro," I answered honestly.

"God damn us both … the same as you."

---

44. Everything Is Samee-Same

*God grant me the serenity
to accept the things I cannot change;
courage to change the things I can;
and wisdom to know the difference.*
—Serenity Prayer

When I first arrived in Nam I didn't know half of what was going on, but after a few months I began to wise up and begin to notice what was going on all around me.

After returning from patrol the potheads would sneak off to various secluded spots to smoke a joint or two. The outer trenches were a favorite location. In the maze of bunkers a small bag of grass could easily be hidden under a sandbag, and it was easy to get rid of a roach if an officer or lifer approached. Another favorite location was the observation tower. No one could climb up without being seen, and there was a wonderful view from the top. Vietnamese grass was potent stuff. After a "J" or two, the heads would wander back into the compound with bloodshot eyes and stupid smiles on their faces.

Sergeant Tom once told me that he once spotted a flashing light coming from inside and gone over to investigate. When he opened the door, he surprised half a dozen men completely wasted. They had attached an emergency strobe light to the ceiling and were sitting back contentedly watching their own light show, completely oblivious to the fact that the container was being used to store ammunition.

"If they hadn't been so stoned, they would have seen that they were sitting in enough ordnance to blow them to kingdom come!" Tom had told me, laughing.

The potheads were a genial, laid-back lot compared with the boozers, some of whom turned nasty when drunk. Alcohol probably led to more problems and non-combat injuries than grass ever did. Hard liquor was available to the officers at their club, but strictly forbidden to enlisted men. This was a hollow restriction however because you could always get a bottle of booze from the gook vendors if you wanted it badly enough and had a little extra dough. Money of course was in short supply for enlisted men.

The base pay for a private was a little over a hundred dollars a month. We got fifty dollars more for being in a combat zone and another fifty added in if you were jump or SCUBA qualified. Not much for risking your life. On top of that, most of us were still paying off the cost of our uniform and other fees. I never wore or even saw my dress blues, but every month the cost of this uniform was automatically deducted from my pay.

We also had to pay for things we couldn't do for ourselves. If we wanted to pass inspection we needed to have our hair cut and our utilities needed to be cleaned and pressed. We had to spend our own money on personal items such as toothpaste, shaving cream and other essentials. Whatever little remained usually went for beer, cigarettes, food from the PX and necessary but extra gear such as poncho liners, and Ho Chi Minh sandals.

If they could have gotten away with it, the Marine Corps would probably have had us buy our own ammunition. To make a little extra dough some of the men turned to gambling, but this was risky business because you never knew who you were playing against. Frenchy, for one, delighted in hustling new replacements. Other men augmented their pay by smuggling in hard liquor or dealing grass, both of which could be bought from the gooks and then resold at a small profit. If the price was right, no one in Nam seemed to care where anything came from.

A scout in the Fourth Platoon pushed the envelope too far. He played the guitar and I would occasionally go over to his tent and listen to him strum away and sing folk songs. One day, while on patrol, he was shot in the leg. Instead of welcoming the Med-Evac however, he pleaded with his sergeant to allow him to continue on the mission, but the wound was serious, and he was flown to the hospital. Everyone was impressed by his Gung Ho attitude. The following day at formation, the major held him up to us as a shining example of Force Recon's military ardor. There were even rumors that he had been written up for a medal.

It was only when the first sergeant broke open his footlocker a few days later to ship out his gear that the reason for his excessive zeal came to light. Inside his footlocker were two stolen M-16 rifles and the pieces of many more. He was augmenting his meager private's pay by disassembling the weapons and shipping them in pieces back to the States to be sold.

"He'll have plenty of time to practice his guitar in Leavenworth,"[1] Truman predicted.

I told him that to me the lifers seemed to be the real pros when it came to feathering their own nests. Our gunnery sergeant was in charge of the enlisted men's club. The clubs were crude, nothing more than plywood shacks with a couple of crates for a counter and a cooler full of beer and ice. The expenses had to be minimal, and the profits must have been considerable. A can of beer at the club cost us twice as much in Nam as it would cost at a bar in the States. Chips, pretzels and nuts were also heavily marked up. Despite the high cost, beer went out of the cooler so fast that the cans didn't even have time to get chilled. The men didn't seem to care about either the price or the warm beer; it was wet and alcoholic.

When someone once asked Gunny Barker why the prices were so high, he told us that he was accumulating a surplus that he would eventually use to buy a decent stereo system and a new refrigerator for the club. It sounded reasonable, but we never saw either one. When his tour was up and he rotated back to the States, whatever surplus there was probably rotated back with him. Barker's replacement, another gunnery sergeant, kept the prices the same. I guess the lifers thought it was one of their perks. Few of the men noticed because most of them never lasted out their full tour of duty.

There was no strict accounting for the money that flowed in and out of the club. Even when I worked at the bar I had no way of knowing where the money ended up and no one to complain to even if I did. There was no cash register to record sales; we simply took the scrip that was thrust into our hands, and put it in a box, which the sergeant took away at the end of the day. The money was never counted before it left the club and therefore there was no way to know if any of it went missing. I knew that it was best to keep my suspicions to myself. The last thing the major would have welcomed would have been a financial inquiry.

There was only a single business authorized to sell civilian clothing on the air base. Men going on R & R griped that they were charged exorbitant prices when they went to buy the civilian clothes they needed to wear when they left Nam. When they got to their destination they were handed a list of approved shops and were strongly encouraged to spend their R & R money only at these locations. Cynic that I was, I couldn't help but wonder how much these businesses had paid to be get on these approved lists and to whom they had paid it.

Our bases ran on gook labor; groups of them were trucked in every morning to work in the kitchens and perform menial jobs. Every day a ramshackle gook truck rolled into our compound to take away the trash. God only knows where it ended up. An elegant Vietnamese lady seemed to oversee the disreputable local work crew. Instead of the drab pajamas and flip-flop sandals worn by the rest of the workers, she was always dressed in an immaculate silk kimono. She carried a parasol and a white pearl–encrusted purse on a strap over her shoulder. We called her the Dragon Lady and recognized that like hard liquor, she was off-limits to enlisted men.

One day when we were still at Camp Reasoner, I came into the club early and saw her speaking sharply to Gypsy. I saw Gypsy reach into her pocket and resentfully pass her a crumpled wad of money, which The Dragon Lady quickly slipped it into her purse. After a few more sharp words, she turned around and saw me standing at the doorway watching them. She held her composure and nodded her head slightly to me as I held the door for her as she left. She was a brazen little hussy and probably knew that she had nothing to fear from a lowly enlisted man like myself.

"Is she shaking you down, Gypsy?" I asked her, concerned about what I had just observed.

Gypsy grabbed a rag and furiously started wiping down the bar. "What 'shakin' down'?" she asked, keeping her head down, obviously still upset.

"You having to give her money," I explained.

"All same same ... you want beer, you give me money ... I want job, I give her money." Gypsy stopped talking and turned to look out the window.

We watched together as the Dragon Lady walked over to the gook barber. He reached into his shirt pocket and with a small bow put some scrip into the opened purse she presented to him. Without saying anything she closed it up and continued walking down the path.

"You see," Gypsy remarked gruffly, turning back to her work.

Aircrews were said to be involved in smuggling drugs, gold, and gems in and out of the country. RVN officers were said to buy their commissions so they could extort money and supplies from the soldiers under them. The Koreans supposedly would take over entire villages, extorting money and stealing as much as they could.

When I first arrived in-country I had tried to ignore these rumors, dismissing them as lies or even outright enemy propaganda. The longer I was in Nam, however, the more I began to realize the whole country was rotten to the core. You only had to open up your eyes and look around.

A few days later at inspection Major Simbul told us that to eliminate "black market profiteering" our old scrip would be replaced with new paper money. The Vietnamese must have already known about the program, because throngs of them were already lined up outside our perimeter offering discounts of a hundred to one. They pushed against our fence and begged us to redeem their money before the deadline made the old scrip they were holding worthless. A squad of MPs appeared brandishing clubs and forced them away from the fence.

The scrip replacement seemed like the mother of all scams. Anyone able to exchange money could make an enormous profit. That didn't include the enlisted men of course. Under the watchful eyes of the MPs, we had to turn in the small amount of scrip we had in our possession and have it replaced with the new script on a one-to-one basis. We were confined to base during the turnover period and could only watch as the officers piled into Jeeps and took off for Da Nang City, hoping to make a quick buck. The following day the black market roared back to life. The vendors knew that it was unlikely that the new scrip wouldn't be replaced anytime soon.

We were supposed to turn in any enemy weapons or gear that we obtained during ambushes or prisoner snatches to G2,[2] but this order was frequently disobeyed, even by officers. Captured items could be bartered for the things we really needed, such as tiger-striped utilities, sturdy RVN packs and other gear that the Marine Corps didn't provide. We had heard that the staff at G2 would gobble up anything we turned over to them and we suspected the backroom boys back at division were making a fortune selling it on the black market. There were even instances where captured South Vietnamese piasters and U.S. scrip vanished into the hands of G2 without a trace, the final inventories mysteriously lacking any mention of the captured funds or valuable weapons. Things sure had a habit of "disappearing" in Nam.

If you took all of the money from the petty theft, the black marketeering, the shakedowns and corruption that went on in Vietnam, and put it all together, you'd still have only pocket change compared to the money being made far from the rice paddies of Nam. The major financial beneficiaries of the war were huge corporations headquartered in the old "US of A." It is estimated that the United States spent nearly a trillion dollars (in 2011 dollars) on the Vietnam War. This was nearly as much as we spent fighting World War II.[3] Throughout the long years of the war a handful of these firms grew enormously fat sucking from the government's teats. These were the companies that built the weapons, supplied and resupplied armaments, and constructed the infrastructure of bases, ports and roads necessary to support the American way of war.

What a juicy time the Vietnam War was for them! The defense industry gobbled up hundreds of billions of taxpayer dollars in lucrative, often no-bid contracts. Corporate lobbyists roamed the corridors of Washington, secure in the knowledge that nearly all of the people they spoke to would eventually be joining them in the same industry. It was such a nice way to do business.

The more C-ration cans we wasted, the more ammunition we expended, the more money the generals spent on new planes, ships and weapons systems, the better the defense industry liked it. It cost America $186,000 to kill a single enemy soldier![4] Forget about trying to win over the hearts and minds of a stubborn, resentful people. Increase bombing campaign! Send in more troops! Why not?

It was only to be expected. Throughout the centuries wars have always been fought for plunder. It made no difference to the captains of industry whether they became rich sacking a city or bleeding the American taxpayer blind. As long as industry turned in a nice profit year after year, the corporate rulers back in America were more than happy to keep the war going.

"Gypsy was right," I thought bitterly to myself. "Everything really was same same."

45. The Bucktoothed Sergeant

Against stupidity the very gods themselves contend in vain.—Friedrich Schiller

I had joined Moose and Frenchy for a trip to Freedom Hill, where the area's PX was located. Freedom Hill was a strange mixture of the military and civilian activities. We could draw our pay at one of the small buildings and immediately spend it getting a haircut or having our uniforms cleaned and pressed at the Vietnamese-run shops located within the compound. The PX also had a cafeteria where we could get a decent meal.

Lieutenant Lord was waiting for us when we returned. He told us that our team had been assigned a new mission and that we would need to get our equipment ready. Almost as an afterthought, he told us that the supply sergeant would be coming with us.

"He needs time in the bush in order to be promoted to staff," Lord explained.

"Oh no ... not him," I thought to myself.

Just looking at the supply sergeant you'd know that he was a loser. His entire being looked like it had been washed out by the streams of life until there was nothing left. Dirty blond hair, pale blue eyes, a parchment skin that the hot sun of Nam failed to darken but did manage to freckle unmercifully. Big buckteeth stuck out whenever he opened his lips, but that wasn't very often, because he had little to say. When he did speak, the words came out in such a heavy southern accent that he was almost impossible to understand.

He was nearly a decade older than the other sergeants and one had to wonder why he hadn't advanced higher in rank. He was supposed to be in charge of supplies, but he left most of the work to the lance corporal unfortunate enough to be assigned to work under him. As far as I could tell he spent most of his time sleeping in a beach chair in the back of the supply shack.

I met him for the first time when I joined Battalion Recon and needed basic equipment. I left his shed with a few pieces of junk: a worn-out flak jacket, a rubber poncho, and a promise of a pair of jungle boots. I had to pick up most of my equipment from extra stuff left behind when other Marines were hospitalized or rotated back to the States.

"Pardon me for asking, sir," Moose asked, "but has the sergeant ever been on a patrol before?"

"No, but the major wants him to go out with us," Lord answered testily." He saw the look on Moose's face and added, "You got any problems with that, Marine?"

"No, sir," Moose answered, looking away.

The team gathered in the operations room where Captain Bilger went over the mission with us. He described it as a standard recon patrol. We'd be looking for enemy activity north of Antenna Valley. This area had been used by the North Vietnamese off and on for many years as a staging area. Our job was to set up an observation post and monitor enemy movement. It sounded like a pretty straightforward recon patrol. We'd be "piggybacking" with the Second Platoon.

Piggybacking was a method where one team would be inserted at the same time another team was extracted. On the plus side, the team being extracted would have secured the LZ, so we didn't have to worry about being shot out of sky coming in. We would also benefit from their activity reports. On the other hand, there was always the possibility that the other team had been followed and we could walk right into an ambush.

As the highest-ranking enlisted man Lieutenant Lord assigned the sergeant to be the assistant patrol leader. As usual, Bo would run point, and I would cover him. We still hadn't been assigned a corpsman and I would also be carrying the Unit 1 medical pack. Moose would be the radio operator with the sergeant and lieutenant on either side of him. Ghant would be the tail-end Charlie.

Frenchy was leaving the following day for his long-awaited R & R to Hong Kong. He assured us that the best tailors in Asia would custom fit him for the best set of suits anyone in New Orleans had ever seen. Ma was recovering from a bad cold. The last thing we needed was someone sneezing in the bush, and he was left behind.

The sergeant didn't say anything during the briefing and it was up to each of us to ask the captain standard questions about radio frequencies, call signs, insertion, extraction points, and artillery coverage in the area. That afternoon I went out with the lieutenant and the sergeant for a high-altitude recon flight over the area that we would soon be patrolling. This was standard procedure, but normally only the patrol leader and assistant patrol leader went on these flights.

I suspected that the lieutenant knew that the sergeant had little experience in the field and wanted another person to go along with him. The flyby enabled us to get familiar

45. The Bucktoothed Sergeant

with prominent terrain features from the air and get a feel for the area. The terrain was rugged, but we saw a number of possible LZs from the air, and the lieutenant and I marked them on our maps. The sergeant spent his time looking down at the jungle through a pair of binoculars that hung around his neck. I couldn't imagine what he was looking at so intently. It was a quick flight, and we returned to base in the late afternoon.

The next morning dawned hot and clear. We saddled up and moved down to the LZ to wait for the birds. I had almost forgotten about the sergeant being with us until Ghant nudged me,

"You're not going to believe this shit," he whispered, pointing toward the trail.

I turned to see the sergeant coming down the path with seemingly every piece of equipment in the supply hut somehow attached to his body. His pack was enormous, bulging with God knows what. The binoculars he had carried yesterday hung from his neck. He had a .45 pistol holstered around his sagging gut. Pencil flares of every color dotted his pocket. Instead of an M-16 he carried a 12-gauge automatic shotgun with two bandoliers of fléchette rounds crisscrossing both shoulders. Everything, from his huge floppy hat to his boots, looked brand-new. He stumbled down the slope with his enormous load of gear and plopped down heavily next to the lieutenant.

"Sorry to be late, sir, couldn't find my knife," he said, gesturing proudly at a bone-handled Bowie knife that hung between his legs like some kind of weird phallic symbol.

"I hope he's not goin' to flash that thing around," Moose warned in a worried voice, looking at the sergeant's shiny Bowie knife. The blades on our Ka-Bars all had a dull gray coating so they wouldn't reflect the sun.

"Wait for me, Wild Bill!"[1] Truman snickered softly, to everyone's amusement.

The lieutenant heard our muffled laughter and turned around looking annoyed, but before he could say anything we heard the sound of the approaching birds and we struggled to our feet. The CH-46 landed with a screaming whoosh. We leaned into the rotor blast and climbed up the ramp into the belly of the craft, sitting crossways on the seats so we could support our packs. As usual, the chopper had the windows knocked out and as we took off cool air blew freely through the aircraft.

I looked out the windows at the clouds passing below and started repeating my mantra to myself. "How beautiful it is … how beautiful." Over time, I began to believe more and more in the protective power of these simple words. Rationally, I knew that repeating these words to myself wouldn't make any difference at all to the jagged piece of steel that might be coming for me, but the words somehow had the power to calm and soothe. The view of the mountains and jungle passing below certainly was beautiful. The rice paddies shimmered like mirrors, reflecting the clouds and the sky, while the jungle that was passing beneath us was patterned in every shade of green imaginable. "How beautiful it is … how beautiful."

On every patrol there was the very real possibility of not coming back, and this feeling of dread grew stronger as the number of patrols I went on increased. Rising above the fear, however, was the pure delicious delight of living life to the fullest. On a mission there was no time, no room, for anything else other than survival. Thoughts about money, girlfriends or home faded away. There was only the *now*.

The piggyback insertion took place in less than a minute. As soon as the chopper landed we were off the bird and the other team took our place. No words were spoken our entire focus was on the jungle around us. After a week or more in the bush, the men on the other team were trying to get into the bird as fast as possible and get out of there. Stinking of the jungle rot, their faces hard and smeared with camouflage paint, they pushed past us. In a few hours we would look and smell the same.

We climbed steadily toward the top of a small hill. I pulled out my map from my front pocket and studied our position. Glancing to my right, I saw the river exactly where it should be. Looking straight ahead, I saw the hill from which we hoped to be extracted poking through the clouds. It looked so close, but there was a deep valley between us, and I knew it would take us days to get there.

We had nearly reached the top of the hill and we stopped just below it, gathered in a protective circle facing out. The sergeant saw me glancing at my map and came over to me, unfolding his entire map and laying it on the ground. I looked at him curiously.

"So where do you think we are?" he asked.

The question annoyed me. Was this some kind of chickenshit test? I knew exactly where we were, as did everyone else on the team. The only time we didn't, was when we moved through cover so dense that we couldn't see any landmarks. Giving the sergeant the benefit of the doubt, I glanced down at his map. He hadn't covered the map in plastic to protect it from the weather. The chart had gotten wet and most of the contour lines had been rubbed off, making it difficult to read. I located the river and a few prominent landmarks and followed them to our position.

"Here." I pointed.

He carefully studied the area where I pointed, took a pencil from a clip on his web gear and circled the location. "Yeah, that where I make it too." He nodded in satisfaction.

"Well shit … numb nuts," I thought turning away. "Why did you bother asking me?"

The sergeant took his map and moved off toward Moose. "The lieutenant wants me to call in the position report," he told Moose in a self-important whisper. Moose, adjusting his radio, established radio contact and handed him the handset.

A warm breeze was flowing up the hill, bringing with it a heavy spicy scent. I closed my eyes and went into my favorite daydream, walking through a college quad, the grass vivid green against old brick, the leaves swirling around my feet, the blessed coolness of a New England autumn.

In the background I heard the sergeant establish radio contact, but then, to my horror, I heard him giving our exact latitude/longitude map coordinates over the radio! Lieutenant Lord must have also heard him, because he scrambled over and tore the handset from his hand.

"What the hell do you think you're doing?" he whispered fiercely.

"You ordered me to call in our position," the sergeant replied defensively in a whining voice.

"Not that way, you asshole!" Lord hissed in an exasperated tone. "Don't you know how to use our rectangular coordinates?"

The sergeant shook his head miserably, and I couldn't help but feel a little sorry for him. The grid system was one of the first things that Chief had taught me, but somehow this sergeant had never learned it.

"Well," the lieutenant sighed, "you've compromised our mission. If the gooks were monitoring our frequencies, they'll know exactly where we are. We've got to get out of here." The sergeant started to say something but then changed his mind and fell silent.

We got our gear on and moved quickly toward the nearest extraction point. I knew it was at least four hours away. We had only traveled a short distance when we heard the sound of automatic rifle fire strafing the position we had just left. It certainly hadn't taken them long; we had just gotten out of there in time! We picked up our pace, running through the jungle trying to find an open spot where a chopper could land, but the jungle canopy was too thick, and we were forced to keep moving.

We finally reached the LZ we had been running toward, but instead of the clearing we had hoped to find we discovered that the area had been reclaimed by the jungle. It would be impossible for the pilot to set down in this tangle of second-growth trees. Far behind us we heard the sound of rifle fire as the NVA tried to trick us into returning fire and revealing our position.

The lieutenant radioed in for a SPIE extraction. We all knew we didn't have much time to get out of there. The CH-46 came in fast and low, dropping two ropes, one from each door. The first line dropped nearly at my feet and I clipped on. The second rope came down by the sergeant. I saw him loop it around him and then pass the free end to Moose, who clipped on with Ghant below him.

The lieutenant was still on the ground with Bo but a second chopper was hovering overhead and Lord waved ours off. I was yanked off the ground with the other men and in few seconds found myself suspended hundreds of feet above the ground. I spun slowly, my hands free, held up by my modified parachute harness. It was a great feeling to have left our pursuers somewhere far below us in the jungle. The second helicopter swooped in to pick up Lord and Ma and I could see them hanging from their own rope as both choppers flew us out of the area.

I was the first person to have clipped on and was on top of everyone else. All the other men were looking down at the ground, searching the jungle and probably hoping to find a target. I was just starting to relax and enjoy the ride when I looked over at the other string of men to see the sergeant pull his knife from the sheath between his legs and begin sawing desperately at the rope above his head!

I couldn't believe my eyes! For a moment I thought he had gone insane and was trying to commit suicide. If he cut through the rope he'd fall to his death and take everyone on his rope along with him. The other men had no idea what was happening above their heads. I was hanging only twenty feet away but powerless to stop him.

I looked up and saw the crew chief peering out the door. I knew he couldn't hear me above the noise of the turbines, but I pointed down and motioned frantically for him to descend. The pilot immediately went into a steep dive, the chopper banking sharply as the pilot headed to a small island in the middle of a river that we were passing over. I looked back again at the sergeant. He had cut the rope nearly in half and I could see the rest of it starting to fray.

"I'm going to have to shoot him; that's all there is to it," I thought to myself, but he suddenly slumped in his harness and the shiny Bowie knife fell from his hands.

As he spun toward me in the air I realized what had happened. The extraction line was cutting him in half! The sergeant had probably never been trained on the SPIE rig and didn't know how to use his harness. Desperate to get out of the jungle, he'd just made a loop in the extraction rope and tied it around his chest, passing the rest of the line down to the other men. When the chopper took off the line tightened and the weight of three men and all their equipment caused the looped line to tighten around his body. There must have been nearly a thousand pounds of pressure squeezing his chest.

The chopper was now over the island and less than a hundred feet up when suddenly the remaining strands of line parted. I could only watch helplessly as my teammates fell through the air, entangled in loops of rope, their equipment and one another. They twisted and spun in the air and finally slammed into the ground. I was close enough to see Moose bounce.

The pilot continued to descend and finally my rope touched the ground. The CH-46 landing beside me in the shallow river.

As soon as my feet hit the ground I detached from the rope and ran over to where my teammates lay in a crumpled heap. The supply sergeant lay on the top of the pile. He was the first person on the other rope to reach the extraction line and he had fallen the greatest distance. As I turned him over, I could feel the bones in his ribs crunch under my hand. He was unconscious and didn't seem to be breathing. His face was a sickening purplish-red color and he looked dead.

The rope was still wound tightly around his chest. The line was cutting into him so deep that I couldn't get the blade of my Ka-Bar under the knot and had to cut it from above. My blade severed rope, web gear, utilities and finally, unavoidably, rolls of his fat that had squeezed up from under the rope. With a final slice I cut him free, blood spurting from the shallow cuts made by my blade.

To my amazement, the sergeant opened his mouth and gasped. He turned his head aside and coughed. A bright stream of blood spurted from his mouth. I suspected that at least one of his lungs had been punctured by a broken rib and he probably had internal injuries as well, but there was nothing more that I could do for him. He needed surgery and he needed it soon. The crew chief and gunner from the chopper ran down the ramp with a stretcher, rolled the sergeant onto it and carried him into the aircraft.

Ghant was sitting in the mud of the riverbank his right foot bent back at an impossible angle. We couldn't move him like that. He must have been in shock, because he didn't say a word as I turned him onto his left side, but when I took hold of his broken leg and tried to pull it back into its normal position he screamed in agony. I flinched but continued to straighten the leg and apply pressure. As the bones slid back into place he sighed in relief and I could feel his body relax.

I removed the medical pack, opened it up and got out bandages and other supplies. I carried morphine ampoules, but pushed them aside. Tony had warned me never to use them if there was any chance of a head injury. Ghant had fallen nearly as far as the sergeant, probably forty feet or more, and I didn't want to take a chance. Using his rifle as a temporary split, I tied it tightly to his leg with bandages. I ran my fingers along his neck and spine but couldn't feel anything else broken

The aircrew only had one stretcher, but they came back with a heavy tarp and the three of us slid Ghant onto it and carried him aboard the chopper, doing our best to protect his back and neck. I was worried about moving him like that, but we didn't have any choice. We were running out of time.

45. The Bucktoothed Sergeant

The crew chief and I ran over to where Moose was lying.

"Don't touch me; please don't touch me!" the big Marine pleaded as we approached. His body was bent backward, extended grotesquely over his pack and the radio he was carrying. He was holding his right arm tenderly with his left, almost like a girl would cradle a doll, It was obvious to me that it was broken, probably in several places, but I was more concerned about his other injuries.

The crew-chief bent down and tried to slip off his equipment.

Moose screamed with pain, "Don't move me!"

"Man, we got to get you out of here," I told him, looking nervously around at the surrounding jungle. We were deep into enemy territory and completely exposed. It was only a matter of time until the enemy found us.

"Can you move your legs?" I asked him, thinking that if we could just get him to his feet we could get out of there, but nothing moved.

The gunner ran over with a poncho liner. I cut down two saplings and made a crude stretcher by winding it around the branches. We carefully moved Moose onto the improvised stretcher and carefully carried him back to the aircraft.

We took off without receiving any fire and the pilot flew directly to the Da Nang hospital. The medics swarmed aboard with stretchers as soon as we landed. There was nothing more we could do and we were flown back to base.

When we got back I told Lieutenant Lord and Ma were both waiting for me on the LZ and I told the lieutenant what I thought had happened. It was now his responsibility to explain everything to the major.

"Wasn't the sergeant wearing an extraction harness?" Ma asked as we walked back.

I couldn't remember if he had worn one or not, but he certainly hadn't used it.

"Even if I were being squeezed to death, I still wouldn't have cut the rope holding me up," I said.

"You don't know what you'd do if you were the one being cut in half," Bo told me in the sergeant's defense.

Ma was waiting for us as we entered our hooch, he was shocked to hear that in a few minutes nearly half of our team had been decimated.

"But why cut the rope above his head?" Ma asked. "He could have cut the rope below him and at least saved himself."

"Maybe he didn't think he could live with himself if he had done that," Bo responded quietly. "I know I couldn't."

We would never know what, if anything, went through the supply sergeant's head as he sawed away at the rescue line until it parted, but we all agreed that the blame for the loss of our teammates had to be placed squarely on our officers and not on him. The major had knowingly sent an unqualified Marine on a dangerous mission just so that he could have a bullshit administrative reason for promoting him. Lieutenant Lord shirked his responsibilities by not objecting to the assignment. It wasn't the sergeant's fault that he had been born a stupid asshole and was expected to fulfill a duty for which he was totally unqualified.

A few weeks later I received a short letter written on Red Cross stationery from Moose. He wrote that he was in a hospital in Japan and that Ghant and the supply sergeant were in the same hospital, but that he had not seen them. The letter concluded with the following words: "They say I broke my back in three places … but I'm doing OK."

---

46. The Silken Boudoir

I said, "You do not show much kindly feeling
for a young man who just saved your life."
"I am happy that he done it," said Lucky Ned Pepper. "I don't say he
wasn't game, I say he was green. All kids is game, but a man will keep
his head and look out for his own self."—Charles Portis, *True Grit*

I was in the mess tent when I first heard the rumor that two teams from Recon Battalion had been ambushed with a few days of one another and that several men had been killed. While Force had been at Reasoner I had occasionally visited my old teammates in the 1st Platoon, but after we moved to An Hoa I had completely lost contact with them. Now hearing the rumor, I was worried, and after formation asked Lieutenant Lord if he could find out anything for me.

He stopped me on my way to the mess tent and pulled me aside. I knew immediately from his demeanor that he didn't have good news. He told me that the rumors about the Battalion Recon teams were true, but that he really shouldn't give out any names until their kin had been notified.

"Anyone from the 1st Platoon?" I persisted anxiously.

He hesitated for a moment.

"I was told they called him Chief."

"How did it happen?" I asked numbly.

"He was shot in the stomach as he jumped off the chopper into a hot LZ." Lord reluctantly told me.

I nodded.

If it was going to happen, that would be the way. Chief had been so good in the bush that I couldn't imagine him ever walking into an ambush, or tripping a booby trap.

Lieutenant Lord said he was very sorry and left me alone with my thoughts.

Chief, who took a new guy under his wing and taught him everything he knew. Chief, whose mother mailed him chili peppers so hot that tears poured out from your eyes. Chief, who might have had the ability to heal me.

I remembered that Chief had once told me that his people believed that combat changes a person's nature, and that warriors need to go through a healing ceremony to be brought back into balance before they can rejoin their families and friends.

"Could you set one up for me?" I asked him.

Chief had looked at me intently for a moment and then shook his head.

46. The Silken Boudoir

"You don't need it yet."

Well, I may not have needed it then, but I sure as hell needed it now.

"Chief my old friend, with you gone, to whom now can I turn to for healing?"

My circle of friends was rapidly shrinking, and I had little desire to make new ones. I'd see the new replacements come into our company, eager young men anxious to prove themselves. I watched them as they slowly lost their idealism and changed into unrepentant killers. I couldn't stop the process, but I hated to watch it.

The newbies were also dangerous to be around. It took months in the bush before you were able to rely on a new guy, and a lot of them just didn't make it that long. When they were still in the process of learning their deadly trade, they were as much a danger to the other men in the team as they were to themselves.

Short-timers were almost as bad, if not worse. They knew too much and had seen too much. Their minds were focused more on getting home than on watching what was going on around them, and they also got themselves killed with alarming regularity.

I was now one of the only men remaining from my original Force Recon team. Sergeant Tom and Stout had been killed. I never found out what happened to Moose, Ghant or the supply sergeant after they fell from the rope. Frenchy had been transferred out after getting a third purple heart. As a "sole surviving son" Mac had never returned to the team after his brother had been killed, and now Chief was gone.

Out of our original platoon of ten men only Truman, Bo, Ma, and myself were left, and I had been in Nam three months before the others had even arrived. Feo, Doc and Polanski had made it through their tour, but nearly all of the men we had gotten into our platoon as their replacements were now also gone.

It seemed to me that the men who remained in the unit as "bush Marines" were too tough to get sick, too lucky to get shot, or, like me, too stupidly proud to think of a way out. Even if bodies were able to absorb the strains and risks of combat, the minds of even the toughest Marines often broke under the strain.

Gowski was a new replacement who had come to us from the grunts. He was a big, broad-shouldered Marine with a rough manner. At first he seemed to fit in well with our team and was assigned to take Ghant's place running tail-end Charlie, but as the number of patrols with us increased, Gowski seemed to become more and more depressed. He would sit for hours on his cot just staring at the wall. When anybody asked him what was wrong he'd just shake his head and turn away. Lieutenant Lord figured that he just needed some time off and when the next mission came up he ordered Gowski to stay behind.

We came back to find our hooch transformed into an Arabian tent. In our absence Gowski had taken a parachute and hung it from the ceiling so that it draped down in graceful folds over his cot. Bizarre symbols and fragments of words written on a piece of scrap plywood were nailed to the side of his bunk.

"What the hell is this, some kind of whorehouse?" Truman joked good-naturedly as he walked into our hooch and pulled Gowski's silk canopy aside.

In one sudden savage motion Gowski rose from his cot and without saying a word grabbed his M-16 and hit Truman in the center of his chest with the butt. Truman sank to his knees in agony.

"Stay out of my area or I'll kill ya!" Gowski warned the rest of us as he, carefully rearranging his silk curtain and settled back on his cot like nothing had happened.

"You bastard, I'll get you for this!" Truman threatened, struggling to his feet and hobbling out the door.

I made myself scarce and the rest of the men followed. The last thing any of us wanted to do was get between two armed maniacs. When Truman got mad he was nearly impossible to control. I was sure he'd return any minute with a loaded weapon, but fortunately he ran into a sergeant from the motor pool who somehow managed to calm him down.

The sergeant returned with Captain Bilger. The two men took one look at Gowski sitting cross-legged on his cot with his rifle in his hands and decided that discretion was the better part of valor. Instead of confronting Gowski themselves, they called in a squad of MPs who somehow managed to remove Gowski from his silken tent. We never saw him again. We left the parachute hanging from the rafters. It added a decorative touch to our spare accommodations.

Slim was also not doing well. He was a private guy and rarely shared his personal life with me or anyone else. Perhaps it would have been better if he had.

I knew that Slim was doing his best to send as much money home as possible. He seldom went to the club and rarely joined us when we went to the PX for some chow or a movie. Even with these small economies however, he would be hard-pressed to support a family on the meager pay of an enlisted man. Many of the men in our unit had girlfriends back in the States, but few were married and fewer still had children.

Slim kept a picture of his pretty wife and chubby little daughter on a shelf above his cot. The baby was sitting up and holding a rattle. The child couldn't have been more than a year old and must have been born shortly after Slim had entered the Marine Corps. The framed photographs stood jarringly next to the anti-personnel mines and ammo cartridges that also lined his shelf.

With each letter from home Slim seemed to grow more and more somber. He did his job in the bush but with every patrol seemed to withdraw further within himself. After being shot out of two LZs in one day Slim must have decided that he had had enough and told me that he was going to ask for a transfer out of Force Recon. A few days later Gunny Barker, our company's administrative NCO, called him in and told him that his request had been denied.

The next morning Slim failed to join our platoon for morning inspection. No one seemed to know where he was. Trying to cover up for him, I told the lieutenant that he hadn't been feeling well and may have gone to sick bay.

Inspection was nearly over when Bo nudged me. Slim was walking down the road toward the parade ground. He was holding his rifle by the barrel with the stock resting on his shoulder. He looked for all the world like some backwoods squirrel hunter going for a stroll down a country lane than an elite recon scout. The major and captain were standing facing us, but everyone in the company was standing at attention and couldn't help but see him as he strolled closer.

"Somebody stop him!" Lieutenant Lord whispered urgently from his place in front of our platoon.

Ma broke ranks and ran toward him, but Slim pushed by and continued walking. He walked directly up to the major, took his rifle from his shoulder, saluted, and in full view of the entire company requested a transfer. The entire company stood there aghast.

46. The Silken Boudoir

Interrupting a morning inspection in such a manner was an unheard-of breach of Marine Corps protocol that we could barely believe it. The major must have also been shocked, but he handled the situation rather well. He asked the first sergeant to escort Slim into his office and then immediately dismissed the company.

Slim never returned to our hooch. The first sergeant packed up his gear and Slim was gone the same day. The next time I saw him he was a gunner on a CH-46. We were practicing insertions using the cargo net and Slim was helping his crew roll up the bulky ladder. The chopper was getting ready to take off and we didn't have time to say anything to each other. Perhaps that was just as well.

From my personal experience the ratio seemed to be about four men wounded to every man killed. Of the wounded, one was wounded seriously and never returned to the unit; the other three went back to their units and were once more put into the meat grinder. Injuries and disease also took a significant toll.

During the rainy season it was impossible to keep dry in the bush. We didn't even try. The grunts could at least wrap themselves up in waterproof ponchos or huddle in bunkers and stay somewhat dry, but the rubberized ponchos made too much noise for our type of patrols, so we simply accepted the fact that we would be completely soaked for days at a time. As long as we kept moving we were OK, but wet clothes eventually drained the heat from our bodies and when we stopped moving we often found ourselves shivering and close to hypothermia.

All of us carried a single silken blanket we bought from the gook vendors clustered around the Da Nang highway. The gook shopkeepers probably bought them from supply sergeants in the rear and then resold them to us. At night we wrapped the thin silk blankets around us and curled up on the ground as the rain poured down. The blankets wouldn't keep out the rain, but the silk did provide some degree of warmth even when wet. On patrols we tried to stop for the night on some kind of an incline so we wouldn't wake up in pool of water, but during the monsoons it rained so hard that there didn't seem to be much difference between a pool and a stream. During the rainy season we lived in water, breathed it, and often died in it. Our weapons rusted; our web gear and clothes rotted. Only by carefully sealing our maps in plastic and then taping the edges of the bag were we able to keep them readable. In these conditions the smallest scratch might quickly become life threatening.

On one patrol we had a new guy from the Third Platoon attached to us as a radio operator. One morning he felt a leech on the inside of his upper arm. No big deal, bloodsuckers were a fact of life in the bush. The slugs would attach themselves anywhere. We usually either pulled them off or hit them with bug juice until they fell away. Maybe the new guy was squeamish and didn't want to touch the leech or maybe he was just fooling around, but he took out his knife and scraping the edge along his inner arm removed the repulsive creature.

The next day he complained to the corpsman that his entire arm and hand were swollen. The small patch of skin where he had removed the leech was red and inflamed. Doc applied some antibiotic cream, but in the wet conditions of the jungle it soon washed away. We wanted to medevac him, but he resisted, telling us that he was OK and wanted to complete the mission. When we got back to base the corpsmen took another look at his swollen arm and sent him off to the hospital at Da Nang. A few weeks later we saw the sergeant from the Third Platoon packing up his gear. He told us that the infection had spread and that the doctors at Da Nang had been forced to amputate his arm at the shoulder in order to save his life.

More commonly, our feet were the problem. We all made fun of jungle rot or the creeping crud, but it was no joke to find yourself limping off the chopper barely able to walk up the hill. We all carried spare pairs of dry socks in plastic bags and every evening when we stopped we would take off our boots, powder our feet with disinfectant powder, and put on the driest pair of socks that we had. Our feet would feel dry and warm for a few minutes, but all too soon the water would wick its way from the wet boots through to our socks. During the rainy season I eventually stopped even using socks; my feet were in just as bad shape one way as the other.

I'd seen some feet so swollen that boots had to be cut off, and the smell when the sodden socks were finally removed would suffocate a corpse. There was no quick cure; we just had to wait for the swelling to go down. Particularly bad cases of jungle rot were sent to the hospital, but the most of the time the infections stopped if we let enough air get to our feet. We knew our feet were getting better when the skin started to dry and crack.

When we got back to our hooch one of the first things we did was change into Ho Chi Minh sandals. These were made out of old tires and they looked like shower shoes on steroids. The open toes allowed air to circulate and they never became saturated with water like our jungle boots.

I wondered why the Marine Corps hadn't simply looked at what the Vietnamese had been using for thousands of years, instead of spending millions of dollars developing inferior substitutes. Why weren't we issued lightweight silk utility jackets that wouldn't absorb water, rubber sandals that allowed our feet to breathe, headgear that shed the monsoon rain? It just didn't make any sense to reinvent the wheel, but I guess the military suppliers back in the United States needed to make as much money as possible before the war ended.

At the next formation the major called me and a half-dozen other Marines up to be awarded various medals. I had completely forgotten about my leg wound and was surprised when I was awarded a Purple Heart. Most of the other guys were up there for the same decoration, but one of the men in the Second Platoon, Corporal Myer, was being awarded a Bronze Star for bravery.

In Force Recon, aside from Purple Hearts, medals for enlisted men were rare. In order to receive a commendation a Marine had to be written up by an officer, and most of our missions were seven-man teams led by NCOs. Force Recon also had the policy of not giving out medals until we had completed our tour of duty. Any possible commendations were supposedly saved in our files to be submitted as "end-of-tour" awards when our time in Nam was over.

After a firefight Captain Bilger would occasionally ask if there was anyone in the team who should be recognized for extraordinary conduct. We were somehow embarrassed by his question and usually just bashfully looked at one another and shook our heads. We felt that were all in it together and basically just doing our job. None of us were looking for medals, and that's probably why we didn't receive them.

In Corporal Myer's case Major Simbul made an exception to his general rule. During a vicious firefight Myer had risked his own life and brought in a wounded comrade. He deserved the decoration, and everyone was pleased to see him receive it. Myer tried to shrug off the attention he received, but we all knew how proud he was to have us congratulate him.

Late that night a single shot rang out from beyond our compound and from somewhere the sudden cry of, "Corpsman!" rang out. We jumped for our weapons and ran for the perimeter as the alert siren began to moan. We waited at our posts peering into the darkness and expecting a larger attack at any moment, but everything was still.

Meyer had been shot in the throat as he lay on his cot writing a letter, perhaps writing home to tell his folks about his decoration. He died within minutes. We never found out who had fired the shot that killed him. Perhaps it had been an enemy sniper, or perhaps it was a random shot fired by the RVN unit down the hill from us. Just when you started to relax and think things were going to be all right the war reached out its claws for you.

"Yea, when your number is up, it's up," Truman intoned, sipping a beer.

"At least he doesn't have anything to worry about anymore," Ma added.

Hearing these trite phrases repeated time and time again was somehow strangely comforting to us. I guess they were true enough.

"What are you going to do with your medal?" Truman asked me, trying to change the subject.

"Probably hock it," I joked, but it was my first medal and in truth I was very proud of it. I took it out of its case and examined it, a heart-shaped piece of gold with a purple stone embossed with the golden image of George Washington.

Frenchy asked to see it. "You know, I don't think this is gold at all," he said, holding it in his hand. "It's too light. I think it's just tin and plastic."

"No way! Give it back to me," I told him, holding out my hand.

Frenchy tossed the medal to Truman, who kept toying with it, playfully keeping it away from me. He placed his fingernail under the purple stone and it suddenly popped off and George Washington flew across the room.

"Jeez, I'm sorry, man; I didn't mean to do that," Truman told me, picking up the pieces and handing them back to me. Looking at what was left of the medal, I realized that Frenchy was right. My Purple Heart really was nothing more than painted tin and plastic.

"Maybe they give the real gold ones to the officers," Truman thoughtfully remarked, looking at the colorful plastic pieces in my hand.

47. CAP

It became necessary to destroy the town in order to save it.
—an unnamed Marine major to military correspondent Peter Arnett in 1968

I wanted to do something in remembrance of Chief, but I didn't know what. I thought about writing to his parents, but I didn't have their address and I was afraid that it would cause them even more grief. I finally remembered that there was a Catholic charity organization that worked with Native American tribes. The duty gopher found me their address and helped me set up an automatic pay deduction that sent a few dollars every month from my pay to that charity.

I went around the compound visiting my friends and asking if they wanted to contribute a little bit each month to the charity. Although the guys in Force didn't even know Chief, every Marine I approached was willing to do so. It was truly remarkable. These guys didn't have a lot of money and some of them were supporting families, but they were all willing to share whatever they could. Every few months we would receive a short hand-written letter from one of the families that our donations had benefited. Usually a photograph of a child was included. It sure made us feel good to get these notes, and I always passed them around to the other guys. I would like to think that the donations we made in Chief's name might have eased the family's grief. Whether or not it did I don't know, but it certainly made us feel better.

I was on a work detail painting the command shack a nice shade of Marine Corps green when I happened to read one of the notices stapled to the bulletin board In bold letters it read: *Make a Difference—Volunteer for CAP!*

The poster was trying to attract volunteers to join the Combined Action Platoon, or CAP. The poster explained that CAP units were small groups of Marines who lived with the Vietnamese in their villages. The poster explained that CAP brought the villagers medical care, helped build schools, dug wells, taught them about democracy and trained them to resist the Communists. The picture on the poster showed a group of smiling Marines working hand in hand with local farmers to dig a well.

It was the first decent idea I had heard since arriving in Nam. After six months all I had seen was destruction. It seemed like everywhere we went we left nothing but a trail of blood and fire. I imagined myself in one of the CAP units giving medical care to a sick kid.

I asked for an appointment with Sergeant Barker, the fat gunnery sergeant who was our company administrative officer. I knew he had turned down Slim's request for a transfer, but CAP was actively looking for volunteers.

He called over the following morning after formation. "Let me get this straight, you want to go live in a gook village?" Barker asked, shaking his head incredulously.

I nodded, pointing to the poster on the bulletin board. He glanced at it dismissively.

"They asked for volunteers to join CAP, gunny, and I'm volunteering."

"Son, I'm tellin' you right now that there ain't a snowball's chance in hell that the major's gonna let one of his scouts babysit some gook villagers. Besides, boy, those CAP guys have some of the highest casualty rates around."

He spit dismissively into the sand and continued, "Shit! Half of the gooks in those villages are VC and the other half would stab you in the back for the bounty money the Cong would put on your head as soon as you stepped through the gate. Why would you want to do anything for them?"

"I'm not just doing it for them. I'm doing it for myself," I answered.

I saw this conversation wasn't getting anywhere and I was getting sick of being called son or boy.

"Shit, boy, I'm only trying to do you a favor. A transfer request won't look good on your record and you can forget about any promotions."

I couldn't tell if Gunny Barker was really trying to look out for my interests or only hoping to get out of doing some extra work.

"I don't care about promotions," I told him.

Barker looked at me as though I had just committed a sacrilege. Lifers lived for their next promotion. "Well, if that's what you really want, I'll look into it, but don't start packing your bags jess yet," he warned.

Despite what the gunny had said, I figured that if CAP needed volunteers then I had a chance at joining them. I thought that if that was going to happen I needed to learn more Vietnamese.

The Second Platoon had a "Kit Carson" scout named Kim assigned to them. My friend Braun had told me that Kim had been an NVA officer who had defected to the South Vietnamese in return for money. Kim was assigned to the Second Platoon. Braun had gone out with him on several patrols. He said Kim was good in the bush but that he never really trusted him. It was hard to trust someone who had proven himself to be a traitor.

I wouldn't have wanted to go out on patrols with Kim, but as long as I paid him he was more than willing to tutor me in Vietnamese. I had always been good at languages and quickly picked up the basic phrases; I enjoyed the sessions and had the feeling that he did also. We would go out to one of the empty bunkers for an hour or so each day to practice speaking Vietnamese with him. He was a good teacher, always cheerful and patient.

I wondered why Kim had to assist his former enemy, but I never presumed to ask. Did he do it for the money or did he truly believe in our cause? Perhaps he simply was trying to pick the winning side.

One day after my lesson ended he leaned over and asked me, "Do you think the Americans will win?"

"What do you think?" I asked.

He just looked at me, shook his head and shrugged.

Kim was given a lot of freedom, much more than we were. When not on patrol he could leave the compound whenever he wished. He bought a new motorcycle with the money he received for defecting. Perhaps the military hoped that money they paid him would entice other NVA officers to defect as well.

Whatever the reason, Kim was taking quite a gamble going out into the field with us. If he was captured and the NVA found that he was a deserter, they would make short work of him. If he was a double agent and Braun or one of the other men even suspected that he had led them into an ambush, he wouldn't last long either.

Gunny Barker called me into his office a few weeks later. He pawed around his cluttered desk and finally pulled my folder out of a big pile.

"Still got your mind set on a transfer?" he asked, tapping my paperwork.

I nodded, fully expecting him to tell me that it had been approved.

"Well, son, I looked into it." He hesitated for a moment for effect. "And you're shit out of luck; you ain't goin' nowhere!"

He held the folder out at arm's length and leaned back in his chair as he pretended to read it. "These here CAP rules say you gotta have four months or more left on your tour."

"But I've got over four months left," I objected.

He nodded in agreement, "Yup, I pulled your records. Four months and twenty-one days to be exact."

"Well, gunny," I persisted, "That's twenty-one days over the limit."

"Just barely," he agreed, smiling again. "But it's gonna take me some time to process your paperwork and by the time I'm finished you'll be ready to catch the big bird back to the world." He leaned back in his chair and regarded me thoughtfully.

"I'm doin' you a favor, son. You should be thankin' me."

"Isn't there anything I can do?" I persisted.

Barker looked annoyed. He had enjoyed his little charade, but now it was over and I was taking up too much of his time.

"Yeah … you can get your ass out of my office!" he ordered, slamming my folder down on his desk.

And so my idealistic dreams about joining a CAP platoon and helping out the Vietnamese and myself even more come to nothing. Thinking about things later, however, I realized that perhaps things had worked out for the best.

During my tour the CAP program and the pacification program in general achieved less than stellar results. The primary emphasis of the U.S. military continued to be on military victories, determined by body counts. CAP units were always underfunded and undermanned. These small thirteen-man units were expected not only to work with the villages to build up their communities but also to engage in offensive activities as well. It was a nearly impossible task, and their casualty rate, as Sergeant Barker pointed out, was extremely high.

The CAP program was based on the concept of Vietnamese "pacification." This involved forcing farmers in contested areas to leave their traditional villages and move into larger fortified camps. Once in the camps they supposedly would be safe from the demands of insurgent forces and the enemy would be deprived of the food supplies they needed to continue the war. Marines sent out on search and destroy missions were told that they were destroying the rice harvest in order to prevent the Vietcong from obtaining supplies. To some extent this may have been true, but it also destroyed the rice that the villages needed to survive. If they wanted to eat, the farmers were forced to move away from their traditional villages and into the fortified camps. This was hardly the way to win the "hearts and minds" of the villagers.

Was it even possible to ever bridge the enormous gulf between our two peoples? I thought of the difference between the Vietnamese rice farmers laboriously planting stalks of rice in their rice paddies and my own family, my father taking the bus to work on the docks in New York City, my mother working as a secretary, me riding my bike and playing Little League baseball. Did we have anything at all in common? Our religion, our language, even our clothes and mannerisms were so different that it just didn't seem possible even in the best of circumstances. Under the trials and tribulations of war, it was probably an impossible goal.

48. The Dog and Pony Show

> *"Good morning, good morning!" the General said*
> *When we met him last week on our way to the line.*
> *Now the soldiers he smiled at are most of 'em dead,*
> *And we're cursing his staff for incompetent swine.*
> —Siegfried Sassoon, "The General"

The following week our compound was a hotbed of activity with anyone not on patrol assigned to work parties. A general was going to be visiting our company for a "dog and pony show"[1] and the major wanted to impress him. I was assigned to fill in the potholes in the road leading to our compound with sandbags so that the general wouldn't be jostled as he rode through our base in his jeep. Other men were given printed instructions and ordered to carefully rake the sand around the headquarters building into something that looked like a Japanese Zen sand garden. Still others spent the day encircling our LZ with tiny American flags. It sure looked nice until they blew away when the first chopper landed. What chickenshit!

The next morning at formation the major asked for volunteers willing to put on a rappelling demonstration for the general and his entourage. I was sick of the ridiculous work parties and stepped forward, and somewhat to my surprise I was one of the four men selected.

We spent the entire afternoon preparing for the general's visit, making sure that our gear was in good shape and practicing fast rope descents on the tower. I had always liked to rappel and considered myself to be good at it. Gunny Barker called us over to the Supply Shack after we had finished practicing and we were issued new camouflage utilities and given the wide-brimmed jungle hats that looked good but were completely useless in the jungle.

The next morning we were all set to go, and actually looking forward to putting on a good show, when Gunny Barker came around to tell us that the general's plans had changed. Instead of coming to Force Recon compound the general had decided to visit Recon Battalion, and that their men would be putting on the show. Barker ordered us to pack up the new uniforms we had been issued so that he could have them delivered to the other team. We stripped off clothes, gave him back the broad billed hats and put away our spit-shined boots. At the time the whole thing was quite a letdown. It was only the following day that we learned how lucky we had been.

During the general's show at Battalion something went terribly wrong. Two members of the rappelling team had jumped out of a hovering aircraft, slid down the rope and landed successfully. Before they could unclip from the rappelling rope, the pilot took off on a low level pass to buzzing[2] the compound and giving an extra thrill to the general and his entourage. The men were dragged screaming along the ground and then literally torn apart when they were pulled through the rolls of razor wire lining the perimeter of the LZ.

We were later told that the reason for the accident was the new rope, which supposedly had kinked and prevented the men from unclipping.

"Sure, blame it on the fuckin' rope," I thought bitterly to myself. "What bullshit!"

I knew exactly what had happened. Everyone was so focused on impressing the top brass that they lost track of what they were doing. The men exited the aircraft, fell through the air and probably reached the ground in seconds. The crew chief saw them land and without waiting for them to unclip immediately gave the pilot the all-clear signal.

A Marine Corps general would probably have had a helicopter assigned for his personal use. I'll bet that that instead calling in one of the aircraft that were typically assigned to Recon, the same chopper that general had flown in on was used for the demo. The pilot and flight crew probably had no experience with our techniques and no idea that it took a few seconds for jumpers to release from the rappelling line. Instead of hovering and allowing the ropes to be pulled in, as was usually done in an actual insertion, once the men hit the ground the pilot immediately took off.

I wondered whether anything would have been different if the general's plans hadn't changed and I had been one of the men rappelling down the line. The only difference probably would have been that I would have been the one ripped limb from limb.

"Thank God it wasn't me," I thought fervently to myself, feeling guilty for the thought and yet unable to stop myself.

"Better them than me."

49. The Fight

A man ... can make an awful lot of easy enemies, but he really isn't in the enemy business until he makes one out of a friend.—Robert Ruark, *The Lost Classics*

It had been months since I had been wounded but my knee it was never really the same again. The shrapnel had done more damage to me than simply physically injuring my leg. It had also shredded the sense of invulnerability that had previously encased me in an imaginary shield. The steel fragments shocked me into the realization that in a firefight there wasn't anything special about me at all. My body was just another target, no different from any of the other pieces of meat moving around me. It was a humbling and frightening lesson to learn.

If we weren't on work parties or going to the bush, we were training. Each morning we stripped to our boots and shorts and went on a five-mile run down the road. We set off, chanting cadence songs as we ran.

Flat shoe, flat fin, look at me,
There's three thing you'll never be:
Airborne, Recon, UDT!

49. The Fight

Everyone in Force Recon not on patrol or actively engaged in duties went on these morning runs. I can't say that I enjoyed PT,[1] but I had to admit that having the entire group together was a good way to build morale. The major himself often led the group and set the pace. He could run like a deer, his long legs effortlessly putting down the miles. With my bum leg I struggled to keep up. It may have been my imagination, but it seemed to me that whenever he saw me falling behind he increased the pace.

After the run Bo and I were dismissed and wandered over to the enlisted men's club where the cooks had set up an outdoor barbeque. They had cut two fifty-gallon oil drums in half lengthwise and had filled them with cubes of charcoal to make two large grills. Hundreds of steaks were stacked up ready for the fire, but the charcoal was just starting to burn when of the men grabbed steaks off the grill and ate them barely seared. Others, even more impatient, dumped a can of kerosene on the fire. As the thick, oily smoke and flame billowed up from the grill they threw on more steaks.

One of the cooks ran over and grabbed the fuel can away. "What the hell are you doing! Trying to poison yourself or blow yourself up?"

"Adds flavor." A young Marine stupidly grinned, his teeth white against a face covered with grease from the steak he was wolfing down and black soot from the fire.

I wasn't about to eat any steak marinated in kerosene and neither was Bo. We left the barbeque and walked into the club. A light rain had begun to fall outside, and the noise level increased as Marines who were hanging around drinking outside made their way into the room. The club was crowded with men from an artillery unit that was moving in down the road and we had to push our way through to the bar. My friend Wilkins was behind the counter, taking in scrip and passing out cold beers from the cooler.

"Crowded tonight," Bo remarked.

"Yup, the major let the cannon cockers use our club. Bad idea," Wilkins grumbled as more artillerymen pushed their way toward the bar. "They've been here most of the afternoon drinking. We're gonna have trouble, just matter of time," he predicted.

I shrugged my shoulders, grabbed a Bud and squeezed in next to Bo. As long as the beer held out I didn't care who was in the club. Every muscle in my body ached from the hours I had spent pounding stakes into the ground that morning. I could still feel the steel rods vibrating in my hands. It sure would have been nice to sit down, but the artillery guys had taken all the tables, so Bo and I stood at the bar talking with Wilkins.

"You're getting pretty short now aren't you?" Bo asked him.

"Only a few weeks left," he responded with a grin. Pulling a short wooden club out of his belt, he pounded it on the bar and yelled, "Twenty-eight days and I'm outta here!"

The other men hooted their approval and raised their cans of beer to him. All of them hoped that soon it would be their turn to make it back to the world. Marines like Wilkins who were nearing the end of their tours proudly carried their "short-timer-sticks" with them wherever they went. These were the bush Marine's equivalent of the officer's swagger stick. Some were carefully carved pieces of art. Wilkins's stick was a simple one, a short staff of wood about two feet long. He had carved his initials into one side and a peace sign on the other

Over on the side of the bar I heard a drinking contest start up:

> Here's to brother Truman, brother Truman, brother Truman …
> Here's to brother Truman who's with us tonight.

> He's happy, he's jolly, he drinks it by golly …
> Here's to brother Truman who's with us tonight.
> So drink chug-a-lug drink chug-a-lug, drink—chug-a-lug.

The "drink chug-a-lug" continued until Truman and the other Marine he was drinking against had downed the can, crushed it in their hand and thrown it to the floor. Truman won the match, but instead of paying up, the other marine started singing another song to the tune of "Camptown Races" under his breath.

> Truman's goin' home in a body bag,
> Body bag … body bag,
> Truman's goin' home in a body bag,
> Oh, the—"

"You're the one goin' home in a body bag, you son of a bitch!" Truman replied hotly as the other scout grinned at him. With his quick temper Truman made an ideal target.

Men from the Second Platoon were sitting around a table by the corner listening to another scout tell about getting shot out of their last patrol. A few artillerymen stood around the table listening, their attempts at entering the conversation contemptuously ignored. The club's stereo system was turned all the way up and with everyone talking the sound level inside was deafening.

The side door slammed open and Uncle walked in, pushing his way through the group that blocked the doorway. He had developed a beer belly since the last time I had seen him, but with his square shoulders and big hands he was still built like a brick shithouse. Tonight his face was flat and expressionless as he contemptuously stared around at the crowded bar. I sensed that he was looking for trouble.

Three of his cronies stood behind him in the doorway. The man next to him was nicknamed Pappy because his lined face made him look much older than he probably was. Pappy was one of our parachute riggers and never went out on patrols. The other two Marines were the Dyer brothers. They weren't identical twins but looked so alike that I had trouble telling them apart. All three of them were nasty pieces of work in their own right. They hung on Uncle's every word, laughing at his jokes and permitting themselves to be alternately mocked and bullied by him.

Now you can't expect to find choirboys in a Marine infantry unit, but most of the guys in the unit were pretty decent. The war and their training might have hardened them, but most didn't have the vicious streak that now seemed to run like a dark thread through Uncle's soul. I watched him move with his small gang to the front of the room. Anyone unlucky enough to be in his way was shoved roughly aside.

"Get the fuck out of my way, shithead; I'm thirsty!" Uncle warned, bullying his way past another Marine. He made his way straight toward the crowded bar and grabbed the shoulder of one of the artillery guys sitting there, pulling him backward.

"You're in my seat. Move it!" he ordered.

Taken by surprise, the man tried to turn, his beer spilling on the counter as Uncle pulled him backward. As the stool tilted I saw a large white plaster cast on the man's foot.

"Uncle … let him be; his foot's broken!" I shouted, reaching over to stop him.

Uncle turned to face me, giving the injured Marine a contemptuous push that sent

49. The Fight

the man sprawling to the floor, his chair rocking back against the bar. Uncle walked slowly up to me, his bloodshot eyes boring into mine.

"What the hell do ya think you're doing?" Uncle asked me his face only a few inches from my own. "Force Recon sticks together." With every slurred word he pushed his index finger into my chest.

"He's got a bum leg," I objected, pushing Uncle away and pointing down to the man on the floor.

Uncle didn't even bother to look down, "So what? Ya don't screw your buddies."

He moved closer to me and I could smell the hard liquor on his breath. I didn't like him so close, it was too easy to get sucker-punched, and I backed away a few steps. He took this as fear and spit contemptuously. "Chickenshit … you ain't Recon."

Bo tried to get between us, "C'mon … let's go; he's drunk." he muttered, pushing me out the door.

We walked back to our hooch and I tried to get some rest. But as I turned and tossed on my cot my mind went back to what had just happened at the club. Part of me wanted to just take Bo's advice and let it go, but lots of men had heard what Uncle said to me. If I didn't stand up to him I'd lose the respect of respect of everyone in the company. In the Marine Corps that's not something you ever want to let happen. I got up from my bunk, took a flashlight and went over to Uncle's tent. I knew where his bunk was and found him wrapped in his blankets snoring away.

I shined the light on his face and shook his shoulder. "Hey, wake up!"

He sat up groggily, rubbing his face. "What the fuck," he swore, rubbing his face and pushing the flashlight away. He recognized me. "Well, if it isn't Chickenshit."

"Meet me outside," I told him.

He came out of his tent a few minutes later followed by the Dyer boys.

"Take back what you said," I told him.

"Take back what you said…. Take back what you said," he mimicked in a high voice as the other two men laughed. "You sound like a pussy."

He walked closer to me and suddenly tried to kick me in the stomach. I dodged and moved backward. It was too late now to back out, and if he wanted to fight dirty that was fine with me.

I saw his two friends circle around behind me and for a moment I thought they were all going to jump me, but Uncle waved them away. "This asshole's mine," he grunted confidently, putting up his hands like a boxer and bobbing his head. He threw a punch with his left, which I blocked, and then followed up with a right that grazed my temple as I backed away. They were both powerful blows that would have ended the fight if they had connected, but the next time he came in I threw a front kick, which caught him square in the chest. It was like kicking a sandbag, but it stopped him for a moment. He grunted and stepped back rubbing his chest, but I could tell that the kick had shaken some of his confidence.

"I'll get you for that, you basta…" Before he could finish I caught him with a solid right hook. It was a good hit. His head snapped back and he doubled over slightly. I saw my chance and threw another kick, which caught him on the side of his head. If I had been wearing boots, that would have ended the fight, but I was wearing a pair of sneakers and he had a head like a rock.

He roared in pain and frustration, swinging wildly as I moved away out of his reach. I knew I had to stay away from him. If he managed to get in closer, he would tear into me. We circled around each other, each of us looking for an opening.

Suddenly he put his head down and charged like a bull, hoping to tackle me. I wasn't expecting him to do that, but I sidestepped and tried to grab his head under my arm as he went past. Using the momentum of his charge, I flipped him onto his back. We both went down, but I was on top and the fall seemed to stun him for a moment. I swung my body around and got him into the judo lock that Sergeant Lewis had taught us in his unarmed-combat session so many months ago.

Despite his struggles Uncle couldn't break the hold, but I needed both of my hands to hold him down as he tried desperately to free himself. He tried punching me in the back of the head with his free hand, but with his head and other arm pinned the blows didn't have any force behind them and he just didn't have the leverage to break my hold.

"You can't do shit now, can you? I could really mess you up!" I gloated, slapping him lightly across the face. I was bluffing. I needed both hands to hold him down. A light slap was all I could manage. If I tried to pull back for a powerful punch, the hold would be broken and he'd free himself. I pushed his right hand down against my leg, applying pressure to his elbow joint. He grunted in pain, but his arms were massive and I couldn't force his arm back any farther. Other than butting him with my head, this was about all that I could do.

"Give up?" I asked, hoping that he would and not really knowing what I'd do if he didn't.

He glared at me with hatred, a trickle of blood running down the side of his mouth from a split lip.

A hand roughly grabbed my shoulder. "Break it up… *Now!* Break it up, I say!" I turned my head to see Gunny Barker standing over us.

"Let him up," he ordered me. Reluctantly I released my grip and quickly rolled away from him. Uncle shook himself like a dog and got up rubbing his upper arm. I must have hurt him more than I thought.

"We were just practicing a little unarmed combat, gunny," Uncle said innocently, wiping the blood from his mouth.

"Shut up! You think I'm stupid? Shake hands and get back in your bunks," he ordered.

"Here it comes," I thought. "He'll grab my hand and then punch me in the mouth."

Fortunately, Uncle must have thought that I'd do the same to him. Both of us stood as far apart as possible and extended our hands for a quick shake.

"I'll remember this," Uncle snarled under his breath, but Barker heard him.

"No you won't! If I hear about either one of you so much as looking sideways at the other, I'll have you both up on charges—understand?

"Understand!" he repeated, looking straight at Uncle, who nodded.

"I'm tellin' you again. If I hear anything more both of you will be in the brig," gunny warned again.

"Jeez, a man's got to get some sleep around here," he said, turning away.

Uncle walked back into his hooch, but as I turned to go back to mine the two Dyer boys followed me.

"Hey, wait up!" one of the little vipers called out.

I stopped and turned around to face them.

"You beat a pretty big man tonight. Think you could take us?" one of them asked, obviously spoiling for another fight.

I knew that I could take either one of these two little shits and probably both together, but I had enough fighting for one night. I pushed by them without saying anything and walked back to my hooch. Everyone in my team was still sleeping. They hadn't even known what was going on a few yards outside the door.

The next morning, I saw Uncle at the formation. His right eye was black-and-blue and his lips were swollen, but considering that I had kicked him as hard as I could in the head he didn't look all that bad. The side of my face was slightly puffy, but other than that I was fine. I didn't say anything to him, and he ignored me. We never spoke again.

As fights go, it certainly wasn't much. I had seen other men beat each other to a bloody pulp over smaller things. I knew that I had done what was I needed to do. In Nam it was far better to get things settled right away than to have them fester. I guess that's what Gunny Barker thought as well.

50. Truckin

The war is going well and will soon succeed.
—Robert McNamara

We finally left An Hua, and good riddance as far as we were concerned. What a hell-hole that place had turned out to be. Our new base was in the foothills southwest of Da Nang. It didn't have a regular name like Camp Reasoner, but was simply called Hill 469. We didn't care if had a name or not. It was set on a level hill overlooking a broad plain, and there were no NVA with rockets looking down our throats. The engineers had built bunkers along the hill and a massive observation tower that overlooked a broad plain to our south. We left our tents behind and moved into regular plywood hooches. Best of all, we now had a decent enlisted men's club!

The only thing the new base lacked was water, Every day the motor pool guys hitched up the water buffalo, a large water tank on wheels, and returned to our base with it. That gave us enough water to drink and wash, but showers for enlisted men were restricted to once a week. The officers, of course, could shower as much as they pleased. We figured the rationing was a small price to pay to be away from An Hoa.

After a week in our new compound we were told that the entire company was going to the R & R center at China Beach to celebrate the military accomplishments of Corporal Doby, who, like Myer, been awarded a Bronze Star for valor, and was now being promoted to sergeant.

Corporal Doby was another exception to what seemed to be the general rule about the awarding of Force Recon decorations. He had manned the tower's .50-caliber machine gun during one of the night attacks at An Hoa. A Marine colonel happened to be visiting our base at the time, and I guess that the firepower Doby was putting out made more of an impression on him than the other guys right next to him firing their M-16s. Doby was written up for the decoration by the colonel himself, and now the major was promoting him to sergeant. We certainly didn't care; good for him! The entire company headed out to China Beach for a celebration party.

China Beach was a beautiful place. The blue waters of the South China Sea lapped against a pristine white sand beach that curved away into the distance. We had quite a celebration party for ourselves. Our trucks pulled right up onto the beach and the cook started making fires in the grills that were set up near a circle of picnic tables. A group of Marines started a volleyball game while the rest of us went for a swim.

It was a great day, lots of free beer and all the steak we could eat. There had been few good times at An Hoa, and I was in no hurry to get back to our compound. Truman and I were sitting around drinking the last of the beer and waiting for the truck that would take us back to our base when Doby appeared. He was smoking a fat cigar and holding a half-empty bottle of whisky. He was wearing his new rank of sergeant and had pinned his Bronze Star to the pocket of his jungle utilities. He patted the medal affectionately from time to time whenever he thought someone was looking.

The driver from our motor pool finally pulled up in a truck and we jumped into the back of it. Truman lowered the tailgate and sat with his feet dangling off the end of the truck bed as the few remaining men still on the beach joined him. I moved to the very front, where I could stand behind the cab and look forward.

Doby started to climb up with us but then, almost as an afterthought, jumped off. He swaggered up to the front of the truck, his bottle of whisky in one hand and his cigar in the other.

"Move over, son, and let a man drive!" he ordered the motor pool driver, opening the door to the cab and pushing him roughly aside. I could hear the driver argue with him, but he eventually gave in and slid over onto the passenger side. Doby climbed in and started up the truck.

"Let's get this show on the road!" he shouted, blowing the horn, revving the engine, and throwing the now empty bottle of whisky out the window.

He popped the clutch and the truck lurched forward, nearly throwing me off my feet. As soon as we reached the main road he floored the gas pedal. The truck steadily gained speed as Doby swerved back and forth across the road and I realized that he wasn't just mildly intoxicated, he was shit-faced drunk. Truman was half-bagged as well and seemed to enjoy being tossed around. He began singing under his breath as the truck lurched back and forth, *Oh ... my name is Sammy Small, fuck 'em all, fuck 'em all...*

The road ran past the huge Air Force base on the southwest side of Da Nang. Ahead of us we could see their living quarters and recreational area where the airmen were playing volleyball. An olympic-sized swimming pool was next to the volleyball courts. As we passed, one of the swimmers climbed the diving tower and did a double flip off the high board. It was hard to believe that we were having our water rationed, and only a few miles away the Air Force guys had their own swimming pool, but that was the way it was. Doby blew a long blast on the truck's horn, and when the airmen turned to look he gave them the finger.

There was another truck ahead of us and Doby stomped on the gas and pulled around it, blasting the horn as he passed. From my position behind the cab I saw that the road ahead made an abrupt right-angle turn not far ahead and I could tell that we were now moving far too fast to make the corner.

"Slow down!" I yelled, pounding on the top of the cab with the butt of my rifle. "For God's sake, Doby! Slow down!"

I don't know whether or not he heard me, but he stood on the brake and the truck skidded violently, nearly leaving the road. Truman and the other men sitting on the tailgate were thrown off as the truck hit the shoulder and nearly overturned. I was still standing up and holding on for dear life. I looked back and saw the other men rolling like logs along the road behind us. The truck had slowed but was still moving far too fast to make the turn. We were hurtling directly toward the huge sausage-shaped tanks filled with aviation gasoline that lined the end of the road.

I jumped, hitting the roadway hard and rolling over and over. I raised my head just in time to see the truck plow through the wire fence protecting the fuel depot. It slammed into the ditch that had been dug around the gasoline bladders and slowly, almost in slow motion, fell over onto its side.

The men from the truck Doby had passed stopped and took us to the hospital. Truman and I were badly scraped and bruised, but neither of us had broken anything. A lot of the men had concussions, a few even more serious injuries that kept them in the hospital longer. Doby and the motor pool driver were banged up but otherwise unharmed.

While we were waiting for the medics to take care of us I couldn't help thinking about the cigar hanging out of Doby's mouth. If the truck had gone a few more feet we would have all been incinerated as thousands of gallons of gasoline exploded. It was too bad that the major couldn't take away Doby's medal, but at least the next time I saw him he had been busted to private.

51. Tiger

Tyger, tyger, burning bright
In the forests of the night,
What immortal hand or eye
Could frame thy fearful symmetry?
—William Blake, "The Tyger"

We were deep in the steep mountain country rising northwest of Da Nang, a place we called Razorback Ridge. The first day of the patrol we had spotted an enemy base camp and had called in multiple air strikes. The NVA must have known we were somewhere around, but they didn't know where. After the air strikes we left our original position and slowly worked our way up to what we thought would be another good observation post. We rarely stayed in the same position for more than a few days; it reduced our chances of being caught.

After about an hour we heard a heavy coughing noise behind us. We immediately stopped, but the sound wasn't repeated.

"Deer?" Bo asked in a questioning whisper.

I didn't know. I had heard deer make lots of sounds in the woods. They would stamp, snort and huff, but I'd never heard them make a noise like that before.

Razorback Ridge was well named. The slope steepened until we were forced to pull ourselves up using the small trees that covered the slope. Several times I was left hanging by my hands as my feet slid out from under me, Wait-a-minute vines sank their three-pronged needle-sharp thorns into my gear, jerking me to a stop every few yards. I kept a small throwing knife taped to the outside of my Ka-Bar's sheath just to have something handy to cut these wire-like vines.

Eventually we made it to the top of the narrow ridgeline. The ground sloped away steeply on two sides. It was a good spot for an observation post and the steep terrain made it reasonably secure. There was a well-used path winding along most of the ridgelines in Nam. If you had the balls to walk these trails, you could cover more ground in an hour than someone slogging through the valleys could cover in days. Unfortunately, you could also run into trouble just as fast.

We decided to move back off the ridge a few hundred feet into the cover of the low bushes growing along the steep slope. It wasn't a great spot to spend the night, because of the steep slope, but it would be impossible for the NVA to reach us.

Bo and I were assigned to watch the trail until nightfall. We set out Claymores at each end to protect ourselves in case of unwelcome visitors. It was a beautiful sunset. As the sun set behind the mountains to the west the entire hillside was bathed in an orange glow. To the east the sky was a deep blue sprinkled with stars. A cool breeze blew up from the valley carrying with it the sweet aroma of some blooming tropical plant.

Night falls quickly in the jungle and when it did we carefully made our way down toward the rest of the team. Instead of our usual circle, with each man facing outward, the men had arranged themselves in an arrowhead formation. The ground was so steep that most had placed their packs against a small tree and then straddled the pack with their heads upward. There was really no other way to stay on the hillside without rolling down. Moving down the hill, Bo and I took up positions at the tip of the arrowhead, about twenty feet above the other members of the unit.

I wedged a small branch under my rifle and secured it by driving my Ka-Bar deep into the ground. We had learned not to fire our weapons at night even if fired upon. Enemy patrols would sometimes shoot randomly into the hillsides in the hope that recon teams would give away their position. At night we were expected to either move away quietly or if that was not possible rely on our knives.

Bo wedged himself into another tree about fifteen feet away and slightly below me. He threw me a short length of parachute cord, which I tied lightly around my arm. We didn't want to have to move around on the steep slope to wake the other for radio watch;

51. Tiger

a slight tug on the line would do just as well. I carefully set the Claymore's igniter next to my rifle and secured it to the ground by a small stick through its handle.

Satisfied that I had prepared my position as well as possible, I took a drink from my canteen and prepared for the night. Leaning back against the hill, propped with the tree and my pack between my legs, I was surprisingly comfortable. I had gotten used to sleeping in absurd positions. The ground was soft and our cover was good. If we couldn't see more than a few feet, neither could the enemy.

It must have been around midnight when I awoke to the sound of thunder. A light rain had fallen during the night and clouds covered the moon; flashes of lightning lit up the sky in the distance. I tried going back to sleep again when I heard the strange coughing noise again, this time much closer.

I sat up and groped for my weapon in the darkness. I had a moment of panic until my fingers closed around my knife and I felt the reassuring barrel of my M-16 next to it. I tugged on the line connecting me to Bo and felt him respond with a jerk of his own. The other men seemed to be still sleeping.

There was the sudden sound of branches breaking above us. Something was moving down the slope directly toward us, and whatever it was didn't care whether it was making any noise or not. Suddenly the sound of the breaking branches stopped, and a fetid smell, sour and feral, filled the air. I peered through a break in the brush in front of me and saw something big moving down the slope toward us, a lighter shadow flowing against the darker background of the jungle. I gripped my Ka-Bar tightly in my hand, but I knew that no knife on earth would stop whatever was now slowly creeping ever closer to me.

"The hell with this!" I thought, dropping my knife and grabbing my M-16. Whatever was coming down the hill was heading right for me and I wanted something more substantial than a thin steel blade in my hands.

Another bolt of lightning struck nearby, and in the sudden flash I saw the silhouette of a tiger crouching in front of me. I fired instinctively, my rifle on full automatic. Awakened by my rifle fire, the rest of the team scrambled around below me, grabbing their gear and moving upward.

Lieutenant Lord was the first to reach me.

"What the hell is going on?" he demanded furiously.

"It was a tiger," I responded shakily, reloading my weapon in the dark.

"Have you lost your fuckin' mind?" he asked incredulously.

"It was a tiger, sir. That's what we heard earlier; it must have been stalking us all day."

"You'd better fuckin' be right," Lord warned. "If I don't see a dead animal tomorrow morning, your ass is gonna be up the creek."

I didn't care what he said to me. I was still alive and I knew that if I hadn't fired I wouldn't be. I had emptied nearly the entire magazine at point-blank range. I felt sure that I had hit the cat and that tomorrow morning we would find its body on the slope below us.

It had now started to rain in earnest, a torrential downpour punctuated by thunder and lightning. All we could do was wait for the dawn. No one got any more sleep.

The next day dawned hot and steamy, but we searched for the tiger in vain. We found a trail of broken bushes leading directly down the hill toward my position, but the heavy rain had washed away any animal tracks or evidence of blood. Bo backed up my story but admitted that he hadn't actually seen the tiger. Lieutenant Lord didn't seem like he believed either one of us.

Shortly after I had left Vietnam, another team ran a patrol on Razorback Ridge. Darkness had just fallen when the men heard a crash in the underbrush followed by screams. In the darkness they discovered that their team leader was missing. The next morning they tracked a trail of blood into a heavily wooded area where they found the half-eaten body of their sergeant being guarded by an enormous Bengal tiger.

They fired at the animal, but the big cat returned several minutes later to challenge them for its kill. The team finally frightened it off. The men called for an extraction, bringing what was left of their sergeant's mutilated body back to base with them. The men on that mission were all hardened combat Marines, but this was too much even for them. None ever went into the jungle again.

A special hunter/killer team armed with sniper rifles was immediately sent out to track down and kill the tiger before any more men were lost. After several weeks scouring the thick jungle for tracks they picked up the trail of a large cat and shot it. They returned to Camp Reasoner carrying the body of a three-hundred-pound tiger on a pole. Perhaps the animal they killed carried my bullets in his body, perhaps not. As the hunters were extracted from Razorback Ridge, they reported that they heard the coughing of another cat stalking them.

52. Don't Blink

> *They'll soon forget their haunted nights; their cowed*
> *Subjection to the ghosts of friends who died,*
> *Their dreams that drip with murder; and they'll be proud*
> *Of glorious war that shatter'd all their pride ...*
> *Men who went out to battle, grim and glad;*
> *Children, with eyes that hate you, broken and mad.*
> —Siegfried Sassoon, "Survivors"

Someone was shaking my shoulder. "C'mon, man, get up!"

I opened my eyes to see my friend Braun standing at the end of my bunk laughing at me. He was a short and wiry guy with blond hair and mischievous blue eyes. I had gone out with him on a number of missions and knew him well. He once told me that he was the youngest Marine ever to be accepted into Force Recon. He was always the consummate professional in the bush, but once back in the rear he loved to party.

"I got you scheduled with Truman and me for guard duty," he told me cheerfully.

I sat up angrily, "I just got back in."

"Trust me, you'll thank me later," he told me confidently.

He breezed out before I could throttle him. Still grumpy, I pulled on my boots and grabbed my web gear, joining Braun, and Truman in front of the command post.

"It's great!" Truman reassured me. The RVN have a small village down in the valley. Once we're away from the compound it's … party time!"

Truman had never been what anyone would consider a spit-and-polish Marine. He liked to party and had a fine disdain for authority, but he was also one of the most skilled and aggressive members of our platoon.

He seemed to enjoy the thrill of a firefight and until recently volunteered to go out on extra patrols, but his former Gung Ho spirit had now left him forever.

A month ago he had gone out as a replacement with Braun's team. This wasn't unusual. From time to time men from one platoon were temporarily assigned to run a patrol with another unit. A few days into the mission they located an enemy base camp hidden deep in a mountain valley. Their sergeant had called in for an air strike, but their request was denied. The men were told that President Johnson had agreed to a cease-fire so that the North Vietnamese could celebrate, he was told, Ho Chi Minh's birthday!

From their hidden observation post high above the valley Truman and the rest of the team watched helplessly as the NVA troops installed a battery of heavy anti-aircraft guns and built up their defenses, a clear violation of the truce agreement. As the days passed and the enemy's position grew ever stronger Truman grew more and more agitated.

One night he grabbed his rifle and set off down the trail leading to the NVA base camp, muttering that this was one birthday that he'd be damned if he was going to celebrate! The other men broke cover and restrained him before it was too late, but he threw his rifle on the ground in disgust and it was all that the Second Platoon's sergeant could do to persuade him to pick it up again. When he returned to our hooch he couldn't even talk about the mission without sputtering with rage and since returning, he seemed to have dedicated himself to drinking, gambling and whoring.

Our new compound was built on a high plateau. Below us was a small RVN village, little more than a cluster of grass huts. A tank had rolled into our compound a few days ago and had maneuvered itself so that its gun overlooked the village below us. As we passed we could smell the sweet scent of marijuana blowing out of its air vents. It wasn't clear to me whether the tank was there to protect the village or to intimidate it. I knew how I would feel if I woke up one morning and saw the barrel of a cannon pointed at my house.

The three of us walked through the barbed wire of our perimeter, carefully following the zigzag footpath leading back and forth through the strands of razor-sharp wire. This path was the only way to pass through our perimeter. It was protected by overlapping fields of fire from machine guns located in the adjacent bunkers. We followed a dirt path downward and finally reached the village shortly before dark. The only people around seemed to be a group of RVN soldiers sitting around a small fire near the end of the compound.

We choose a spot a few hundred yards away, dropped our packs and relaxed as Braun called in and made radio contact with our base. One of the RVN soldiers stood up and slowly walked over to us. Pulling on a cigarette, he squatted down next to Braun, who nodded to him.

"What you want ... grass ... girls...?" he asked in a conspiratorial voice.

"Man, we want it all," Braun replied, smiling.

"Girl ten dolla. Grass five dolla," he replied, his face impassive.

Broun shook his head firmly. "No, man. Grass two dolla ... girl five dalla."

They bargained for a few minutes and finally came to an agreement. The soldier wheeled a small Honda motorbike from beside the fence and took off down the trail.

"You think he'll be back?" I asked as he drove away.

"Of course. I didn't give him the money yet."

Braun was right; after only fifteen minutes or so he came back with a woman sitting sidesaddle on the motorbike clutching the soldier tightly around the waist. Truman got up eagerly, but as they got closer I saw his enthusiasm begin to fade. The woman on the backseat was so fat and old that she could barely climb off the seat.

"Is that the best you can do?" Truman asked in a disappointed voice.

"She numba one!" the RVN replied indignantly, holding out his hand. "Ten dolla!"

"We should have just gotten the grass," Braun muttered bitterly, handing the soldier some scrip.

I could tell the soldier thought it wasn't enough, but he pocketed the bills and drove with his woman to a small tent at the other end of the compound. I busied myself lighting a small fire and starting to cook up the rations we had brought with us. Braun rolled a fat roach from the grass he had just bought and sat back contentedly.

"Oh, man," he moaned in satisfied delight. "This is good shit."

"You think so?" Truman asked, taking a drag from the roach that Braun offered him.

Braun nodded. "I'm the connoisseur of grass, man," taking another deep hit, "definitely numba one."

"You'd better take another toke before taking on that lady," I advised Truman, pointing back to the tent where she was motioning to him.

Braun offered a roach to me, but I shook my head. I had tried smoking grass a few times, but it never really did much for me. I preferred my beer any day.

"I'll take his," Truman said, holding out his hand.

"Smokin' more after your're already high don't get you any higher," Braun counseled.

"I'm gonna see how high I can get tonight and function," Truman told us, getting up and walking toward the tent.

My attention was caught by the RVNs gathered around the hooch at the other end of the clearing. They had gotten up and were looking our way.

"You know, I don't like the feel of these guys," I warned Braun as they suddenly started walking over to us.

"Let's not get paranoid; they probably just want more money," Braun muttered, but I noticed that he had picked up his M-16.

The soldiers squatted down facing us across the fire. They all held rifles loosely in their hands.

Braun nodded to them in a friendly way. They looked back impassively.

"Cam hute twook?"[1] I offered.

They glanced at their leader and shook their heads. This was unusual in itself. I had never known an RVN soldier to refuse a free cigarette. They never refused anything at all. Two more men appeared from behind their hut, one moving to our left, the other to our right. I didn't know what their game was, but I didn't like it.

Their leader said something in Vietnamese and the other men laughed. Pointing his finger at me like it was a gun, he pretended to squeeze off a shot. The men surrounding him smirked. He made another remark, then suddenly raised his rifle and pointed it at my stomach. I clicked the safety off my M-16, and pointed it at his head.

Time stopped as we looked into each other's eyes. A slight tightening of my finger on the hair trigger of my M-16 would blow him away, but he might still be able to get me. If he fired first, I was determined to waste him before I died. Long seconds passed, and we both pulled ourselves back from the abyss. With a look almost of respect, he lowered his rifle, straightened up and walked away. The rest of his men followed behind him.

"What the hell was that all about?" Braun asked. Unbeknownst to me, he had been covering my back the entire time.

"I have no fuckin' idea," I replied.

For the first time in Nam my hands began to shake, and I couldn't seem to stop them.

I heard giggling behind me and Truman came out of the tent, oblivious to everything except the state of his dick. The radio crackled, and he picked up the handset. He motioned us over and said we had been ordered to return to base. This was very unusual; never before had we been ordered back before morning.

"Crossing the wire in the dark? We've never done that before," Braun objected in a concerned voice.

"Shit… I know the trail like the back of my hand. I've been coming down here for tail twice a week," Truman boasted dismissively.

"Yeah, let's get out of here," I agreed, keeping a worried eye on the RVN soldiers.

We packed up our gear and walked back up the trail. There was a full moon and it was easy for us to find the path that led through the wire. We called in and were told to proceed, but when we reached the middle of the wire a searchlight suddenly turned on and blinded us. A few seconds later we heard an order blared from a bullhorn.

"Just keep on coming!"

"What the hell do you think you're doing?" Truman yelled as we stumbled in the sudden glare. "Get that fuckin' light out of our eyes!"

"This is the captain. Drop your weapons, turn out your pockets and step aside."

"Oh shit," Truman muttered as he turned out his pockets and half a dozen small silvery packets fluttered to the ground.

"What are these, Marine?" Captain Bilger asked ominously, moving over to Truman and picking up one the packets he had dropped from the ground.

"Condoms, sir," Truman replied with a straight face.

I started to laugh, but things were about to turn ugly. While the captain's attention was focused on Truman, Braun had stealthily dropped something else to the ground and stepped on it, but the first sergeant had seen him.

"Well … well… what do we have here?" he asked softly, picking the small bag of grass off the ground and holding it up in front of him. Braun just stood there without saying anything.

With a sudden savage motion the first sergeant slammed the butt of his rifle into Braun's stomach and then clipped him across the head with the barrel as he doubled over in pain. Truman and I surged forward only to face four MPs who suddenly appeared out of the shadows. We had been set up.

The MPs dragged Braun to an empty hooch. For nearly an hour we heard them working him over. One group combat Marines hated even more than the Cong was the military police. These guys took every opportunity to ride roughshod over enlisted men. We heard the MPs yelling questions and the thump of their fists, but Braun never uttered a word.

"You can stop it. Just tell me who else was involved," the first sergeant told us calmly, raising his voice just enough for the captain to hear.

I never saw Braun selling any dope; as far as I knew he had always given it away.

After an hour everyone seemed to tire of the farce. When the sun came up, the MPs went through our gear one more time and then loaded Braun onto a Jeep and dragged him away in handcuffs. The rumor had it that he was going to be court-martialed, but I heard later that he was so beat up that the lifers got scared and simply had him transferred into a grunt unit. Damn shame; he was one of the best scouts in the company. What a waste, and all over a small bag of pot. Charlie was probably laughing all the way to Hanoi.

53. Sentry Post Alpha

But Achilles was angry still. Once more he addressed the King in violent words: "You drunkard, with eyes like a bitch and heart like a fawn! You never arm yourself with your men for battle, you never go out on a raid with the fighting men— no pluck in you for that! You think it is certain death! It is much better, isn't it, to stay in camp and rob anyone who tells the truth to your face."—Homer, *The Iliad*

My serious problems with the "powers that be" in the Marine Corps began the unlucky day I was assigned guard duty at sentry post Able. The post was a small guard shack that the Seabees had built just outside the barbed wire that encircled our new compound. During the day the sentry box was unmanned and anyone could drive in or out of our base unchallenged, but at night it was manned by those Marines selected for sentry duty, and one unlucky night it was my turn.

Up to that point in my tour, aside from Lieutenant Lord, I hadn't had any real contact with officers. I just did my job, tried to stay squared away and out of their sight.

We had come back from an uneventful patrol from an area we called the Arizona Territory a few days before when I found myself selected for guard duty. After supper I grabbed my gear and walked down the road to the guard shack. As darkness descended,

53. Sentry Post Alpha

I sat down on the bench that ran along the inside wall of the shed, put my gear on the floor and looked out, but I couldn't see a thing. Someone had installed an electric light directly over the doorway. It was blindingly bright and there was no switch to turn it off. The light prevented me from seeing anyone coming down the road, but anyone coming down the road could certainly see me. I felt like an insect caught in a circle of white light, the perfect target for any gook sniper worth his salt.

"Whose great idea was this?" I asked myself, getting more and more nervous.

I got up and tried to adjust the light so that it wasn't shining directly down on me, but it was bolted into place, and covered in a protective steel frame. I didn't have any tools and had no way to get at it. I walked up the road about thirty feet until I was outside the glare. The base was settling down for the night. One by one the other lights in the compound finally went out. There was no moon, but the sky was brilliant with stars.

Around midnight I saw headlights were moving down the dirt road leading to our compound. I grabbed my rifle and starting walking back toward the guard post when the lights on the approaching vehicle suddenly went out and the sound of its engine died.

I had a bad feeling and stayed where I was, outside the cone of light. The vehicle was coasting toward me down the hill, now completely silent. I could now see that it was a Jeep and could just make out three figures sitting in it.

"Halt!" I called out when it was a couple of hundred feet in front of from me.

"Halt! Identify yourself!" I yelled louder, but the Jeep kept coming.

I took the safety off my M-16. "Halt!" I yelled for a third time, dropping to my knee and bringing my M-16 up to my shoulder.

"Fuck it! I'm not going to just stand here and get run over," I thought to myself. Aiming low, I squeezed off a single round, which ricocheted off the ground a few feet in front of the vehicle. I heard the squeal of brakes and the Jeep skidded to halt less than fifty feet in front of me.

"Don't fire! Don't fire! We're Americans!" I heard a terrified voice call out.

I kept my weapon raised and moved closer.

Under the light I saw Captain Bilger sitting next to Blake, one of the drivers in the motor pool. A new lieutenant from the Fourth Platoon sat stiffly in the back of the vehicle.

"What the hell! Why didn't you stop?" I shouted, angry and deeply frightened by what had nearly occurred. "I nearly wasted you!"

The captain tried to stand up and say something, but fell back in his seat. Even from a distance I could smell the whisky on his breath. The lieutenant said something to Blake that I didn't hear. Blake looked at me without a word, started up the engine, and the Jeep moved past me. Bilger tried sitting up again, but as he turned to look back at me the Jeep lurched forward and he once again fell back in his seat. My shot had alerted the entire compound and the Jeep proceeded down the road through a gauntlet of armed and nervous men.

Less than half an hour later Truman came up to relieve me, "You're in deep shit; what the hell happened?" he asked.

I shook my head and tried to explain.

"Well, you'd better get your act together," Truman advised. "The first sergeant is really pissed and wants to see you in the command bunker!"

I picked up my gear and walked down the road until I got to the headquarters building. The first sergeant was waiting for me by the door.

"Get in here!" he shouted as soon as he saw me. "What the hell were you doing, firing at an officer?"

"I couldn't see who it was. I called three times for them to halt. They didn't, so I fired a warning shot in front of them."

"Didn't you see who was in the Jeep?" he asked angrily.

I shook my head, "No, I couldn't see anything with that goddamned light shining on me. The Jeep could have been loaded with gooks for all I knew."

"Why did you leave your post?" he asked ominously, switching his questioning.

"What?"

"They said you weren't in the guard shack. Why did you leave your post?" he repeated.

I took a deep breath and chose my words carefully, knowing what I said could easily lead to a court-martial.

"I didn't leave my post, first sergeant," I told him, defending myself. "I positioned myself so that I would be outside of the light and could see down the road."

I wondered afterward if he was the one responsible for ordering the lights to be installed. It was just the chickenshit sort of thing he would have concerned himself with.

"They had turned off their lights and engine. I think they were trying to sneak by me," I explained, realizing as I spoke just how lame my excuse sounded.

"And why would they do that?" he asked skeptically.

"How the hell would I know? The captain was drunk, probably the lieutenant as well.... Ask Blake."

"Already did," he replied. "Go on … get out of here," he ordered gruffly.

I never found out if Blake had supported my account or not. When I asked him he told me that he was under orders not to talk to me about it until the "investigation" was completed, but I knew Blake well enough to know that he wouldn't jeopardize his easy job as an officer's driver just to stick up for me. It was only months later when I was nearly ready to rotate back to the States that he finally confided to me that Captain Bilger had thought it would be fun to coast through the gate and "catch some asshole sleeping." His confession came far too late for it to do me any good.

The next morning at inspection the captain found my rifle dirty, and that day and for many weeks afterward I found myself on a continuous round of work details, stringing barbed wire, clearing brush and burning shit. No matter how well I polished my boots or cleaned the barrel of my M-16, they always found something. I had loved being a Recon Marine, but now I began to realize that Force Recon didn't seem to care all that much for me. I found myself working alongside the dregs of the outfit, the slackers, stoners and other shit birds of the company. These men had an entirely different outlook from the well-disciplined Marines I had previously been associated with.

"What's your hurry, man?" one of the men on the work detail asked me as I jumped up on a truck to unload crates of rations. He sat down next to the tailgate. "We've got all morning."

"Just trying to finish up," I responded.

"Shit, man, we finish early and they just find something else for us to do."

He pulled a roach from his pocket and, lighting it, up took a long pull and offered it to me. I shook my head and looked around nervously, It was early morning, and we were right in the middle of the compound. He passed it on to the other Marine in our work detail, who cupped it in his hands and inhaled deeply.

"Maybe later we'll all be dead," the Marine he had passed it to replied meditatively, taking another long draw.

---

54. Murder

A voice is heard in Ramah, weeping and great mourning, Rachel weeping for her children and refusing to be comforted, because they are no more. —Jeremiah 31:15

Since the incident with Captain Bilger at the sentry post I had been on his hit list, and no matter what I did there didn't seem to be any way to get off it. Even Lieutenant Lord seemed to grow tired of having me written up time and time again at inspections. It didn't reflect well on him. He probably knew that I was as squared away as anyone in the company and that Captain Bilger was just busting me. He finally offered me the job of cleaning up the enlisted men's club every morning when we were not on patrol. This would at least get me out of formation and out of the captain's sight.

The next day, I found myself sweeping up the money that had fallen out of the pockets of drunken Marines at the enlisted men's club. While everyone else was standing for inspection, I was listening to music on the radio and wiping down the bar. I began to think that things might be getting better, but they continued to go downhill.

That night on sentry duty, I saw the major walking slowly toward our bunker. He had his head down and seemed to be in deep thought. I hesitated to disturb him and simply watched as he made his way closer. When he got near I said, "Good evening, sir," to him. He nodded but kept walking and didn't say anything in response. In the morning, however, I was told to report once again to the first sergeant. He told me that the major had complained to him that he had walked past my post without a challenge.

"What?" I asked, hurt and bewildered by the accusation. "I saw as soon as he turned toward our bunker. I wished him a good evening as he got closer. I said "good evening," what more did he want?"

"The *major* said you weren't alert," the first sergeant repeated dryly, emphasizing the word "major" and ordering me to report for another work detail.

Ah, the irony of life as an enlisted man. First the officers complained when you challenged them; then they complained when you didn't.

I knew if the major had a choice of believing his second in command about what happened at the sentry post or me, his decision would be obvious. I had never seen him walking around the outside bunkers before; perhaps he was testing me? Perhaps I was getting paranoid, but I began to think that he might have been trying to set me up. I didn't know what was going on in his head. I had never even spoken to him before.

I was assigned to repair the barbed wire and clear out the grass between the rows of wire. We burned it out, spraying kerosene on the weeds from tanks of kerosene strapped to our backs. Once the fire was lit, the flames on the ground could be directed by spraying on more kerosene. It was hot, dirty work. The wire had to be lifted up in sections so that we could work underneath it. Our heavy gloves were soon cut to pieces by the razor-sharp wire and most of the men were bleeding before the sergeant called off the work party around noon. I was still fuming about being put on another punishment detail for no reason.

"It just ain't fair," I complained to one of the black guys working beside me as we picked up our shovels and headed back.

"Man, you think the world is fair?" he said, laughing at me. "Where you ever get that idea?"

As I walked back to our hooch I passed a group of Seabees busily constructing a stage in front of the movie screen that was set up near the parade ground. Westerns and guts-and-glory war movies, particularly about Vietnam, were the favorites. One would think that we would have had our fill of violence, but that was not the case; the more savage the movie the better. Perhaps the Marine Corps believed that showing war movies would accustom us to the brutality all around us. More likely, we were seeing projected on the screen images of the men we imagined ourselves to be. What fools we were, gaping like sheep at images projected on a white plywood screen, applauding movie stars who had managed to avoid the draft and were profiting handsomely from the war stories coming out of Vietnam.

There were no movies this particular evening. The Seabees told me that they were constructing a stage for a USO[1] tour that was going to be performing at our base. It was the first I had heard about it, but at the time I was too hot to care. All I was looking forward to was a shower and a long drink of water. After I had gotten both I stretched out on my cot and tried to rest. When I awoke it was evening and I heard the sounds of a band warming up. A large group of Marines were milling around in front of the small stage that the Seabees had built that afternoon.

The band was made up of five or six Vietnamese singers playing guitars and drums. When I walked up they were singing old Beach Boy songs. They played with a lot of enthusiasm, but California surfing songs sung with Vietnamese accents sounded simply awful. While I watched, one of the singers, a tiny Vietnamese girl who looked like she should have been in grade school began stripping down to a bikini. The men whooped and howled.

I was certainly no prude, but this was too much even for me. I turned my back on the spectacle and climbed up the hill toward our club, hoping to get a beer. The place was almost deserted; everyone was at the show. I fished a cold beer out of the ice bucket and walked over to pay our new bartender, Corporal Wilkins, who was now counting the days until he his tour was up.

"How's the show?" he asked.

54. Murder

"Terrible, you're not missing a thing," I told him irritably.

"Why don't you see if you can sneak by the officers club? I heard that they have an Australian singer coming over."

"I hope she's better than the ones they have down there," I told him, pointing to the sad Vietnamese band and their teenage stripper.

"Don't worry about that. Officers and lifers always have the best ... liquor, women, you name it."

I took his advice and walked down the hill toward the club, sipping my beer as I went. Enlisted men were not allowed inside, however, a group of men were peering in through the large screened window. I pushed my way closer and looked inside the building.

The room was decorated in a Hawaiian decor. It was packed, with men sitting around small tables or standing at the bar. Bottles of hard liquor lined the shelves. Many of the faces were strange to me and I assumed that officers from other units had come down for the show. To the right of the bar was a stage, and in a spotlight I saw a beautiful young girl picking up the microphone. She smiled, acknowledging the applause, and then began to sing, her voice delightfully low and sweet.

After a few songs, I saw our major get up from the table and move toward the stage. Taking the microphone out of her hand, he began to thank her when I heard a soft popping sound. Heads turned toward it, and then back to the stage, to where the singer was reaching out to grasp the microphone. She took a step forward and then a spray of blood burst from her mouth. Her drummer lunged forward and caught her around the waist as she fell to the floor. Someone yelled, "Incoming!" as the lights were cut and everyone dove for the floor.

The compound was in turmoil. Within a few seconds alarms were sounding and everyone was running for their weapons. Flares were popping up into the sky, lighting up the perimeter. I grabbed my gear and stumbled into the bunker behind our hooch, Any minute I expected to be fighting for my life, but nothing further happened. After an hour or so the order was given to stand down. As I gathered my gear together and walked back to our hooch I fell in with Bo, who told me that he had heard that the singer had died instantly from a single gunshot wound to the heart.

Bo shook his head in disbelief. "A girl."

I felt the same way. It was always terrible to watch men killed alongside you, but for a lovely young girl to be shot while singing to us? It was so outside the normal order of things that it was hard to believe. I told Bo that I thought that the major had been the target and that the singer had just happened to step into the line of fire.

We passed a group of Marines talking to one of the snipers in the Third Platoon. Like an oracle of old, he sat back basking in their attention. "Naw ... if I set in the brush eight or nine hundred yards back with Daisy here"—he patted his long rifle affectionately—"why, you'd hardly even hear the shot."

I kept remembering the strange popping sound that came from my left. It didn't sound like a long-range shot to me. It seemed to come from somewhere close to where I was standing.

Throughout the day the stories grew. Most of the men believed that the major had been the target and that the girl had been killed by accident. Others swore that they had seen one of the Vietnamese kitchen staff suspiciously duck into one of the trenches shortly before the shot was heard.

The next morning after inspection we noticed an older man standing next to the major. His wore civilian clothes, dark pants and white shirt instead of a regular uniform. A large pearl-handled pistol was strapped to a holster around his rather portly hip.

"Who's this cowboy?" Truman asked under his breath as the unknown man advanced with major.

"At ease," the major commanded. We stood at the at ease position, legs spread, hands locked behind our backs.

"This is Captain Green from the Criminal Investigation Division, CID," Simbul told us, nodding to the pudgy man by his side. "He is here to conduct an investigation into the murder which occurred here last night."

I could feel the tension spread throughout the company.

"Shit," Truman muttered under his breath, "just what we fuckin' need."

The CID captain began to speak. "Last night a young woman was shot and killed. We believe from a shot fired at close range from a silenced weapon." He paused for a moment. "I am in charge of the investigation and will be here on base all week. I urge anyone with any information to come forward and speak to me."

We were dismissed.

Knowing all too well how the Marine Corps operated, I hated the thought of getting involved at all. I was worried that somehow I might draw attention to myself and because of my interaction with the major the previous night, perhaps even find myself becoming the scapegoat. In the end, however, I decided to meet with Green and tell him the little I knew. That afternoon I gave him my story about the popping noise that I heard. He asked where I was standing and if I noticed anything else suspicious. I told him that was all I knew and felt relieved to be dismissed.

A few days later everyone was called together once again. The CID captain announced that they had identified the murderer and would be taking him to the brig that afternoon. He added that if convicted the man would likely be executed by a firing squad. In the distance we could see Reilly, the Third Platoon's sergeant, sitting in a Jeep, handcuffed and guarded by two MPs. I had been on a couple of patrols with Reilly and knew him well. He was one of the nicest guys in our outfit. Everyone liked him. I couldn't imagine him ever doing such a thing.

Walking back to our hut, I told Bo that it might be a ploy by Green to have the real murderer confess, but in the weeks that followed no one came forward and Reilly didn't return. It wasn't until nearly a month had passed before another arrest was made and Reilly finally returned to the company. My guess had been correct. His arrest had been apparently nothing more than a ruse to get the real killer to come forward.

A Marine we called Pappy was charged for the murder. He was a rigger, one of the men responsible for packing our parachutes. I never knew him to go out in the field. I always hoped that I wouldn't draw one of the chutes that Pappy had packed because he seemed to spend most of his time drinking in the club.

Pappy's court-martial took place well after I had returned to the States, but I read about it. Two other Marines had apparently confessed to actually stealing the weapon but told the investigators that they had given it to Pappy. When I read this, I couldn't help but wonder if the other two men were the Dyer brothers. I knew that the three of them were close friends, and it was just the type of thing I could see the little bastards doing.

Pappy admitted having the pistol in his possession but said that he had only used it to shoot at a herd of feral pigs that had been nosing around the perimeter of our base. This was a lame, bullshit excuse if I ever heard one. If there had been any pigs nosing around our compound, sentries like myself would have seen them. I didn't believe Pappy's story, and apparently neither did anyone else at his trial. He was convicted and sentenced to twenty-five years of hard labor.

I thought that was the end of the matter, but years later I found that Pappy's murder conviction was eventually overturned. His lawyer argued that the immunity offered to the two other Marines called into question their incriminating testimony. By that time years had passed since the murder had taken place, the Vietnam War was winding down, and no one in the military wanted to reopen the case. Pappy was released and reinstated into the Marine Corps, He kept his rank and received back pay for the time he had spent in prison. As far as the military is concerned, and to the best of my knowledge, the murder of the young Australian singer remains unsolved to this day.

55. Short-Timer

So much a long communion tends
To make us what we are:–even I
Regain'd my freedom with a sigh.
—Byron, *The Prisoner of Chillon*

Every morning as soon as I awoke I went over to my short-timer calendar hanging on my wall and carefully inked in another day. There were several versions of the calendar in use in Nam. The duty gofer had a bunch them in his files and would give you a copy if you treated him right. Mine was a drawing of the Snoopy comic strip character twirling around happily with his ears flying out. Every part of his body was divided up into little numbered squares, first months, then weeks, and then days. When Snoopy had been completely colored, my tour of duty would be over. It was particularly satisfying to come in from a patrol and be able to fill in a big block of days.

Truman presented me with a short-timer stick, a piece of wood about the size of a riding crop. He had hammered a .50-caliber shell casing on to one end. Each member of the team had carved part of it. Initials and crudely incised symbols crisscrossed its surface. The stick was supposed to bring good luck, and I cockily carried it with me everywhere, a swagger stick for a burnt-out bush Marine. I had heard that in other units there was only one stick, which was given to the person with the least amount of days left in Nam and then, when he left, passed along to the next Marine in line. There was no such restriction in our unit and men often made their own when they got down to a month or so left in-country.

"Hey, short-timer!" my friends called out when I entered the mess hall carrying it. I'd nod happily and reply, "Shorter than your dick," or whatever silliness popped into my head at the moment. I knew that each of them knew to the day how long he had left on his own tour and like prison inmates each of them looked forward to being set free. I knew what they were thinking because I had thought the same thing myself: "Hell, if this shithead made it, maybe I can too."

I had less than five weeks left to go. Over a year in Nam, now a little over a month left. So many of my teammates had been either killed or wounded, but it looked like I was going to make it. Out of my original platoon only Bo, Truman and Ma were left and I had been in-country several months longer than they had. I considered it a miracle to have survived this long.

There was a belief in Nam that most soldiers got killed within either their first few weeks in-country or their last. I heard it called "the light bulb theory." Most light bulbs either burned out when they were first plugged in, or failed at the end of their life expectancy. I believed in the theory. At the beginning of their tour the new guys didn't know enough to stay alive. They would trigger booby traps, bumble into ambushes, or hesitate to kill a fraction of a second too long. At the end of their tour even the best of men became a danger to the team as well as themselves. Their focus changed from doing their job to simply staying alive and running out the clock. Spooked by the slightest sound, living only partly in the present, short-timers did their best to act normally and hide from their teammates the fact that their nerves were completely shot.

Toward the end of my previous patrol, I had been so convinced that I would be killed in my sleep that I stayed awake for three days and nights. I offered to take radio watches from the other men and a few foolishly let me do it. In the past I had always trusted the other team members to watch my back. Now with my tour of duty coming to an end I trusted only myself.

I found myself daydreaming more and more about home and what I would do when I got there. I thought about going back to college. I saw myself walking along tree-lined roads to my classes as autumn leaves swirled around my feet. I pictured myself quietly studying late at night in a room of my own. Immersed in my new life as a scholar, I would be able to forget everything about my months in Vietnam. It was a simple dream but very precious to me.

Usually short-timers were taken out of the bush and given a job in the rear a month or so before their tour ended. I remembered my friend Wilkins. At one time he was one of the best scouts in Force Recon. When he had about six weeks left he got so jumpy that even after being taken out of the bush and put on guard duty he started seeing Vietcong behind every shadow. Night after night he'd open up with the .50-caliber, screaming, "gooks in the wire!" Nothing anyone could say or do would calm him down. He swore he saw them.

After a series of sleepless nights and repeated warnings, the exasperated first sergeant gave him the lowest job in the company, burning out the latrine pots. These were fifty-gallon drums cut in half and placed beneath the latrine seats. Every morning Wilkins would drag the quarter barrels of waste out to the burning area, pour in a gallon or so of kerosene and light it with a piece of toilet paper. The disgusting mixture of shit and piss would smoke and stink, but as long as it was constantly stirred with a long stick everything would eventually burn off. It was hot, dirty, somewhat humiliating work. It was a job usually assigned as a punishment detail, but Wilkins seemed to thrive on it.

After a couple of weeks on latrine duty Wilkins's eyes lost their haunted look. As he worked, stripped to his shorts in the ungodly heat of the Asian sun, his skin lost its jungle pallor and turned a deep golden brown. He was assigned to be the club bartender and after a few weeks he gained back some of the weight he had lost humping the bush and even began to develop a beer belly. This wasn't surprising, because he was liked by everyone and at the end of the day was always treated to cold beer by the other men.

We held a party for him just before he was due to rotate back to the States. In the middle of the festivities we made our way to the nearest latrine with Wilkins in tow. Nailed to the side of the latrine was a large wooden plaque that we had all signed. Written in gold letters against a blue background were the words *Wilkins Memorial Shitter*. He stared at it in amazement. For a moment I was afraid that he might take offense. At one time he was known to have quite a temper, but now he just shook his head and laughed. Blinking and smiling in the sunlight, he reminded me of a benign Buddha.

I had no wish to take over Wilkins's job, but I was looking forward to being taken out of the bush and spending my remaining weeks in Nam back in the compound on mess duty or something just as safe. The officers in control of my destiny had other ideas.

Lieutenant Lord ordered our team to report to the intelligence tent for a briefing. When we got there members of the Second Platoon was already waiting. We barely had time to seat ourselves when Captain Bilger entered. We got to our feet and snapped to attention. He proceeded to tell us that our two teams would be doing a joint prisoner snatch. Our objective was the capture or elimination of a Caucasian-looking soldier who had been spotted moving toward a Montagnard village a few weeks ago.

"I thought the Montagnards were our friends?" Truman asked uneasily.

"We thought they were." The captain nodded. "That's why we've got to know what that Russian bastard is doing in their village." How he knew the soldier was Russian was something he didn't bother explaining to us.

He turned the briefing over to Lieutenant Lord, who started giving us our assignments. I was shocked to be told that I was assigned to be one of the three men on the grab team. This was the most dangerous role of the whole operation. I was expecting to be pulled from the bush, not assigned to another mission, especially not something as dangerous as a prisoner snatch.

I couldn't stop myself from thinking about all of the men I had known who had been killed as they got really short, and a dull foreboding welled up inside me. I knew with absolute certainty that if I went on this operation I wouldn't return. I sat through the rest of the briefing in a numb silence. As soon as Lord dismissed us I went over to talk to him as he was leaving the room and asked to talk to him as he tried to push past me.

"Later, " he responded impatiently, still trying to get by me, but I persisted.

"Sir, I've gone out more times than anyone else in the company…"

He must have guessed what I was going to ask and interrupted me.

"I don't have time for this bullshit. If I say you're going … you're going!" he interrupted, pushing past me and walking out the door. I wondered if he didn't know how short I was or just didn't care. Didn't he realize how much I needed to go home?

If he had said something like, "It's because of your experience that we need you," or anything even remotely similar, I would have accepted the assignment despite my misgivings and would have gone on the mission. His offhand dismissal, however, made me realize how completely someone I didn't even respect could control the rest of my life.

The lieutenant however must have thought about what I had told him and had second thoughts, because the next day I was taken off the mission roster and told to report for mess duty. Whether he made the decision out of compassion or self-preservation is not for me to say. Perhaps he saw my anger and just didn't trust me being around him with a loaded weapon.

During the Vietnam War there were more than a thousand episodes of enlisted men "fragging"[1] their own officers. This is truly an appalling statistic as it stands, but the true number is probably many times higher. This number is a shameful blot on the military heritage of the men who served honorably in Vietnam, and one that I suggest has never been adequately examined. For a soldier to take such an extreme action against his own commander would have meant that he had been driven to madness. During my entire tour I never heard of such an action even mentioned. There was however, the incident of the murdered singer, so I guess I didn't know everything that was going on in the company.

It was true that I didn't particularly like the lieutenant as a person, and I was wary of his decisions in the bush, but I certainly didn't hate him. I figured we were both on the same team, and each of us had our own roles. I was probably reading too much into the reason for Lord's decision, he probably just needed someone to go on mess duty and picked me.

Like other bush Marines who had been in-country for many months my body had reacted to the sweltering heat and constant patrols by paring itself of any excess fat. I wasn't sick or weak but was terribly thin. I had lost nearly fifty pounds, nearly a quarter of my body weight.

I reported to the staff sergeant in charge of the kitchen. He was a tall blond guy who kept things running with a quiet efficiency. Everyone seemed to like him. When I reported in he was sitting down in a small office built on the end of one of the mess halls writing in a green ledger. He saw me looking down curiously at what he was doing and confided that he was writing a novel about Vietnam.

"The only thing wrong is that I have not seen anything more than the inside of the kitchen." He smiled ruefully.

"Well, there's lot of guys that would take your place in a heartbeat," I awkwardly responded.

"I know, but even if I got to go out on one patrol at least I could say that I did something."

"Yeah, you could get yourself killed and take a lot of other men with you," I thought to myself, remembering the supply sergeant.

"You could probably talk to the major," I suggested halfheartedly, hoping he wouldn't take my advice.

"Already did; he told me that my job was here." He looked around at his neat little office with distaste.

I didn't know what else to say, so I just stood there. He stood up wearily and put aside his book.

"Anyway ... you'll be with us for a few weeks. You'll work breakfast unless something special's going on. I'll introduce you to the crew."

The "crew" turned out to be two young Vietnamese girls who helped prepare the meals and an older papa-san who helped clean up after each meal. Four other Marines were on mess duty with me helped dole out the food. The young girls were as perky as young squirrels. They chattered away, laughed, teased, and kept their distance from us. My duties were light. I reported every morning at dawn to start the water heaters and wipe down the tables, helped put out the food and occasionally served.

Once I assisted the cook in laying out a fancy steak dinner in the officer's lounge, complete with china, candles, wine and an ice sculpture of an American eagle. The fancy setting flamed the dull resentment I had built up toward officers and authority in general. I recognized my attitude for the sour-grapes feeling that it was and put such thoughts aside. In my own mind I outranked them all—I was a short-timer!

Less than a week later Foresight returned from the prisoner snatch without a prisoner and without Ma. Bo told me that the metal casing from an illumination round fell out of the sky and hit him on the back of his head, knocking him unconscious. I started to laugh at the sheer improbability of such a thing happening.

"Its not funny," Bo admonished me sternly. "That canister probably weighed ten pounds; he was lucky it didn't kill him!"

His words only caused me to laugh harder and Bo couldn't help but join me.

"He's all right, isn't he?" I finally gasped.

"Yeah, he'll be fine after a couple of days," Bo replied, rubbing tears of mirth from his own eyes.

---

56. Trinkets

Mistah Kurtz—he dead.
A penny for the old guy.
—T.S. Eliot, "The Hollow Men"

Another three weeks on mess duty passed. My team came back from yet another unsuccessful prisoner snatch. The day after they returned, the lieutenant told me to report to the command bunker after I had finished my mess duties. Thinking back to the incident with Captain Bilger at the sentry post, I feared the worst. I took off my mess duty apron and the foolish white paper hat that we were forced to wear in the kitchen and reported as ordered.

The duty gofer told me to wait for a minute and then showed me into the major's office. The room was large and rather cozy; a window looked out over the parade ground, and a leather easy chair sat next to a well-stocked bookcase. There was even a braided woolen rug on the floor. If it weren't for the American flag standing in the corner, I would have thought that I was standing in the study of a college professor.

Major Simbul got up from behind his large desk and stood in front of it. The first sergeant was on his left and Lieutenant Lord stood by his right. I could tell they had been talking about me but had stopped when I entered. I saw my personnel file open on the desk.

"What now?" I thought to myself, saluting and standing at attention.

To my surprise, the major held out his hand, gave me a rather forced smile and congratulated me on completing my tour of duty. He handed me the orders that would return me to the States. He looked at me as if waiting for me to say something, perhaps thank him, but my mind went blank and I couldn't think of a thing to say.

"At ease," the first sergeant barked.

I spread my feet and clasping my hands behind my back stared straight ahead.

The lieutenant walked over and also shook my hand, pressing something into the palm as he did so. I looked down at what he had given me in such a furtive manner. It was a large silver-coated coin; the disk was engraved with the words *First Force Recon* on one side and *First Marine Division* on the other. I had never seen anything like it before and just stared at it. Lord saw me looking down at the coin in confusion and in an annoyed voice told me that it was a challenge coin. It would prove to others that I had been a member of First Force Recon.

"I need this piece of tin to prove that I was in Recon?" I asked myself.

The sergeant handed me a Zippo lighter with the Force Recon emblem embossed on the front. I didn't smoke, but I figured I could give it to my father when I returned home. The three men stood there looking at me.

I wanted to say something, to tell them that I had done my best and that I had been a good bush Marine. I wanted to remind them that I had survived twenty-seven patrols, more than anyone else in the company. I wanted to tell them that I was grateful to be going home. Instead I simply stood there like the resentful, dangerous dumb beast I had become. Were they expecting me to thank them, and if so for what? I could tell they were growing annoyed with me, but I didn't know why. I had done my duty. What more did they want from me?

"Dismissed," the major finally ordered.

I saluted, turned on my heel and left with my handful of trinkets and my orders out of Nam. I returned to the hooch and packed up my gear. The rest of the team had left for another prisoner snatch. I would be gone before they returned.

I sat down on my cot, pulled my footlocker over and gazed at the top where there were twenty-seven names written on the top of the wooden cover, Elephant Valley, Happy Valley, Charlie Ridge, Razorback Ridge, Antenna Valley, The Arizona Territory, The Garden of Eden and so many more. I took out my Magic Marker and added one final entry in bold black letters: **HOME!**

56. Trinkets

I remembered Chief pushing the footlocker over to my cot the first time we met. My fingers traced the black square where he had blanked out Mariner's name so many months ago. The footlocker he had given me had served me well, safely carrying my personal gear from firebase to firebase as Force Recon moved around Nam. I took a Magic Marker and scratched out my name. As I did so, it seemed as though an oppressive weight was finally being lifted from my mind. In removing my name perhaps I could free the worst part of myself from the person I had become after thirteen months of combat. I later learned that it wouldn't be that simple.

I began removing clothes and other gear from the footlocker, stuffing dry socks, clean utilities and my good boots into my duffel bag, and putting my old worn bush gear into a plastic garbage bag. My old jungle clothes still carried the smell of sweat, bug juice and jungle mud on them. I wrote #1 on a tag that I put around the neck of the garbage bag so that the gooks taking away our garbage would know there was something inside that bag they might be able to use. I left my throwing knives, a spare K-Bar, my bush hat, a compass, a tube of camo paint, a bottle of bug juice, a few pencil flares, and a few more odds and ends in the footlocker for the next poor soul to take my place.

My flak jacket, web gear and helmet hung by a nail from the wall and I took them down for the last time. The flak jacket was ripped and one of the protective plates had fallen out. I had always intended to get it replaced, but I never did, and now I didn't need to. I picked up the helmet that had protected me during the An Hoa rocket attacks. The Marine who had it before me had drawn a crude peace symbol on the front of the helmet and had written the words *Don't follow me.... I'm lost too!* on the back of it. I smiled one final time at the saying and put the helmet one last time on my head.

I took down my rifle from its rack and walked down to the path to turn in my gear. I told the private taking my flak jacket at the supply shack about the missing panel. He took one look at it and threw the entire thing in the trash. I gave him my helmet and the rest of my web gear and went next door to the armory to turn in my rifle.

There was a new armorer behind the counter, a young corporal. He took a look at my battered M-16 and grimaced. "Man, this baby's had a lot of hard use," he told me, running his hands over the battered stock.

"Best damn rifle in the company!" I told him defensively as he looked at it skeptically. "Now don't you go issuing it to a fuckin' pogue," I warned him. "Give it to someone going out in the bush. It'll keep 'em alive."

The corporal stepped back and nodded, startled and perhaps a little frightened by the veiled threat in my voice.

I returned to our hooch. My area was nearly stripped, and I felt naked without my rifle. It had been a part of me for such a long time that I missed the reassuring weight in my hand. I took the green notebooks that I had written in every day and carefully put my Snoopy calendar inside the cover so that he would be protected. The books themselves went into the duffel bag. I put my priceless orders carefully on top and clipped the duffel bag shut.

That was it. I was done. Except for my footlocker, the area looked like I had never been there. My cot was ready for the Marine who would take my place. I wish that I could have known him. Maybe I could have passed along a few of the things that Chief had taught me, but it was too late now.

I picked up my duffel bag. I now knew how Polanski, Feo, Doc and the other men had felt when their tour was over. I would never again have friends like the ones I had known. They were like brothers to me, we would have died for one another.

I left the compound as quietly and as lonely as I had arrived, hitching a ride from a truck that was going into the Da Nang air base. We drove part of the way along the same road that I had come in on, but a lot of things had changed in the thirteen months since I had first made my first trip.

The ammunition depot that had been there when I first arrived was destroyed several months ago. At first, it was thought that the depot had been hit by NVA sappers or destroyed during a rocket or mortar attack, but eventually the truth came out. Someone in authority had complained that the grass was growing too high on the top of one of the ammunition bunkers and had ordered it removed. Another idiot had the bright idea of burning it off with one of the kerosene flamers instead of cutting it. The exploding bombs and other ordnance shook the entire valley. Nearly a quarter of a mile away from the ammunition depot the steel fence posts around the Freedom Hill PX had been bent over by the blast. The steel buildings where we had drawn our pay and gotten our uniforms pressed had collapsed completely.

"Damn shame," I thought as we rode past the wrecked PX. I had spent good times there with Chief, Slim, and—I forced my runaway memories to a stop. I couldn't go there now. I had to focus on getting away while I still could. I felt that my luck was running out and that time was not on my side.

The rice paddies were still there, shimmering in the sunlight and reflecting the sky and clouds like huge mirrors. The young boys were guiding their water buffalos with their small sticks. The farmers were knee-deep in the water of the paddies, bending over their stalks of rice as they had done for the generation before we came and would continue to do for generations after the last Americans had left.

"How beautiful ... how beautiful" I found myself repeating my mantra one last time.

57. Ho...Ho...Ho Chi Minh

For it's Tommy this, an' Tommy that, an' "Chuck him out, the brute!"
But it's "Saviour of 'is country" when the guns begin to shoot;
An' it's Tommy this, an' Tommy that, an' anything you please;
An' Tommy ain't a bloomin' fool—you bet that Tommy sees!
—Rudyard Kipling, "Tommy"

They had just started boarding us for our flight out of Nam to Guam when a group of rowdy half-drunk Air Force officers pushed through the line and forced their way ahead of us onto the plane. We were forced to wait until the next plane, which left the following morning. I could have followed the other men and spent the night in Air Force barracks, but I was afraid of missing the flight. I spent the night in the open, sleeping like a bum on a bench outside the terminal, sipping on a small bottle of Southern Comfort that I had picked up from one of the gook vendors.

I drank my bottle of whisky and remembered the happy times, sunlit days filled with friends and laughter. I tried to push away the dark memories, but in the same way that the highest waves on the ocean are always joined to the deepest troughs the bad times came flooding back into my mind as well. I thought back about my tour of duty, how when I first arrived in Nam I had risked my life over and over again in the most casual manner, before finally realizing almost too late how very precious a gift it truly was. I finally went to sleep, thinking about how great it would be when I finally made it back home.

The night slowly faded and the sun rose hot and clear. It was my last day in Nam. I stood my now empty bottle of whisky against the fence and walked down to the staging area to finally board an early morning flight to Guam. We landed and were taken over to a large supply depot to retrieve the uniforms and personal gear that we had left there thirteen months ago. After they searched through my records I was told that they had nothing for me. My uniforms and personal effects had apparently been destroyed in a fire several months earlier. Other Marines were given different stories. The uniforms and personal effects that they had stored in Guam before leaving for Nam had been lost in a hurricane or had been accidentally mislabeled and destroyed. They sure had a lot of accidents in that outfit.

We were flown from Guam to Hawaii and then to San Diego, where we were taken to the Marine Corps base at Camp Pendleton for final processing. After we were shown our quarters we were given a physical. I felt in pretty good shape, but even with my month of gorging myself on mess duty I had lost over thirty pounds. My mental state was something else, but they didn't examine us for that. I was easily startled and yet feeling strangely detached from what was going on around me. My thoughts of Nam were vivid, my memories of my earlier life hazy. I didn't know what would become of me in the future, but I knew I had made it out of Vietnam alive, and for the moment that was enough.

We were given passes to go off base, but none of us had any U.S. currency. The few pieces of scrip that we had in our pockets were worthless in the States. If there was any way for us to exchange them no one told us about it. A fat staff sergeant came in and told us that if we went to provide the audience for a TV show afterward we would be taken to a restaurant and given all the pizza and all the beer we could hold. We piled eagerly into a waiting bus and were taken to a movie studio where we suffered through the horrors of a comedy quiz show. Large signs were held up whenever they wanted us to "Clap" or "Laugh." Finally, we were led back onto the bus, but instead of being taken for pizza and beer we were unloaded back at the base, no pizza, no beer, no nothing. We never saw the sergeant again, and it was a good thing for him that we didn't.

The following day a recruiting sergeant came around trying to get us to re-up. He glanced at my paperwork. "With your record you could make another grade if you re-enlisted and you'd get a nice bonus as well."

"No thanks," I responded, shaking my head at the offer.

"Well, at least you had a taste of the Marine Corps," he said cheerfully, not upset in the least by my refusal.

"Sergeant … I've had more than a taste. I've had a bellyful!"

He wrote something on my paperwork and handed it back to me. When I looked at the pages later he had written: *"Marine is UNDECIDED about Re-Enlistment."*

In a feeble effort to find jobs for thousands of returning GIs, the Marines had invited local companies to come onto the base to talk to us about civilian employment. A representative from a bus company in San Diego described the openings they had for drivers and mechanics. At the end of his talk one of the Marines stood up and asked if he had any work for a machine gunner. The recruiter laughed uncomfortably and left without anyone taking him up on his jobs. I guess we all figured that as veterans we wouldn't have any problem finding work, an assumption that turned out to be overly optimistic, to say the least.

A few days after arriving in California I had tickets to the East Coast, my back pay in my pocket, and my discharge papers clutched in my hand. I was told that I still had some time left on my enlistment but that it was unlikely that I would be called back into active service. Having taken years of our lives, the Marine Corps now seemed that it couldn't get rid of us fast enough.

I phoned my parents and told them I was back in the United States and that they could expect to see me in a day or two. There was such joy in their voices.

My tickets were for a late-night flight from San Diego to Newark, New Jersey. Newark was the hub for returning troops who lived in the Northeast. We had undergone a final inspection before we left the base, and we were all spit-and-polish in our stateside Marine Corps uniforms. I was surprised at the number of combat ribbons I was entitled to wear on my uniform; they hung heavily on my chest. We were issued AWOL bags[1] to hold our orders and some civilian clothes.

I finally boarded the plane with a small group of other soldiers, most of whom were also returning from Vietnam. Compared with the raucous group of nervous Marines on the outgoing flight to Nam, the return flight consisted of a quiet group of men who were immersed in their own thoughts. We had just settled down in our seats when a gunnery sergeant entered the plane.

"Listen up," he ordered. "You guys have been away for quite a while, and things may not be exactly the same as when you left."

We looked around at one another in confusion, uncertain as to what he could possibly mean. We hadn't been gone that long had we?

"You'll arrive late evening in Chicago and around two a.m. in Newark because at that time of day there's less chance of anti-war protesters, but there are always a group of these bastards hanging around. I strongly advise you to ditch your uniforms and change into civilian clothes before you land if you don't want to get into a confrontation with them."

"Not me! I'm proud of these," a young corporal objected, pointing to the rows of combat ribbons on his chest.

"Suit yourself," the sergeant replied with a shrug. "You're civilians now. You can do what you want. I'm just warning you, that's all."

None of the rest of us said anything. We'd all had our fill of confrontations. I just wanted to get home, see my folks and friends. The last thing I needed was to get into a hassle with anyone.

When we had joined up, the anti-war movement was just getting started. The only radio we heard in Nam was propaganda from the Armed Forces stations. The only paper we received was the *Stars and Stripes,* which was more of a military rag than an actual newspaper. During our tour we were led to believe that the nation was still behind us. We were about to find out that this wasn't the case at all.

Halfway into the flight I went into the small lavatory in the tail of the plane. There was a pile of uniforms on the floor, nearly blocking the door. I took off my combat ribbons and held them in my hand for a moment before dumping them into the trash. I had only worn the insignias for a couple of days and their colors and emblems were still foreign to me. I took off my uniform and crammed it into the small trash receptacle alongside the sink. I opened up my travel bag and put on blue jeans and a T-shirt. The only items I kept were my golden jump wings and my dog tags, which were still taped up on their frayed parachute cord with my can opener. I slipped both of these into the side pocket of my jeans.

The aircraft landed in Chicago and most of the men departed. By the time we got to Newark there were only a handful of men left on the plane. The aircraft landed on schedule and pulled into the terminal.

Despite the early morning flight a dozen scruffy-looking anti-war protestors were waiting for us to disembark. The men sported disheveled beards and long hair. I thought it strange that many of them were wearing military utility jackets and combat boots. The two long-haired women in the group were both very attractive; they wore low-cut blouses, strings of beads and colorfully patterned loose skirts. One of them held up an American flag. The police had set up a barrier between us and the demonstrators and there was a bored-looking cop standing off to one side. As soon as the demonstrators saw us coming down the ramp they started yelling and waving signs.

"Baby killers, murderers!" they shouted, and then started chanting, "Ho … Ho … Ho Chi Minh."

I was the first to go down the ramp, and managed to push my way through to nearest exit before the protestors could really get organized. Most of the other men weren't as fortunate. The men who still wore their Marine uniforms found themselves to be the focus of the protestors attention, cursed by the men and spit upon by the women as they tried to leave the terminal. We would have been better off if we had stuck together as a group, but we were now civilians and on our own. Each of us was anxious to avoid a fight and go our separate ways.

The cop just stood there looking on with a bored expression on his face. He didn't make the slightest attempt to do anything. Why should he? He had probably been standing vigil with them for weeks. He probably even knew them by name. We were the outsiders, arriving like packages a few times a night.

Had they asked, the protestors would have found that my views of the war were probably not that much different from their own, but that wouldn't have made any difference. They wouldn't have cared what I thought. They needed something to protest against and we were readily available.

I made my way to the bus and taxi area. The buses weren't running at that hour of the morning, and the taxi drivers didn't want to go out of the city and miss out on other fares. I had drawn five hundred dollars in back pay and offered one of the taxi drivers a hundred bucks to drive me home. It was a lot for a short ride, but money meant nothing to me. I was so anxious to get home and see my parents that I would probably have given the driver everything in my wallet if he had insisted. I settled in the backseat and peered out the window as we drove through the city.

"I just got back from Vietnam." I mentioned to the driver as he extended his hand for my money.

"Dat so?" he replied in a bored voice, folding the bills and putting them in his shirt pocket.

58. Homecoming

God's law it is that he who learns must suffer.
Even in our sleep the pain "that cannot forget" falls drop by drop
upon the heart and by the awful grace of God gives us wisdom. —Aeschylus

The taxi driver left me off on the corner in front of my house. The sun hadn't come up yet, but the darkness was beginning to fade and the birds had started to sing. How often during the previous year had I awoken to this same half-light and wondered if I would survive the day? It was very quiet as I walked down the sidewalk to my home. The key to the back door was still under the flowerpot by the back steps.

I heard a scuffling noise from behind the door as my old dog heard my steps on the porch and scratched at the door. She was having eye problems when I left and in the thirteen months since I was gone she had grown blind, but she recognized me by smell, whined excitedly and wagged her tail. I buried my face in her warm fur and hugged her. She licked me and whimpered with pleasure, turning from side to side in my arms.

"Good girl," I whispered, petting her head and rubbing her ears. "Good girl."

I stepped into the kitchen and was immediately enveloped by the familiar smells I had grown up with. The warm, sweet scent of tobacco from my father's pipe, the smell of flowers my mother had picked from her garden and placed in a vase on the table, the warm, musty smell from the dog bed by the stove, mingled with a hundred others, each brining back so many memories. How strange that smell, perhaps the weakest of all the senses, can evoke such vivid memories.

My dog ran into my parents' bedroom, whining and crying. I heard my father get up and came into the kitchen. He didn't have his glasses on and his weak blue eyes filled with tears as he gave me a quick hug. He told me that he had stayed up until midnight waiting for me but then went to bed because he thought I wouldn't be able to get home until the morning. I told him that I had taken a taxi from the airport. My parents had

58. Homecoming

never had much money and he raised his eyebrows at the extravagance. The light on my mother's night table turned on.

"Go in and see her," my father urged softly. "She's been waiting for you for such a long time."

I went in to find my mother unable to leave her bed. My father told me later that she had recently been diagnosed with the cancer that would soon take her life. She raised herself up slightly as I entered the room and smiled, but a few seconds later she began to cry softly. I sat on the side of her bed and held her hand. I was shocked by how much she had aged. Her hair was now streaked with gray and she was terribly thin. She settled back against her pillow; her face was pale, but her eyes brimmed with pleasure at my return.

After a few minutes my father said that we should let her rest. I followed him back into the kitchen, where he started making coffee. I told him that I hadn't even known that my mother was sick. He replied slowly that she hadn't wanted to worry me.

"You know, don't you, that by going into the Marine Corps you caused her cancer."

I froze with the coffee in my hand as he continued, "She was never a strong person and her worrying about you every minute of every day ... well, it eventually made her sick."

"I just got home. How could you say something like that to me?" I asked him, shocked and deeply hurt by what he had just said.

He dropped his eyes, but I knew in my heart that he was probably right. My joining the Marines and going into combat probably did kill her. My father wasn't an educated man, but he had a good head on his shoulders and always said what he thought. In this case what he thought was probably correct. I must have put both of them through hell.

"Why couldn't you have gotten out of the war?" he finally asked.

I didn't know what to say. I could have avoided the draft like so many others if I had really wanted to do so. I certainly could have chosen a safer service than the Marine Corps. I didn't have to volunteer for paratrooper training or try to join a long range reconnaissance team. Every choice that I made was mine alone.

"I was very young and very foolish," I told him as honestly. He accepted my answer, nodded and turned away.

What I told him was certainly true. Like many young men I had craved excitement and even danger. I was drawn to the Marine Corps by the potent lures of patriotism and military glory. I yearned to experience life to its fullest. I wanted to prove myself as a man and so I joined the most elite combat unit I could find. Looking back on my decisions, I now realized that I had just been a foolish child cloaked in a sense of his own invulnerability and focused only on himself.

I don't feel particularly proud of what I did as a Force Recon scout in Vietnam, but I don't feel guilty about it either. I did my best to fulfill my obligations to my country. I remained true to my teammates. I never did anything in combat that the enemy wouldn't have gladly done twice over to me. What I did feel guilty about was the unnecessary grief and worry I caused to the people back home, to those who loved me, but there was nothing I could do about that now. I had been another person then. Now I had to live with the choices that foolish younger person had made for me.

Epilogue

The Vietnam War is ancient history, and I've kind of divorced myself from it over the years. —General William Westmoreland

I returned from Nam with lethal skills that were completely useless in civilian life, a leg full of shrapnel fragments that wandered around my body as if they had a life of their own, and an almost pathological distrust of authority.

I was hoping to put the Vietnam War behind me, but America was still in the process of tearing itself apart over it. There had been too many photographs of burning villages and crying children. Too many muddy body bags had somehow been transformed into gleaming bronze coffins and returned to the States draped in the American flag. Vietnam vets were being stigmatized as drug-crazed killers and seemed to be easy targets for the wrath that was now consuming America.

I went to a birthday party when I first returned. There was an awkward silence as I first walked into the room. Someone I had thought of as a friend suddenly called out a sarcastic greeting: "Welcome back … baby killer!"

The girls sitting next to him giggled, as the other men looked at me impassively.

"I never killed anyone who wasn't doing their best to waste me first," I responded.

Even as I spoke to them, my words seemed out of place. They were ill suited to a birthday party, fit more to a firebase. Everyone was looking at me and the looks weren't friendly. I turned to leave, but another high school classmate came in, took me aside and offered me a drink. We sat down on the porch as I tried to relax. After a few minutes I told him how upset I was by what had just been said to me.

He looked at me closely for a moment, took a drink of his beer, and responded in a superior voice, "Yeah, the truth really hurts, doesn't it?"

I felt a hot flush come over my face and tried to restrain myself from punching him in the teeth.

"No, God damn it! The truth doesn't hurt. It's assholes like you who don't have a clue. That's what hurts!"

I stormed out the door and I roamed the street for hours, but it didn't really help. Like thousands of other Vietnam vets, I just had to learn to keep my mouth shut. After trying for months to find a job without even a callback I realized that if I ever wanted to find work I had to remove any mention of military service from my résumé.

It was years before anyone asked me about the war. When I first got back from Nam the protest movement was in full swing and no one was interested in learning about what we went through over there. My father told me that sometime we'd have to get together over a couple of beers and talk about it, but then he died and we never did get a chance to have that talk.

About six months after being discharged I received a small cardboard box in the mail from the Marine Corps. When I opened it up I found it contained the Navy Achievement Medal. In stilted military language the attached citation read: *Awarded for meritorious service while acting as a grenadier in an action resulting in the killing of thirty-four enemy soldiers.*

I was confused. The only action that even came close to the citation's wording was the mission where we led the grunts into battle. In that fight the enemy had taken most of their dead with them as they retreated, leaving us with only a dozen or so confirmed kills. Could it have been the time we called in the *New Jersey*? During that action I hadn't even fired a shot.

I wasn't even sure exactly what a "grenadier"[1] was. The phrase sounded to me like some archaic title from Napoléon's day. During my entire Marine Corps career I had never even heard the word used. Perhaps this was my "End of Tour" award? I put the medal and my citation on my bookcase and several weeks later a friend of mine saw it sitting there.

"Hey, I got one of these," he told me, picking up my medal and examining it.

"You did?" I asked, impressed. "I thought you were in the Reserves."

"Yup," he agreed cheerfully. "I spent my time typing up forms in Philadelphia, never even saw a ship."

"And you got a medal for doing that?"

"Sure did! They give the Navy Achievement Medal out to electricians, cooks, typists, nearly anybody who stayed in long enough," he explained happily.

After he left I took the damn thing off my mantle and threw it in the trash. It made me angry just to look at it.

There was a VFW post right down the road from me and I stopped in one evening. I thought it might be a good place to relax and meet some other veterans. The bar was filled with older men. The bartender reluctantly gave me an application form to fill out and I paid my fee but never got my membership card and was never even issued the key that would let me in the door. I went back a couple of times before realizing that the VFW was a private club run for the World War II guys, and they didn't want any Vietnam vets disturbing their cozy little boozing hole.

I tried to put my life back together. I went back to school and married a wonderful lady. I found menial work painting, working as a plumber's assistant, doing whatever it took to pay the rent. It wasn't easy, but with both of us working my wife and I struggled along and managed to make ends meet. I finally got a job that I liked in a chemical factory. I did everything, from working the paint machine to assisting in the laboratory. Computers were just starting to be used within the company and I got involved with programming them. It turned out that I had talent for this work and I began to take courses in computer science at a local university. I kept my time in Nam out of my résumé and was eventually hired to work full time as a programmer. My wife and I bought a house and soon had a little baby daughter. My life seemed to be finally coming together.

After a number of years, I was put up for a promotion and a young executive was assigned to evaluate me. He was my age but several levels above me in the corporate structure. Vietnam vets were never able to catch up. The war and its aftermath had taken too many critical years away from the men and women who did serve. While the draft dodgers were moving up the corporate ladder and prospering economically, educationally, and professionally we had been slogging through jungle mud just trying to stay alive. Those missing years could never be reclaimed.

Holding up my résumé, the young man asked me about the nearly four-year gap in my employment record. When I told him that I was in the service, he asked me why I hadn't put it down on my résumé. I told him that I probably wouldn't have been hired if I had done so.

"You seem like a really smart guy; what happened? You probably could have gotten a deferment. I know lots of guys that did."

"Things that you wouldn't understand," I answered gruffly.

"Such as?" he persisted.

"Patriotism, loyalty, honor," I answered angrily—damned if I was going to kowtow to this little snot.

He pulled back in his chair as if I had slapped him, and terminated the interview and turned down my promotion. When would I ever learn?

A few weeks later, I read in the paper about a Vietnam vet in our town who suffered from combat fatigue and committed suicide. I mentioned to my wife how fortunate I was never to have suffered from shell shock or anything like that.

She looked at me incredulously. "Are you kidding? It took you more than a year before you were able to climb down out of the trees! How about those nightmares and hallucinations you keep having? You really need to get some help."

"Hallucinations? I don't hallucinate," I objected.

"The spider," she reminded me.

"Oh, that."

A few days ago, I had woken up in the middle of the night to see a huge black spider slowly lowering itself down a web toward my head.

"Get out of the bed!" I yelled, pushing my wife to the floor and rolling away.

I turned on the light to see … nothing. There was no spider and no web hanging over the bed. I didn't understand and searched under the bed with a broom. Where could it have gone? If I hadn't rolled away it would have bitten me in the face.

I decided to take my wife's advice and made an appointment to see a psychologist at the VA clinic near my home. She was a sweet young thing, probably just out of graduate school. She began by asking whether I had any anger issues.

"No, I try to avoid confrontations. I'm afraid that if I ever really got angry I might hurt someone. That's probably why I chose a career as a programmer. It's a solitary profession."

"That's a very powerful insight," she remarked in an encouraging voice as I nodded. She was a really such a nice young lady.

"Do you ever get flashbacks?" she asked.

"No, not really … well, maybe sometimes," I finally admitted. "If I hear a helicopter passing overhead or hear a loud noise I sometimes find myself getting a little nervous. Nothing to worry about," I added defensively.

I didn't tell her about the sudden noises that made my heart race and my palms sweat. I didn't mention how I'd suddenly freeze at an unexpected sound, my trigger finger twitching, my eyes involuntarily searching for movement. I didn't tell her about looking at a vacant field and seeing in my mind's eye places to set up an ambush.

I had said that I was afraid of hurting someone. If I had been honest with her, I would have said that I was afraid not only of hurting, but of killing someone. My calm demeanor was only a mask covering some dark part of my soul that clawed to be set free. No… I had probably told her too much already.

The psychologist made marks on her pad and asked me if she could sign me up for a therapy group that met in her office once a month. I could tell that she really wanted me to join her group, but I didn't like the idea. I explained to her that I tried not to dwell on my time in the service. She seemed slightly disappointed but accepted my answer and moved on to another question.

"Can you describe one of the worst things to happen to you in Nam?" she asked.

My mind went back to the jungle, the spiders, the rats, the smell of the mud and the feeling of dread that shadowed my every step. I couldn't tell someone young enough to be my daughter about these things and suggested that I tell her a humorous story instead. She agreed and sat back as I began telling her the story of the bucktoothed sergeant. The thought of someone stupid enough to cut the rope he was hanging from seemed pretty funny to me.

She sat there listening intently and making notes. I had just gotten to the part of my story where the weight of the other team members started cutting into him when she suddenly placed her hands over her ears, shook her head and said she had heard enough. She turned her chair away from me, looked out the window and tried to compose herself. I was embarrassed and felt terrible that I had upset her. We had been getting along so well.

"How could you think that something like that was amusing?" she asked angrily, dabbing at her eyes with a handkerchief.

I shook my head. I didn't know the answer to her question.

A few weeks later I received a letter from the VA stating that I had been diagnosed with PTSD and had been awarded a small disability pension from the government. I joked to my wife that this meant that I was now certifiably nuts, but she didn't think my remark was funny.

Every few years I would come across someone who might have been in the war. Within a few minutes, some part of me recognizes a fellow combat veteran and our casual conversation turns into a strange sort of mating dance.

"Serve in the military?"

"Air Cav, the Delta. You?"

"Marines ... Da Nang, An Hoa."

We would sit quietly for a minute, each of us wrapped in his own thoughts.

"Well ... welcome back, bro." We would shake hands and turn away.

We don't need to carry around a stupid challenge coin. We know who we are.

Considering the number of men who had served in Nam, such meetings are rare. Most of the time if I see another gray-haired guy driving around with a Vietnam bumper sticker on his car it will turn out to be someone who spent his entire tour on a ship miles offshore or in some other support role. One time I spoke to someone with a Vietnam license plate who told me that he had been in the Reserves during the Vietnam era and had never even left the States. Not to take anything away from his service, but it's no wonder that we lost the fucking war. It seems as though there were only a handful of guys over there doing the actual fighting.

Bo and I talk every year or so. I'll get a call around the holidays and hear his gravelly voice on the phone asking me how things are going. After Nam he went back home and married his childhood sweetheart. He got his job back in the steel mill, but like many other companies, it went bankrupt in the downturn of the eighties. Unable to find work in the steel industry Bo became a custodian in a Catholic school and became a beloved part of it.

Over the years Bo has had more than his share of health problems, cancer and other illnesses. It seemed to me that many of his medical issues were likely due to his exposure to Agent Orange. At the time we had been told that the chemicals were completely harmless to humans. We had been fed lies. Even then, the military knew that these powerful herbicides caused cancers and other health problems. Whenever I brought up Agent Orange, however, Bo would change the subject and talk about coaching the local Little League team or tell me about his kids and eventually his grandkids. He was still the same old Bo; he hasn't changed at all.

Bo told me that Truman had lived with him for a few weeks when he first got out of the Marines and that as a civilian he had been wilder than ever. His drinking and carousing got so bad that Bo eventually threw him out of the house. Truman had always kidded that his father had told him that if he continued in his dissolute, violent ways he'd come to live in a "big house with high walls." I hope that didn't happen.

One time I asked Bo about Lieutenant Lord. He told me that after I had left the team Lord had settled down and become quite good in the bush.

"You never liked him, did you?" Bo asked me.

I thought about his question. No, I didn't like him, but I didn't need to like him, and he didn't need to like me. Each of us only needed to do our jobs. When I was with Recon Battalion, I hadn't particularly liked Sergeant Blaze, I don't think any of the men did, but we respected him. I told Bo that from the time he had taken over our platoon Lord hadn't done anything to earn my respect, let alone my friendship.

Bo told me that I was being too hard on Lieutenant Lord, and I had to admit that he had a point. Sergeant Tom had been a very special leader and at the time I was still shaken by his loss. If the legendary Marine hero Chesty Puller had magically been pulled down from Marine Corps heaven and put in charge of our team, I probably would have resented him just as much.

It was also true that by the time that Lord first joined our unit I had become disillusioned with the war and my place in it. Instead of the eager gung ho Marine the lieutenant had been expecting to heroically lead into battle, he found himself saddled with a sullen, resentful brute who questioned his every order and only obeyed them reluctantly. It was no wonder we didn't become the best of buddies.

Bo continued to stick up for Lieutenant Lord and told me that he had eventually even gotten to like him. I found this comment really a bit much and reminded him about the dry-shaving incident. I told him that he would give the devil himself the benefit of the doubt, but he just laughed at me.

He told me that he had heard that Lord had been decorated for bravery, but didn't know the details. I wasn't surprised. I never questioned Lord's courage, only his judgment. He wasn't a stupid man, quite the opposite, but he seemed to lack the ability to imagine the really bad things that could happen if you weren't really careful in the bush. After I had seen so many of my friends killed or injured, my own imagination had been on permanent overdrive. I certainly wasn't willing to be sacrificed on the altar of Lord's military ambitions.

The Greek military historian Thucydides once wrote: "The bravest are surely those who have the clearest vision of what is before them, glory and danger alike, and yet notwithstanding, go out to meet it."[2] For Thucydides, true bravery consisted in consciously overcoming your fears, not reacting in the almost instinctual way that often occurs in the heat of battle.

The grunts, following us toward a hill where they knew many of them would die; the tunnel rat, climbing into a tiny hole with nothing more than a flashlight and a .45; Luchini, deathly afraid of heights but willing to be dropped from a helicopter in order to retrieve the body of his friend. These acts of steady courage still fill me with awe, and yet medals are seldom awarded for deeds like these.

To my everlasting regret, I had lacked the courage to even stay with Stout while he lay in his hospital bed. I'm sure that it would have made a big difference to him to have someone he knew remain with him for a while, but I had failed the test. I just couldn't bear to sit there and watch him suffer.

I did retrieve the radio that I had told Truman to leave behind. That was certainly a dangerous enough thing to do, but it wasn't courage that drove me; it was desperation. We needed a working radio and I was the person responsible for our not having one. It was my duty to go back and retrieve it. I didn't have any choice, and as Thucydides knew, without choice there is no true bravery.

The most courageous thing that I ever did in Vietnam was climbing back on top of the officers' shower to kick away a flaming fuel can. I was certain that the damned thing was going to explode in my face at any moment, but no one was going to put me up for a medal for that. I was lucky enough to not end up in the brig!

I never found out what happened to my friend Moose who so wanted to return to his hometown, become a teacher, and "make a difference to his people." For that matter, I don't know what happened to any of the men who were lost when they fell from that chopper so many years ago, but the images of their young faces remain vividly clear in my mind and always will.

Frenchy had somehow gotten a third Purple Heart for a minor shrapnel wound and he was sent back to Guam before his tour was complete. His last injury occurred when the rest of our team was in the bush and I never had a chance to say good-bye to him. He always said that once he got out he planned to make a living as a pimp in New Orleans. We never knew if he was kidding or not, but he did spend all of his R & R money on fancy Hong Kong suits, so he must have been planning well ahead. I'm not worried about Frenchy, he always knew how to take care of himself.

About five years ago I was surprised to receive a phone call from Gowski, the Marine who had turned his sleeping area into a boudoir. He told me that after leaving the Marines he had enlisted in the Army and when that enlistment expired he went into the Navy. When I spoke with him he was operating heavy equipment and spending his weekends practicing marksmanship at a local shooting range. He told me that he had just bought a .22-caliber pistol as a Christmas present for his seven-year-old son. I shook my head and had to laugh as I hung up the phone. He sounded as crazy as ever.

I tried for years without success to get in contact with Ma, and found him living not far from me in Maine and I went over to visit him. He told me that he had originally gotten a job as a tree trimmer for a lumbering company, but had quit because he felt that the job was too dangerous! He must have moved shortly after and I lost contact with him. Too bad; he was a decent guy and a good friend.

I often think of the men in my Battalion Recon team. I wondered what they thought when they first shuffled into their hooch to find a newbie sitting nervously on a cot waiting for them. In my mind I see them still, a wild band of young Marines led by a stone-cold teenage killer, humping the jungle trails of Nam in search of prey.

Looking through the pages of an old magazine one day, I saw photographs of the ancient Cambodian city of Angkor and with a shock of recognition realized that the swirling images carved into these temples were the same as those I had seen during our patrol in the Garden of Eden. The abandoned stone temple we had stumbled upon must at one time have been a far-flung outpost of the ancient Khmer civilization. After the war ended, An Hoa was also abandoned, and our base has now returned to the jungle. Perhaps in some future time someone will stumble upon our crumpled bunkers and the wreckage of our planes and wonder what could possibly have happened there.

On July 15, 1974, the decision was made to deactivate First Force Recon. The intelligence community was pushing their new satellite surveillance technologies, which they believed would eliminate the need for the deep reconnaissance patrols that Force specialized in. It was also well known that the Marine Corps brass never liked the idea of having such an elite group within the Marine Corps in the first place, arguing that every Marine was "elite." Most of the men and women in the Corps, however, serve in supporting roles, from truck drivers to cooks. All Marine recruits are given basic riflemen training, but let's be honest, support personnel are not combat troops. The generals came to regret their decision when Navy SEAL teams eagerly stepped in and took over the type of missions that had traditionally been performed by Force Recon Marines.

Whatever the true reason for the deactivation, the men of First Force were instructed to turn in their gear and were quickly transferred out to other units. The records of classified missions were burned, while unclassified information was simply tossed into the trash.[3] Cynic that I am, I can't help but think that that the unit's deactivation and the associated destruction of these *Top Secret* records was simply the best way of forever concealing our clandestine missions.

One of the few items saved from the carnage was a simple sign that had hung in the operations center, which read: *If everyone could be Force Recon—it wouldn't be Force Recon!*[4]

I can't deny that I had my share of issues with the Marine Corps, but I did my best to fulfill my duty. I probably never fully achieved the lofty principles I accepted to become a Recon Marine, "Honor, Perseverance, Spirit and Heart," but I never forgot them. My left arm is tattooed with an image of the golden jump wing insignia, with *1st Force Recon* inked above and the letters *USMC* boldly lettered underneath it. The tattoo reminds me of my service and what we endured. Whatever my deficiencies back in the rear, I knew that I had finally earned Sergeant Blaze's ultimate compliment: "He was a damn good bush Marine."

The old saying "Once a Marine always a Marine" is certainly true; sometimes I wish it were not so. The Marine Corps molded me into the person I am, but it also destroyed forever the person I might have become. My tour in Vietnam has scarred me, body and soul. My fellow Vietnam veterans continue to suffer from the effects of wounds, Agent

Orange exposure, and shell shock. What can be said of our sacrifices? All of us believed that we were serving our country, but if so how?

When the Vietnam War finally ended more than fifty-eight thousand American troops had died, fifty thousand of them enlisted men. More than three hundred thousand were wounded, many of them so seriously that they would never be the same again. At the end of the war nearly two thousand men were still unaccounted for and by 2014 nearly one hundred thousand Vietnam veterans had taken their own lives.[5]

It is estimated that the number of people killed in Indochina during the war years ranged from two and a half to more than four million people.[6] An even greater number were maimed, orphaned, displaced, or forced to flee the fighting. The war was truly one of the greatest humanitarian tragedies of the twentieth century, a tragedy that continues to haunt us to this day. Herbicides such as Agent Orange still continue to poison the environment of Southeast Asia, causing birth defects, cancers and other health problems. Hundreds of thousands of unexploded cluster bombs dropped from American aircraft in an ultimately futile attempt to cut the Ho Chi Minh Trail continue to kill and maim innocent civilians.

Americans should have learned at least some lessons from the cauldron of the Vietnam War. We should have learned that it is easier to start a war than to end one. We should be wary of supporting corrupt governments that lack the support of the people. We should not assume that technology will necessarily translate into battlefield effectiveness. We should have learned that it is difficult, if not impossible, for an outside force to defeat an enemy who look like the local population, speak their language and worship the same God.

Have we learned any of these lessons? Examining the American experiences in Iraq, Syria, Afghanistan, and the other recent conflicts, I doubt that we have learned anything at all. It seems that the "powers that be" believe that America's new all-volunteer army is there to be used. American combat troops are now in so many countries, fighting against so many different groups, that it is impossible for me to keep track of them. Before sending the children of their constituents into battle, members of Congress need to get some "skin in the game." I doubt they would be so eager to initiate conflicts in foreign lands if their own children and grandchildren would be put into danger. It simply isn't right for the blue-collar working classes to be expected to fight and die when the privileged members of our society have no such obligation.

My thoughts and prayers go out to the brave men and women of the Marine Corps who are serving our country in foreign lands. They must be made of tougher stuff than I was. My tour of duty in Vietnam was thirteen months, and I literally counted the days until I returned home. I can't imagine how the men and women serving our country in the Armed Forces today can possibly cope with being deployed over and over again with no end in sight. I know I couldn't.

Neither the pills the VA once sent me nor the alcohol I buy on my own has done anything to stop my nightmares. Once or twice a month I wake up in the middle of the night dreaming about Nam. I hear the warning siren and someone screams, "Incoming!" I reach for my rifle, but it's not there. I search desperately through enormous piles of ammunition and combat gear without finding it. The explosions get closer and closer. Someone yells, "gooks in the wire!" and I wake up sweaty and trembling.

I dream that I am crawling up a long muddy hill toward an enemy sentry, my Ka-Bar in my hand. As he turns toward me I stab downward. My knife hand sinks in until it feels like it is scraping the inside of a coconut.

I dream that I am suddenly alone in the jungle, fleeing down the trails, looking for cover where there is none to be found. I try to hide from the enemy soldiers, but they find me. Sometimes I kill; sometimes I am the one who is killed. It doesn't even seem to matter.

Every once in a while I will have a good dream and find myself back once again with my long-dead teammates.

"Hey, man, how's it going, man? We thought you left us."

I look around me at the smiling young faces and answer truthfully.

"No way, man…. No fuckin' way."

My Team

Reconnaissance Creed

Realizing it is my choice and my choice alone
to be a Reconnaissance Marine,
I accept all challenges involved with this profession.
Forever shall I strive to maintain the tremendous reputation
of those who went before me.
Exceeding beyond the limitations
set down by others shall be my goal.
Sacrificing personal comforts and dedicating myself
to the completion of the reconnaissance mission shall be my life.
Physical fitness, mental attitude, and high ethics.
The title of Recon Marine is my honor.
Conquering all obstacles, both large and small,
I shall never quit.
To quit, to surrender, to give up is to fail.
To be a Recon Marine is to surpass failure;
To overcome, to adapt and to do whatever it takes
to complete the mission.
On the battlefield, as in all areas of life,
I shall stand tall above the competition.
Through professional pride, integrity, and teamwork,
I shall be the example
for all Marines to emulate.
Never shall I forget the principles
I accepted to become a Recon Marine.
Honor, Perseverance, Spirit and Heart.
A Recon Marine can speak without saying a word
and achieve what others can only imagine.

Navaho Blessing

Happily may their roads back home be on the trail of pollen
Happily may they all get back
In beauty I walk
With beauty I walk
With beauty before me I walk
With beauty behind me, I walk
With beauty below me, I walk
With beauty above me, I walk
With beauty all around me, I walk
It is finished in beauty…
'Sa'ah naaghéi, Bik'eh hózhó."

Chapter Notes

Preface

1. Charlie—the name Marines gave to our enemies, the Communist soldiers. These could be regular North Vietnamese soldiers (NVA) or local Vietcong.
2. I Corps—the northern region of South Vietnam extending to the border with North Vietnam.

Chapter 1

1. Puff—the Douglas AC-47, a fixed-wing propeller-driven aircraft used for close infantry support. The nickname Puff was taken from "Puff the Magic Dragon," but it was also called Snoopy.
2. Claymore mine—a deadly anti-personnel mine.

Chapter 2

1. GUAM—the initials vulgarized as "Give Up And Masturbate."
2. Tour of duty—The amount of time Marines would have to spend in Vietnam, usually thirteen months.

Chapter 3

1. Newbie—someone new to Vietnam.
2. Tet Offensive—launched on January 31, 1968, seventy thousand North Vietnamese soldiers and Vietcong forces attacked positions throughout South Vietnam
3. RVN—Republic of Vietnam.
4. Twook—cigarettes.
5. Deedee Mao—"Get lost" or "Go away."
6. PX—Post Exchange. A place where you could buy food, watch a movie, relax for a while.
7. Dogpatch—the hometown of the comic strip characters in "Li'l Abner."
8. Camp Reasoner—camp named after First Lieutenant Frank Reasoner, who was killed leading a reconnaissance team in 1965. He received the Medal of Honor for his actions in that fight.
9. PFC—Private First Class—the next to the lowest rank for an enlisted man.

Chapter 4

1. Noted on maps as Hill 327, the number designating the number of feet above sea level.
2. HQ—headquarters.
3. "Taps"—the bugle call that marked the end of the day. It usually meant "lights-out."

Chapter 5

1. M-60—an air-cooled belt-fed machine gun.
2. Papa-san—an elderly Vietnamese man. An older Vietnamese lady would be called Mama-san.
3. LAW—Light Antiarmor Weapon, basically a handheld rocket launcher similar to the bazooka of World War II vintage, but able to fire only a single rocket.
4. It seems like the Army stole this cheer from us several years ago, but they pronounce it more as "OooRah," and it doesn't sound the same at all.

Chapter 6

1. Bud—Budweiser. I never saw any other brand sold in Nam. I guess they had the contract locked up.
2. NCO—Non-Commissioned Officer (Corporal rank or above).

Chapter 7

1. Lifer—someone who is making a career in the Marine Corps.
2. R & R—Two weeks of Rest and Relaxation, usually taken in one of the Asian cities.

Chapter 8

1. Muc Luc—a fermented fish sauce.
2. *Click Click*—during the Normandy invasion paratroopers were given little tin "clickers" that they used to identify themselves to one another. Placing the tongue against the roof of the mouth and drawing in a slight breath also produced a soft *click-click* sound that could be used as an alert signal.

Chapter 10

1. Huey—Bell UH-1 Iroquois helicopter, originally designated HU-1, hence the name Huey.

Chapter 12

1. Arc Light—a B-52 bombing run.

Chapter 14

1. RIP—Recon Indoctrination Platoon.
2. Cover—Marines prided themselves on having a unique "cover," or hat. It was different from the Army baseball cap and starched until it received a distinctive "Marine Corps" look.

Chapter 15

1. Sight in—set the mechanical sights on our rifles for various distances.
2. LRRP—Long-Range Reconnaissance Patrol.
3. Fléchette rounds—shotgun shells loaded with steel projectiles. The name comes from the French *fléchette*, or "little arrow." About twenty of these darts were packed into a single shell.

Chapter 16

1. Unit 1—the basic field medical kit.

Chapter 17

1. Chi-Com—Chinese-Communist.
2. Ray Stubbe and Michael Lanning, *Inside Force Recon: Recon Marines in Vietnam* (Ivy Press), p. 202.

Chapter 19

1. Heads—potheads.
2. Det cord—detonation cord, an explosive wire used to set off a larger explosive.

Chapter 22

1. Gunnery Sergeant—a Senior NCO rank (E-7) in the Marine Corps.
2. Pogue—a pejorative term for rear-echelon support personnel who are not involved in combat operations.
3. Green Machine—our term for the Marine Corps.

Chapter 24

1. *Stars and Stripes*—the military newspaper that was published in Vietnam.

Chapter 27

1. RPG—Rocket-Propelled Grenade.
2. Slick—a version of the standard Huey helicopter configured to transport troops.

Chapter 28

1. SITREP—situation report.

Chapter 30

1. OCS—Officer Candidate School.

Chapter 31

1. Agent Orange—a herbicide used extensively in Vietnam to defoliate the jungle. Named for the orange stripe on the chemical drum, it is a potent mix of two herbicides. During the war these chemicals often included dioxin. These chemicals are known to cause cancer, neurological problems, skin conditions and even birth defects.

Chapter 33

1. "M"—Corpsmen would write the letter M on the foreheads of patients to whom they had administered morphine so that the hospital would know how many doses were given.

Chapter 34

1. Nemo residio—"no one left behind."
2. Swiss harness—a rappelling harness made out of heavy rope.
3. Carabineer or "biner"—a steel "D" or coupling ring used by rock-climbers.
4. SPIE—Special Insertion and Extraction rig.

Chapter 37

1. Koan—a Zen riddle intended to bring enlightenment to Buddhist monks.

Chapter 41

1. Bangalore torpedoes—metal cylinders filled with explosives.
2. Blighters—a World War I term for wounds serious enough to get someone taken out of the front but not bad enough to result in permanent injury.
3. If the chance of being killed in a single mission was 1 percent, the chance of being killed before completing twenty-five missions would be 25 percent.

Chapter Notes

Chapter 42

1. Years later I saw photographs of the Cambodian kingdom of Angkor and realized that the small temple was probably an outpost of the ancient Khmer civilization, which flourished between the ninth and thirteen centuries.

Chapter 44

1. Leavenworth—the Navy Brig was located at Leavenworth prison. The criminal John Dillinger reportedly said that the hardest time he ever spent in prison was while he was locked up at Leavenworth.
2. G2—division intelligence
3. http://thevietnamwar.info/how-much-vietnam-war-cost/.
4. Ibid., p. 80.

Chapter 45

1. "Wait for me, Wild Bill" was what Wild Bill Hickok's comical sidekick used to say on a 1950s TV show.

Chapter 48

1. Dog and pony show—a staged demonstration of our capabilities.
2. Buzz—make a low-altitude pass.

Chapter 49

1. PT—Physical Training.

Chapter 52

1. Cam hute twook—bastardized Vietnamese (spelled various ways) meaning "Do you want a cigarette?"

Chapter 54

1. USO—United Service Organizations—an organization that put on shows for the troops.

Chapter 55

1. Frag—to kill a fellow American soldier with a fragmentation grenade.

Chapter 57

1. AWOL [Absent without leave] bags—small gym bags that could hold a few items of clothing. They were also referred to as "bugout" bags.

Epilogue

1. Grenadier—a specially selected foot soldier in certain elite units.
2. Thucydides, *History of the Peloponnesian War*.
3. At least some records were retrieved from the trash by Lieutenant Commander Ray Stubbe, who turned them into a book: *Inside Force Recon: Recon Marines in Vietnam*.
4. *Ibid.*, p. 103 (see notes).
5. http://history-world.org/vietnam_war_statistics.htm.
6. http://alphahistory.com/vietnamwar/costs-of-the-vietnam-war/.

Recommended Reading

Albanese, Marilia. *Angkor: Splendors of the Khmer Civilization.* Vercelli, Italy: White Star, 2006.
Bohrer, David. *America's Special Forces: Weapons, Missions, Training.* Osceola, WI: MBI, 1998.
Fall, Bernard. *Street Without Joy: The French Debacle in Indochina.* Harrisburg, PA: Stackpole, 1961.
Finlayson, Andrew. *Killer Kane: A Marine Long-Range Recon Team Leader in Vietnam, 1967-1968.* Jefferson, N.C.: McFarland, 2013.
FitzGerald, Francis. *Fire in the Lake: The Vietnamese and the Americans in Vietnam.* New York: Vintage, 1968.
Greenberg, Rick. *Silent Heroes: A Recon Marine's Vietnam War Experience.* CreateSpace, 2016.
Guidebook for Marines, 11th rev. ed. Washington, D.C.: The Leatherneck Association, 1967.
Karnow, Stanley. *Vietnam: A History.* New York: Viking, 1983.
Kidder, Tracy. *My Detachment: A Memoir.* New York: Random House, 2006.
Lee, Alex. *Force Recon Command: 3rd Force Recon Company in Vietnam, 1969–70.* New York: Ballantine, 1995.
Mason, Robert. *Chickenhawk.* New York: Penguin, 1984.
Norton, Bruce. *Force Recon Diary, 1969: The Riveting, True-to-Life Account of Survival and Death in One of the Most Highly Skilled Units in Vietnam.* New York: Ivy Books, 1991.
Norton, Bruce. *Force Recon Diary, 1970: A True Account of Courage in Vietnam.* New York: Ballantine, 1992.
O'Brien, Tim. *The Things They Carried.* New York: Broadway Books, 1990.
Peters, Bill. *First Force Recon Company: Sunrise at Midnight.* New York: Ivy Books, 1999.
Pushies, Fred. *Marine Force Recon.* Osceola, WI: MBI, 2003.
Spector, Ronald. *After Tet: The Bloodiest Year in Vietnam.* New York: Free Press, 1993.
Stubbe, Ray. *Inside Force Recon: Recon Marines in Vietnam.* New York: Ivy Books, 1989.
Vetter, Lawrence C. *Never Without Heroes: Marine Third Reconnaissance Battalion in Vietnam, 1965–70.* New York: Ivy Books, 1999.

Index

Agent Orange 111, 112, 127
AhOooRah 13
Air Calvary 142
AK-47 53
An Hoa 94
Antenna Valley 3
anti-personnel mines 55
arc light 39, 42
armory 11, 52

B-52 bomber 42, 111
banana clip 53
Battalion Recon 8
beach survey 148
beanies and weenies 21, 54
Ben Giang 20
black market 172, 175
booby traps 55, 56, 81, 130
boots 12
bug juice 27

"C" rations 9
C-4 explosive 3, 96, 102, 136
CH-46 Sea Knight 13
C-114 Flying Boxcar 63
Cam Ranh Bay 72, 116
camouflage paint 24
Camp Reasoner 8
CAP 187, 190
CAR-15 rifle 54
cargo net extraction 128
challenge coin 218, 229
Charlie Ridge 3, 83
chi-com grenade 59
China Beach 197
Chosin Reservoir 122
Chu Lai 62
CIA 102
Claymore mine 14, 24, 37, 60, 95
click click (warning) 26, 84, 153
Cobra attack helicopter 123
concertina wire 18
Criminal Investigation Division (CID) 212
crossbow 165

Da Nang 4, 5
det cord 70

Dien Bien Phu 95
dog and pony show 191
Dog Patch 7
dog tags 22
Dragon Lady 173

elephants 163
extraction harness 125

flares 14
flechette rounds 55
footlocker 16
Force Recon 44, 45, 232
Fort Benning 63
fragging 216
Freedom Hill 20
freeze-dried food 21

G2 174
Garden of Eden 3, 153
Giap (General) 93
golden wings 62
grass, marihuana 171, 205, 206
grid (MAP) 22, 23
grunts 87, 134, 135
Guam 221

Happy Valley 3, 62
Hawaii 4
heat stroke 113
Hill 469 197
Ho Chi Minh Trail 107
Hong Kong 49
hooch 9
HUEY (helicopter) 31, 142

I Corps 3
illumination rounds 140

jungle penetrator 70, 125
jungle rot 15, 49, 186

Ka-Bar Knife 12, 24, 25, 57
Khe Sanh 150
Kit Carson scout 189
Koreans 88

ladder, extraction 75
leeches 104, 185
LZ, LZ Finch 13

M-14 rifle 11
M-16 rifle 10, 12
M-18A1 Claymore 14, 24, 37, 60, 95
M-19 60mm mortar 142
M-60 machine gun 11, 54, 83, 85, 125
M-72 LAW 12
M-79 grenade launcher 55, 125
machine gun, 50 caliber 11, 61, 83, 100
magazines, M-16 22
mantra 30
Medevac 70
monsoon 3
mortar attack 56,
Motivational Platoon 48

Navy combat medics 49, 129
New Jersey (ship) 81
NVA 20, 59, 68, 86, 96, 200

parachute jumps 62, 65
Phuac Hao 20
piggybacking 176
pistols 55, 212, 213
poncho 21
PRC-25 radio 65, 107
prisoner snatch 55, 165
protestors 223
PTSD 228, 229
Puff gunship 3, 115

R & R 49, 175
Raiders (WWII) 24
rappelling 123, 124, 126, 191
rats 142
Razorback Ridge 199
Reasoner, Lt. 8
Red Beach 63
river patrol 90
rockets (enemy) 97
RVN 6, 57, 170

SCUBA 90, 146, 172
Seabees 99, 210
SEALS 232
short timer calendar 47
silk blanket 21, 185

241

SLICK (helicopter) 99, 142
smoke, identification 43, 78
snakes 159
sniper 39, 100
Song Cai River 20
songs 46, 47, 66, 80, 192, 193, 194
special forces 26, 87, 99
spiders 42, 156

SPIE ("The Rope") 127, 128, 179, 180
Stars and Stripes 48, 88
Swedish K 125

tear gas 122, 126
Tet Offensive 6
tiger 199
tunnel rat 144

UNIT 1 (medical) 57, 113

VFW 227
Vietminh 95

water buffalo 7, 65
white phosphorous, Willie Peter 60, 144

www.ingramcontent.com/pod-product-compliance
Ingram Content Group UK Ltd.
Pitfield, Milton Keynes, MK11 3LW, UK
UKHW050534150426
5217IPUK00026B/1933